RIN-NE

Story and Art by
Rumiko Takahashi

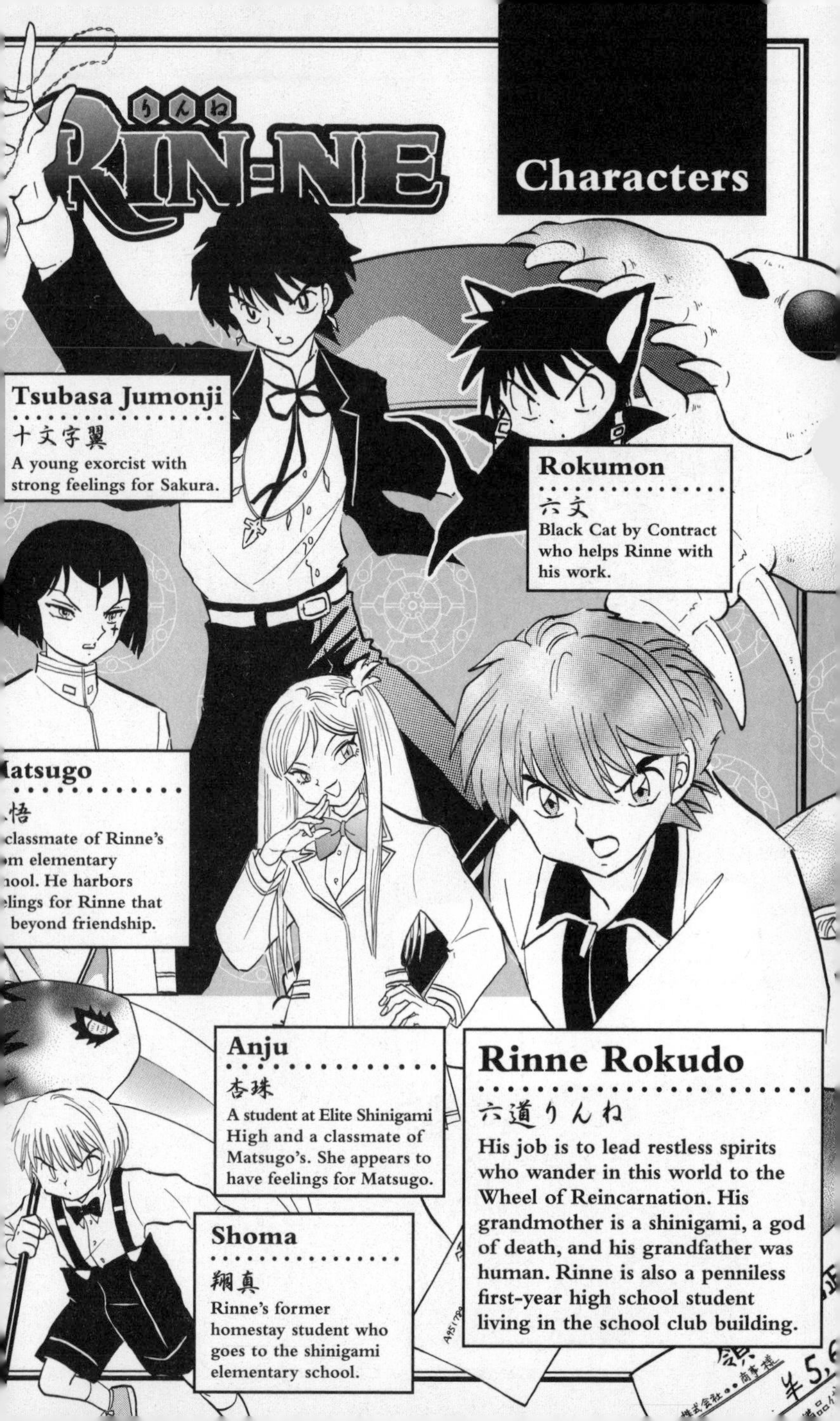
RIN-NE
りんね
Characters
Rokumon
六文
Black Cat by Contract who helps Rinne with his work.
Tsubasa Jumonji
十文字翼
A young exorcist with strong feelings for Sakura.
Rinne Rokudo
六道りんね
His job is to lead restless spirits who wander in this world to the Wheel of Reincarnation. His grandmother is a shinigami, a god of death, and his grandfather was human. Rinne is also a penniless first-year high school student living in the school club building.
Anju
杏珠
A student at Elite Shinigami High and a classmate of Matsugo's. She appears to have feelings for Matsugo.
Shoma
翔真
Rinne's former homestay student who goes to the shinigami elementary school.
latsugo
悟
classmate of Rinne's
m elementary
hool. He harbors
lings for Rinne that
beyond friendship.

Raito and Refuto

来兎＆零不兎

Fraternal twins and proprietors of the Crescent Moon Hall scythe shop. Raito handles sales and Refuto does the manufacturing.

Beautiful Secreta

秘書

She works as Sabato's secret and she's Ageha's older sister

Ichigo

苺

A first grader who is the reincarnation of Rinne's mother, Otome.

Sakura Mamiya

真宮 桜

When she was a child, Sakura gained the ability to see ghosts after getting lost in the Afterlife. Calm and collected, she stays cool no matter what happens.

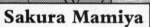

Sansei Kuroboshi

黒星三世

The grandchild of Tamako's Black Cat by Contract, Kuroboshi. Even though he's supposed to aid shinigami with their duties, he is deathly afraid of ghosts.

Ageha

鳳

A devoted shinigami who has a crush on Rinne.

The Story So Far

Sakura, the girl who can see ghosts, and Rinne, the shinigami (sort of), spend their days together helping spirits that can't pass on reach the Afterlife and dealing with all kinds of strange phenomena at their school.

When Ayame Sakaki's feelings for Jumonji manifest as a disobedient disembodied spirit, she decides it's time to get her crush under control once and for all. But the disembodied spirit guesses her scheme and asks Rinne to cut off the spiritual bonds binding her to Ayame…with disastrous results! As springtime approaches, the spirits are acting even more boisterous than usual, and Rinne's got to work 24-7 to handle all the exorcisms that come his way!

Contents

Chapter 369: I Am Not Afraid......5

Chapter 370: Putting One's Affairs in Order......23

Chapter 371: The Telling Voice......41

Chapter 372: A New Friend......61

Chapter 373: Red Bride Church......79

Chapter 374: This Is an Investment!......97

Chapter 375: The Phoenix Scythe.......115

Chapter 376: Crescent Moon Hall Forever.......133

Chapter 377: Something Fell in the Pool......151

Chapter 378: Dress from the Future......169

CHAPTER 369: I AM NOT AFRAID

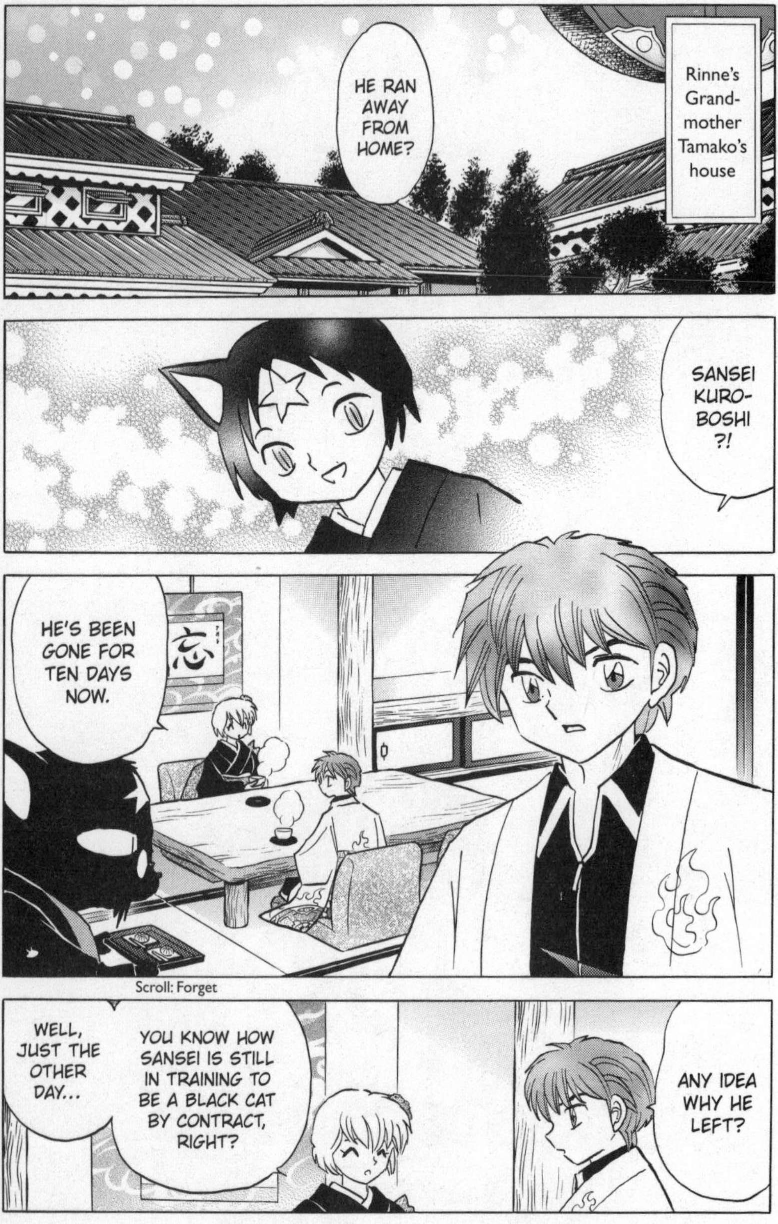
Rinne's Grandmother Tamako's house
HE RAN AWAY FROM HOME?
SANSEI KURO-BOSHI ?!
HE'S BEEN GONE FOR TEN DAYS NOW.
ANY IDEA WHY HE LEFT?
YOU KNOW HOW SANSEI IS STILL IN TRAINING TO BE A BLACK CAT BY CONTRACT, RIGHT?
WELL, JUST THE OTHER DAY...

Scroll: Forget

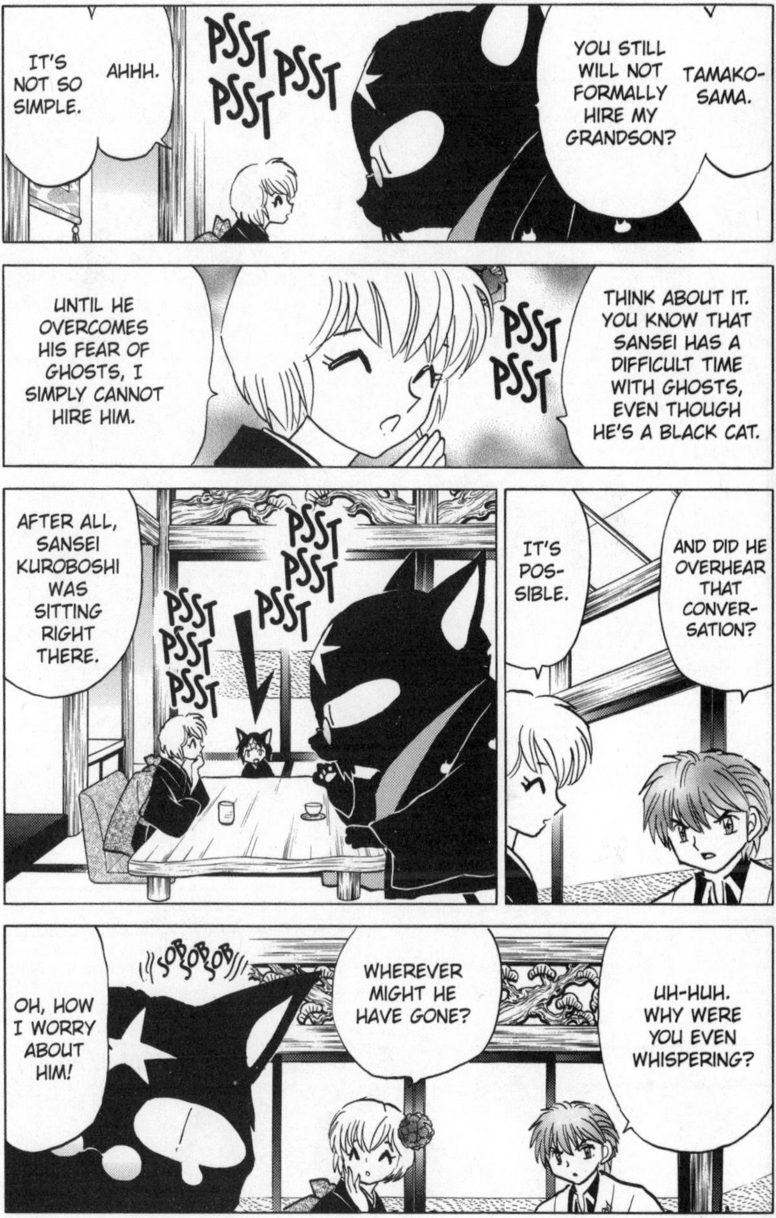
TAMAKO-SAMA.
YOU STILL WILL NOT FORMALLY HIRE MY GRANDSON?
PSST PSST PSST
AHHH.
IT'S NOT SO SIMPLE.
THINK ABOUT IT. YOU KNOW THAT SANSEI HAS A DIFFICULT TIME WITH GHOSTS, EVEN THOUGH HE'S A BLACK CAT.
PSST PSST
UNTIL HE OVERCOMES HIS FEAR OF GHOSTS, I SIMPLY CANNOT HIRE HIM.
AND DID HE OVERHEAR THAT CONVERSATION?
IT'S POS-SIBLE.
PSST PSST PSST
PSST PSST PSST
AFTER ALL, SANSEI KUROBOSHI WAS SITTING RIGHT THERE.
UH-HUH. WHY WERE YOU EVEN WHISPERING?
WHEREVER MIGHT HE HAVE GONE?
SOB SOB SOB
OH, HOW I WORRY ABOUT HIM!

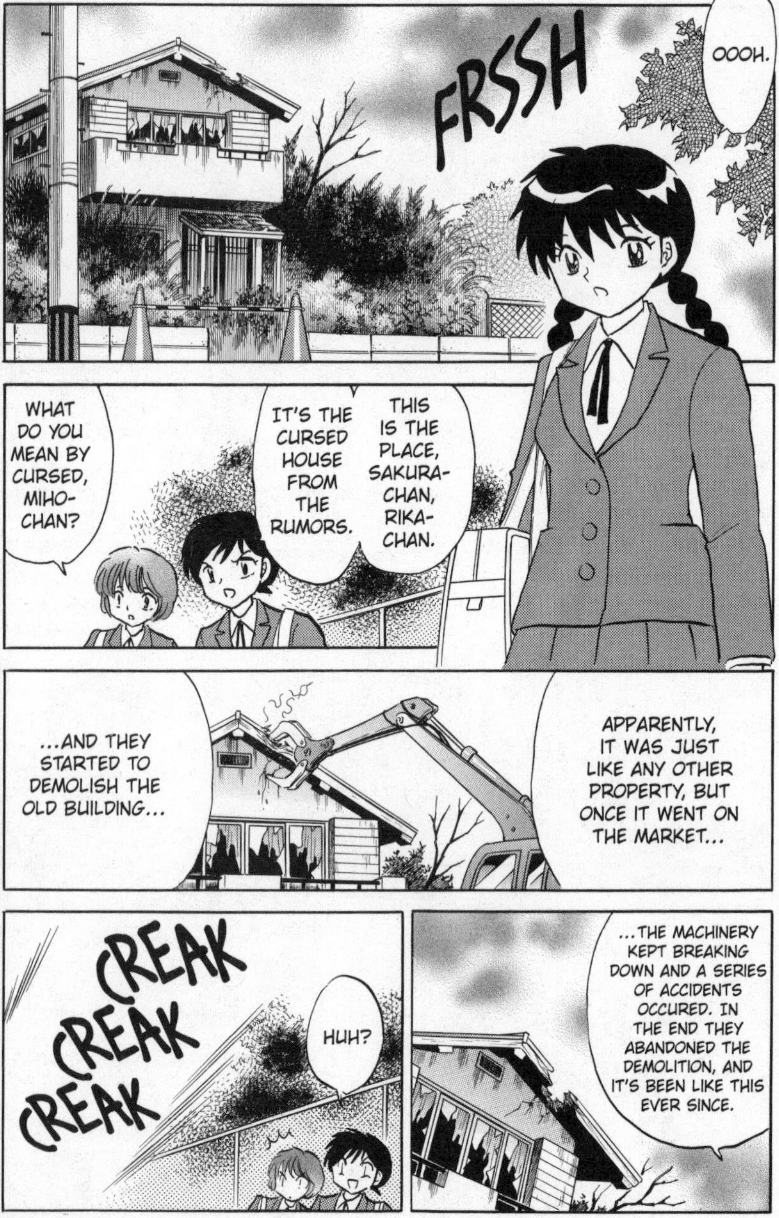
FRSSH
OOOH.
THIS IS THE PLACE, SAKURA-CHAN, RIKA-CHAN.
IT'S THE CURSED HOUSE FROM THE RUMORS.
WHAT DO YOU MEAN BY CURSED, MIHO-CHAN?
APPARENTLY, IT WAS JUST LIKE ANY OTHER PROPERTY, BUT ONCE IT WENT ON THE MARKET...
...AND THEY STARTED TO DEMOLISH THE OLD BUILDING...
...THE MACHINERY KEPT BREAKING DOWN AND A SERIES OF ACCIDENTS OCCURED. IN THE END THEY ABANDONED THE DEMOLITION, AND IT'S BEEN LIKE THIS EVER SINCE.
CREAK
CREAK
CREAK
HUH?

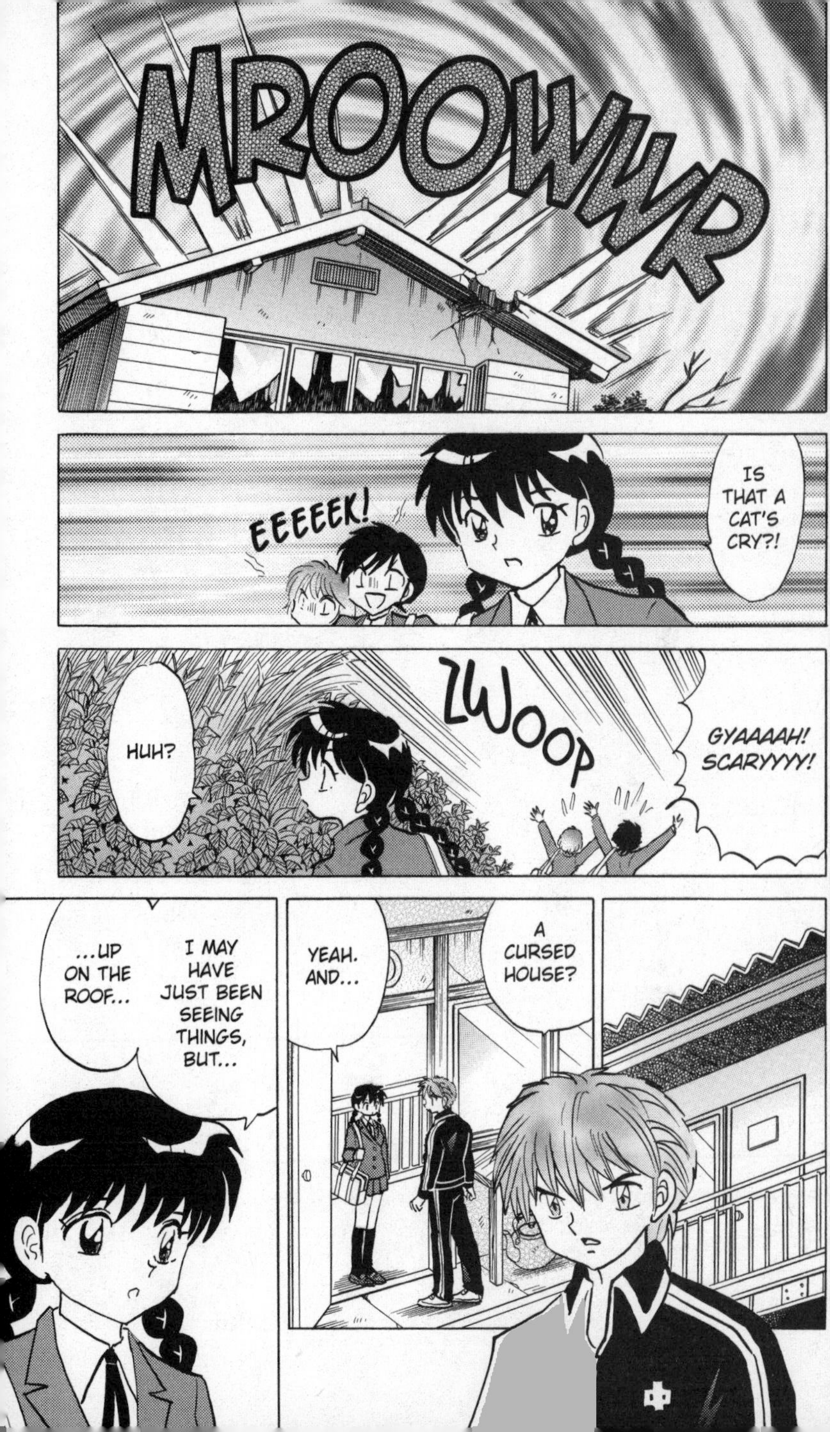
MROOWWR
IS THAT A CAT'S CRY?!
EEEEEK!
ZWOOP
GYAAAAH! SCARYYYY!
HUH?
A CURSED HOUSE?
YEAH. AND...
I MAY HAVE JUST BEEN SEEING THINGS, BUT...
...UP ON THE ROOF...

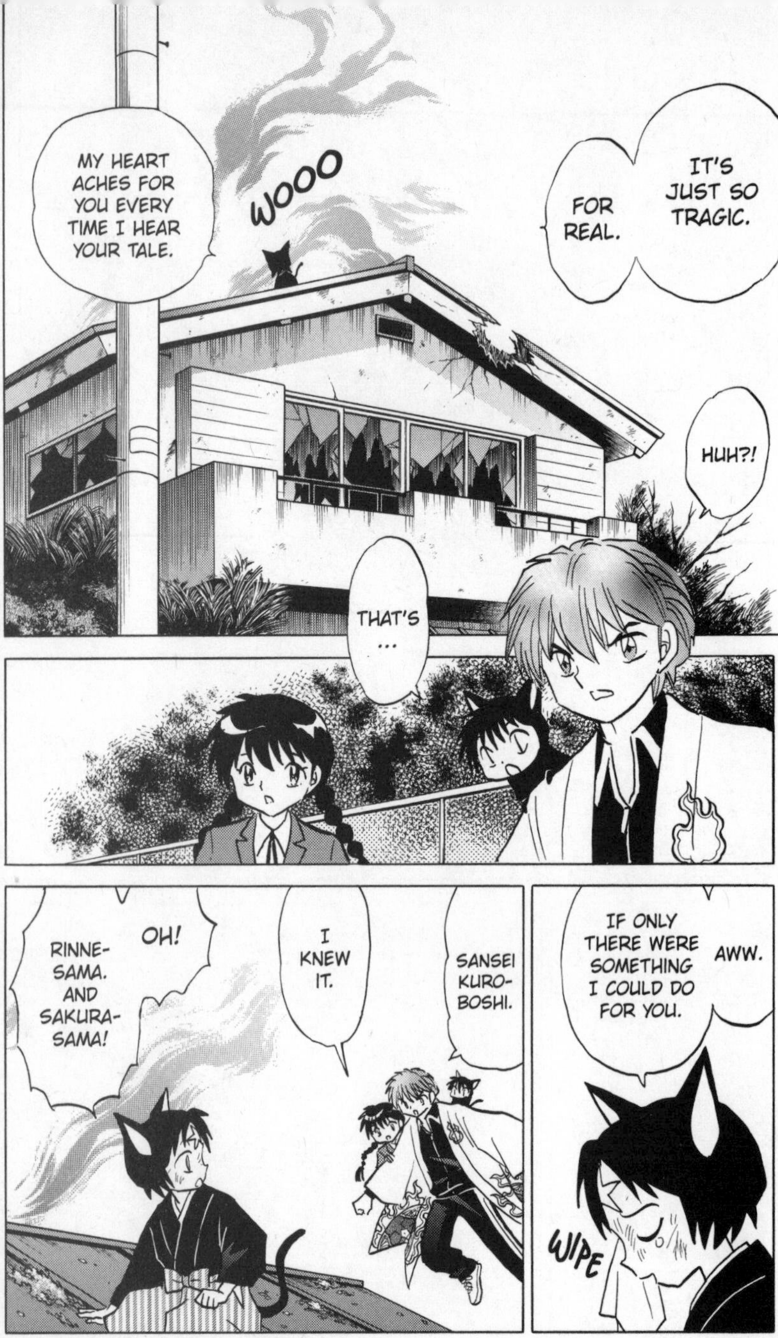
IT'S JUST SO TRAGIC.
FOR REAL.
MY HEART ACHES FOR YOU EVERY TIME I HEAR YOUR TALE.
WOOO
HUH?!
THAT'S ...
AWW.
IF ONLY THERE WERE SOMETHING I COULD DO FOR YOU.
WIPE
SANSEI KURO-BOSHI.
I KNEW IT.
OH!
RINNE-SAMA. AND SAKURA-SAMA!

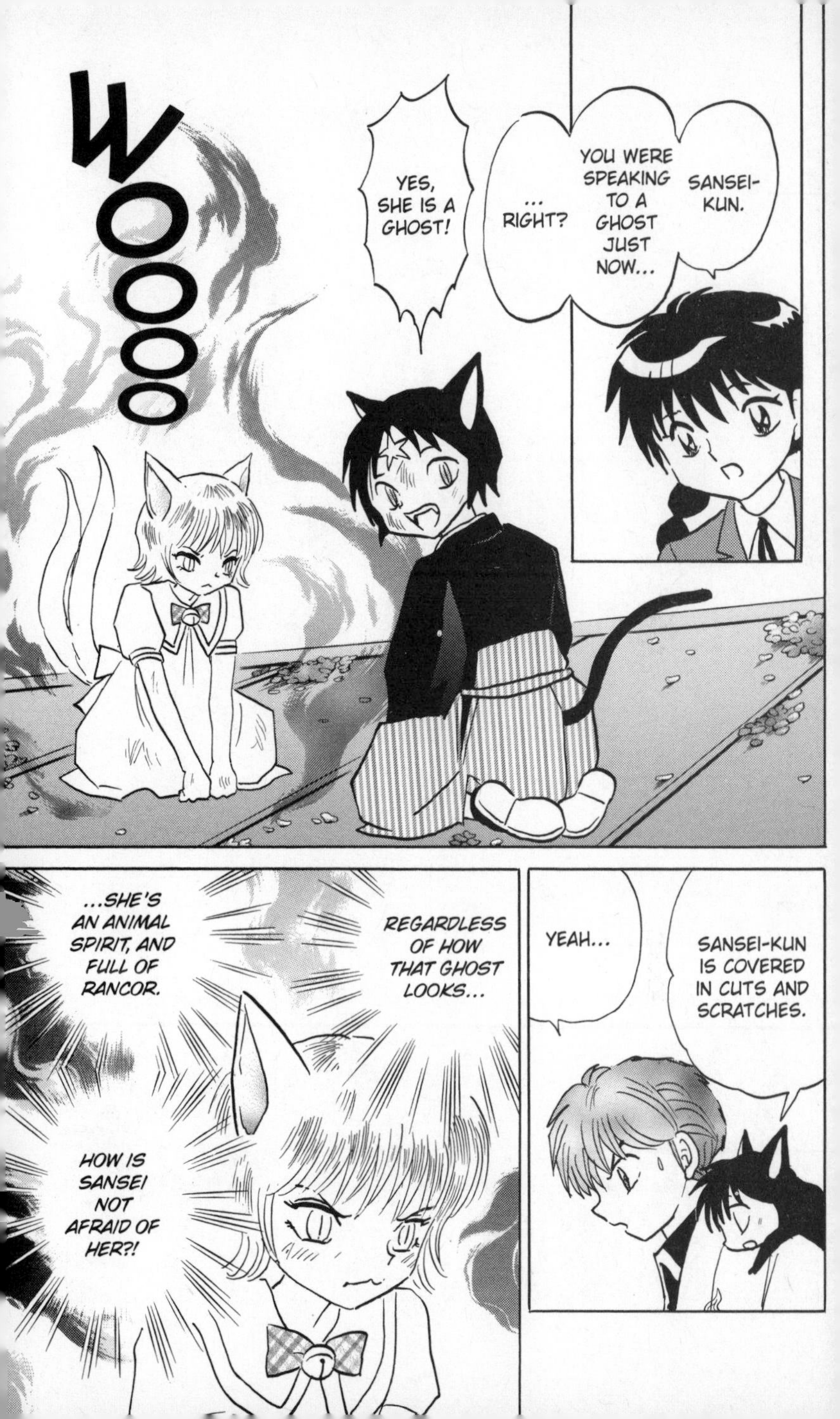
SANSEI-KUN.
YOU WERE SPEAKING TO A GHOST JUST NOW...
...RIGHT?
YES, SHE IS A GHOST!
WOOOOO
SANSEI-KUN IS COVERED IN CUTS AND SCRATCHES.
YEAH...
REGARDLESS OF HOW THAT GHOST LOOKS...
...SHE'S AN ANIMAL SPIRIT, AND FULL OF RANCOR.
HOW IS SANSEI NOT AFRAID OF HER?!

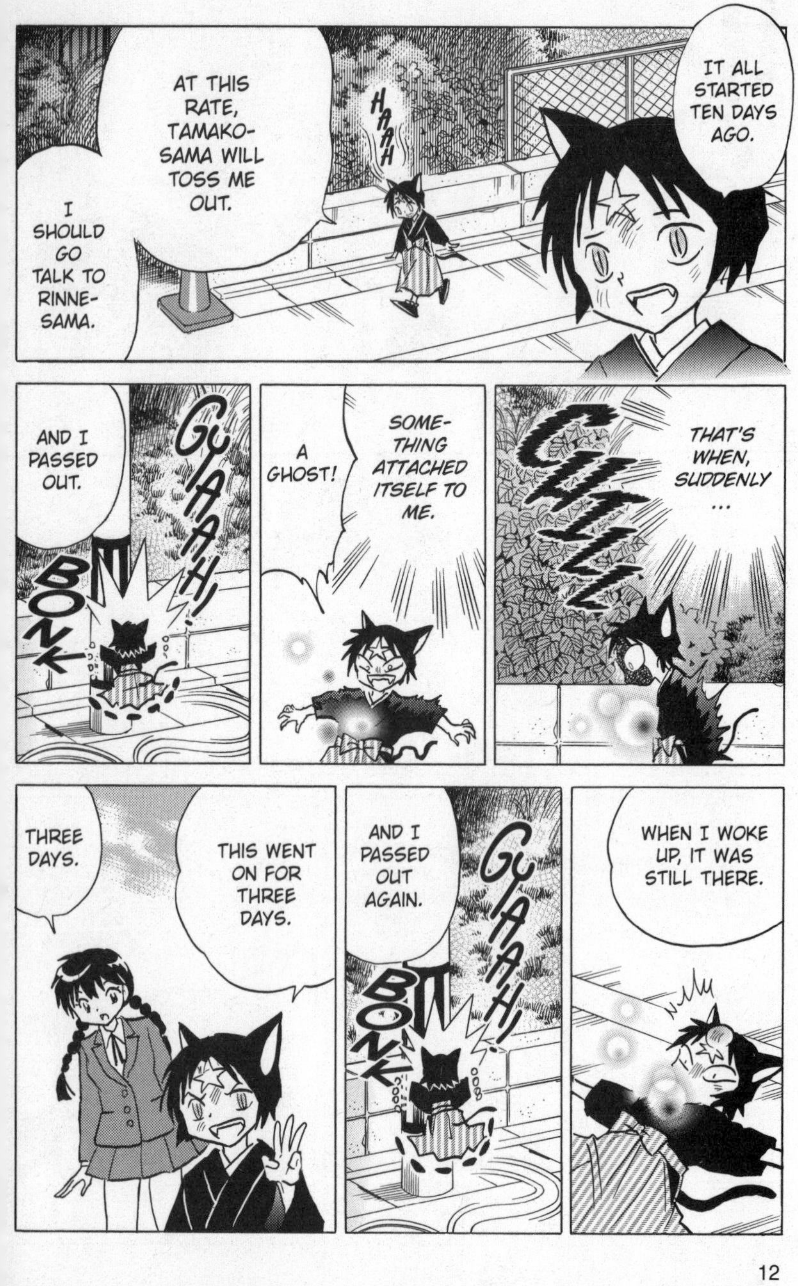
IT ALL STARTED TEN DAYS AGO.
AT THIS RATE, TAMAKO-SAMA WILL TOSS ME OUT.
HAAAH
I SHOULD GO TALK TO RINNE-SAMA.
THAT'S WHEN, SUDDENLY...
CHILL
SOME-THING ATTACHED ITSELF TO ME.
A GHOST!
GYAAAH!
AND I PASSED OUT.
BONK
WHEN I WOKE UP, IT WAS STILL THERE.
GYAAAH!
AND I PASSED OUT AGAIN.
BONK
THIS WENT ON FOR THREE DAYS.
THREE DAYS.

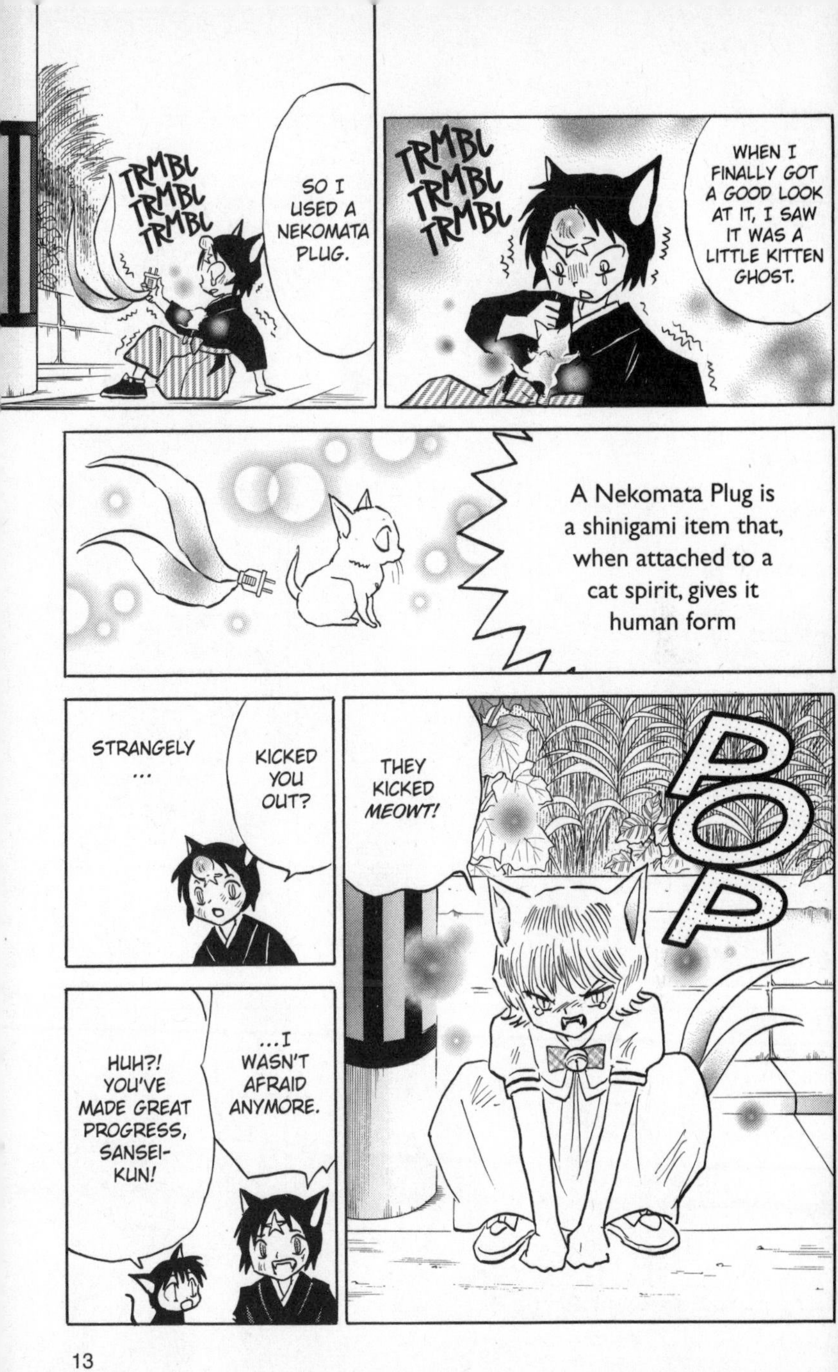
TRMBL TRMBL TRMBL
WHEN I FINALLY GOT A GOOD LOOK AT IT, I SAW IT WAS A LITTLE KITTEN GHOST.
TRMBL TRMBL TRMBL
SO I USED A NEKOMATA PLUG.
A Nekomata Plug is a shinigami item that, when attached to a cat spirit, gives it human form
POP
THEY KICKED MEOWT!
KICKED YOU OUT?
STRANGELY ...
...I WASN'T AFRAID ANYMORE.
HUH?! YOU'VE MADE GREAT PROGRESS, SANSEI-KUN!

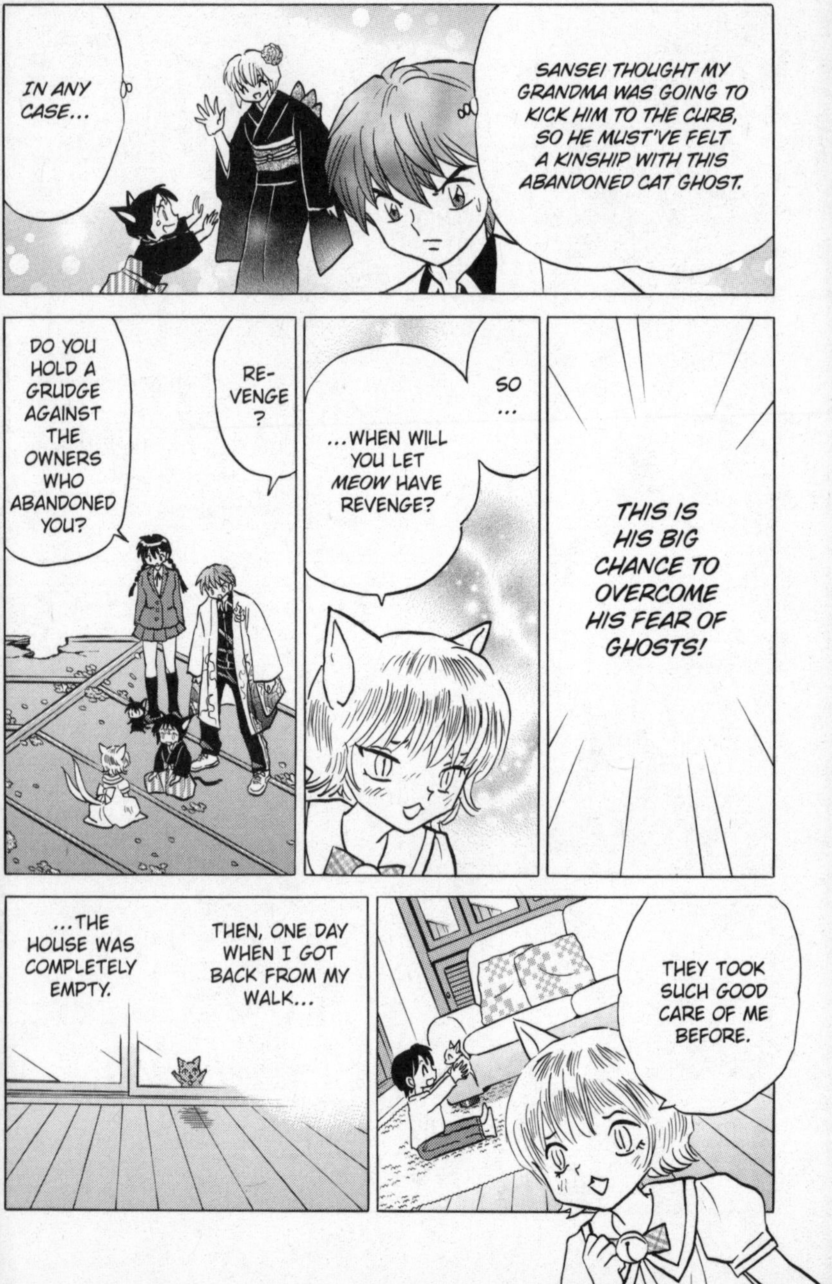
SANSEI THOUGHT MY GRANDMA WAS GOING TO KICK HIM TO THE CURB, SO HE MUST'VE FELT A KINSHIP WITH THIS ABANDONED CAT GHOST.
IN ANY CASE...
THIS IS HIS BIG CHANCE TO OVERCOME HIS FEAR OF GHOSTS!
SO ...
...WHEN WILL YOU LET MEOW HAVE REVENGE?
RE-VENGE?
DO YOU HOLD A GRUDGE AGAINST THE OWNERS WHO ABANDONED YOU?
THEY TOOK SUCH GOOD CARE OF ME BEFORE.
THEN, ONE DAY WHEN I GOT BACK FROM MY WALK...
...THE HOUSE WAS COMPLETELY EMPTY.

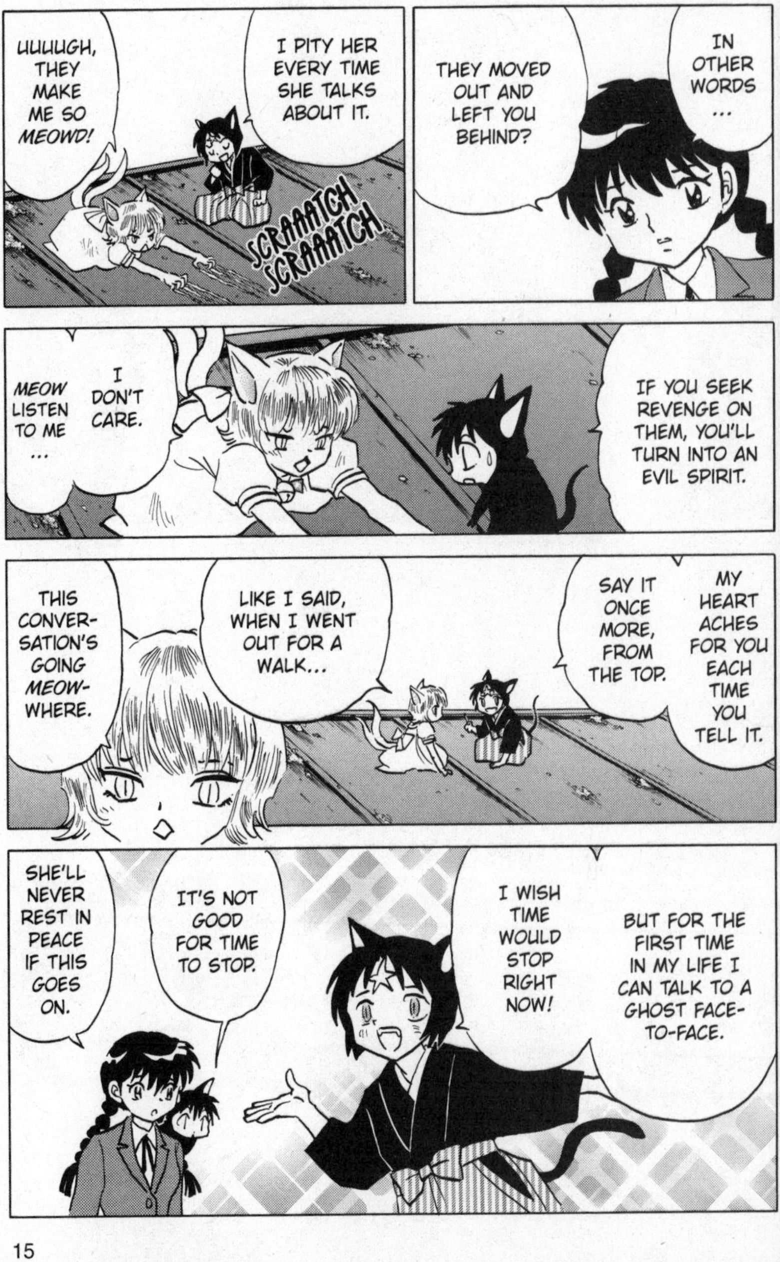

IN OTHER WORDS...
THEY MOVED OUT AND LEFT YOU BEHIND?
I PITY HER EVERY TIME SHE TALKS ABOUT IT.
UUUUGH, THEY MAKE ME SO *MEOWD!*
SCRAAATCH SCRAAATCH
IF YOU SEEK REVENGE ON THEM, YOU'LL TURN INTO AN EVIL SPIRIT.
I DON'T CARE.
MEOW LISTEN TO ME...
MY HEART ACHES FOR YOU EACH TIME YOU TELL IT.
SAY IT ONCE MORE, FROM THE TOP.
LIKE I SAID, WHEN I WENT OUT FOR A WALK...
THIS CONVERSATION'S GOING *MEOW*-WHERE.
BUT FOR THE FIRST TIME IN MY LIFE I CAN TALK TO A GHOST FACE-TO-FACE.
I WISH TIME WOULD STOP RIGHT NOW!
IT'S NOT GOOD FOR TIME TO STOP.
SHE'LL NEVER REST IN PEACE IF THIS GOES ON.

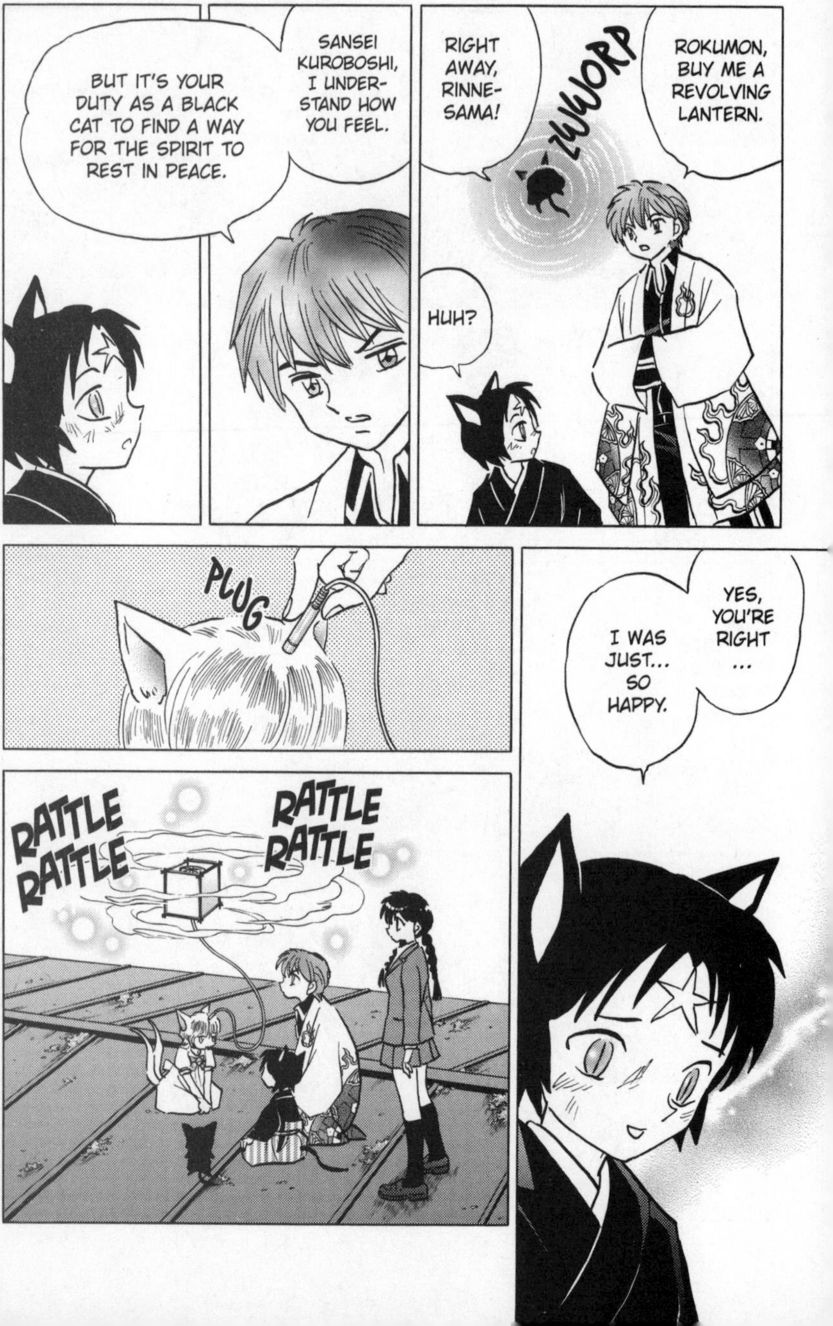
ROKUMON, BUY ME A REVOLVING LANTERN.
ZUWORP
RIGHT AWAY, RINNE-SAMA!
HUH?
SANSEI KUROBOSHI, I UNDER-STAND HOW YOU FEEL.
BUT IT'S YOUR DUTY AS A BLACK CAT TO FIND A WAY FOR THE SPIRIT TO REST IN PEACE.
YES, YOU'RE RIGHT ...
I WAS JUST... SO HAPPY.
PLUG
RATTLE RATTLE
RATTLE RATTLE

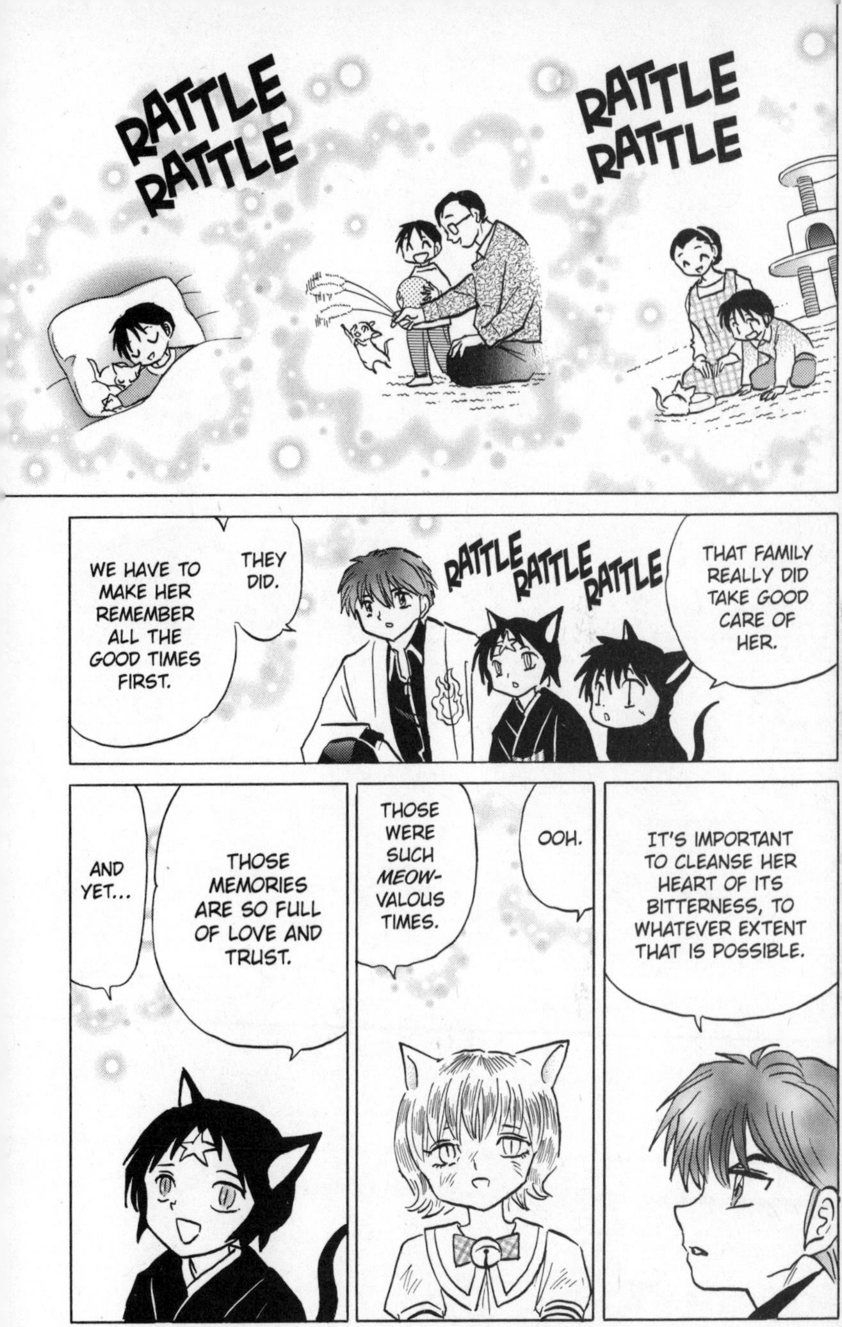
RATTLE RATTLE
RATTLE RATTLE
THAT FAMILY REALLY DID TAKE GOOD CARE OF HER.
RATTLE RATTLE RATTLE
THEY DID.
WE HAVE TO MAKE HER REMEMBER ALL THE GOOD TIMES FIRST.
IT'S IMPORTANT TO CLEANSE HER HEART OF ITS BITTERNESS, TO WHATEVER EXTENT THAT IS POSSIBLE.
OOH.
THOSE WERE SUCH *MEOW-VALOUS* TIMES.
THOSE MEMORIES ARE SO FULL OF LOVE AND TRUST.
AND YET...

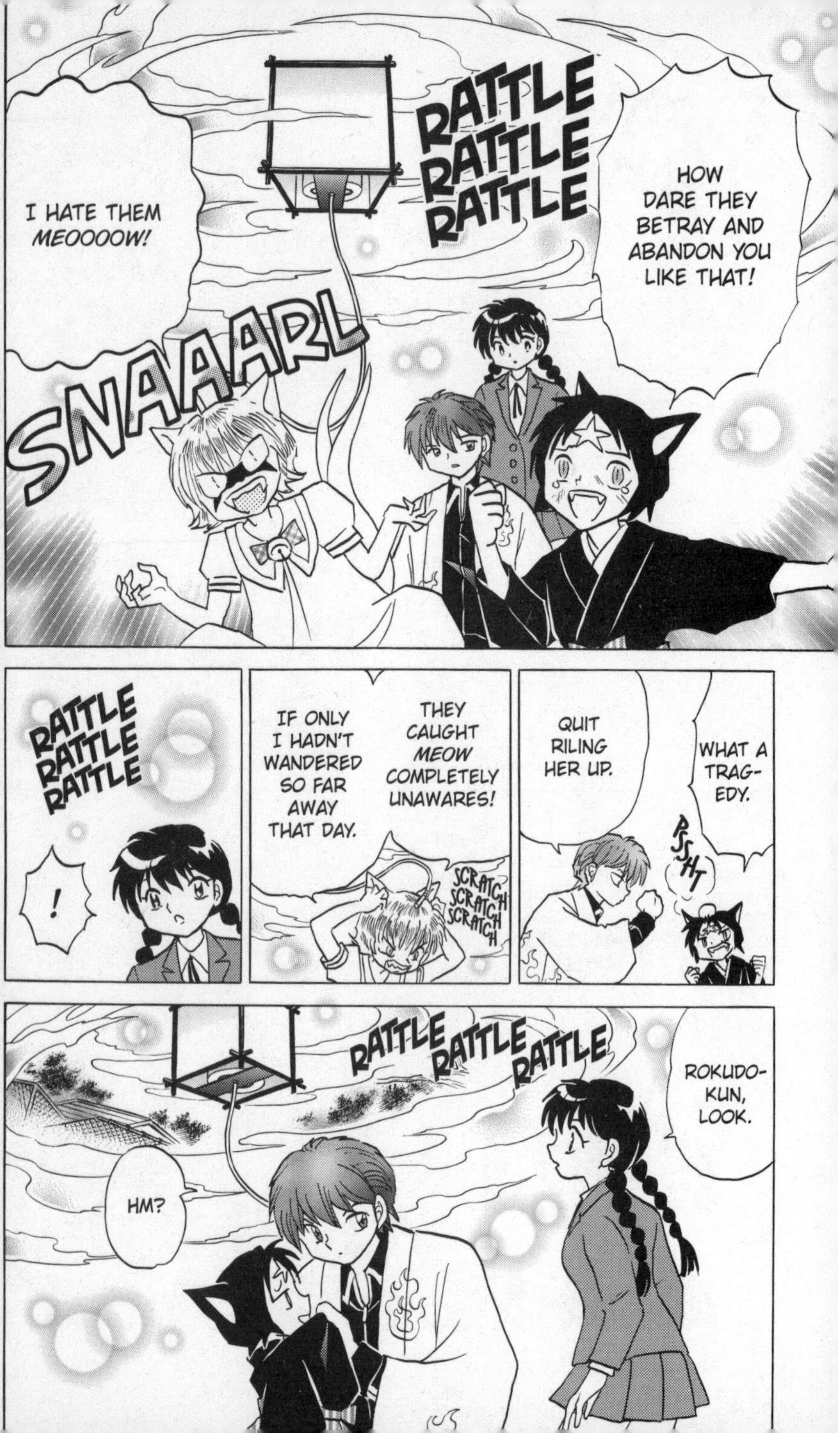
HOW DARE THEY BETRAY AND ABANDON YOU LIKE THAT!
RATTLE RATTLE RATTLE
I HATE THEM *MEOOOOW!*
SNAAARL
WHAT A TRAG-EDY.
QUIT RILING HER UP.
PSSHT
THEY CAUGHT *MEOW* COMPLETELY UNAWARES!
IF ONLY I HADN'T WANDERED SO FAR AWAY THAT DAY.
SCRATCH SCRATCH SCRATCH
RATTLE RATTLE RATTLE
!
ROKUDO-KUN, LOOK.
RATTLE RATTLE RATTLE
HM?

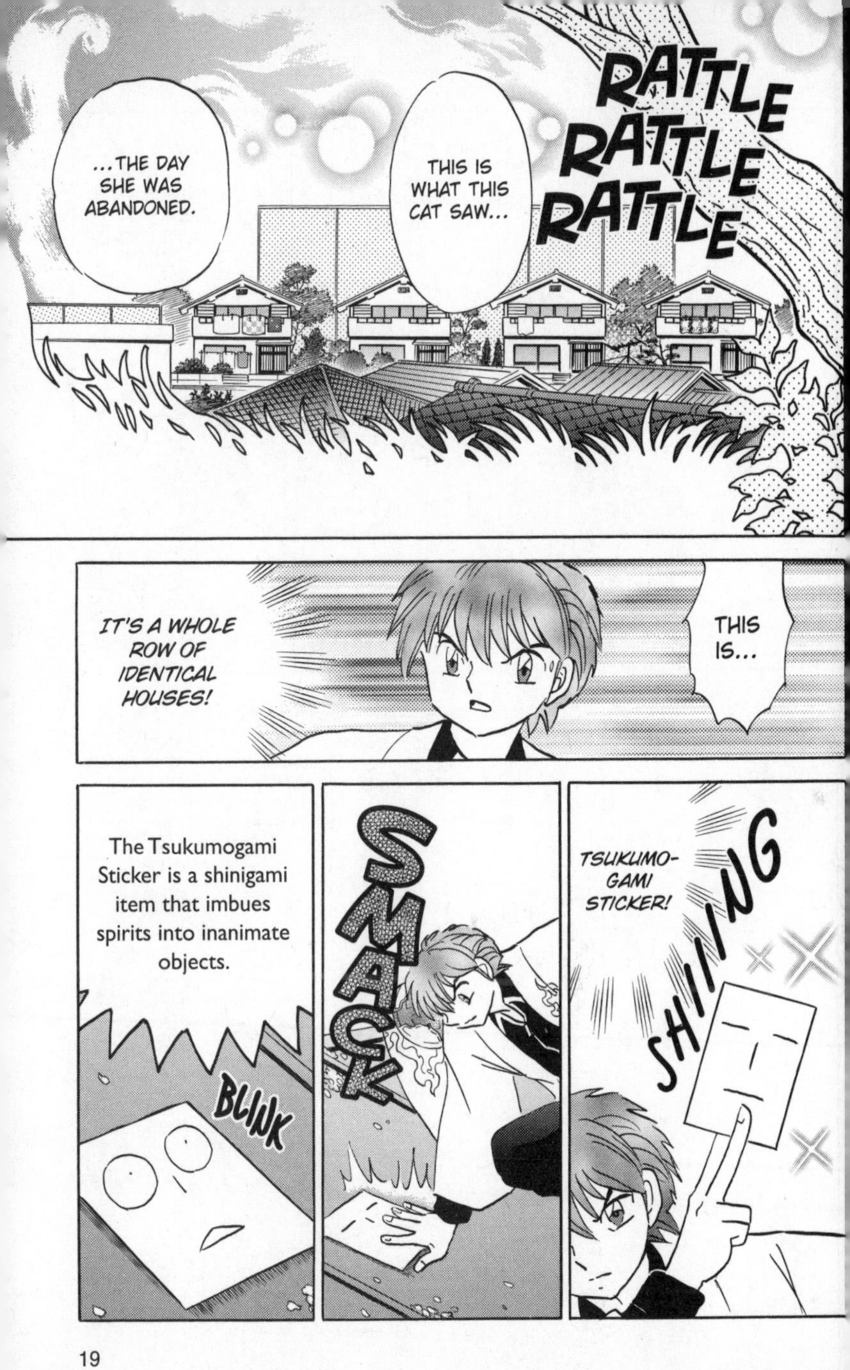
RATTLE RATTLE RATTLE
THIS IS WHAT THIS CAT SAW...
...THE DAY SHE WAS ABANDONED.
THIS IS...
IT'S A WHOLE ROW OF IDENTICAL HOUSES!
TSUKUMO-GAMI STICKER!
SHIIING
SMACK
The Tsukumogami Sticker is a shinigami item that imbues spirits into inanimate objects.
BLINK

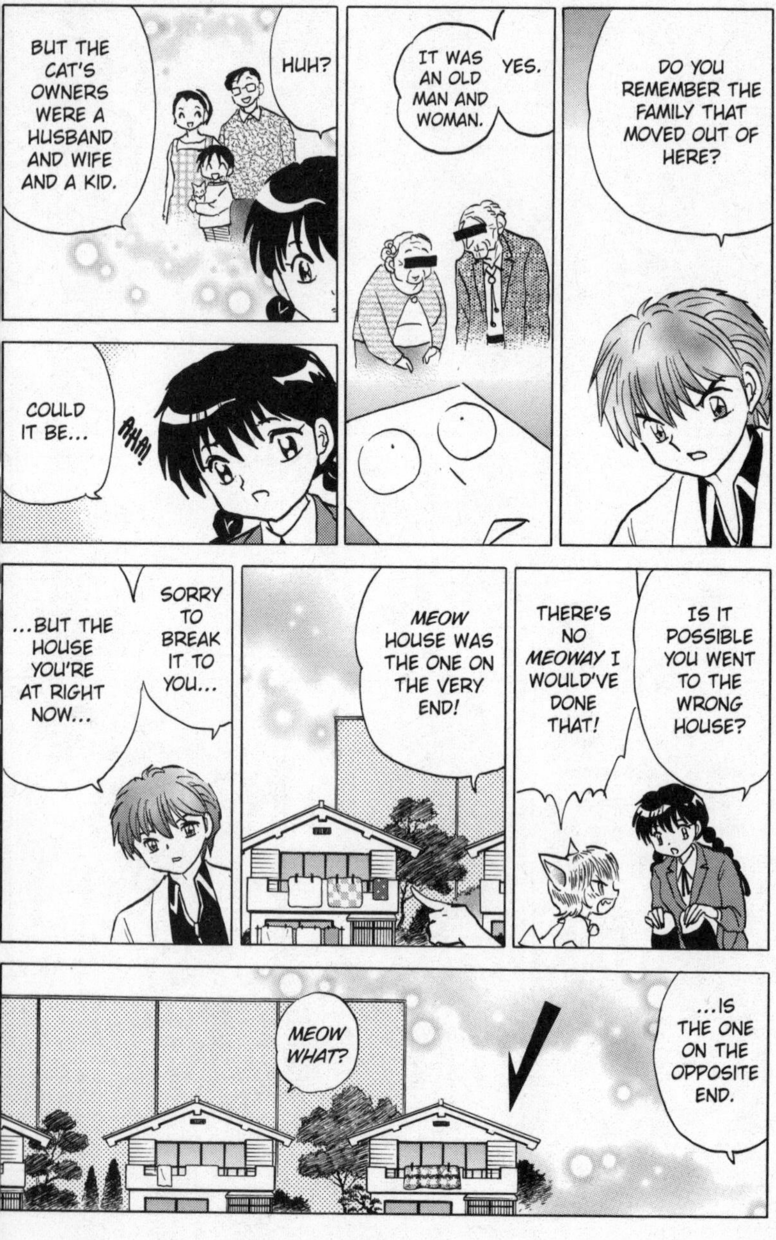
DO YOU REMEMBER THE FAMILY THAT MOVED OUT OF HERE?
YES.
IT WAS AN OLD MAN AND WOMAN.
HUH?
BUT THE CAT'S OWNERS WERE A HUSBAND AND WIFE AND A KID.
AHA!
COULD IT BE...
IS IT POSSIBLE YOU WENT TO THE WRONG HOUSE?
THERE'S NO *MEOWAY* I WOULD'VE DONE THAT!
MEOW HOUSE WAS THE ONE ON THE VERY END!
SORRY TO BREAK IT TO YOU...
...BUT THE HOUSE YOU'RE AT RIGHT NOW...
...IS THE ONE ON THE OPPOSITE END.
MEOW WHAT?

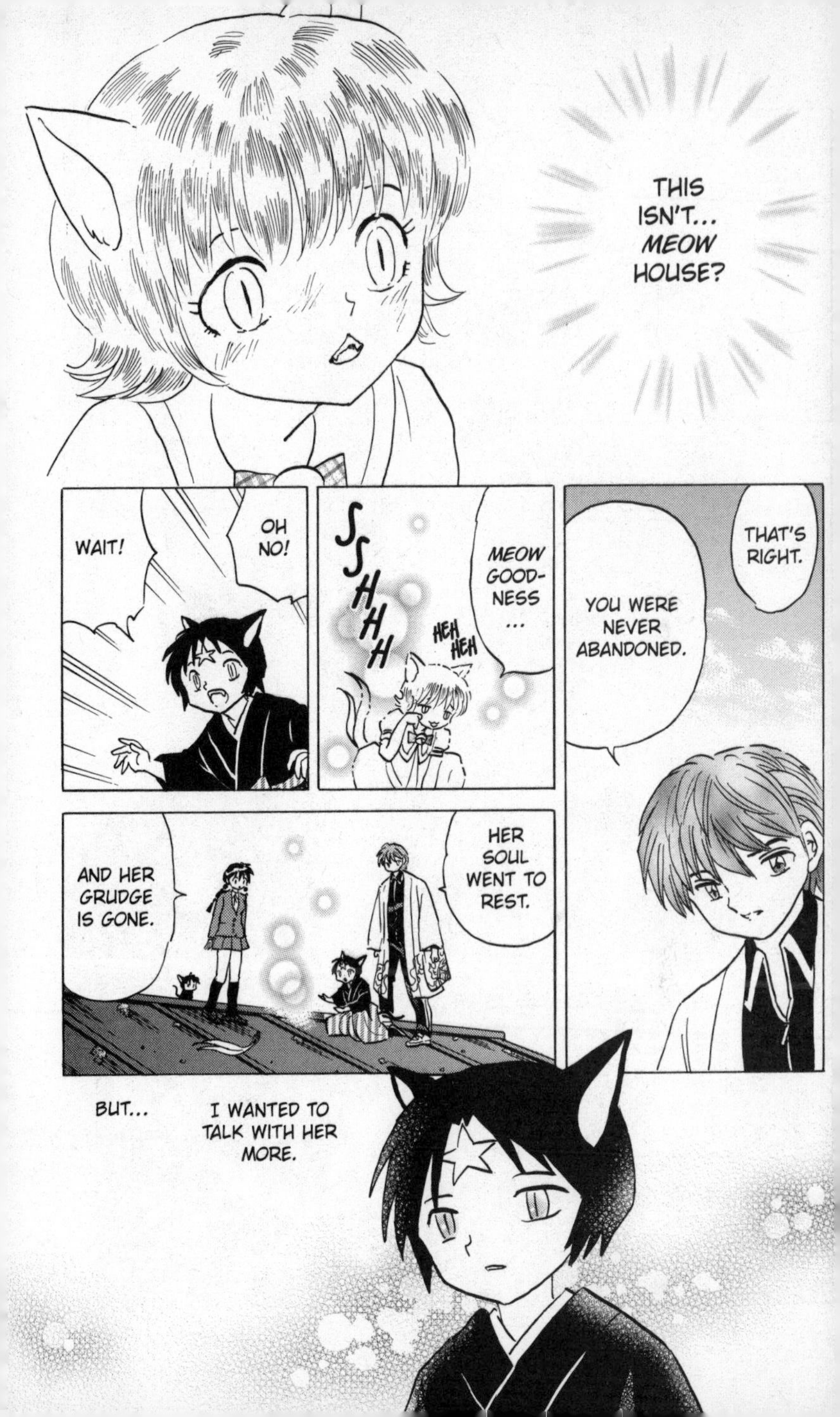
THIS ISN'T... MEOW HOUSE?
THAT'S RIGHT.
YOU WERE NEVER ABANDONED.
MEOW GOODNESS ...
SSHHH
HEH HEH
OH NO!
WAIT!
HER SOUL WENT TO REST.
AND HER GRUDGE IS GONE.
BUT...
I WANTED TO TALK WITH HER MORE.

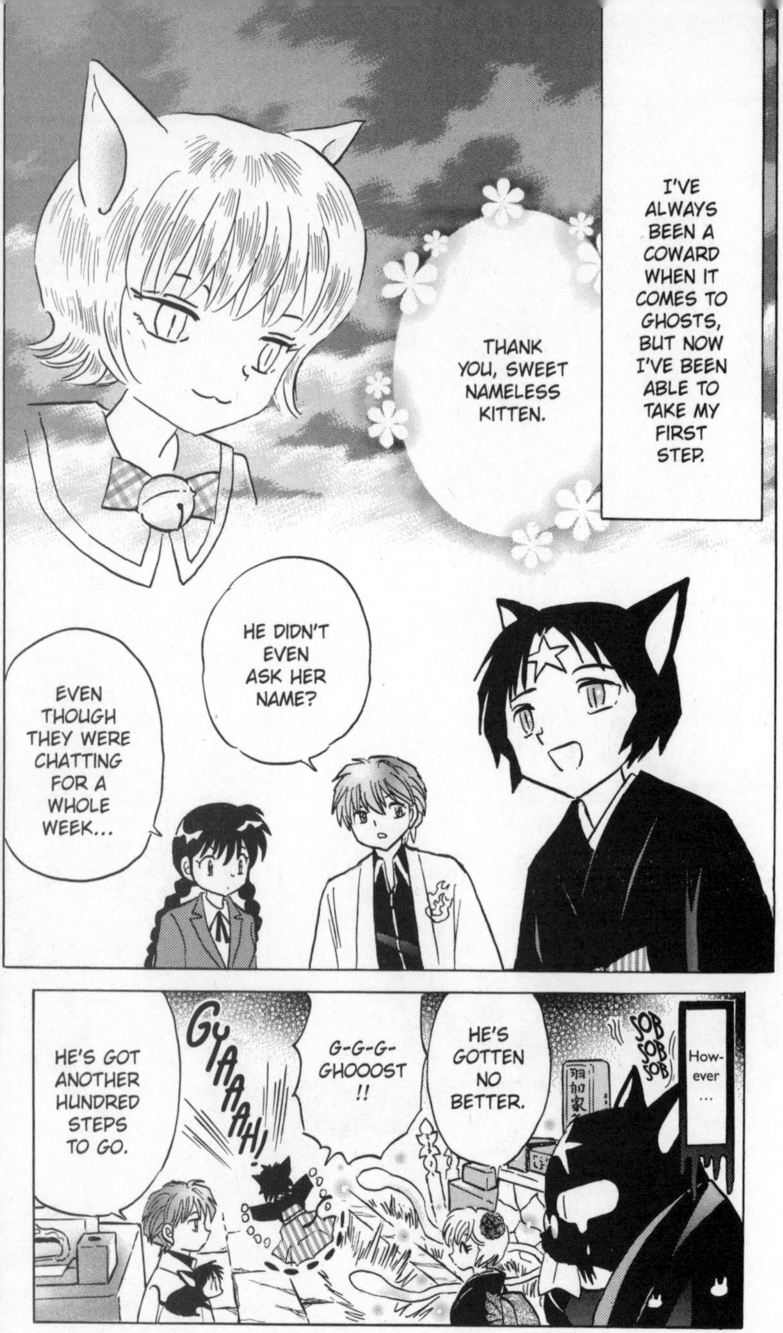
I'VE ALWAYS BEEN A COWARD WHEN IT COMES TO GHOSTS, BUT NOW I'VE BEEN ABLE TO TAKE MY FIRST STEP.
THANK YOU, SWEET NAMELESS KITTEN.
HE DIDN'T EVEN ASK HER NAME?
EVEN THOUGH THEY WERE CHATTING FOR A WHOLE WEEK...
However...
SOB SOB SOB
HE'S GOTTEN NO BETTER.
G-G-G-GHOOOST!!
GYAAAAH!
HE'S GOT ANOTHER HUNDRED STEPS TO GO.

CHAPTER 370: PUTTING ONE'S AFFAIRS IN ORDER

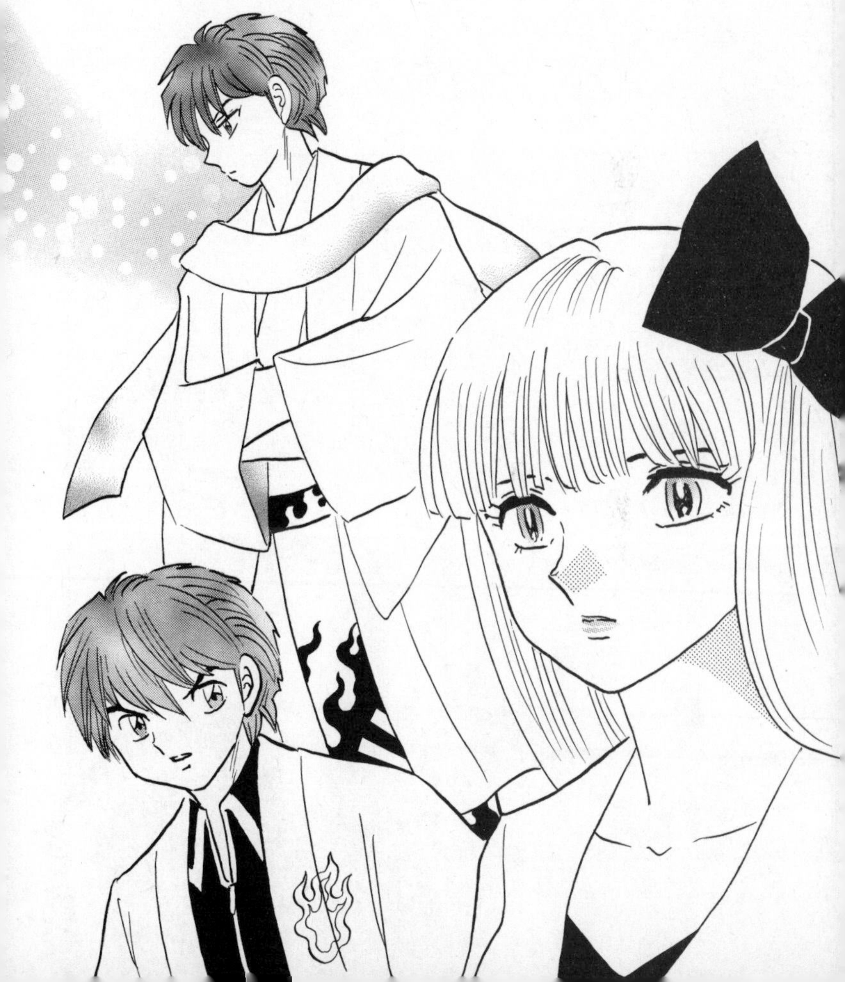

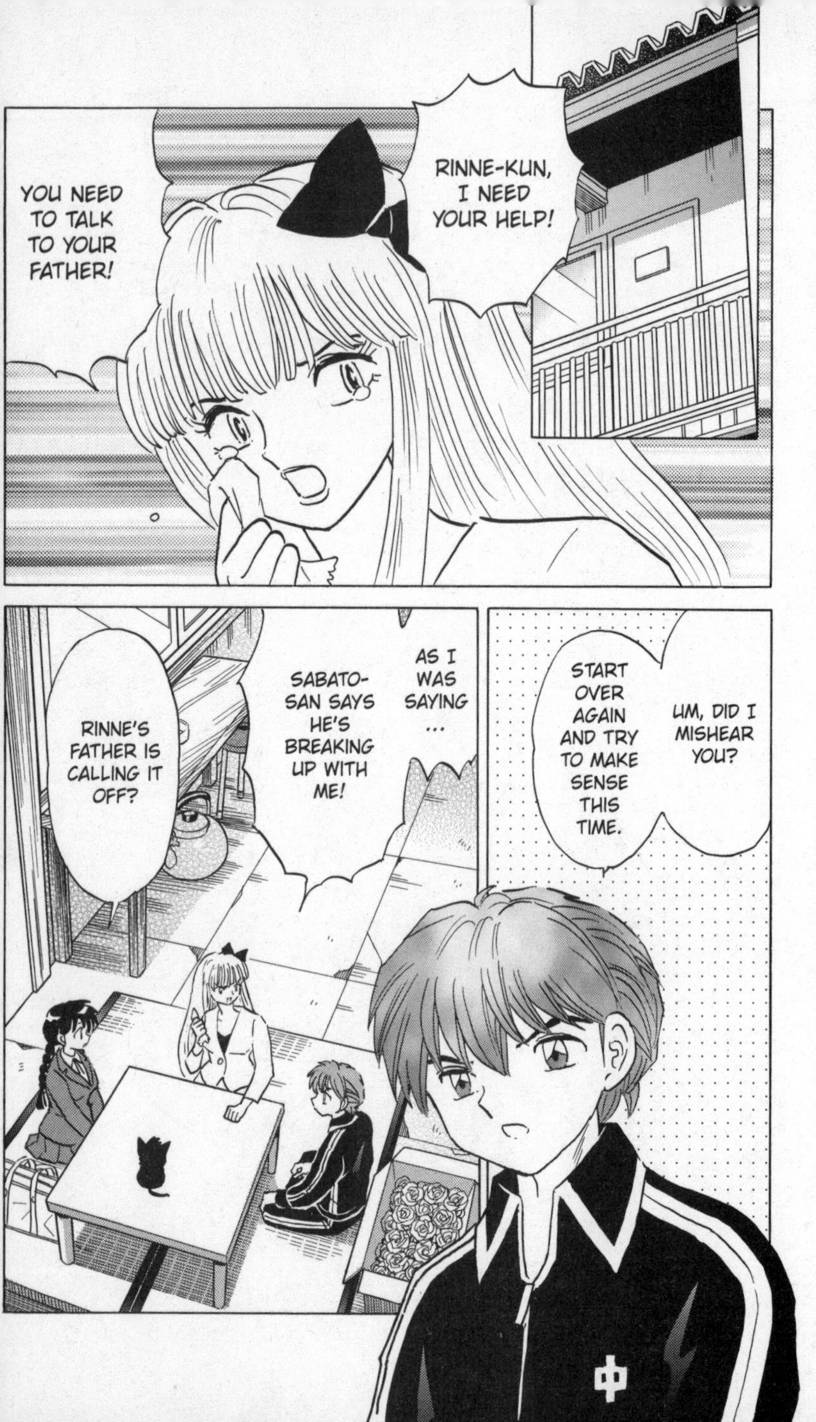

RINNE-KUN, I NEED YOUR HELP!
YOU NEED TO TALK TO YOUR FATHER!
UM, DID I MISHEAR YOU?
START OVER AGAIN AND TRY TO MAKE SENSE THIS TIME.
AS I WAS SAYING...
SABATO-SAN SAYS HE'S BREAKING UP WITH ME!
RINNE'S FATHER IS CALLING IT OFF?

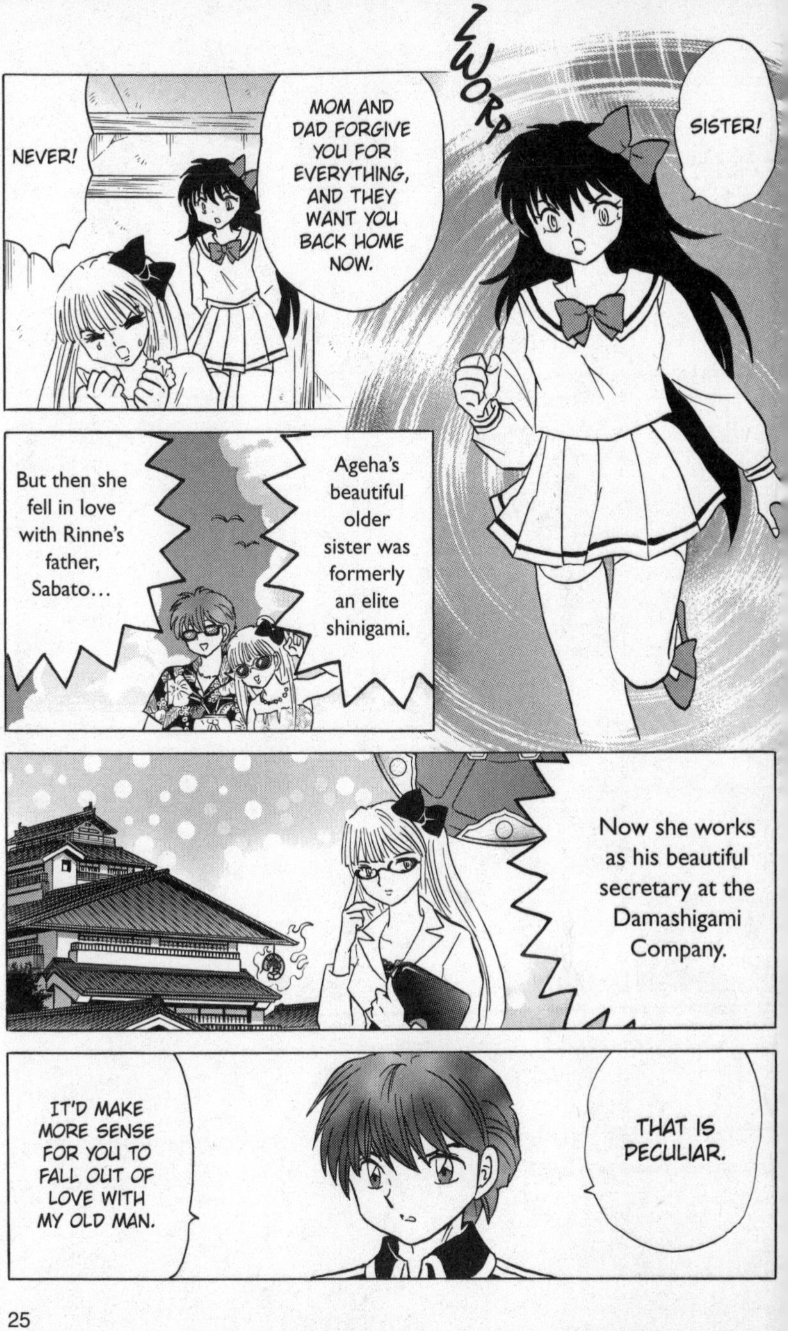
ZWORP
SISTER!
MOM AND DAD FORGIVE YOU FOR EVERYTHING, AND THEY WANT YOU BACK HOME NOW.
NEVER!
Ageha's beautiful older sister was formerly an elite shinigami.
But then she fell in love with Rinne's father, Sabato…
Now she works as his beautiful secretary at the Damashigami Company.
THAT IS PECULIAR.
IT'D MAKE MORE SENSE FOR YOU TO FALL OUT OF LOVE WITH MY OLD MAN.

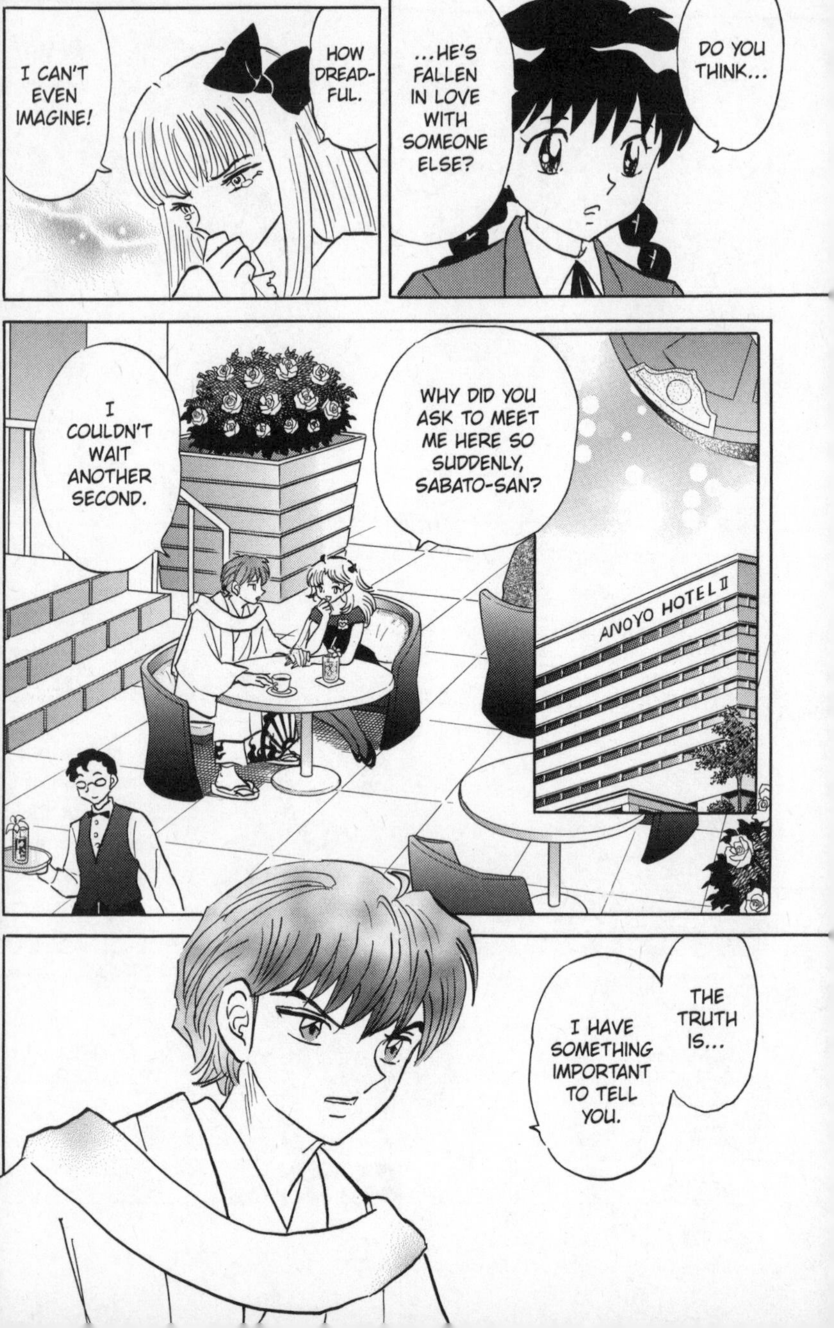
DO YOU THINK...
...HE'S FALLEN IN LOVE WITH SOMEONE ELSE?
HOW DREAD-FUL.
I CAN'T EVEN IMAGINE!
WHY DID YOU ASK TO MEET ME HERE SO SUDDENLY, SABATO-SAN?
I COULDN'T WAIT ANOTHER SECOND.
ANOYO HOTEL II
THE TRUTH IS...
I HAVE SOMETHING IMPORTANT TO TELL YOU.

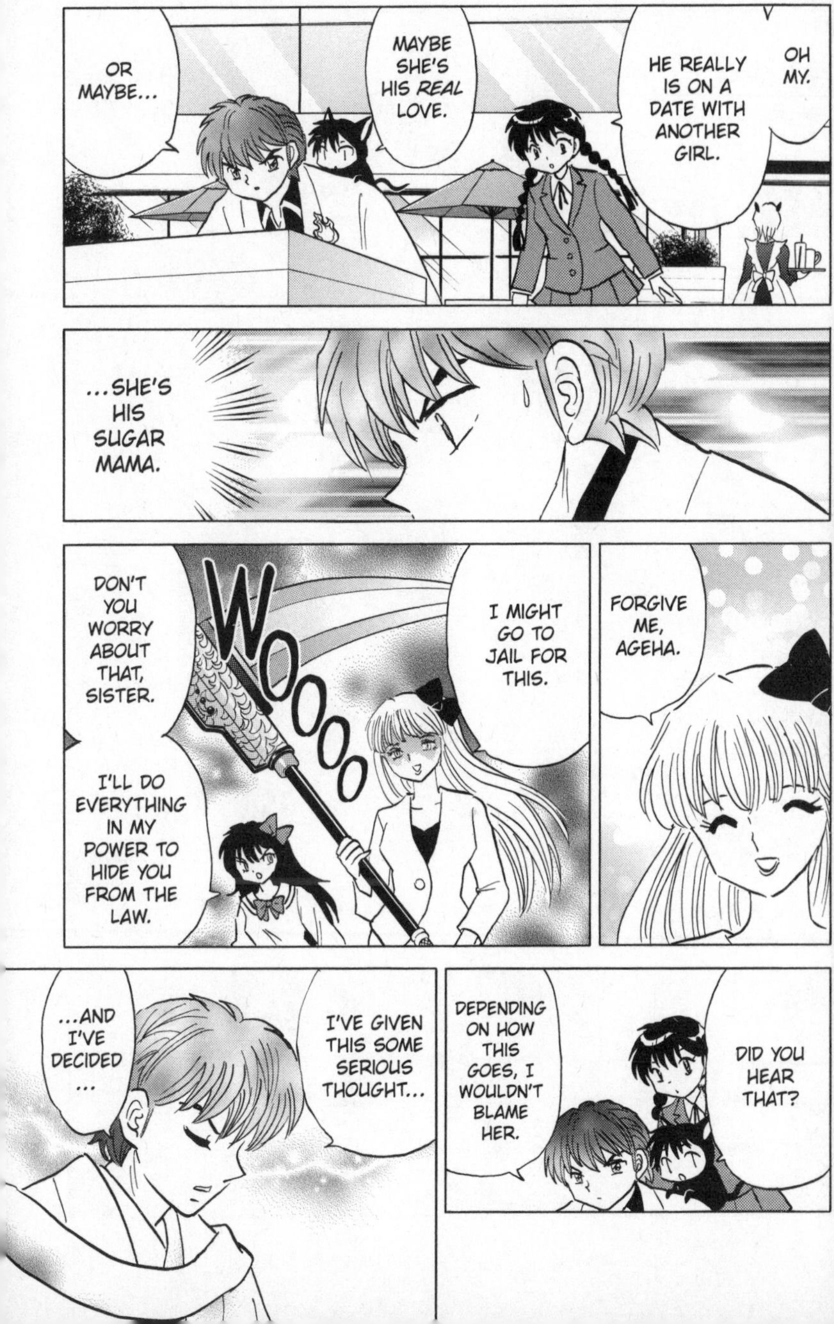
OH MY.
HE REALLY IS ON A DATE WITH ANOTHER GIRL.
MAYBE SHE'S HIS *REAL* LOVE.
OR MAYBE...
...SHE'S HIS SUGAR MAMA.
FORGIVE ME, AGEHA.
I MIGHT GO TO JAIL FOR THIS.
WOOOOO
DON'T YOU WORRY ABOUT THAT, SISTER.
I'LL DO EVERYTHING IN MY POWER TO HIDE YOU FROM THE LAW.
DID YOU HEAR THAT?
DEPENDING ON HOW THIS GOES, I WOULDN'T BLAME HER.
I'VE GIVEN THIS SOME SERIOUS THOUGHT...
...AND I'VE DECIDED...

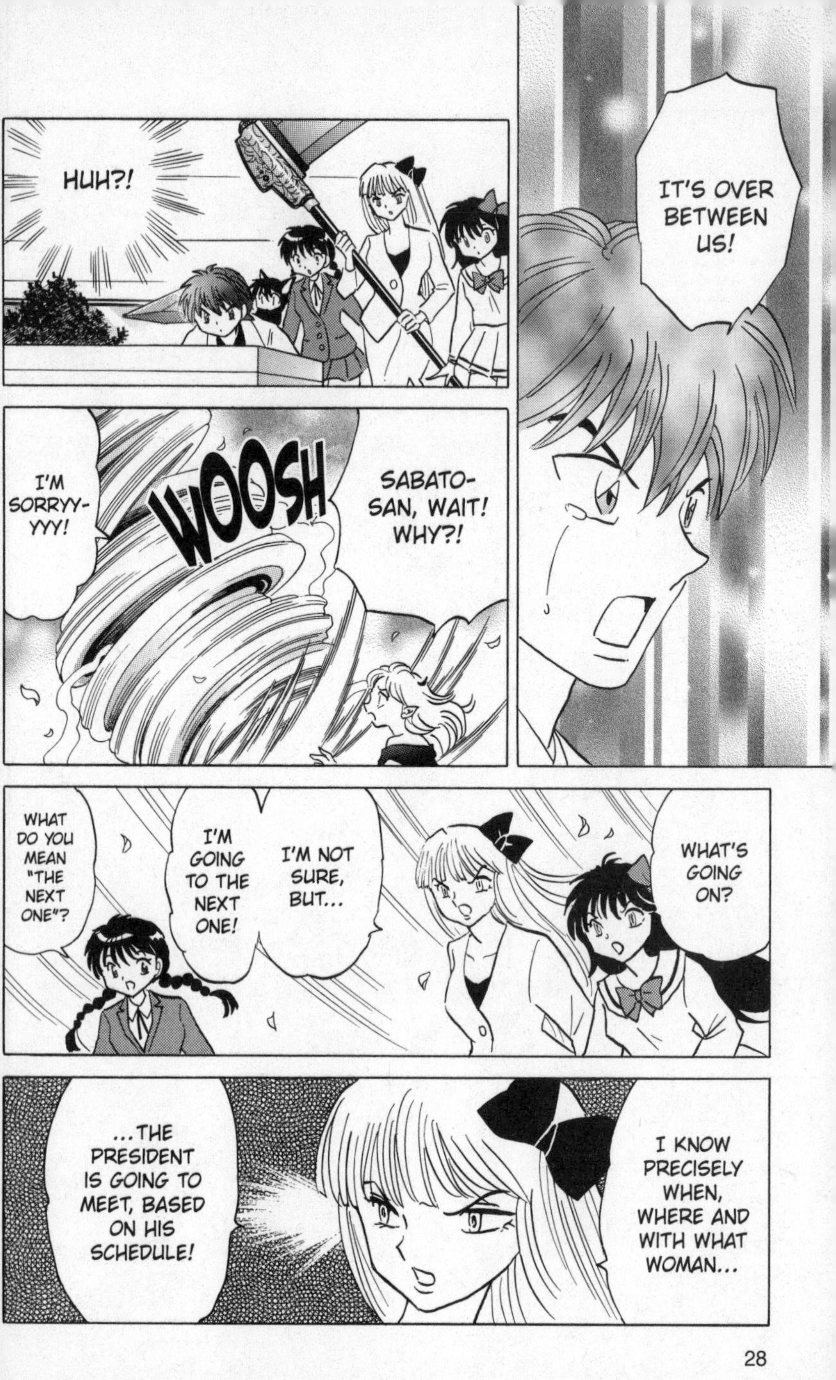
IT'S OVER BETWEEN US!
HUH?!
SABATO-SAN, WAIT! WHY?!
WOOSH
I'M SORRYY-YYY!
WHAT'S GOING ON?
I'M NOT SURE, BUT...
I'M GOING TO THE NEXT ONE!
WHAT DO YOU MEAN "THE NEXT ONE"?
I KNOW PRECISELY WHEN, WHERE AND WITH WHAT WOMAN...
...THE PRESIDENT IS GOING TO MEET, BASED ON HIS SCHEDULE!

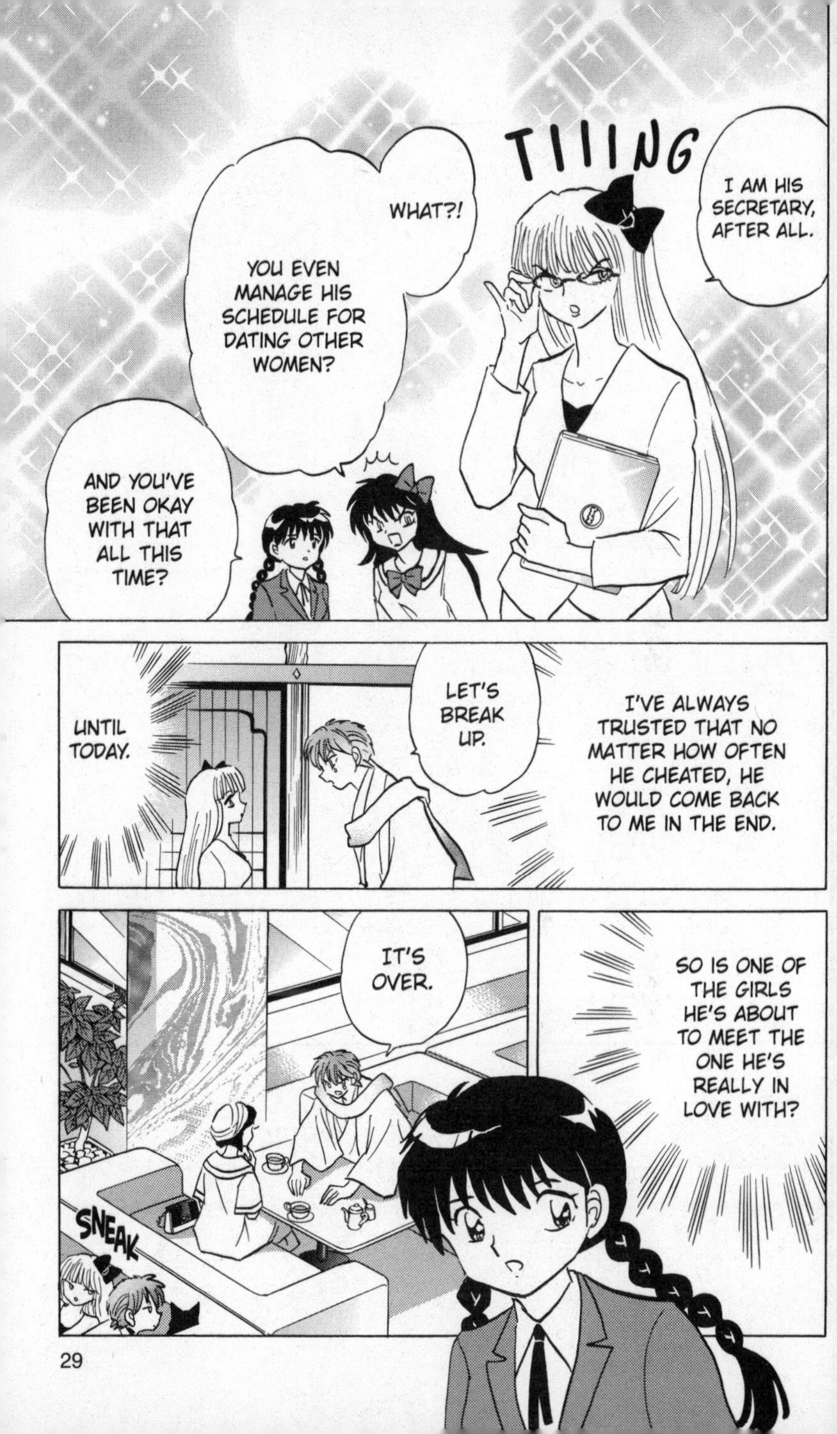

I AM HIS SECRETARY, AFTER ALL.
TIIING
WHAT?!
YOU EVEN MANAGE HIS SCHEDULE FOR DATING OTHER WOMEN?
AND YOU'VE BEEN OKAY WITH THAT ALL THIS TIME?
I'VE ALWAYS TRUSTED THAT NO MATTER HOW OFTEN HE CHEATED, HE WOULD COME BACK TO ME IN THE END.
LET'S BREAK UP.
UNTIL TODAY.
SO IS ONE OF THE GIRLS HE'S ABOUT TO MEET THE ONE HE'S REALLY IN LOVE WITH?
IT'S OVER.
SNEAK

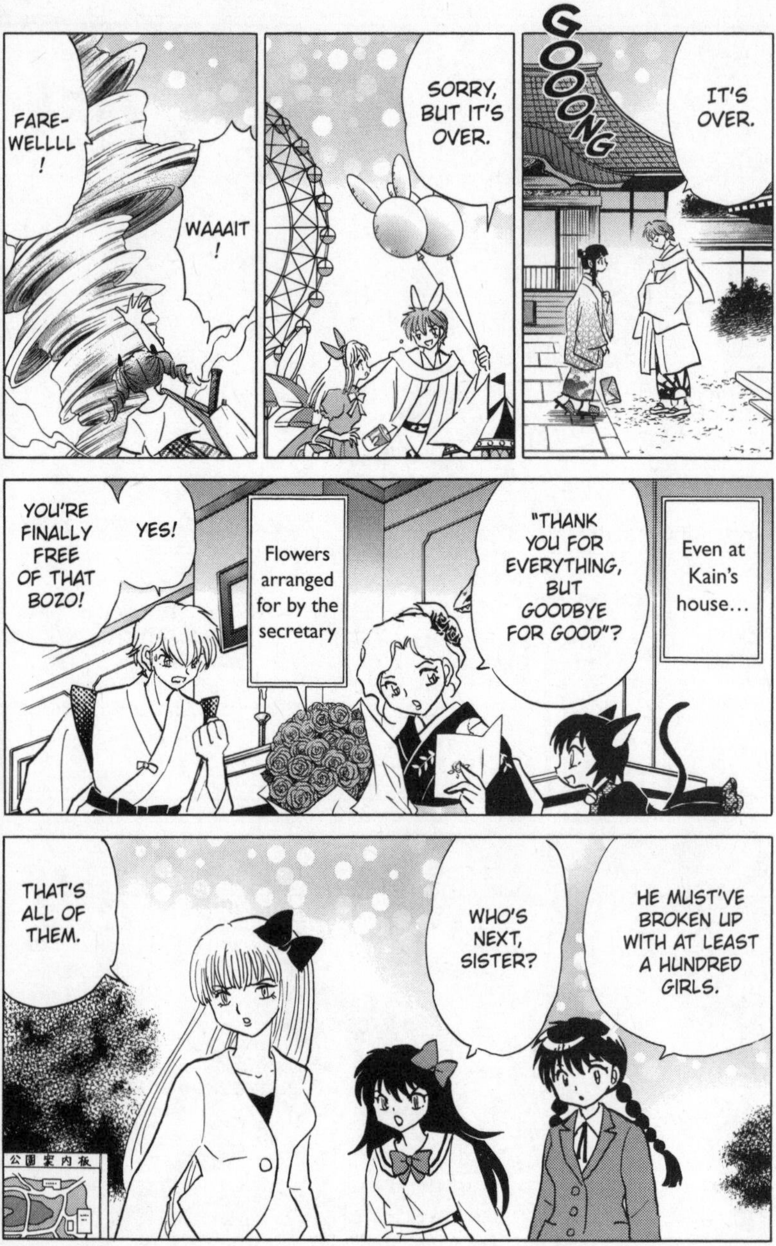
GOOONG
IT'S OVER.
SORRY, BUT IT'S OVER.
FARE-WELLLL!
WAAAIT!
Even at Kain's house…
"THANK YOU FOR EVERYTHING, BUT GOODBYE FOR GOOD"?
Flowers arranged for by the secretary
YOU'RE FINALLY FREE OF THAT BOZO!
YES!
HE MUST'VE BROKEN UP WITH AT LEAST A HUNDRED GIRLS.
WHO'S NEXT, SISTER?
THAT'S ALL OF THEM.
公園案内板

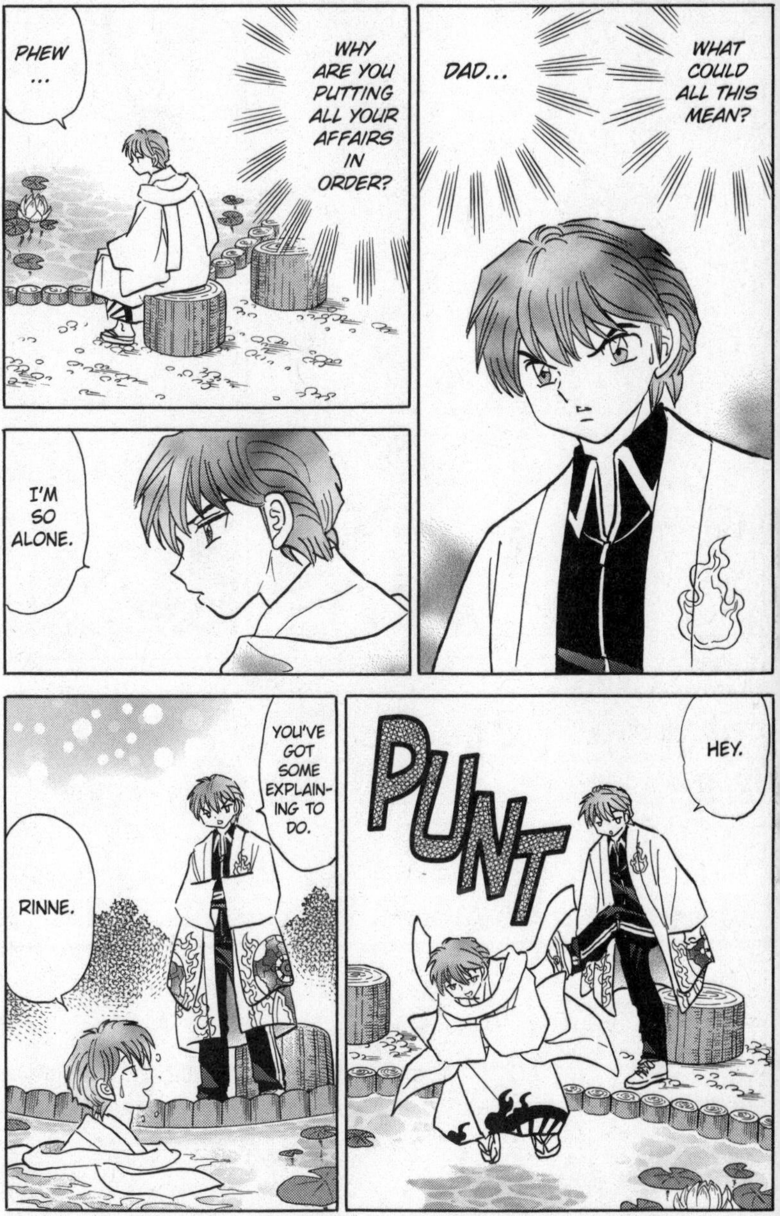
WHAT COULD ALL THIS MEAN?
DAD...
WHY ARE YOU PUTTING ALL YOUR AFFAIRS IN ORDER?
PHEW ...
I'M SO ALONE.
HEY.
PUNT
YOU'VE GOT SOME EXPLAIN-ING TO DO.
RINNE.

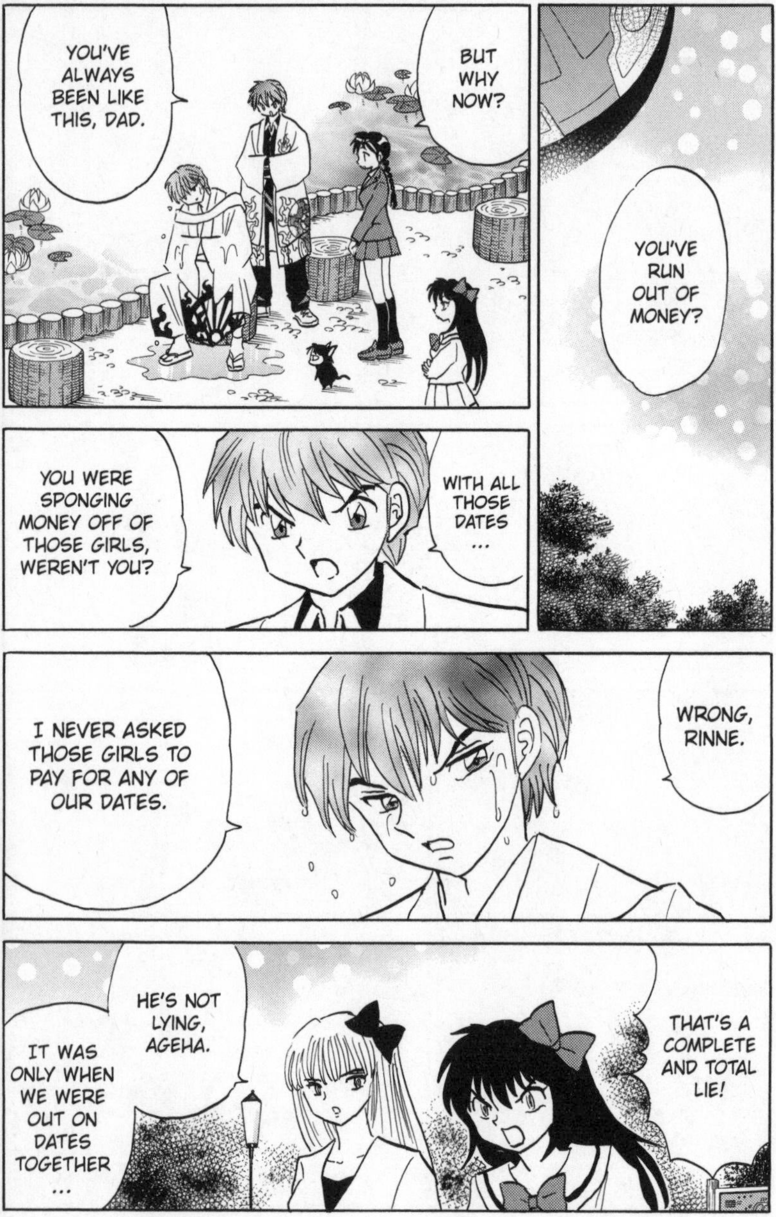
YOU'VE RUN OUT OF MONEY?
BUT WHY NOW?
YOU'VE ALWAYS BEEN LIKE THIS, DAD.
WITH ALL THOSE DATES ...
YOU WERE SPONGING MONEY OFF OF THOSE GIRLS, WEREN'T YOU?
WRONG, RINNE.
I NEVER ASKED THOSE GIRLS TO PAY FOR ANY OF OUR DATES.
THAT'S A COMPLETE AND TOTAL LIE!
HE'S NOT LYING, AGEHA.
IT WAS ONLY WHEN WE WERE OUT ON DATES TOGETHER ...

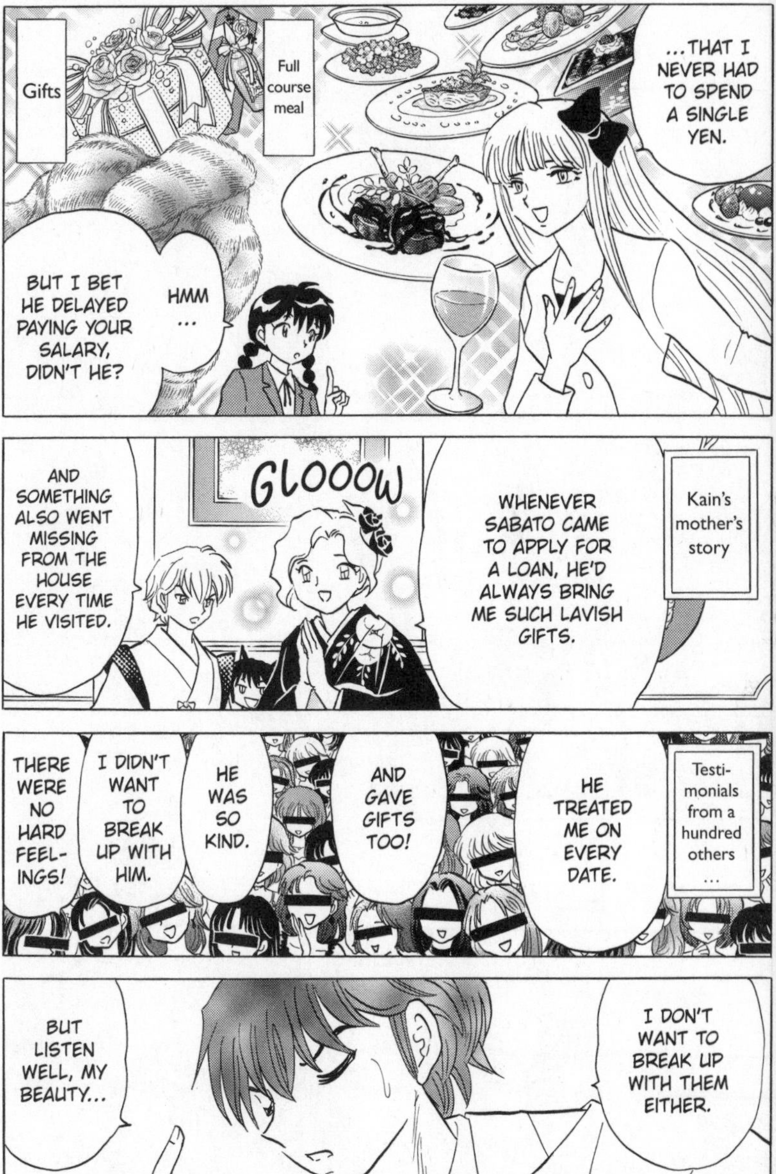
...THAT I NEVER HAD TO SPEND A SINGLE YEN.
Full course meal
Gifts
HMM...
BUT I BET HE DELAYED PAYING YOUR SALARY, DIDN'T HE?
Kain's mother's story
WHENEVER SABATO CAME TO APPLY FOR A LOAN, HE'D ALWAYS BRING ME SUCH LAVISH GIFTS.
GLOOOW
AND SOMETHING ALSO WENT MISSING FROM THE HOUSE EVERY TIME HE VISITED.
Testi-monials from a hundred others...
HE TREATED ME ON EVERY DATE.
AND GAVE GIFTS TOO!
HE WAS SO KIND.
I DIDN'T WANT TO BREAK UP WITH HIM.
THERE WERE NO HARD FEEL-INGS!
I DON'T WANT TO BREAK UP WITH THEM EITHER.
BUT LISTEN WELL, MY BEAUTY...

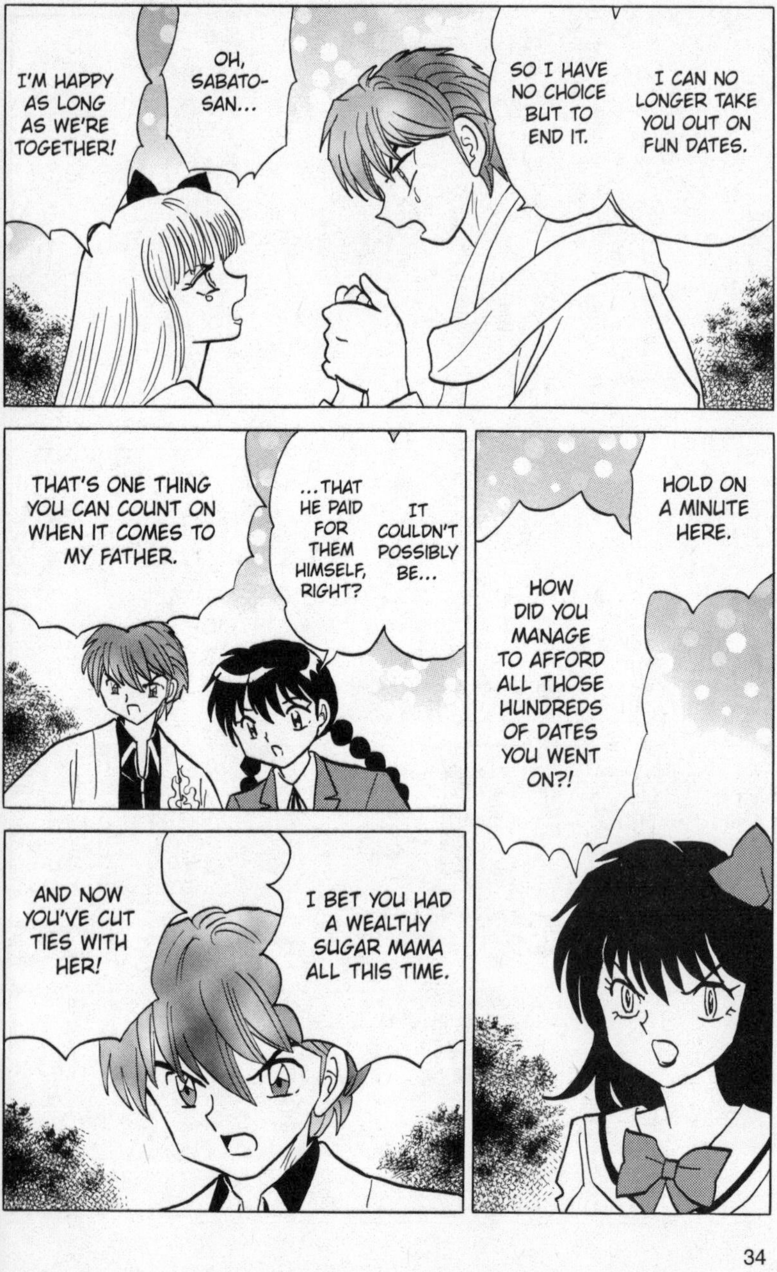
I CAN NO LONGER TAKE YOU OUT ON FUN DATES.
SO I HAVE NO CHOICE BUT TO END IT.
OH, SABATO-SAN...
I'M HAPPY AS LONG AS WE'RE TOGETHER!
HOLD ON A MINUTE HERE.
HOW DID YOU MANAGE TO AFFORD ALL THOSE HUNDREDS OF DATES YOU WENT ON?!
IT COULDN'T POSSIBLY BE...
...THAT HE PAID FOR THEM HIMSELF, RIGHT?
THAT'S ONE THING YOU CAN COUNT ON WHEN IT COMES TO MY FATHER.
I BET YOU HAD A WEALTHY SUGAR MAMA ALL THIS TIME.
AND NOW YOU'VE CUT TIES WITH HER!

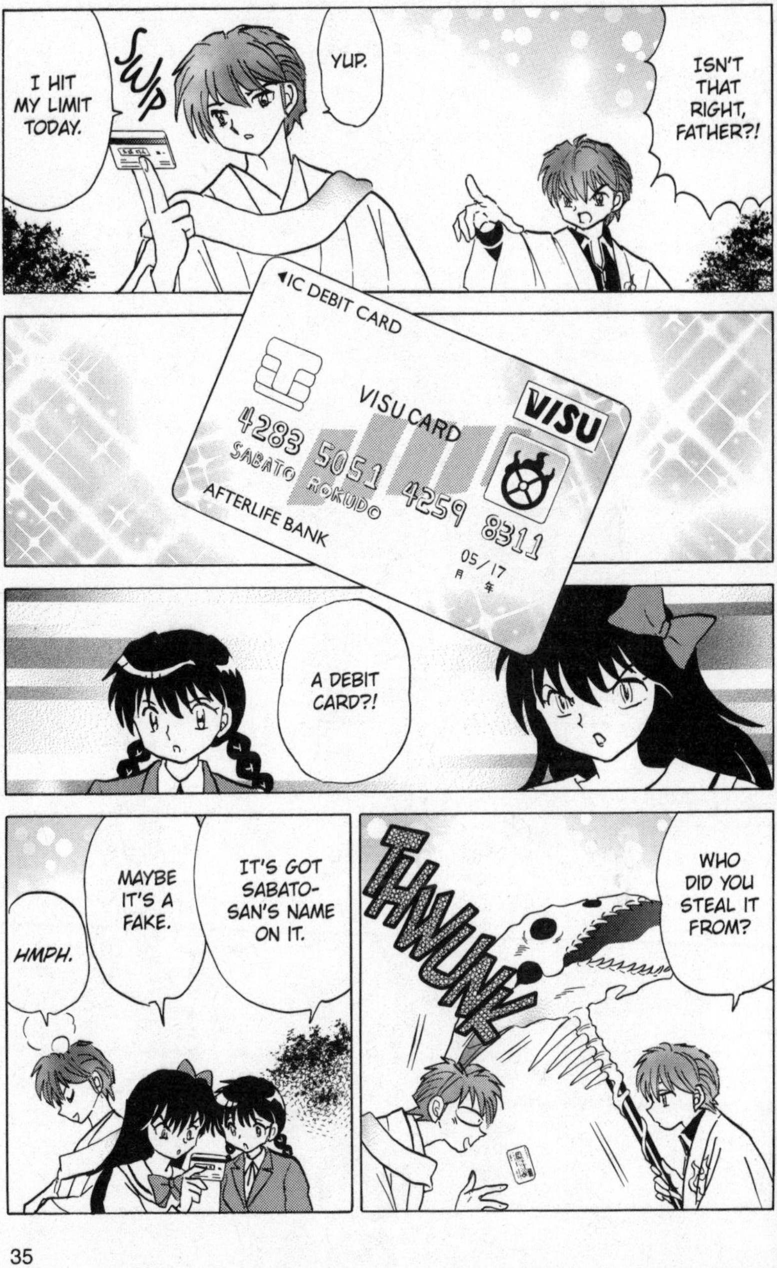
ISN'T THAT RIGHT, FATHER?!
YUP.
SWIP
I HIT MY LIMIT TODAY.
IC DEBIT CARD
VISU CARD
VISU
4283 5051 4259 8311
SABATO ROKUDO
AFTERLIFE BANK
05/17
A DEBIT CARD?!
WHO DID YOU STEAL IT FROM?
THWUNK
IT'S GOT SABATO-SAN'S NAME ON IT.
MAYBE IT'S A FAKE.
HMPH.

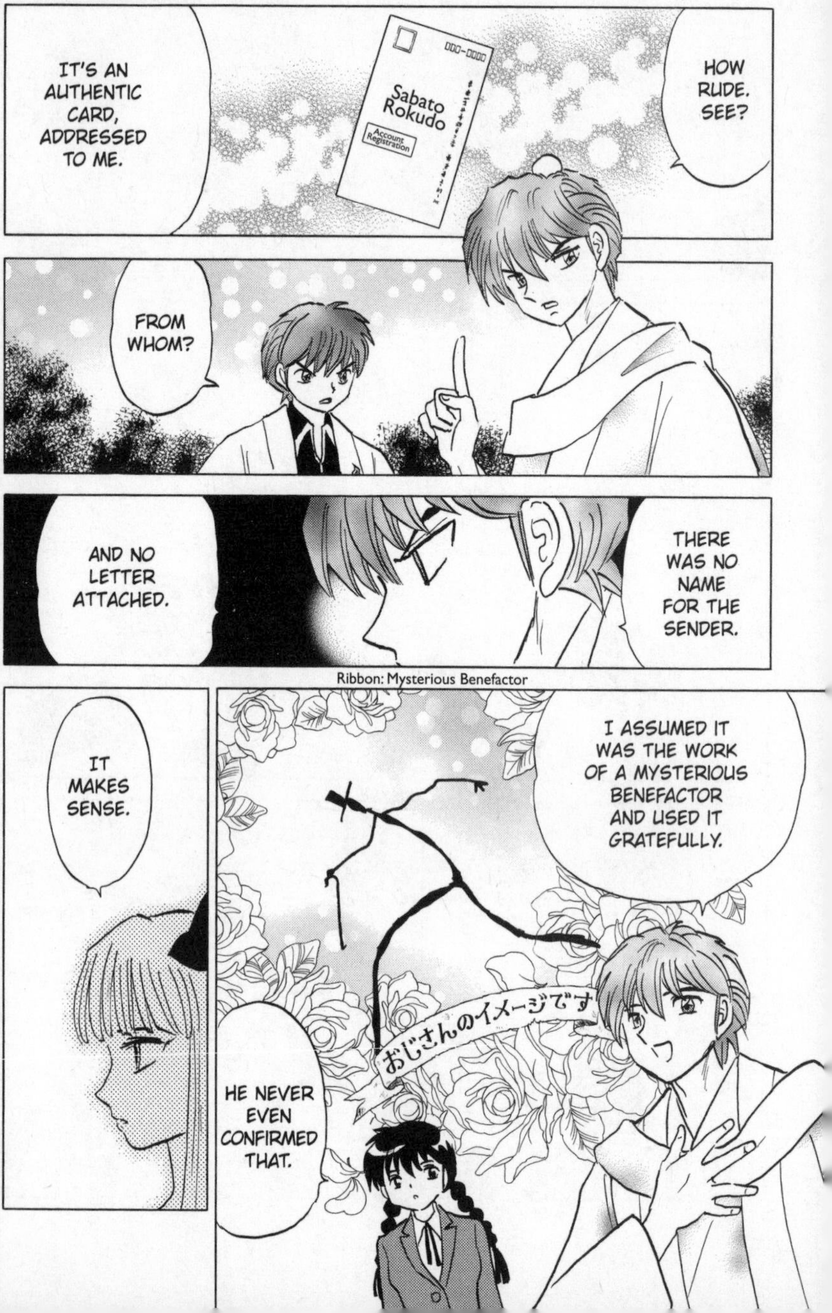
HOW RUDE. SEE?
Sabato Rokudo
Account Registration
IT'S AN AUTHENTIC CARD, ADDRESSED TO ME.
FROM WHOM?
THERE WAS NO NAME FOR THE SENDER.
AND NO LETTER ATTACHED.
Ribbon: Mysterious Benefactor
I ASSUMED IT WAS THE WORK OF A MYSTERIOUS BENEFACTOR AND USED IT GRATEFULLY.
おじさんのイメージです
HE NEVER EVEN CONFIRMED THAT.
IT MAKES SENSE.

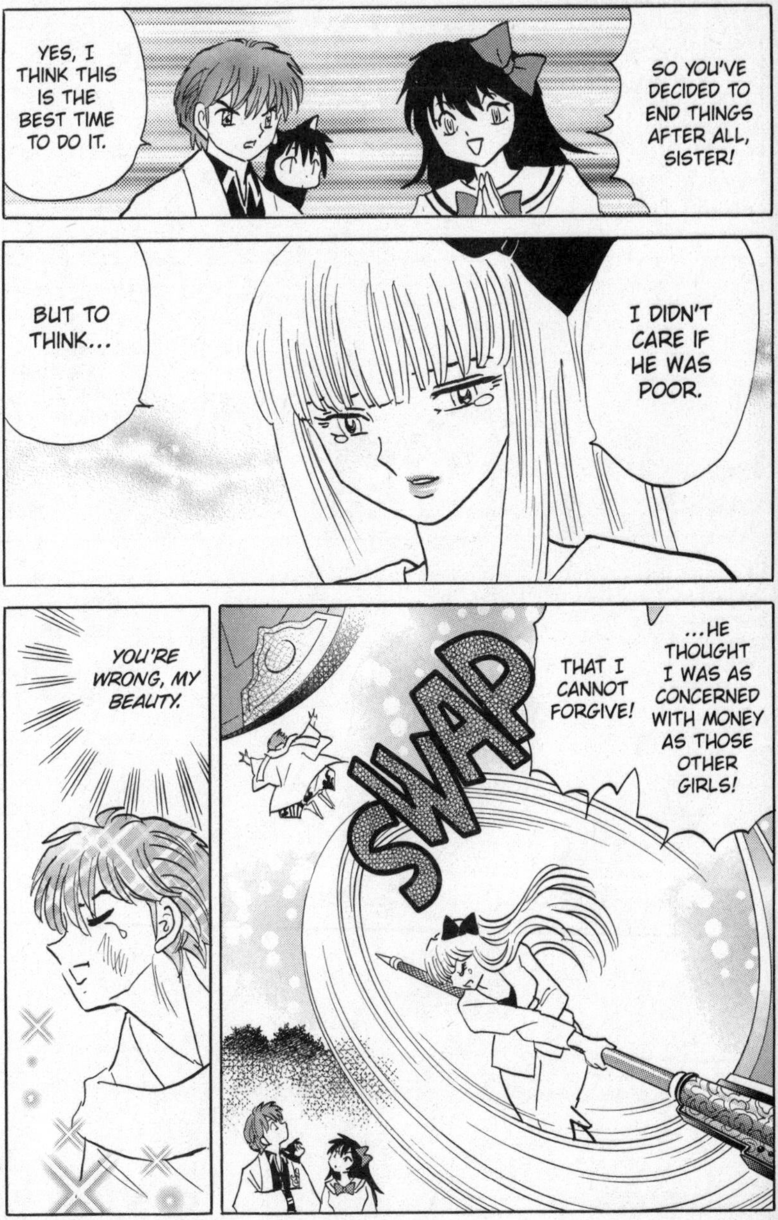
SO YOU'VE DECIDED TO END THINGS AFTER ALL, SISTER!
YES, I THINK THIS IS THE BEST TIME TO DO IT.
I DIDN'T CARE IF HE WAS POOR.
BUT TO THINK...
...HE THOUGHT I WAS AS CONCERNED WITH MONEY AS THOSE OTHER GIRLS!
THAT I CANNOT FORGIVE!
SWAP
YOU'RE WRONG, MY BEAUTY.

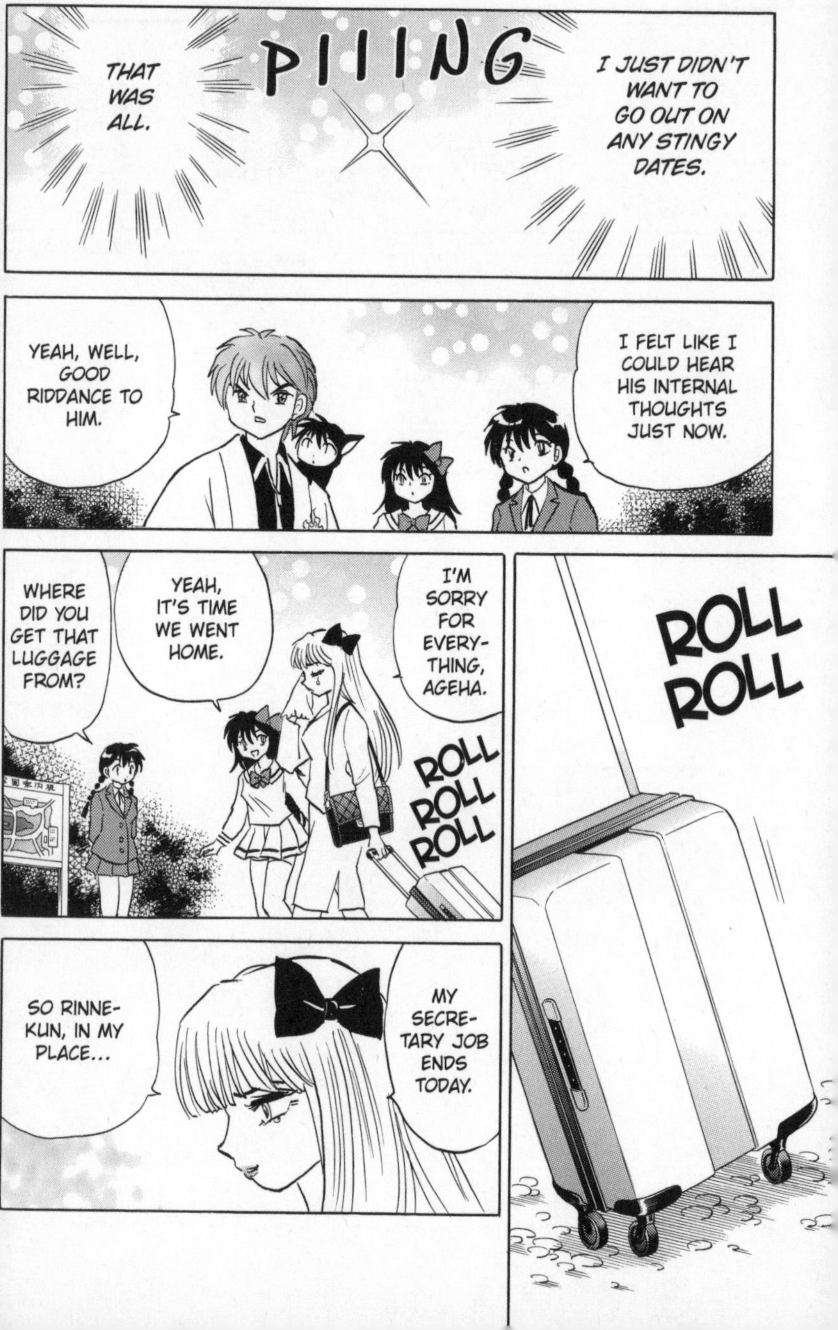
I JUST DIDN'T WANT TO GO OUT ON ANY STINGY DATES.
PIIING
THAT WAS ALL.
I FELT LIKE I COULD HEAR HIS INTERNAL THOUGHTS JUST NOW.
YEAH, WELL, GOOD RIDDANCE TO HIM.
ROLL ROLL
I'M SORRY FOR EVERY-THING, AGEHA.
ROLL ROLL ROLL
YEAH, IT'S TIME WE WENT HOME.
WHERE DID YOU GET THAT LUGGAGE FROM?
MY SECRE-TARY JOB ENDS TODAY.
SO RINNE-KUN, IN MY PLACE...

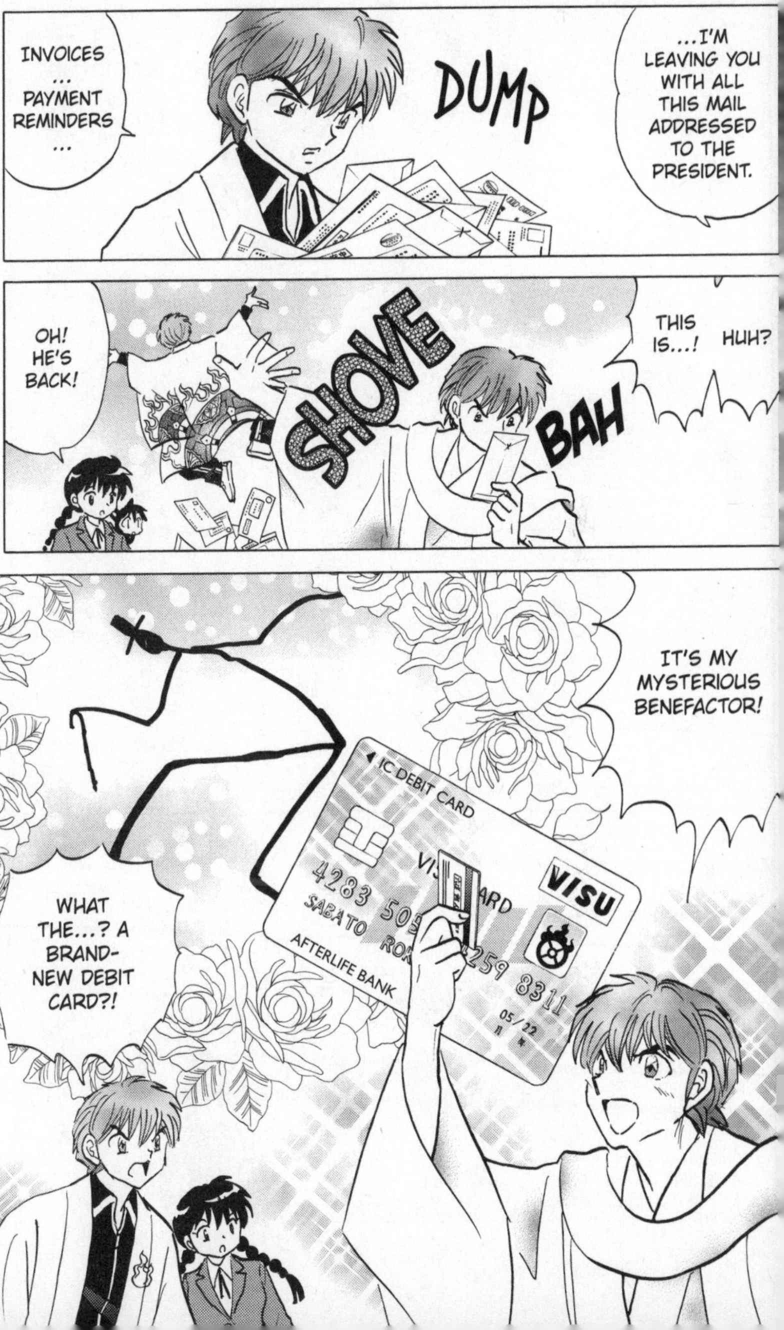
...I'M LEAVING YOU WITH ALL THIS MAIL ADDRESSED TO THE PRESIDENT.
DUMP
INVOICES ... PAYMENT REMINDERS ...
HUH?
THIS IS...!
BAH
SHOVE
OH! HE'S BACK!
IT'S MY MYSTERIOUS BENEFACTOR!
IC DEBIT CARD
VISU
AFTERLIFE BANK
WHAT THE...? A BRAND-NEW DEBIT CARD?!

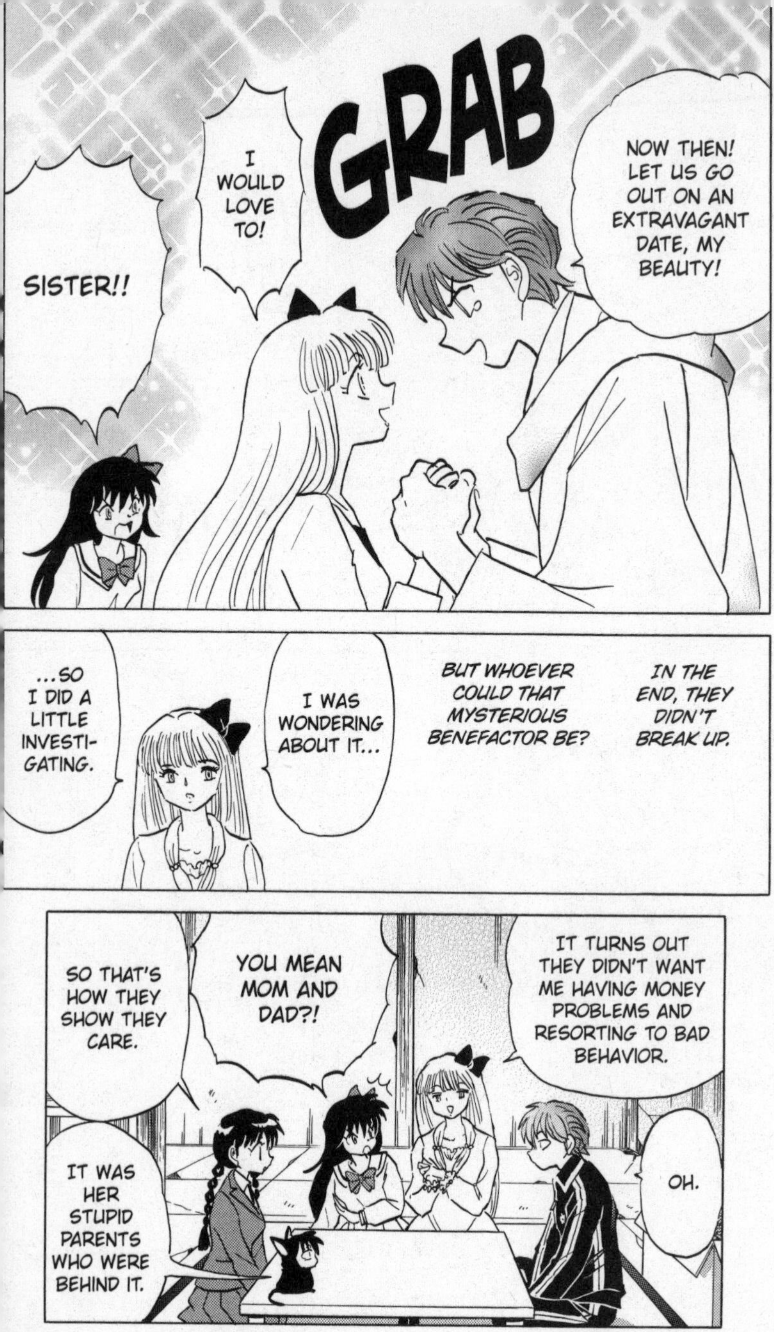
NOW THEN! LET US GO OUT ON AN EXTRAVAGANT DATE, MY BEAUTY!
GRAB
I WOULD LOVE TO!
SISTER!!
IN THE END, THEY DIDN'T BREAK UP.
BUT WHOEVER COULD THAT MYSTERIOUS BENEFACTOR BE?
I WAS WONDERING ABOUT IT...
...SO I DID A LITTLE INVESTI-GATING.
IT TURNS OUT THEY DIDN'T WANT ME HAVING MONEY PROBLEMS AND RESORTING TO BAD BEHAVIOR.
YOU MEAN MOM AND DAD?!
SO THAT'S HOW THEY SHOW THEY CARE.
OH.
IT WAS HER STUPID PARENTS WHO WERE BEHIND IT.

CHAPTER 371:
THE TELLING VOICE

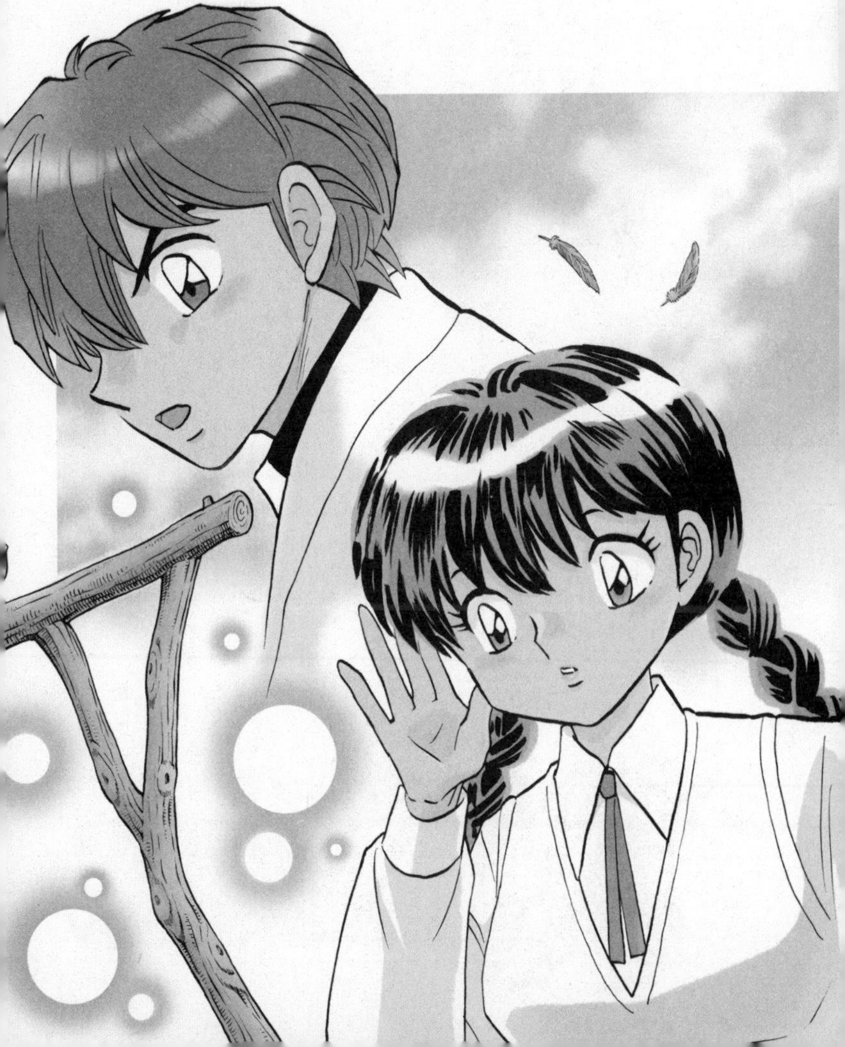

りんね

RIN-NE

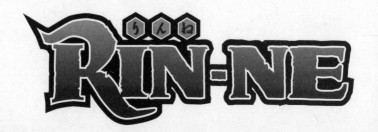

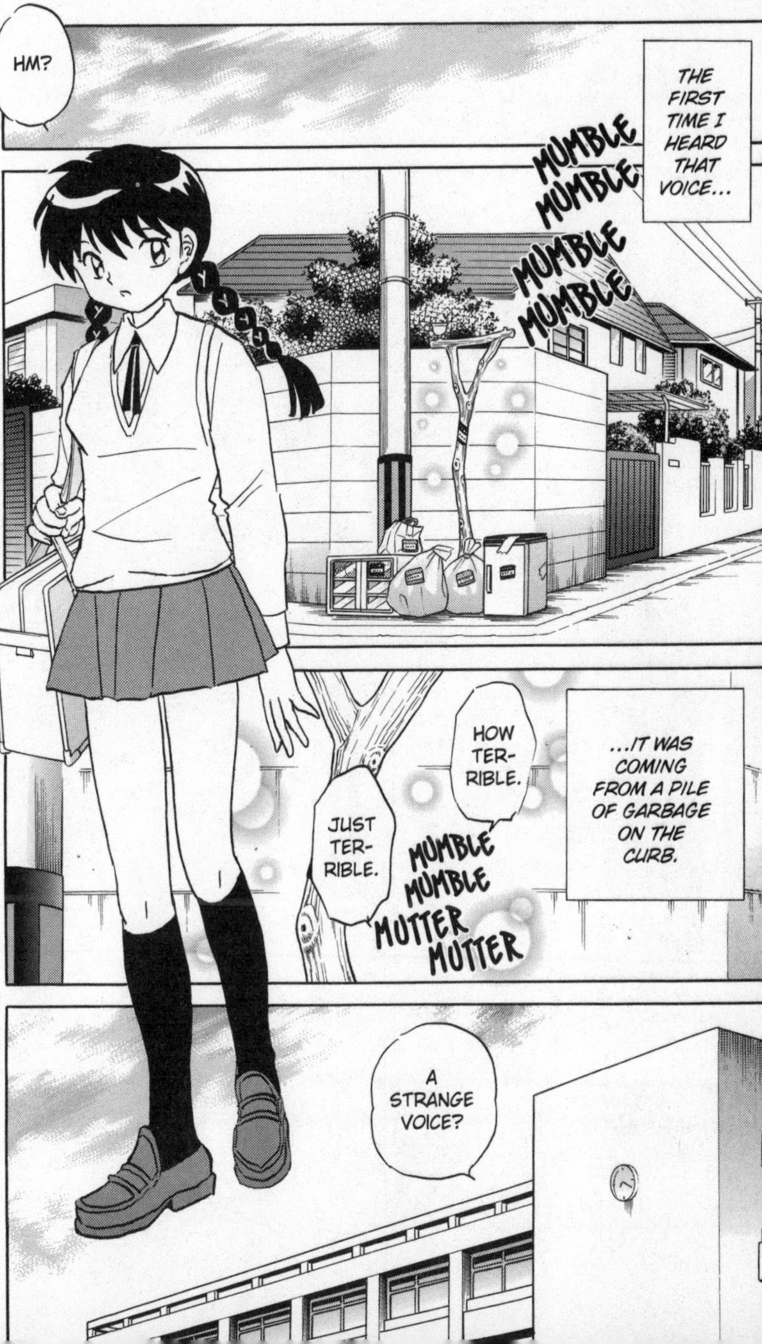
THE FIRST TIME I HEARD THAT VOICE...
HM?
MUMBLE MUMBLE
MUMBLE MUMBLE
...IT WAS COMING FROM A PILE OF GARBAGE ON THE CURB.
HOW TER-RIBLE.
JUST TER-RIBLE.
MUMBLE MUMBLE MUTTER MUTTER
A STRANGE VOICE?

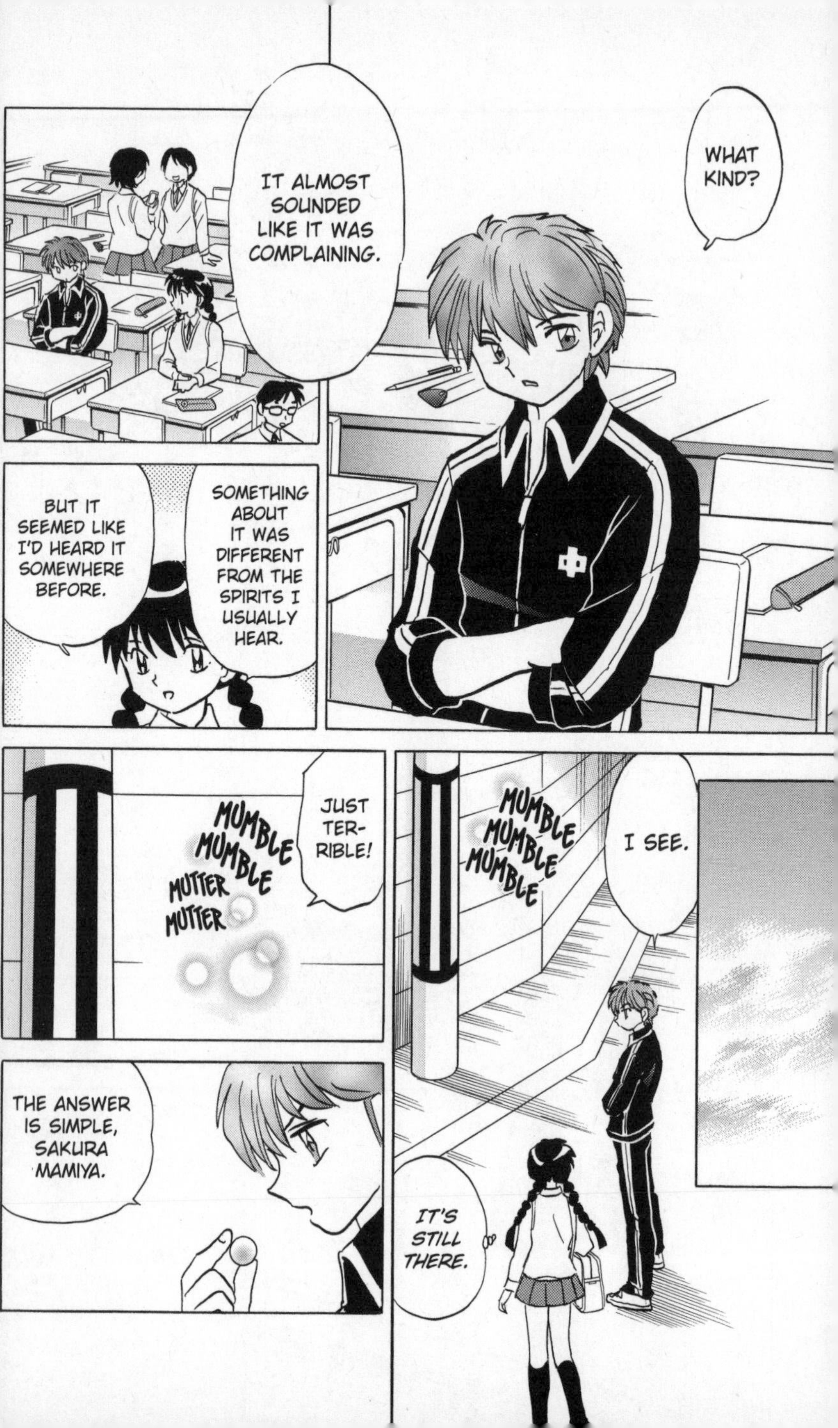
WHAT KIND?
IT ALMOST SOUNDED LIKE IT WAS COMPLAINING.
SOMETHING ABOUT IT WAS DIFFERENT FROM THE SPIRITS I USUALLY HEAR.
BUT IT SEEMED LIKE I'D HEARD IT SOMEWHERE BEFORE.
I SEE.
MUMBLE MUMBLE MUMBLE
IT'S STILL THERE.
JUST TER-RIBLE!
MUMBLE MUMBLE
MUTTER MUTTER
THE ANSWER IS SIMPLE, SAKURA MAMIYA.

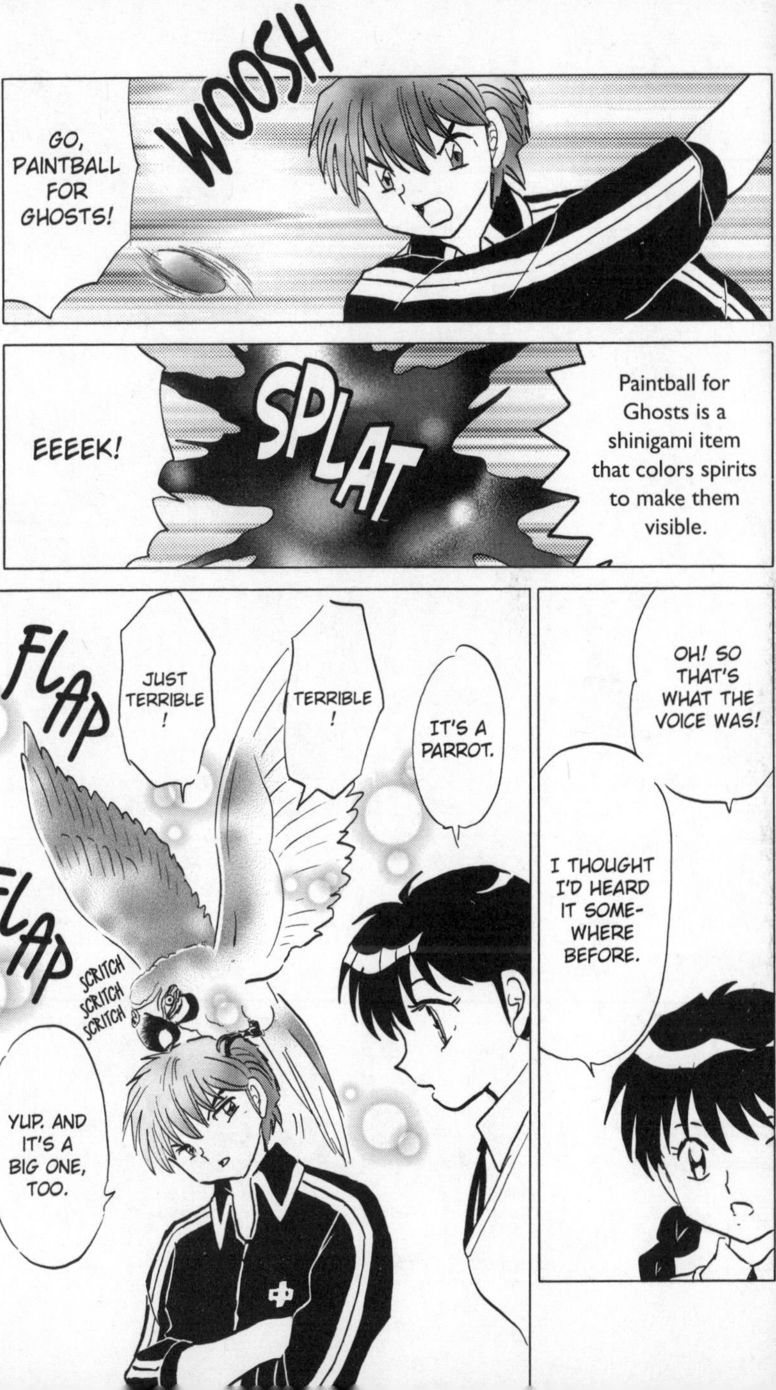
WOOSH
GO, PAINTBALL FOR GHOSTS!
Paintball for Ghosts is a shinigami item that colors spirits to make them visible.
SPLAT
EEEEK!
OH! SO THAT'S WHAT THE VOICE WAS!
I THOUGHT I'D HEARD IT SOME-WHERE BEFORE.
IT'S A PARROT.
TERRIBLE!
JUST TERRIBLE!
FLAP
FLAP
SCRITCH SCRITCH SCRITCH
YUP. AND IT'S A BIG ONE, TOO.

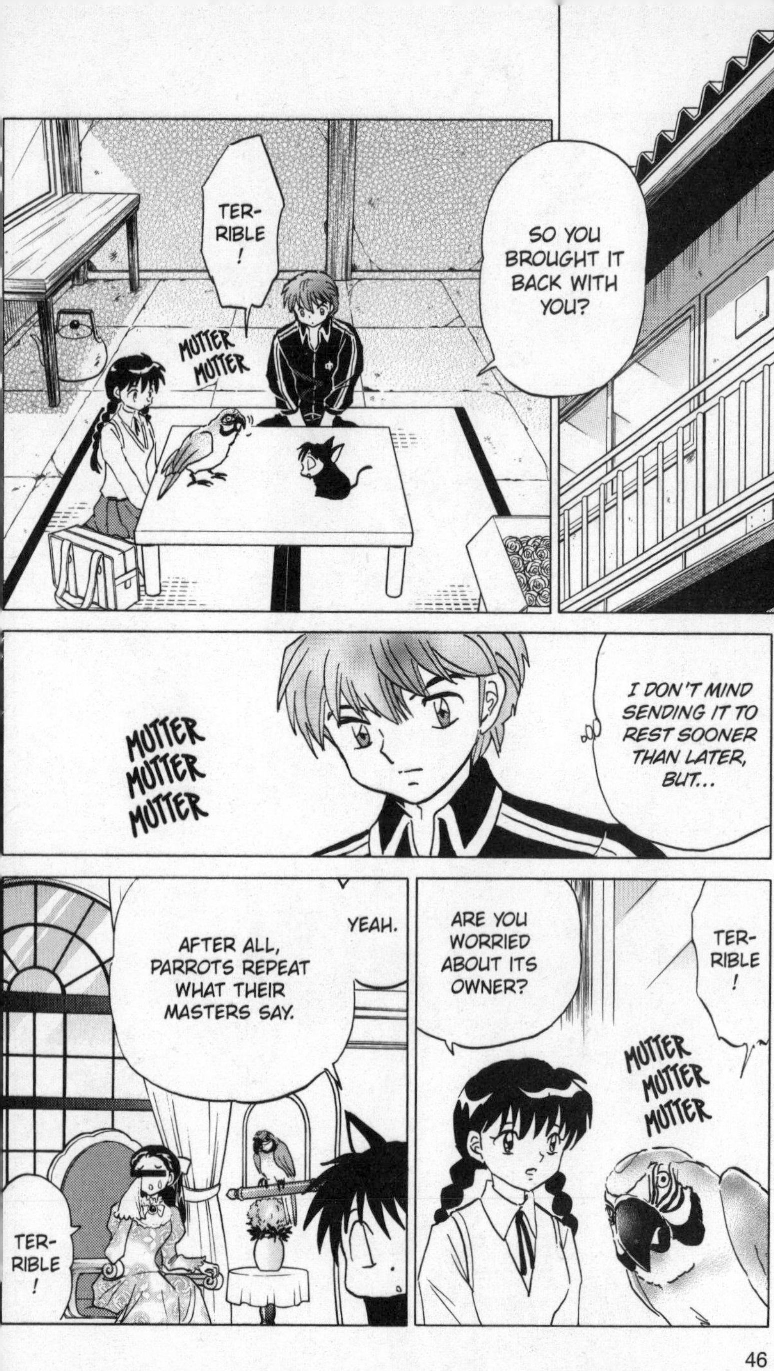
SO YOU BROUGHT IT BACK WITH YOU?
TER-RIBLE!
MUTTER MUTTER
I DON'T MIND SENDING IT TO REST SOONER THAN LATER, BUT...
MUTTER MUTTER MUTTER
TER-RIBLE!
ARE YOU WORRIED ABOUT ITS OWNER?
MUTTER MUTTER MUTTER
YEAH.
AFTER ALL, PARROTS REPEAT WHAT THEIR MASTERS SAY.
TER-RIBLE!

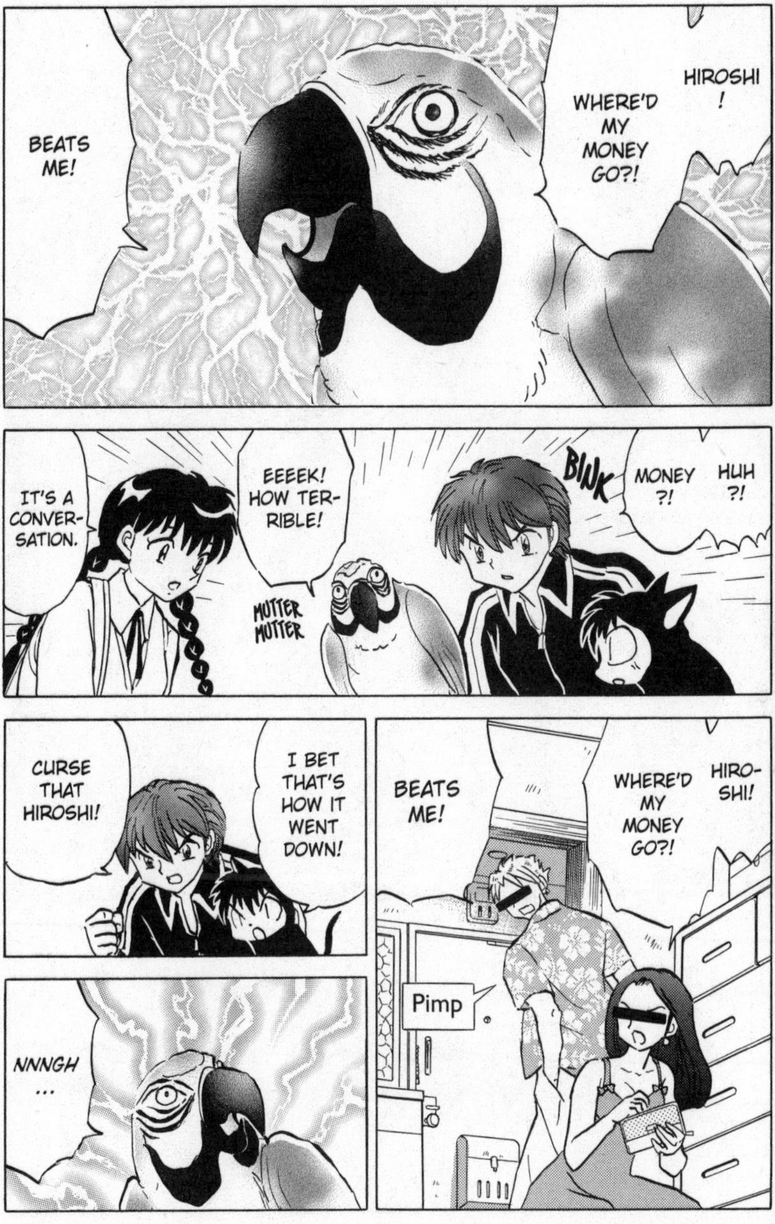
HIROSHI!
WHERE'D MY MONEY GO?!
BEATS ME!
HUH?!
MONEY?!
BLINK
EEEEK! HOW TERRIBLE!
MUTTER MUTTER
IT'S A CONVERSATION.
HIRO-SHI!
WHERE'D MY MONEY GO?!
BEATS ME!
Pimp
I BET THAT'S HOW IT WENT DOWN!
CURSE THAT HIROSHI!
NNNGH...

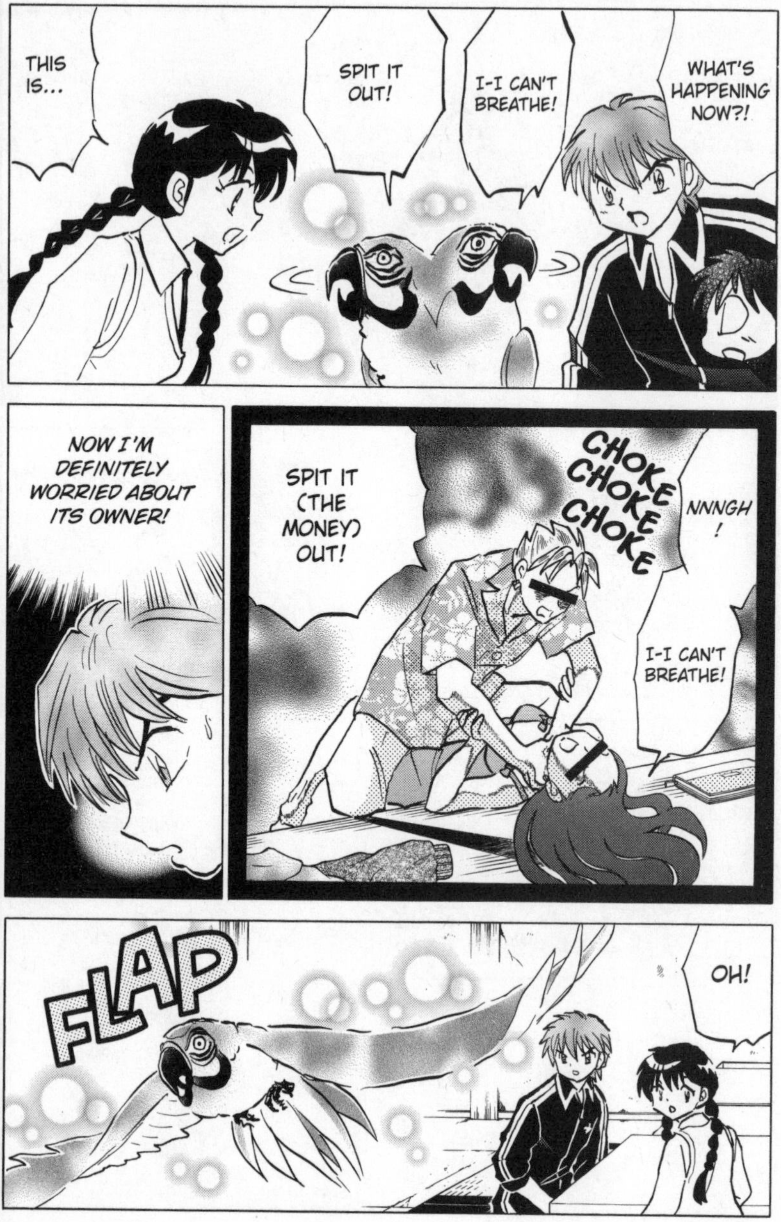
WHAT'S HAPPENING NOW?!
I-I CAN'T BREATHE!
SPIT IT OUT!
THIS IS...
NNNGH!
CHOKE CHOKE CHOKE
SPIT IT (THE MONEY) OUT!
I-I CAN'T BREATHE!
NOW I'M DEFINITELY WORRIED ABOUT ITS OWNER!
OH!
FLAP

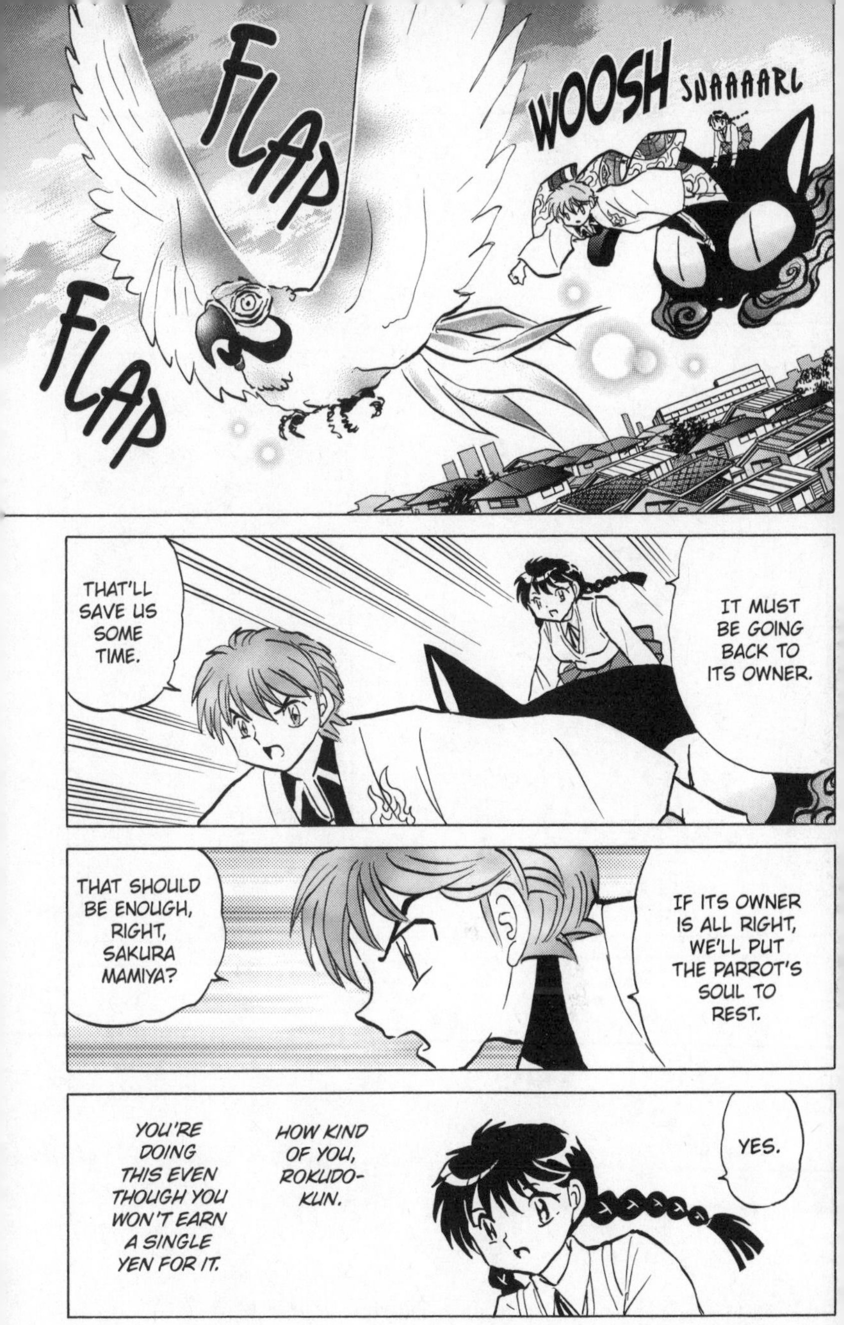
SNAAAARL
WOOSH
FLAP
FLAP
IT MUST BE GOING BACK TO ITS OWNER.
THAT'LL SAVE US SOME TIME.
IF ITS OWNER IS ALL RIGHT, WE'LL PUT THE PARROT'S SOUL TO REST.
THAT SHOULD BE ENOUGH, RIGHT, SAKURA MAMIYA?
YES.
HOW KIND OF YOU, ROKUDO-KUN.
YOU'RE DOING THIS EVEN THOUGH YOU WON'T EARN A SINGLE YEN FOR IT.

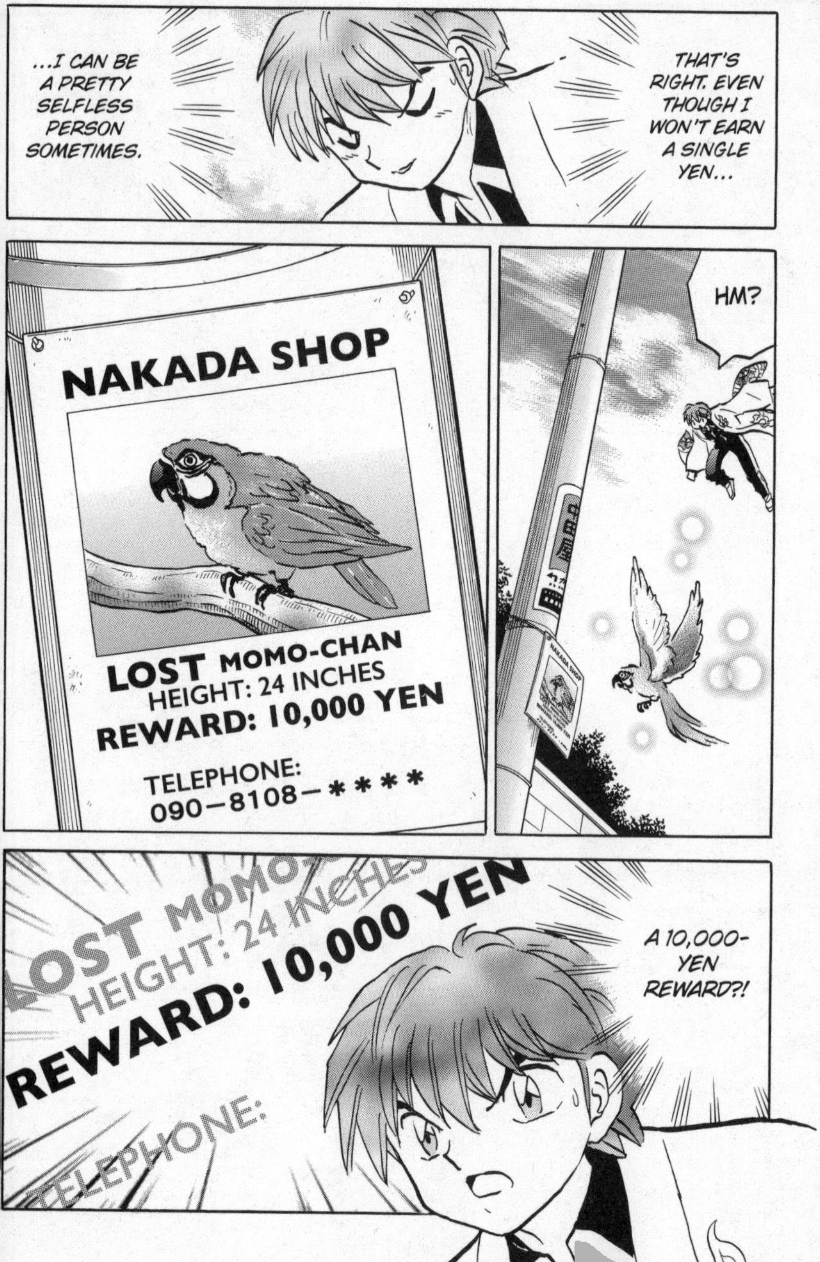
THAT'S RIGHT. EVEN THOUGH I WON'T EARN A SINGLE YEN...
...I CAN BE A PRETTY SELFLESS PERSON SOMETIMES.
HM?
NAKADA SHOP
LOST MOMO-CHAN
HEIGHT: 24 INCHES
REWARD: 10,000 YEN
TELEPHONE:
090—8108—****
A 10,000-YEN REWARD?!
LOST MOMO-
HEIGHT: 24 INCHES
REWARD: 10,000 YEN
TELEPHONE:

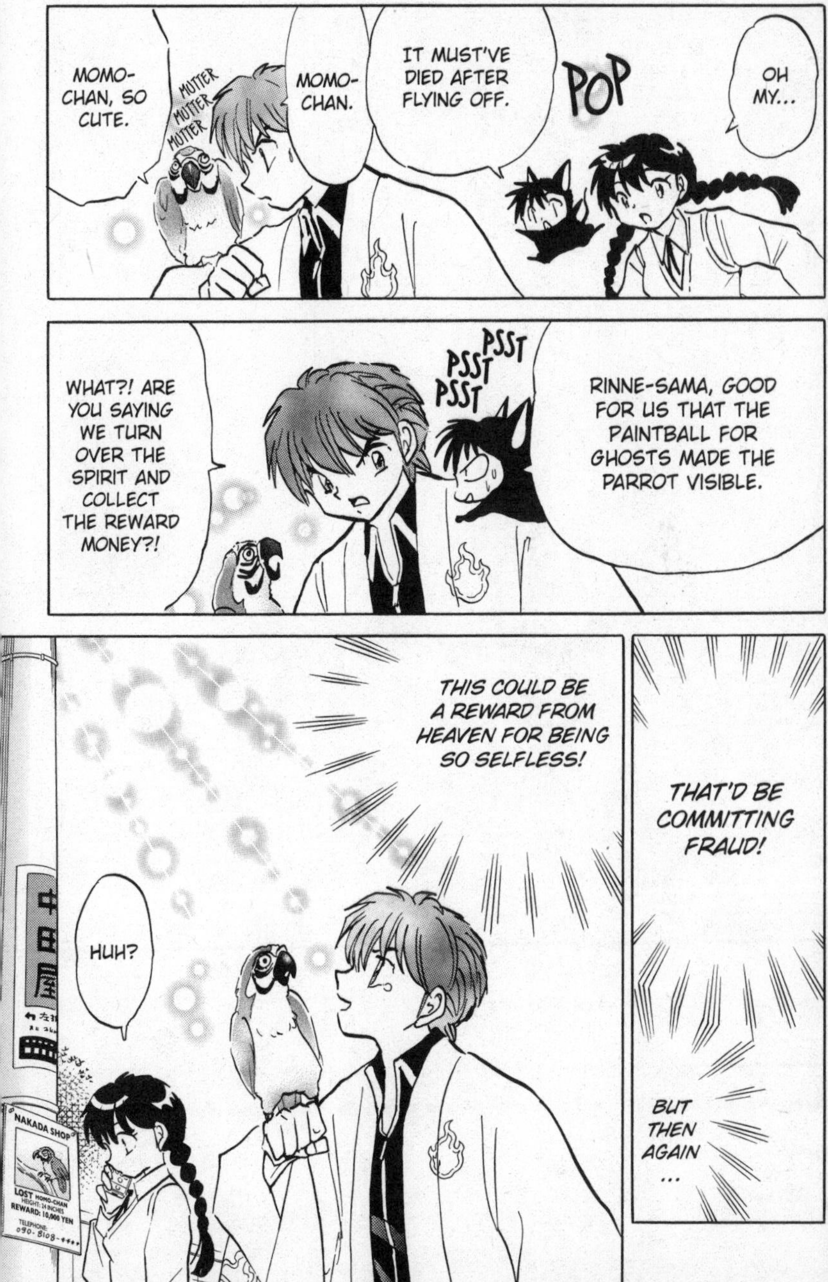
OH MY...
POP
IT MUST'VE DIED AFTER FLYING OFF.
MOMO-CHAN.
MUTTER MUTTER MUTTER
MOMO-CHAN, SO CUTE.
RINNE-SAMA, GOOD FOR US THAT THE PAINTBALL FOR GHOSTS MADE THE PARROT VISIBLE.
PSST PSST PSST
WHAT?! ARE YOU SAYING WE TURN OVER THE SPIRIT AND COLLECT THE REWARD MONEY?!
THAT'D BE COMMITTING FRAUD!
BUT THEN AGAIN ...
THIS COULD BE A REWARD FROM HEAVEN FOR BEING SO SELFLESS!
HUH?
中田屋
NAKADA SHOP
LOST MOMO-CHAN
HEIGHT: 24 INCHES
REWARD: 10,000 YEN
TELEPHONE:
090-8108-****

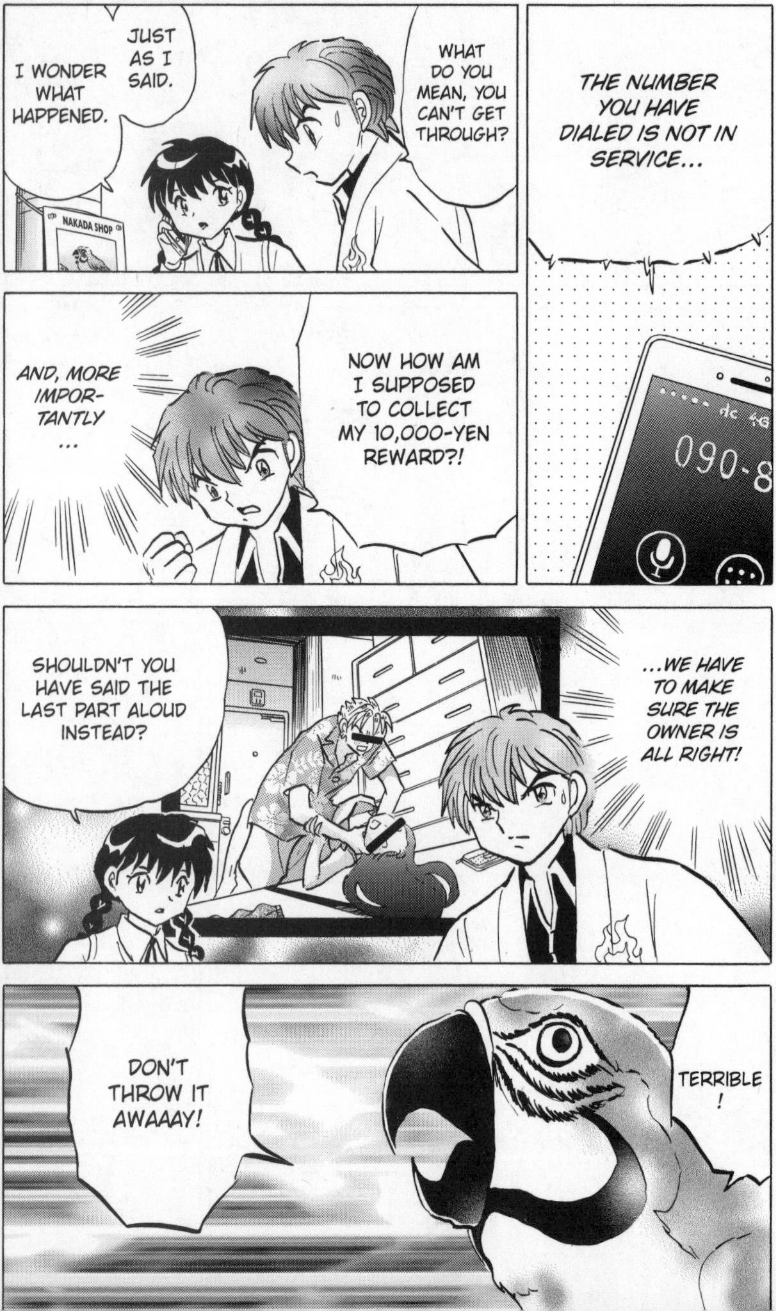
THE NUMBER YOU HAVE DIALED IS NOT IN SERVICE...
090-8
WHAT DO YOU MEAN, YOU CAN'T GET THROUGH?
JUST AS I SAID.
I WONDER WHAT HAPPENED.
NAKADA SHOP
NOW HOW AM I SUPPOSED TO COLLECT MY 10,000-YEN REWARD?!
AND, MORE IMPOR-TANTLY...
...WE HAVE TO MAKE SURE THE OWNER IS ALL RIGHT!
SHOULDN'T YOU HAVE SAID THE LAST PART ALOUD INSTEAD?
TERRIBLE!
DON'T THROW IT AWAAAY!

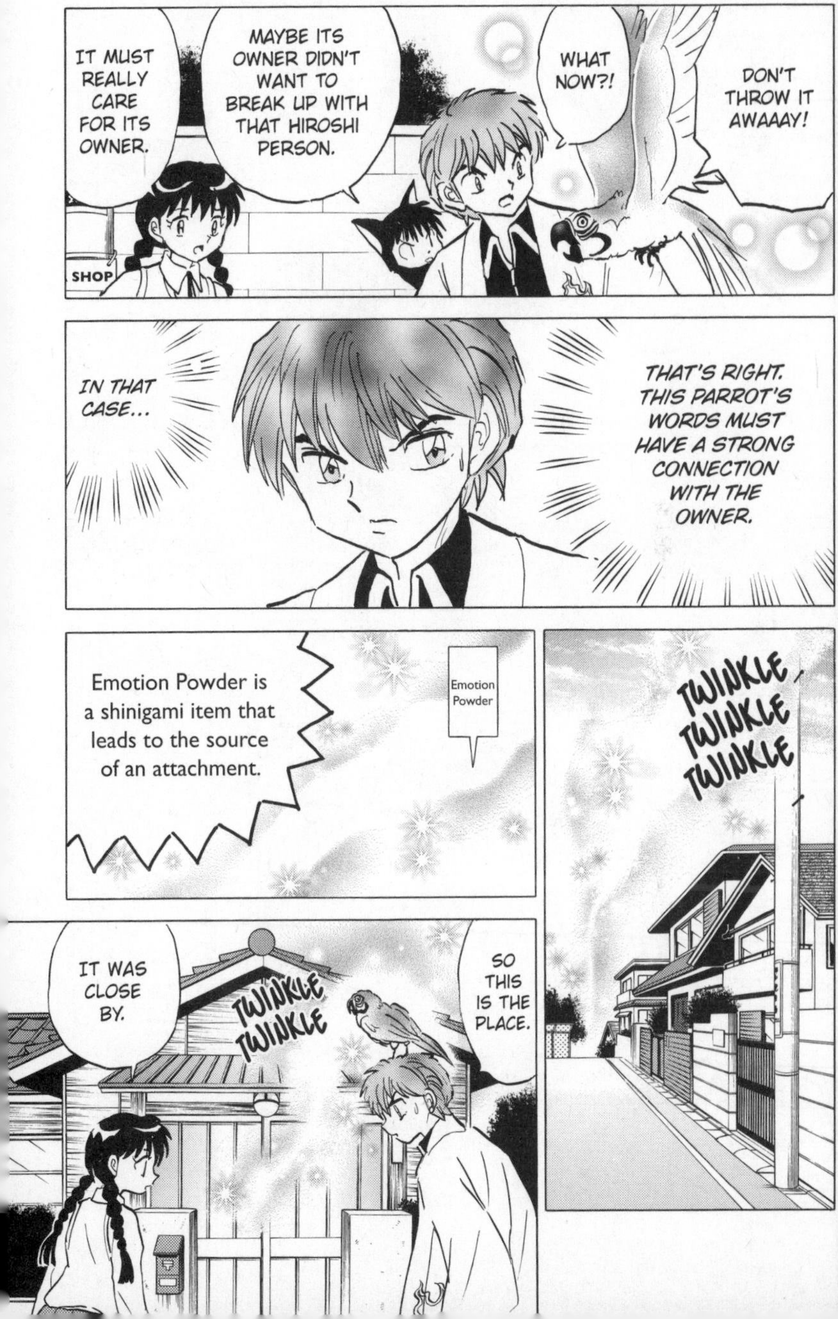
DON'T THROW IT AWAAAY!
WHAT NOW?!
MAYBE ITS OWNER DIDN'T WANT TO BREAK UP WITH THAT HIROSHI PERSON.
IT MUST REALLY CARE FOR ITS OWNER.
SHOP
THAT'S RIGHT. THIS PARROT'S WORDS MUST HAVE A STRONG CONNECTION WITH THE OWNER.
IN THAT CASE...
TWINKLE TWINKLE TWINKLE
Emotion Powder
Emotion Powder is a shinigami item that leads to the source of an attachment.
SO THIS IS THE PLACE.
TWINKLE TWINKLE
IT WAS CLOSE BY.

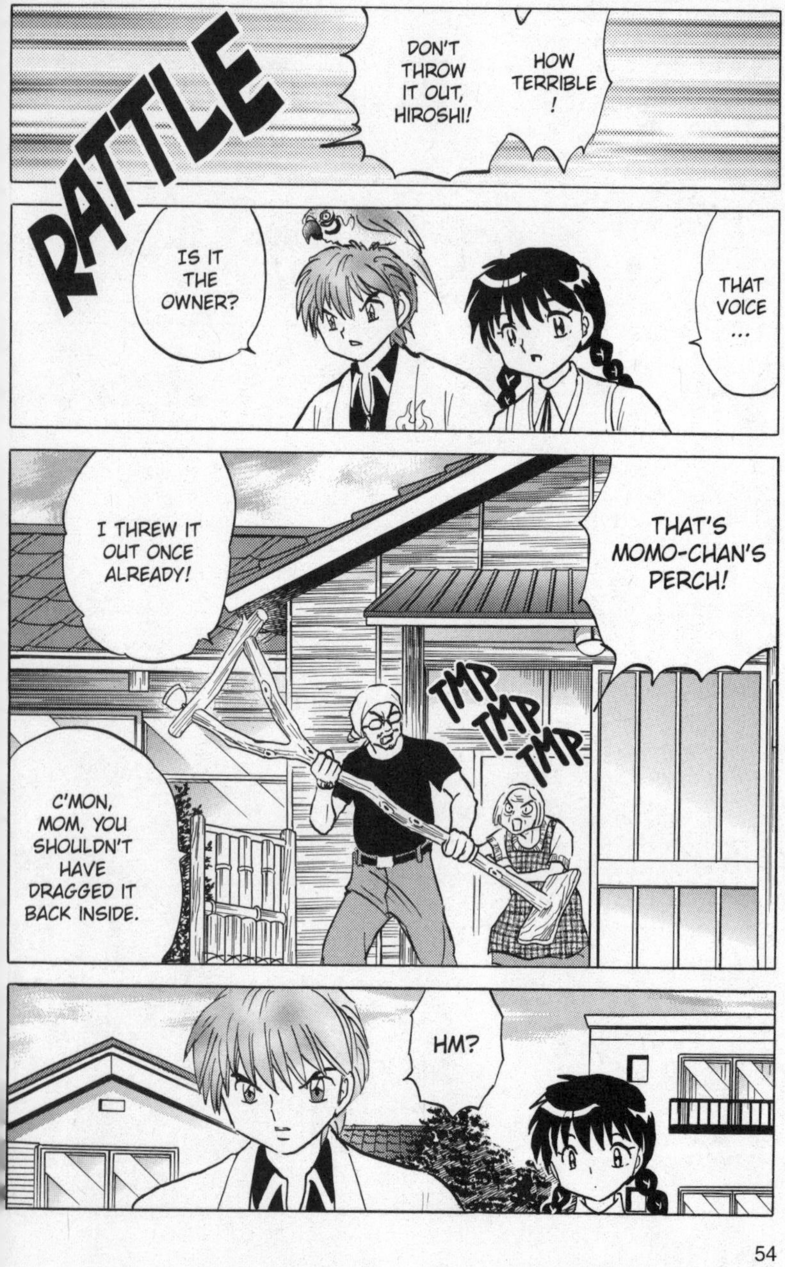
HOW TERRIBLE!
DON'T THROW IT OUT, HIROSHI!
RATTLE
THAT VOICE...
IS IT THE OWNER?
THAT'S MOMO-CHAN'S PERCH!
I THREW IT OUT ONCE ALREADY!
TMP TMP TMP
C'MON, MOM, YOU SHOULDN'T HAVE DRAGGED IT BACK INSIDE.
HM?

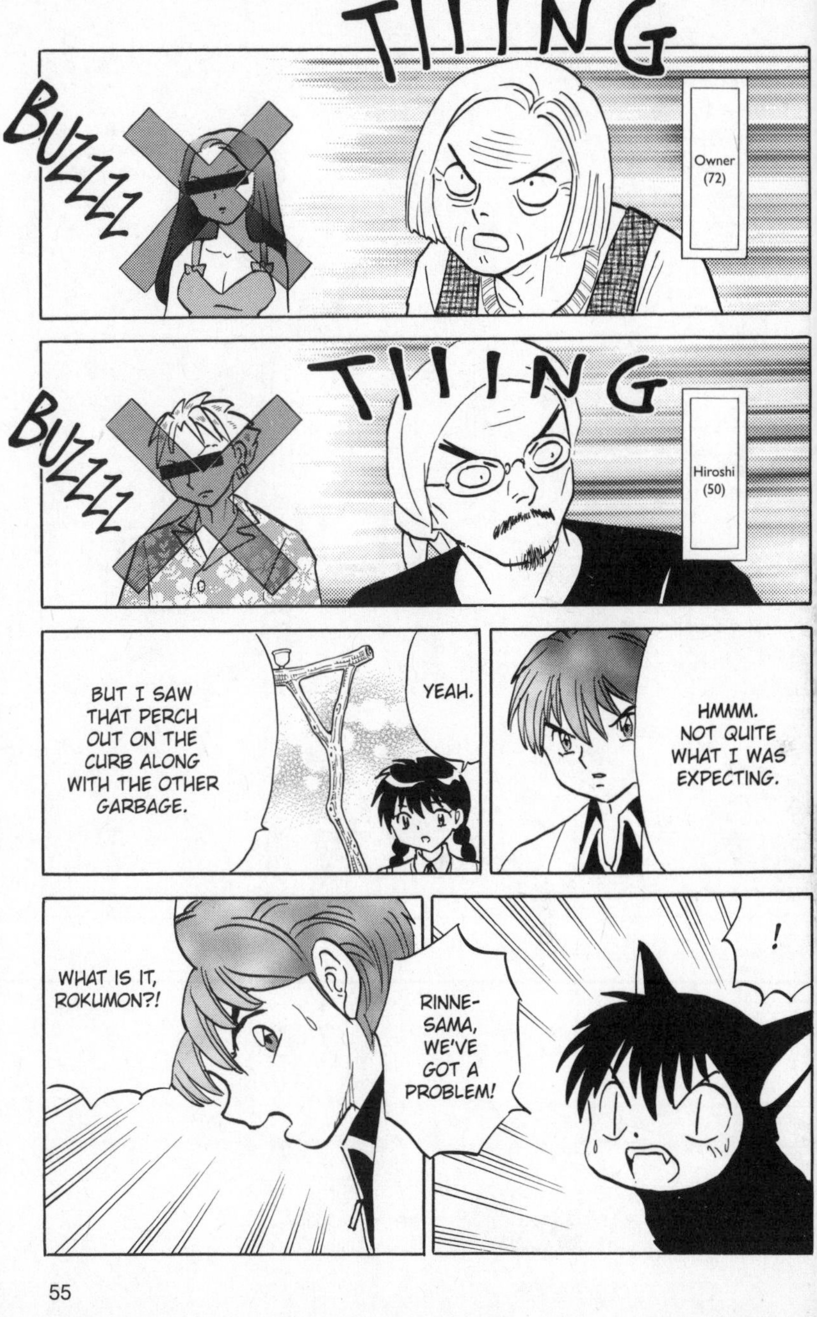
TIIING
Owner (72)
BUZZZZZ
TIIING
Hiroshi (50)
BUZZZZZ
HMMM. NOT QUITE WHAT I WAS EXPECTING.
YEAH.
BUT I SAW THAT PERCH OUT ON THE CURB ALONG WITH THE OTHER GARBAGE.
!
RINNE-SAMA, WE'VE GOT A PROBLEM!
WHAT IS IT, ROKUMON?!

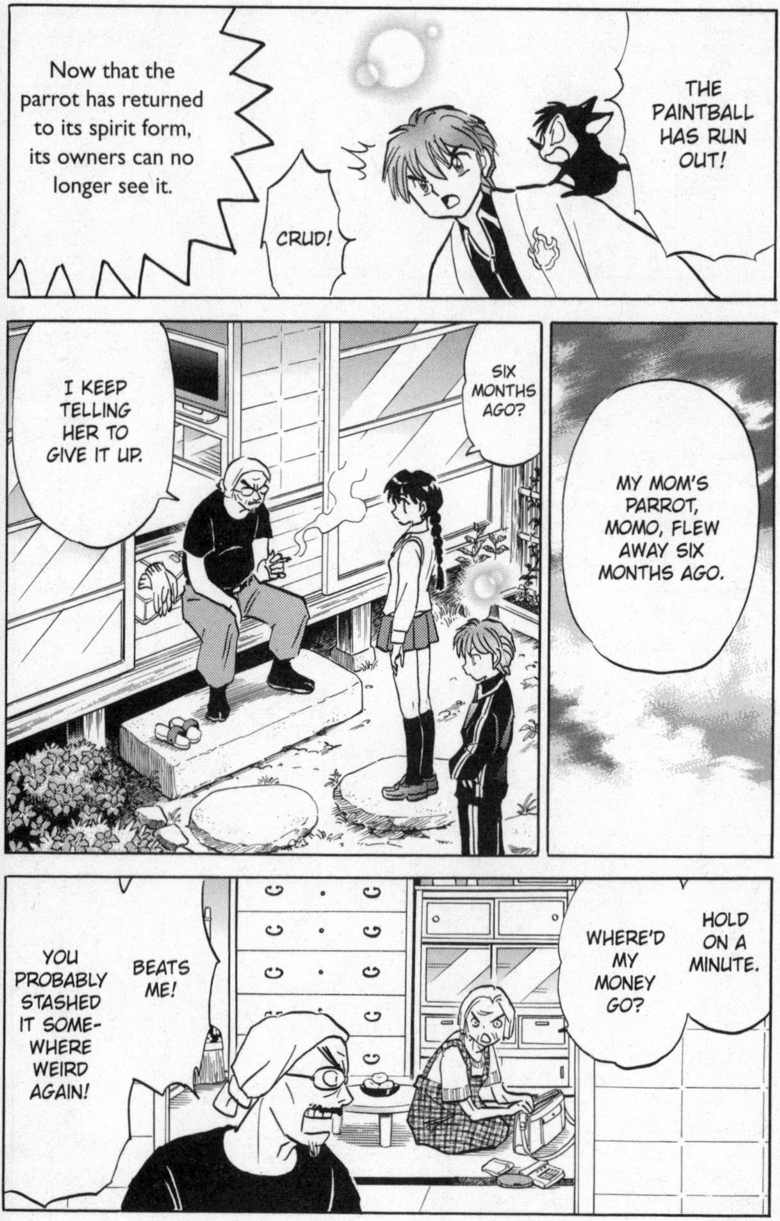
THE PAINTBALL HAS RUN OUT!
Now that the parrot has returned to its spirit form, its owners can no longer see it.
CRUD!
MY MOM'S PARROT, MOMO, FLEW AWAY SIX MONTHS AGO.
SIX MONTHS AGO?
I KEEP TELLING HER TO GIVE IT UP.
HOLD ON A MINUTE.
WHERE'D MY MONEY GO?
BEATS ME!
YOU PROBABLY STASHED IT SOME-WHERE WEIRD AGAIN!

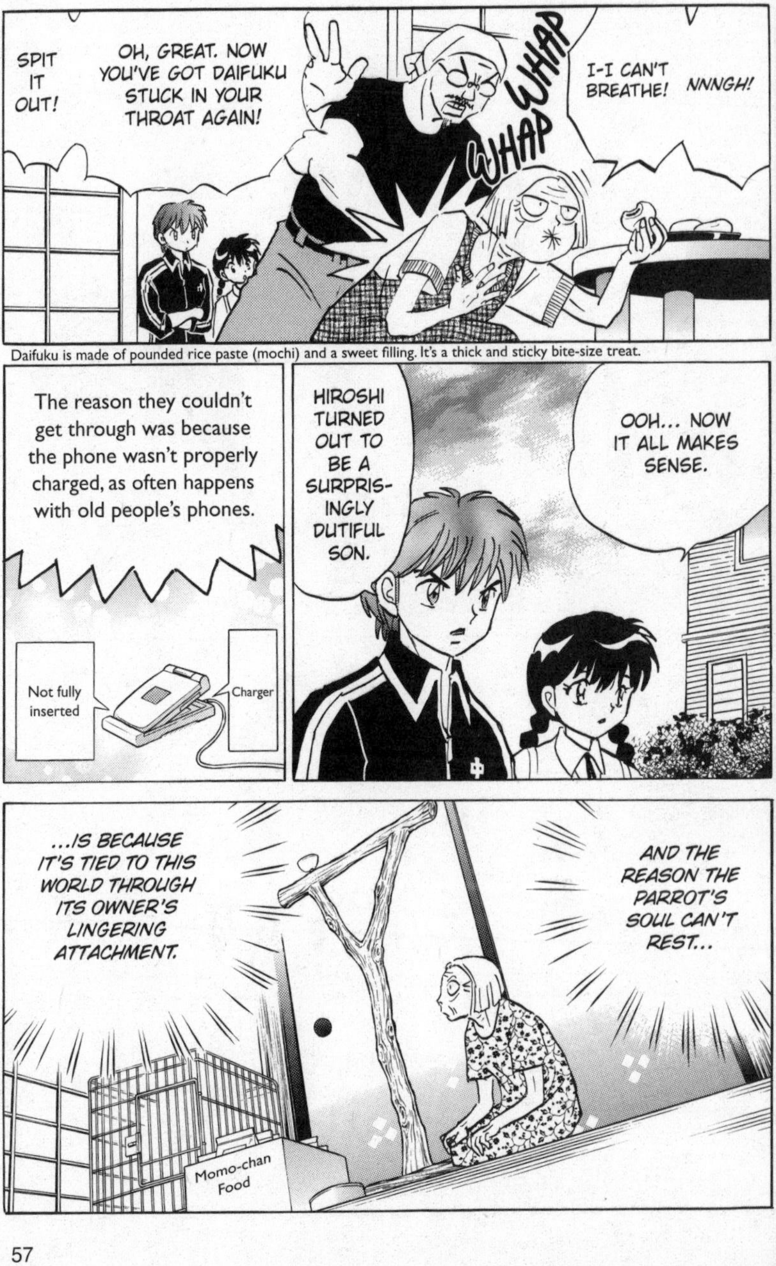
NNNGH!
I-I CAN'T BREATHE!
WHAP WHAP
OH, GREAT. NOW YOU'VE GOT DAIFUKU STUCK IN YOUR THROAT AGAIN!
SPIT IT OUT!
OOH... NOW IT ALL MAKES SENSE.
HIROSHI TURNED OUT TO BE A SURPRISINGLY DUTIFUL SON.
The reason they couldn't get through was because the phone wasn't properly charged, as often happens with old people's phones.
Charger
Not fully inserted
AND THE REASON THE PARROT'S SOUL CAN'T REST...
...IS BECAUSE IT'S TIED TO THIS WORLD THROUGH ITS OWNER'S LINGERING ATTACHMENT.
Momo-chan Food

Daifuku is made of pounded rice paste (mochi) and a sweet filling. It's a thick and sticky bite-size treat.

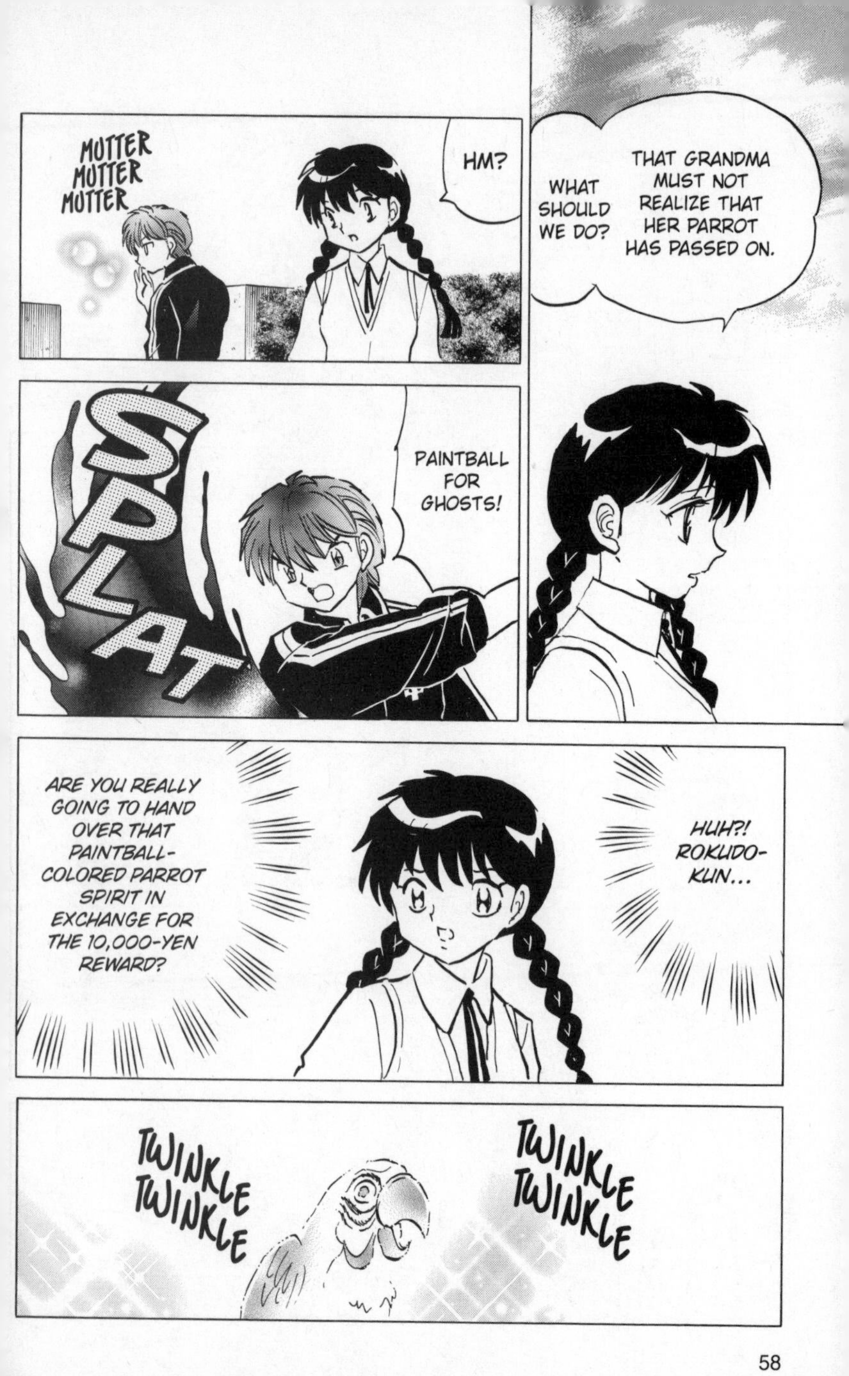
THAT GRANDMA MUST NOT REALIZE THAT HER PARROT HAS PASSED ON.
WHAT SHOULD WE DO?
HM?
MUTTER MUTTER MUTTER
PAINTBALL FOR GHOSTS!
SPLAT
HUH?! ROKUDO-KUN...
ARE YOU REALLY GOING TO HAND OVER THAT PAINTBALL-COLORED PARROT SPIRIT IN EXCHANGE FOR THE 10,000-YEN REWARD?
TWINKLE TWINKLE
TWINKLE TWINKLE

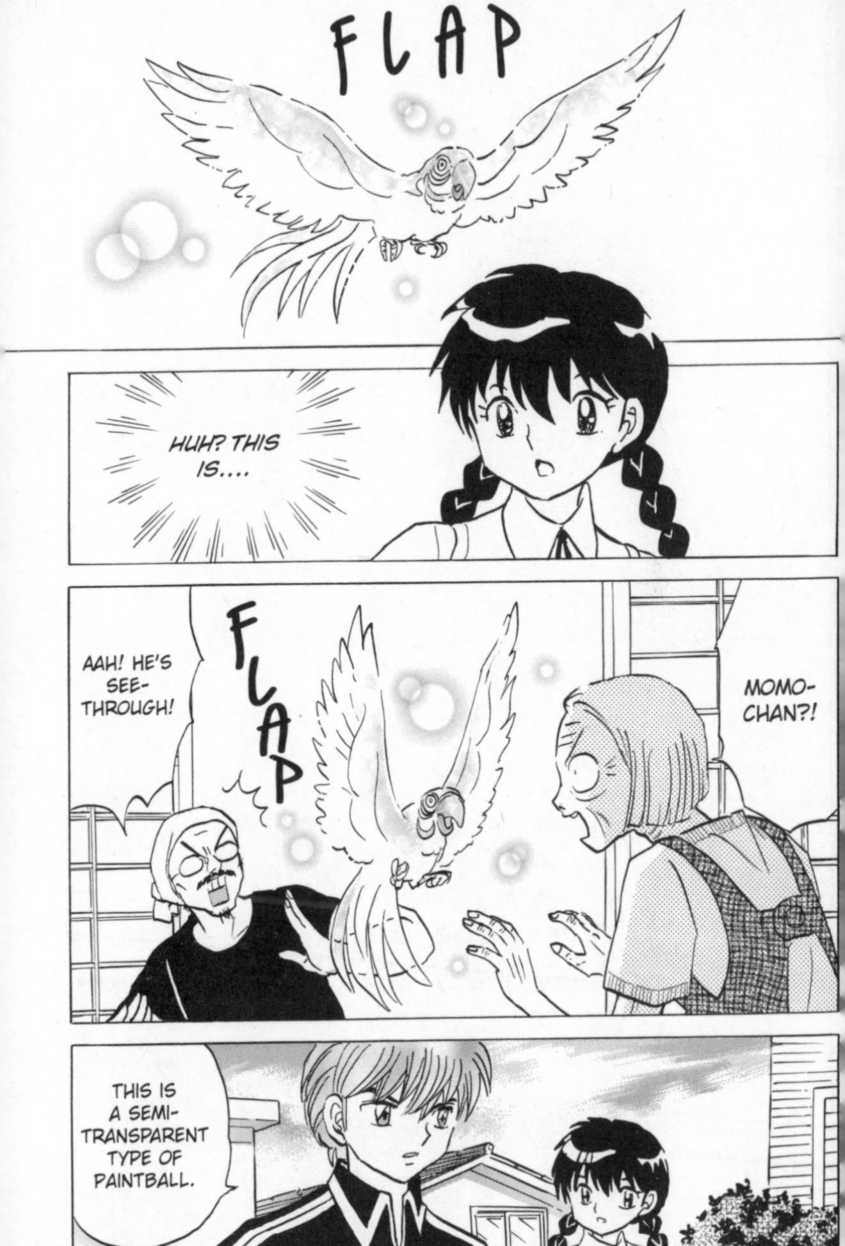
FLAP
HUH? THIS IS....
MOMO-CHAN?!
FLAP
AAH! HE'S SEE-THROUGH!
THIS IS A SEMI-TRANSPARENT TYPE OF PAINTBALL.

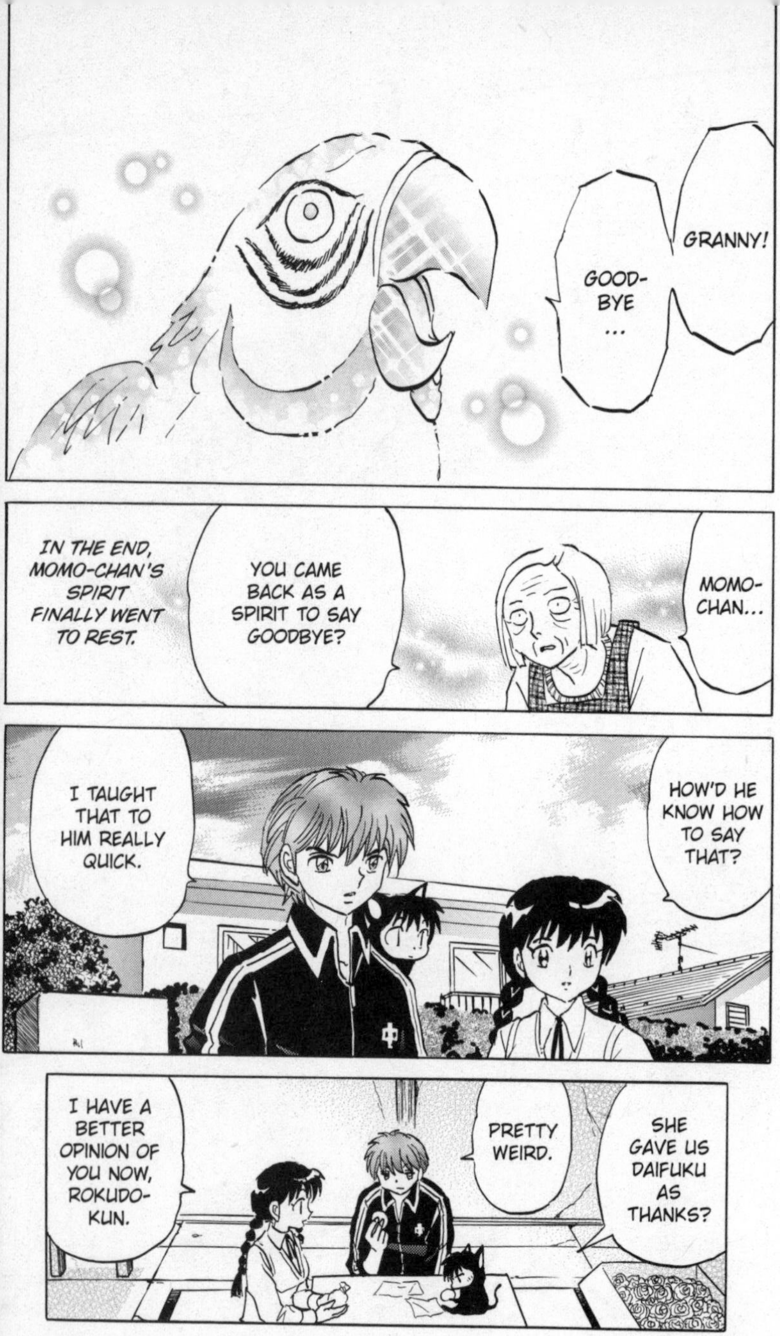
GRANNY!
GOOD-BYE ...
MOMO-CHAN...
YOU CAME BACK AS A SPIRIT TO SAY GOODBYE?
IN THE END, MOMO-CHAN'S SPIRIT FINALLY WENT TO REST.
HOW'D HE KNOW HOW TO SAY THAT?
I TAUGHT THAT TO HIM REALLY QUICK.
SHE GAVE US DAIFUKU AS THANKS?
PRETTY WEIRD.
I HAVE A BETTER OPINION OF YOU NOW, ROKUDO-KUN.

CHAPTER 372:
A NEW FRIEND

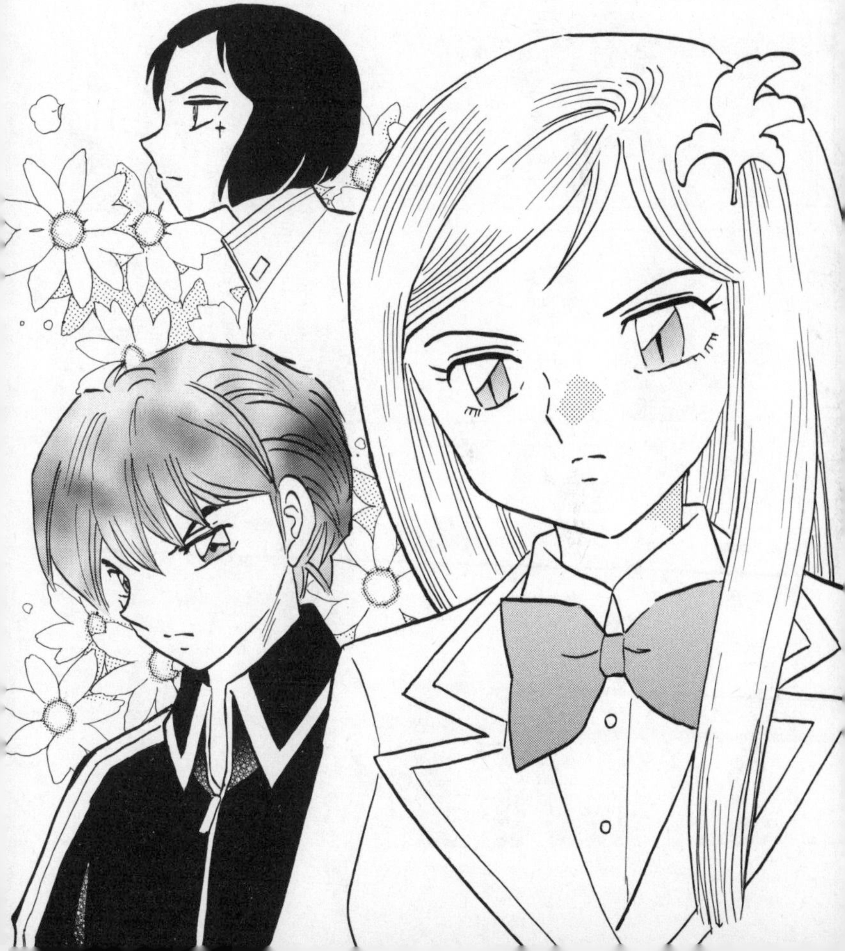

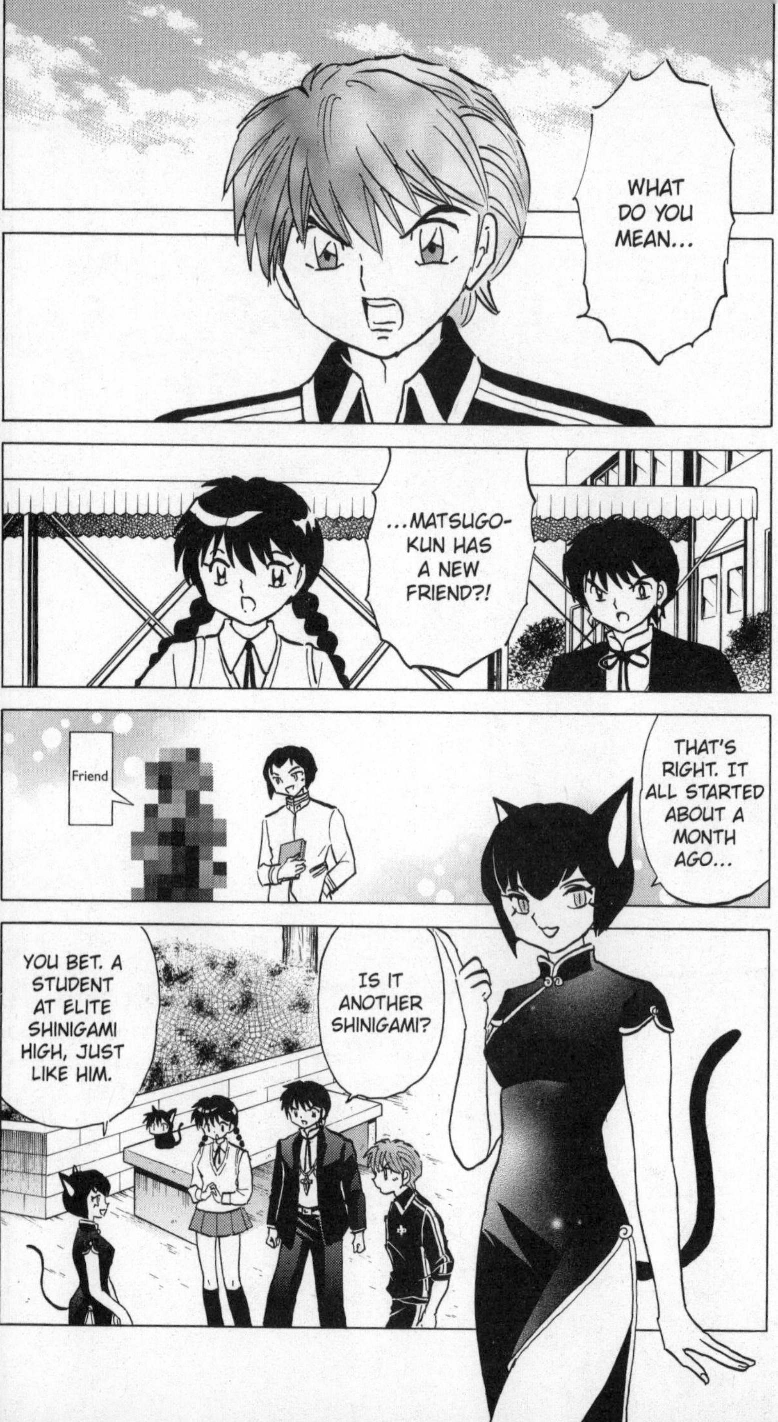
WHAT DO YOU MEAN…
…MATSUGO-KUN HAS A NEW FRIEND?!
THAT'S RIGHT. IT ALL STARTED ABOUT A MONTH AGO…
Friend
IS IT ANOTHER SHINIGAMI?
YOU BET. A STUDENT AT ELITE SHINIGAMI HIGH, JUST LIKE HIM.

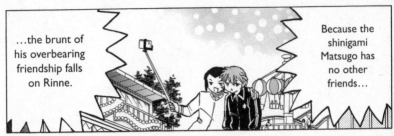

Because the shinigami Matsugo has no other friends…
…the brunt of his overbearing friendship falls on Rinne.
GOOD FOR HIM.
AND THANK YOU TO WHOEVER THIS NEW FRIEND IS!
HE MUST FEEL INCREDIBLY RELIEVED.
CONGRATULATIONS, ROKUDO-KUN.
KUROMITSU-SAN, DID YOU COME ALL THIS WAY JUST TO TELL US THAT?
YUP. AND NOW…
…I'D LIKE TO INTRODUCE YOU TO HIS NEW FRIEND.
ZWORP
OH, RINNE-KUUUN …

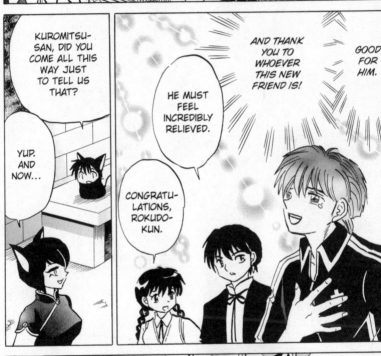

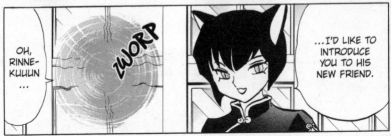

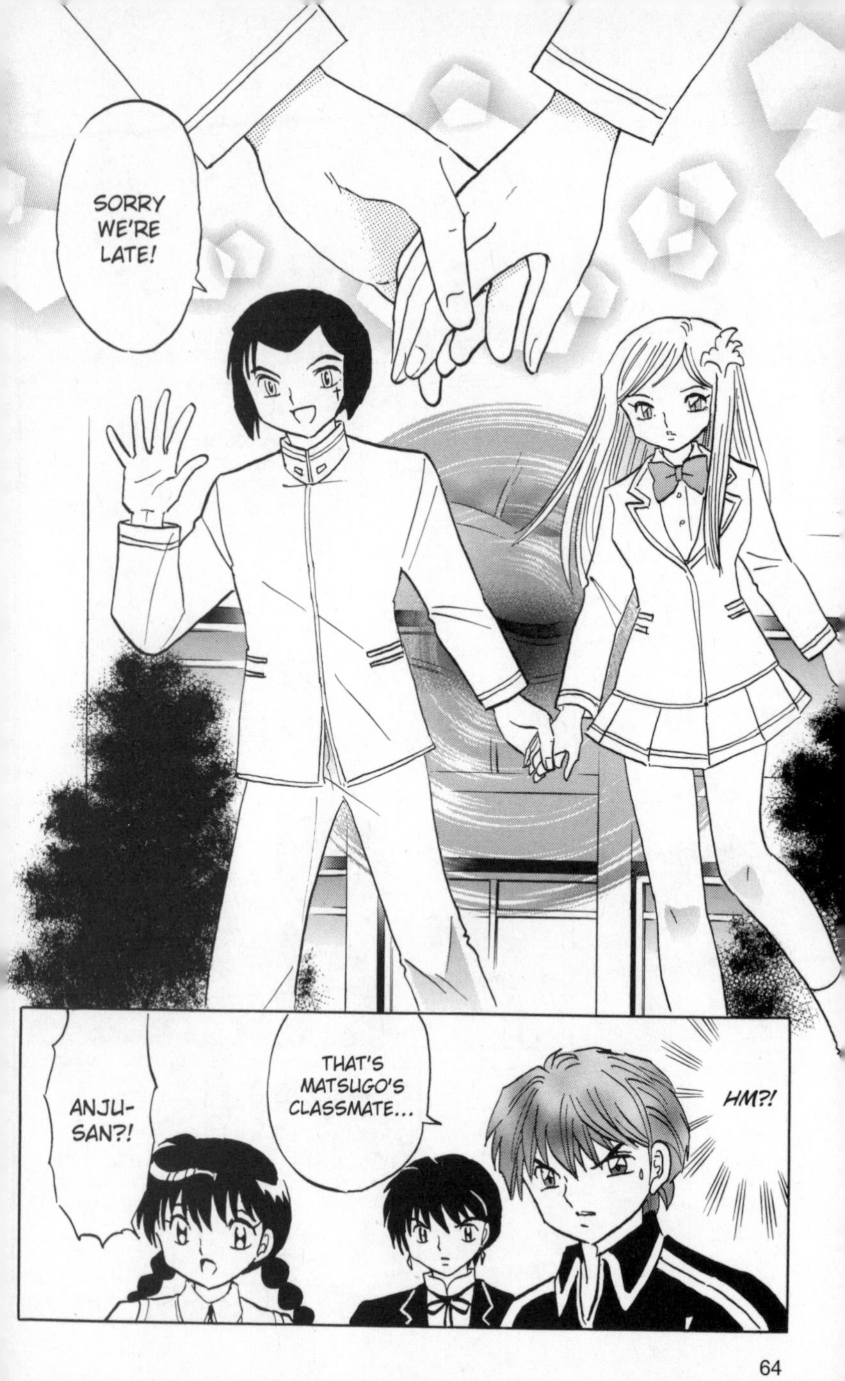
SORRY WE'RE LATE!
HM?!
THAT'S MATSUGO'S CLASSMATE...
ANJU-SAN?!

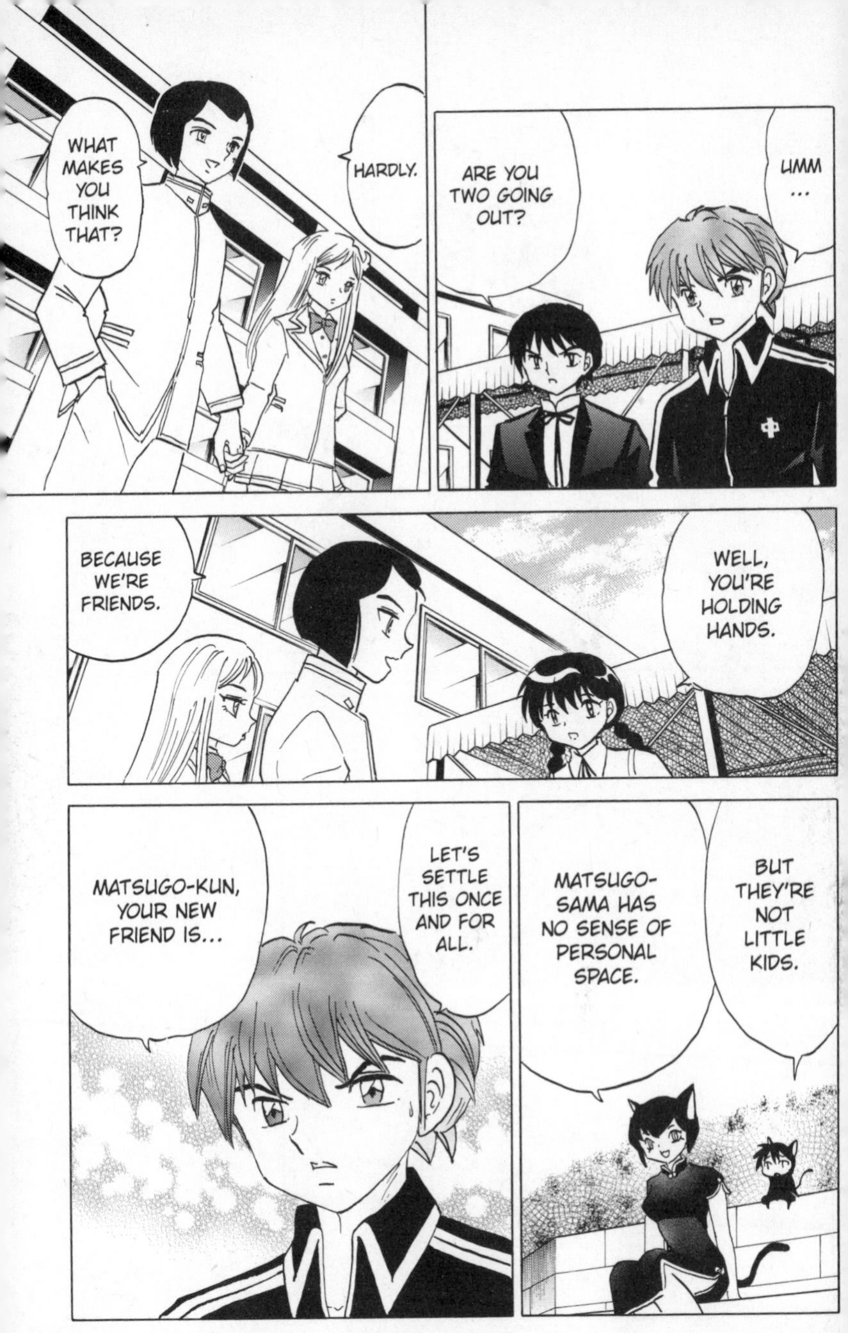
UMM...
ARE YOU TWO GOING OUT?
HARDLY.
WHAT MAKES YOU THINK THAT?
WELL, YOU'RE HOLDING HANDS.
BECAUSE WE'RE FRIENDS.
BUT THEY'RE NOT LITTLE KIDS.
MATSUGO-SAMA HAS NO SENSE OF PERSONAL SPACE.
LET'S SETTLE THIS ONCE AND FOR ALL.
MATSUGO-KUN, YOUR NEW FRIEND IS...

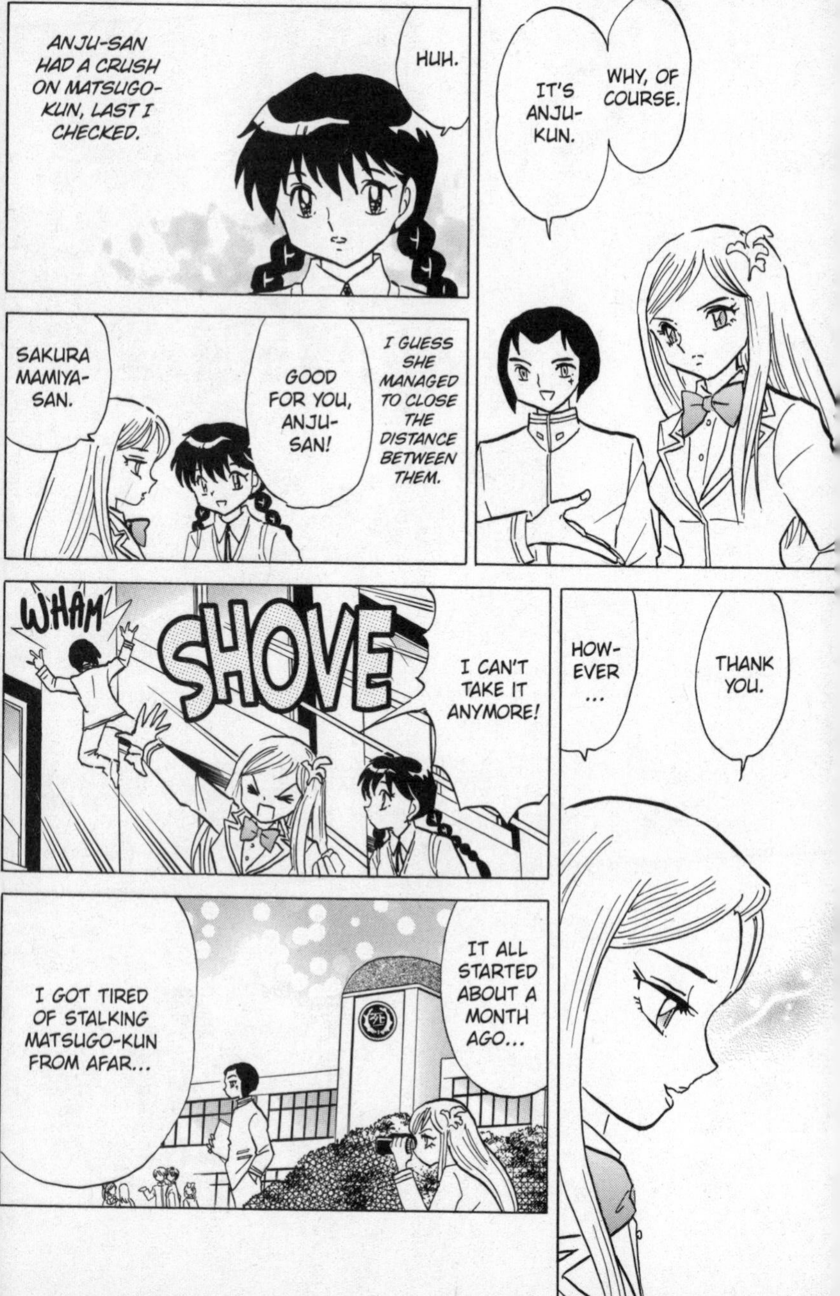
WHY, OF COURSE.
IT'S ANJU-KUN.
HUH.
ANJU-SAN HAD A CRUSH ON MATSUGO-KUN, LAST I CHECKED.
I GUESS SHE MANAGED TO CLOSE THE DISTANCE BETWEEN THEM.
GOOD FOR YOU, ANJU-SAN!
SAKURA MAMIYA-SAN.
THANK YOU.
HOW-EVER...
I CAN'T TAKE IT ANYMORE!
SHOVE
WHAM
IT ALL STARTED ABOUT A MONTH AGO...
I GOT TIRED OF STALKING MATSUGO-KUN FROM AFAR...

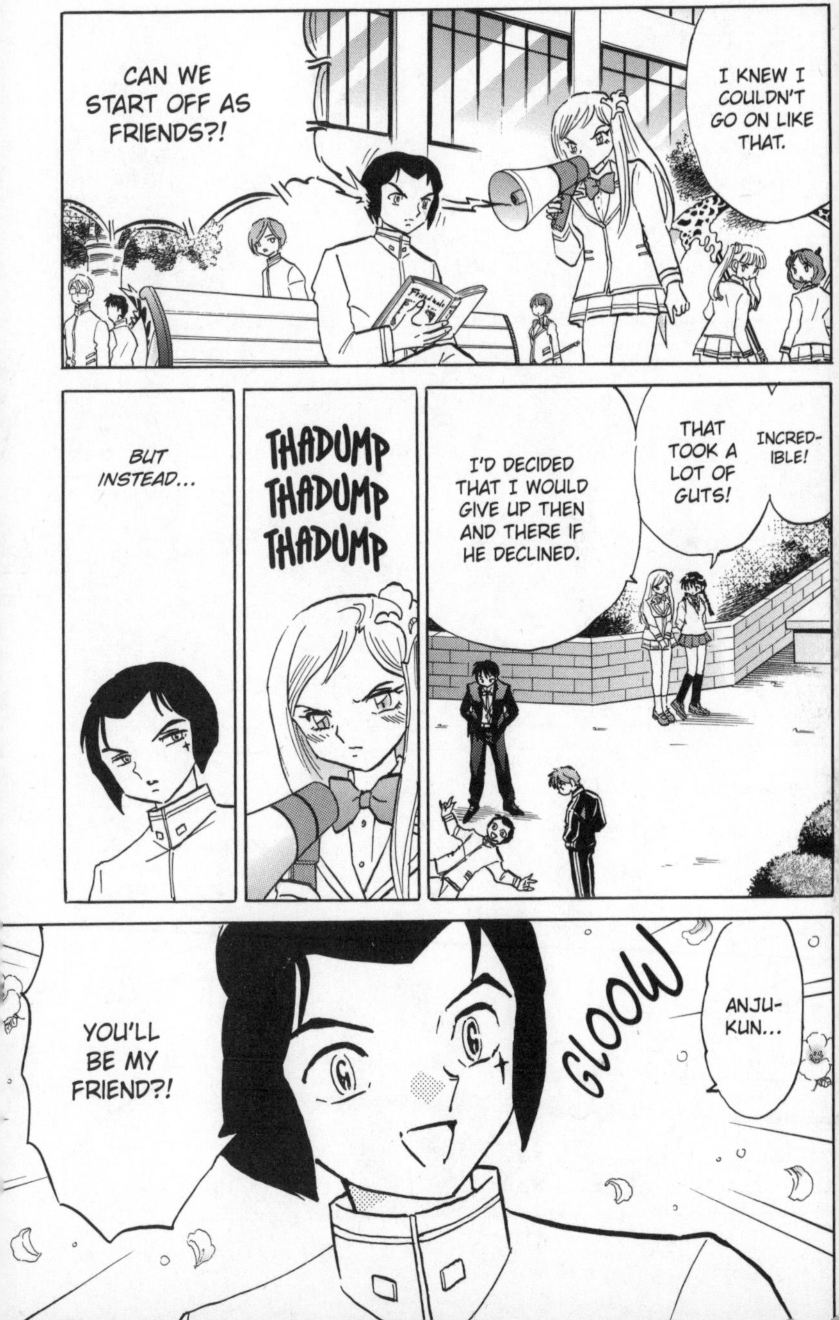
I KNEW I COULDN'T GO ON LIKE THAT.
CAN WE START OFF AS FRIENDS?!
INCRED-IBLE!
THAT TOOK A LOT OF GUTS!
I'D DECIDED THAT I WOULD GIVE UP THEN AND THERE IF HE DECLINED.
THADUMP THADUMP THADUMP
BUT INSTEAD...
ANJU-KUN...
GLOOW
YOU'LL BE MY FRIEND?!

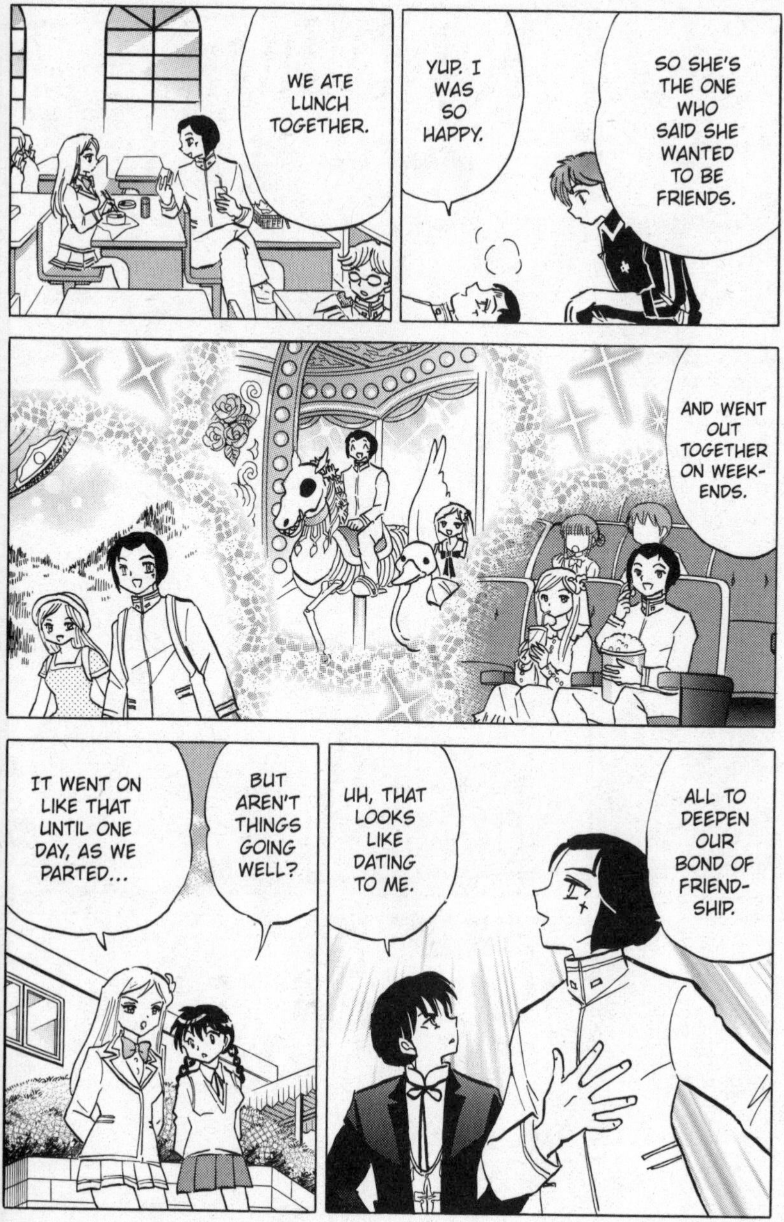
SO SHE'S THE ONE WHO SAID SHE WANTED TO BE FRIENDS.
YUP. I WAS SO HAPPY.
WE ATE LUNCH TOGETHER.
AND WENT OUT TOGETHER ON WEEK-ENDS.
ALL TO DEEPEN OUR BOND OF FRIEND-SHIP.
UH, THAT LOOKS LIKE DATING TO ME.
BUT AREN'T THINGS GOING WELL?
IT WENT ON LIKE THAT UNTIL ONE DAY, AS WE PARTED...

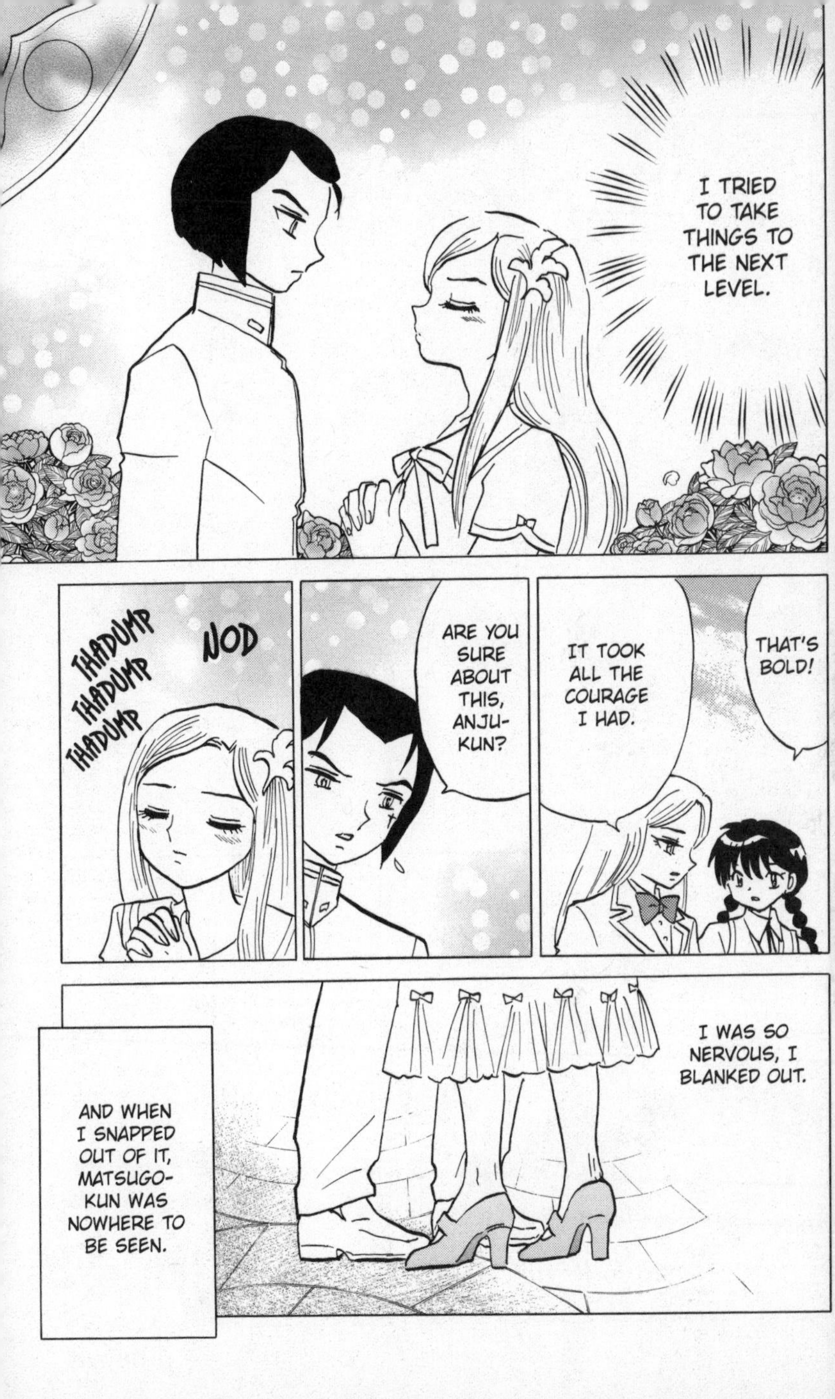
I TRIED TO TAKE THINGS TO THE NEXT LEVEL.
THAT'S BOLD!
IT TOOK ALL THE COURAGE I HAD.
ARE YOU SURE ABOUT THIS, ANJU-KUN?
NOD
THADUMP THADUMP THADUMP
I WAS SO NERVOUS, I BLANKED OUT.
AND WHEN I SNAPPED OUT OF IT, MATSUGO-KUN WAS NOWHERE TO BE SEEN.

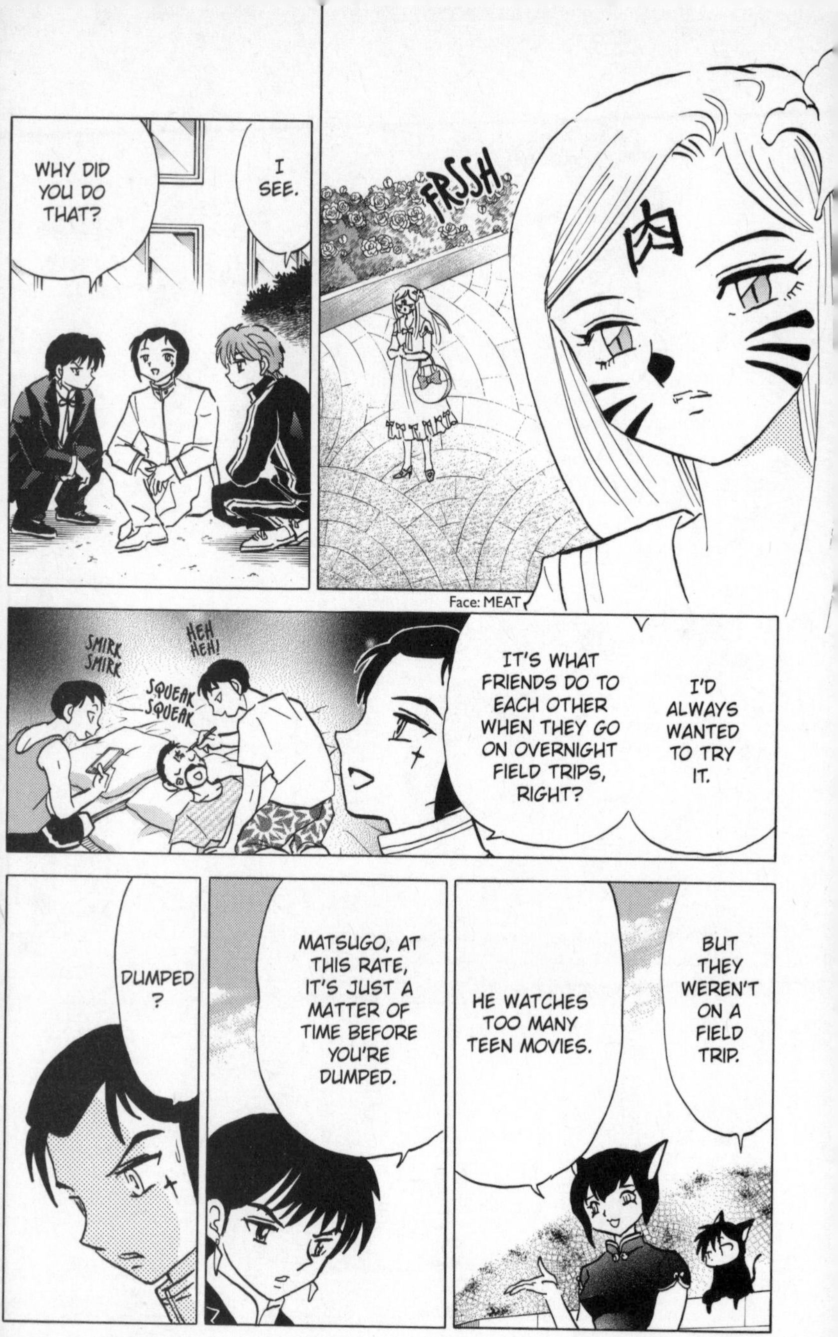
Face: MEAT
FRSSH
I SEE.
WHY DID YOU DO THAT?
I'D ALWAYS WANTED TO TRY IT.
IT'S WHAT FRIENDS DO TO EACH OTHER WHEN THEY GO ON OVERNIGHT FIELD TRIPS, RIGHT?
HEH HEH!
SQUEAK SQUEAK
SMIRK SMIRK
BUT THEY WEREN'T ON A FIELD TRIP.
HE WATCHES TOO MANY TEEN MOVIES.
MATSUGO, AT THIS RATE, IT'S JUST A MATTER OF TIME BEFORE YOU'RE DUMPED.
DUMPED?

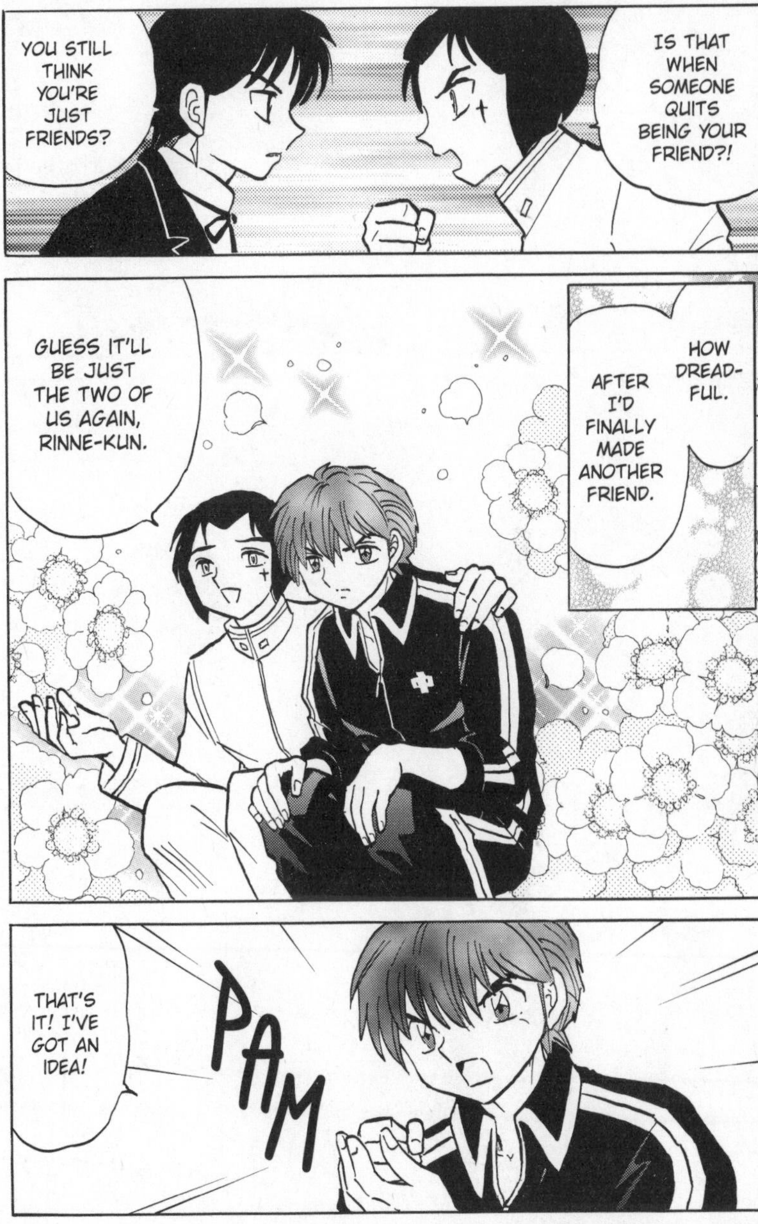
IS THAT WHEN SOMEONE QUITS BEING YOUR FRIEND?!
YOU STILL THINK YOU'RE JUST FRIENDS?
HOW DREAD-FUL.
AFTER I'D FINALLY MADE ANOTHER FRIEND.
GUESS IT'LL BE JUST THE TWO OF US AGAIN, RINNE-KUN.
PAM
THAT'S IT! I'VE GOT AN IDEA!

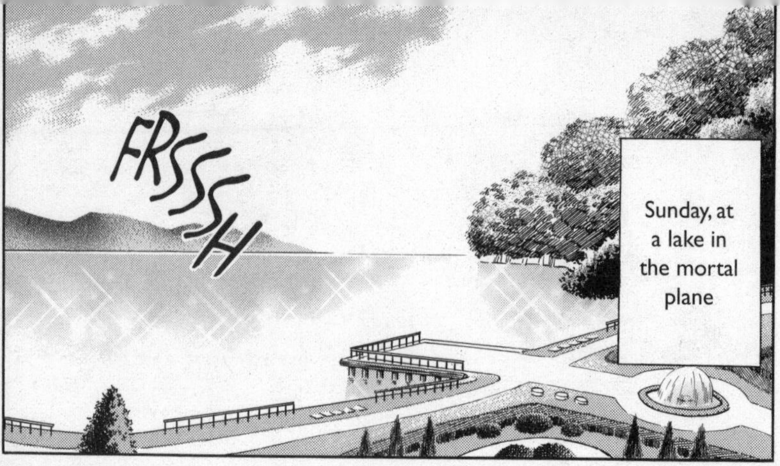
Sunday, at a lake in the mortal plane
FRSSSH

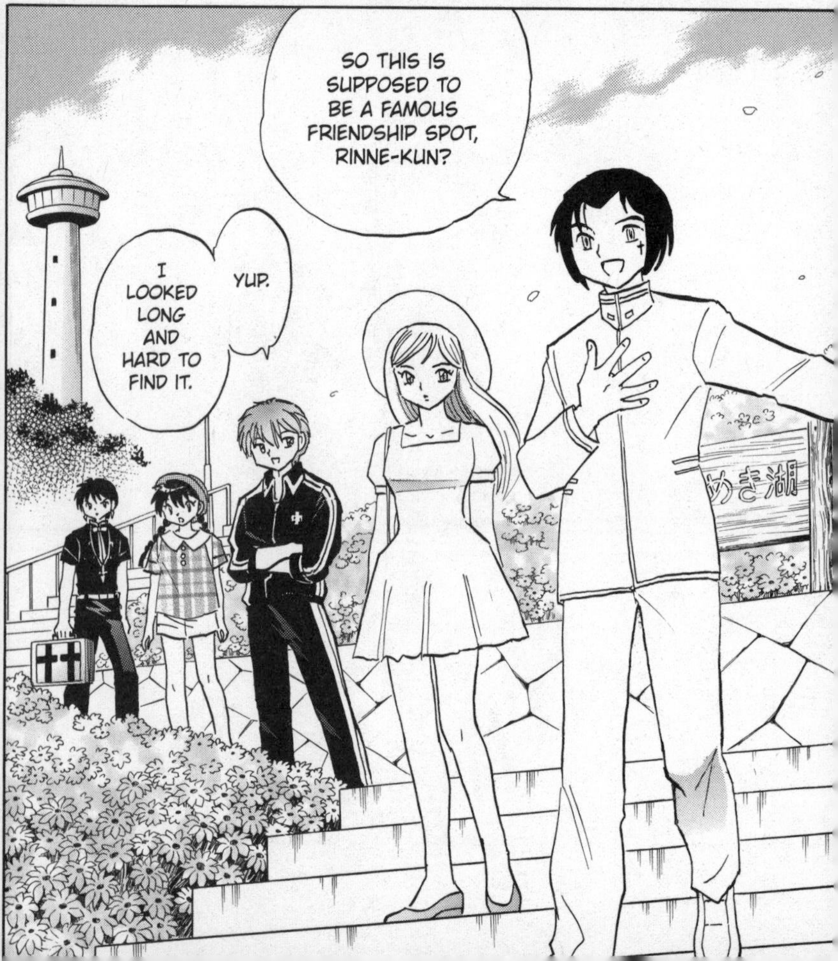
SO THIS IS SUPPOSED TO BE A FAMOUS FRIENDSHIP SPOT, RINNE-KUN?
YUP.
I LOOKED LONG AND HARD TO FIND IT.

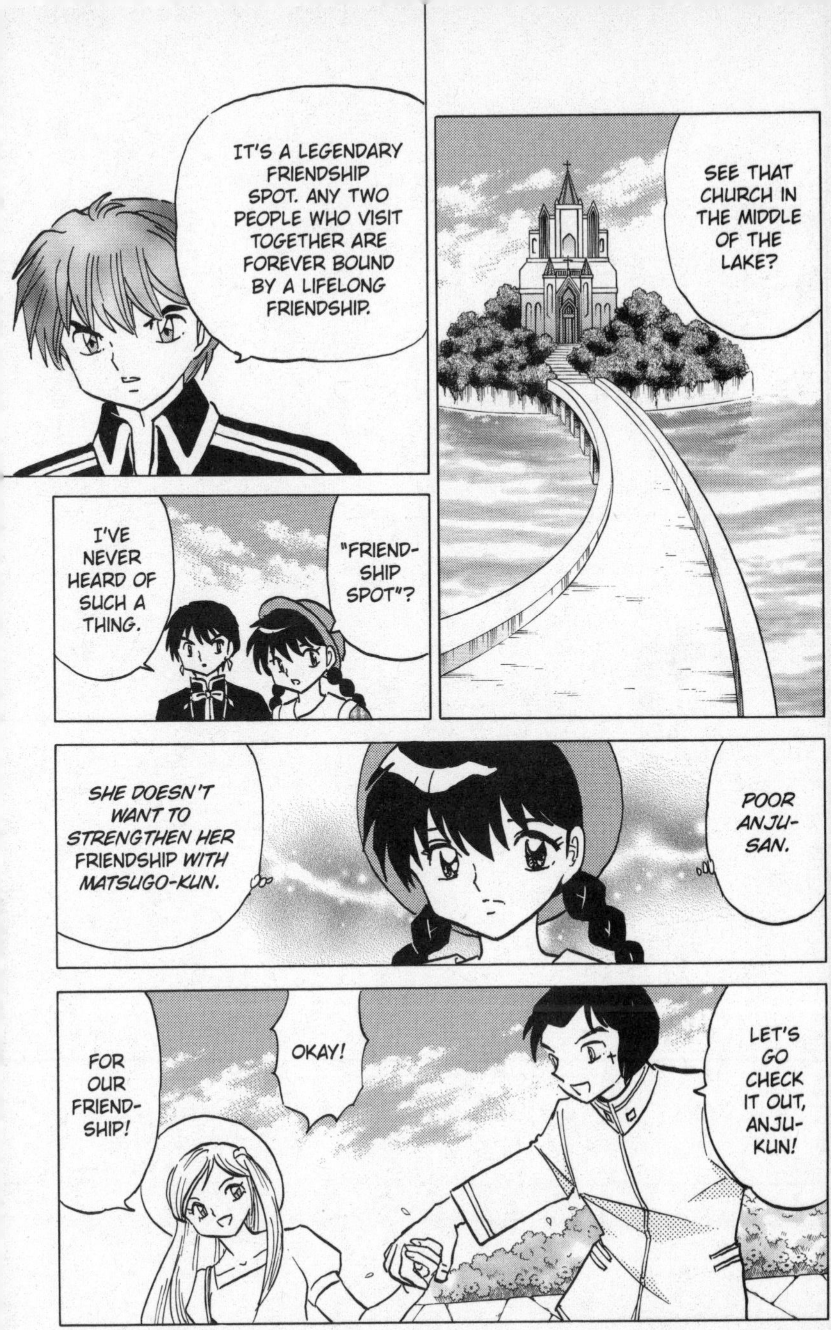
SEE THAT CHURCH IN THE MIDDLE OF THE LAKE?
IT'S A LEGENDARY FRIENDSHIP SPOT. ANY TWO PEOPLE WHO VISIT TOGETHER ARE FOREVER BOUND BY A LIFELONG FRIENDSHIP.
"FRIEND-SHIP SPOT"?
I'VE NEVER HEARD OF SUCH A THING.
POOR ANJU-SAN.
SHE DOESN'T WANT TO STRENGTHEN HER FRIENDSHIP WITH MATSUGO-KUN.
LET'S GO CHECK IT OUT, ANJU-KUN!
OKAY!
FOR OUR FRIEND-SHIP!

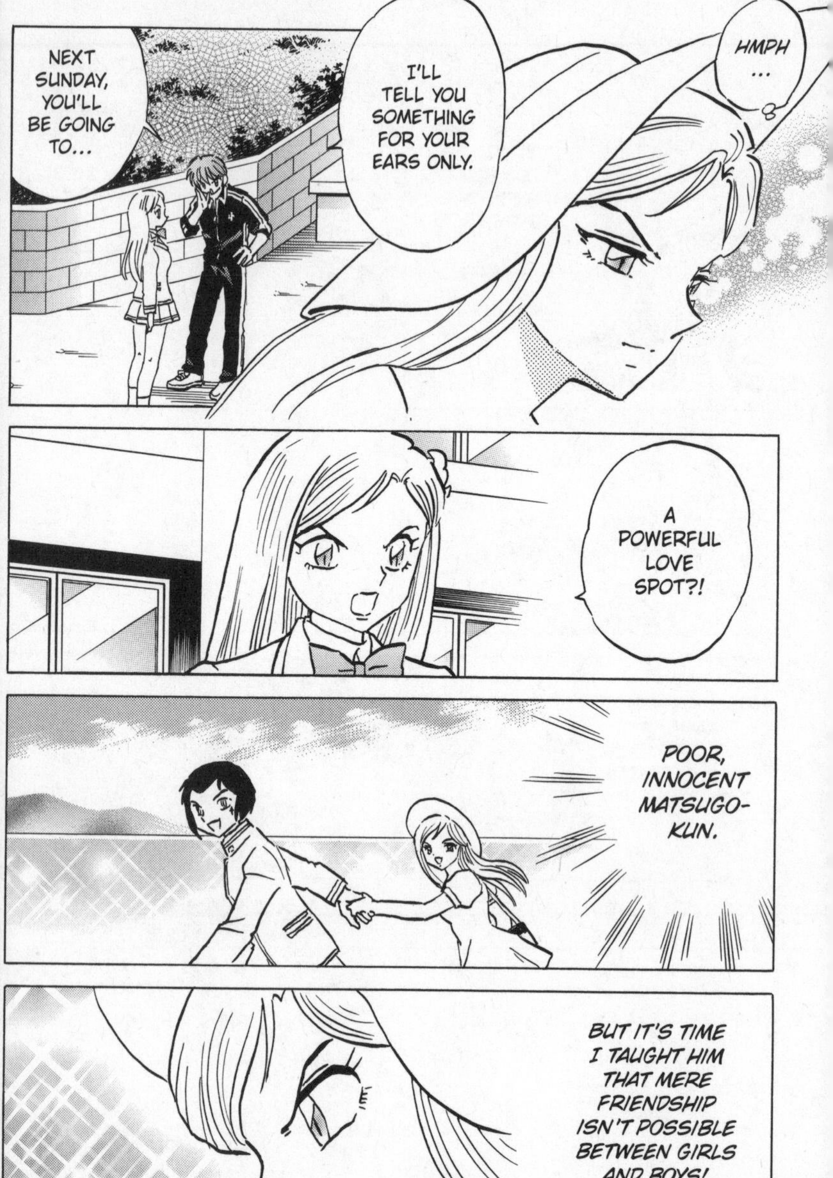
HMPH ...
I'LL TELL YOU SOMETHING FOR YOUR EARS ONLY.
NEXT SUNDAY, YOU'LL BE GOING TO...
A POWERFUL LOVE SPOT?!
POOR, INNOCENT MATSUGO-KUN.
BUT IT'S TIME I TAUGHT HIM THAT MERE FRIENDSHIP ISN'T POSSIBLE BETWEEN GIRLS AND BOYS!

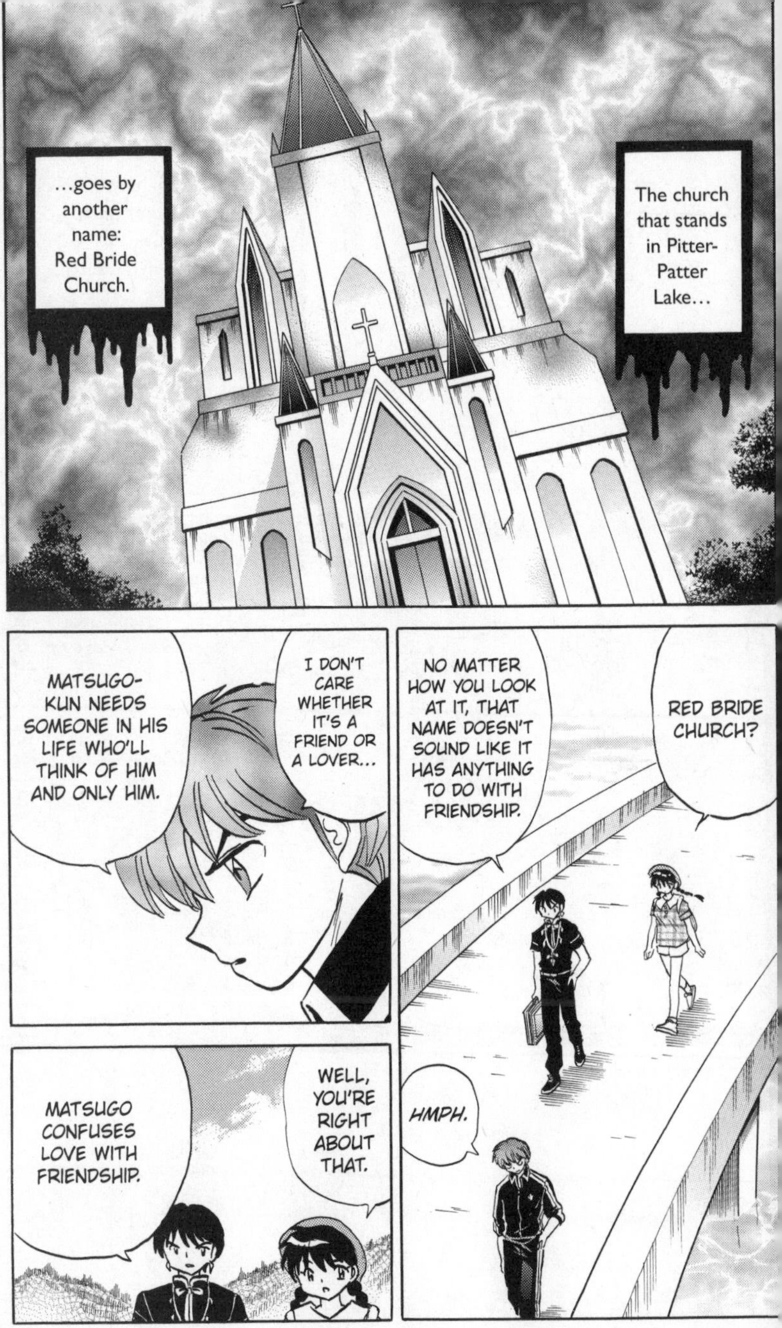
The church that stands in Pitter-Patter Lake…
…goes by another name: Red Bride Church.
RED BRIDE CHURCH?
NO MATTER HOW YOU LOOK AT IT, THAT NAME DOESN'T SOUND LIKE IT HAS ANYTHING TO DO WITH FRIENDSHIP.
HMPH.
I DON'T CARE WHETHER IT'S A FRIEND OR A LOVER…
MATSUGO-KUN NEEDS SOMEONE IN HIS LIFE WHO'LL THINK OF HIM AND ONLY HIM.
WELL, YOU'RE RIGHT ABOUT THAT.
MATSUGO CONFUSES LOVE WITH FRIENDSHIP.

In the middle of the 20th century, a couple who had eloped because their family wouldn't accept their marriage...

...arrived on the steps of this church.

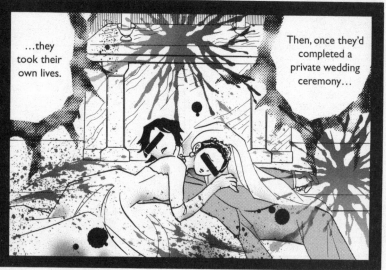

Then, once they'd completed a private wedding ceremony...

...they took their own lives.

WHEN THEY WERE DISCOVERED, THE BRIDE'S WEDDING GOWN WAS STAINED RED.

RED?

THAT'S WHY...

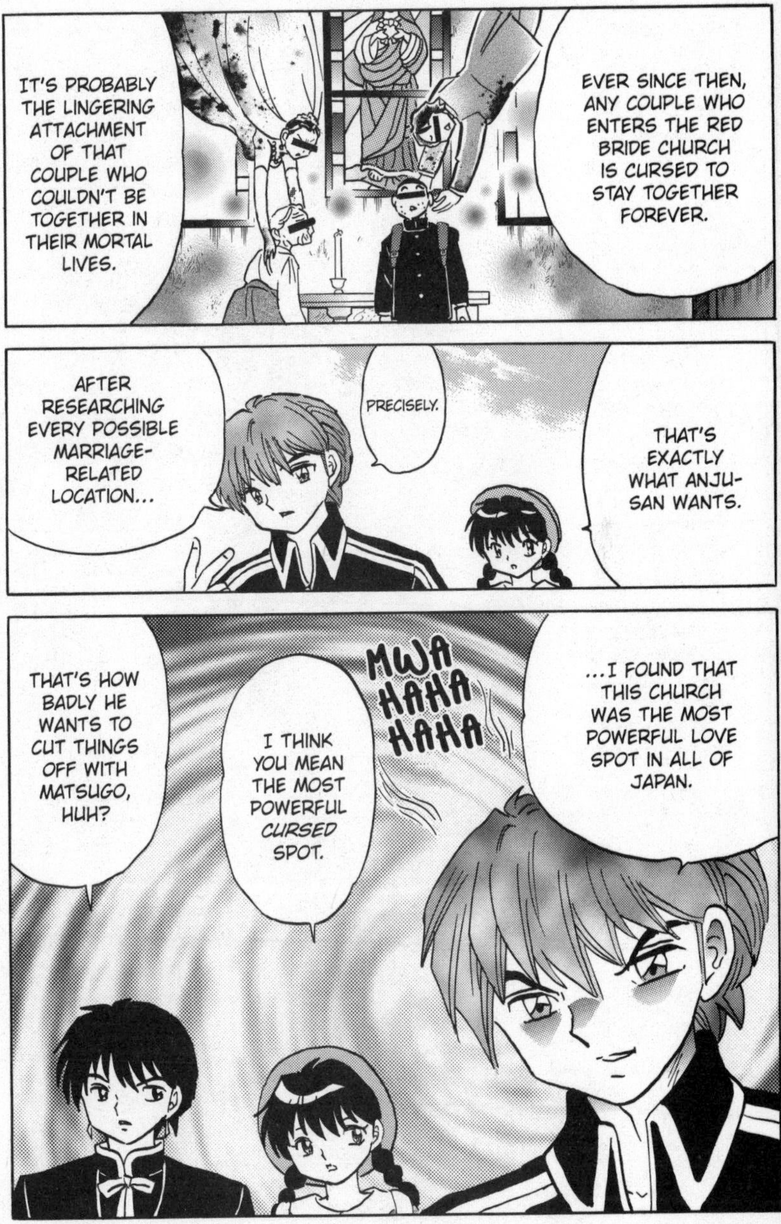
EVER SINCE THEN, ANY COUPLE WHO ENTERS THE RED BRIDE CHURCH IS CURSED TO STAY TOGETHER FOREVER.
IT'S PROBABLY THE LINGERING ATTACHMENT OF THAT COUPLE WHO COULDN'T BE TOGETHER IN THEIR MORTAL LIVES.
THAT'S EXACTLY WHAT ANJU-SAN WANTS.
PRECISELY.
AFTER RESEARCHING EVERY POSSIBLE MARRIAGE-RELATED LOCATION...
...I FOUND THAT THIS CHURCH WAS THE MOST POWERFUL LOVE SPOT IN ALL OF JAPAN.
MWA HAHA HAHA
I THINK YOU MEAN THE MOST POWERFUL *CURSED* SPOT.
THAT'S HOW BADLY HE WANTS TO CUT THINGS OFF WITH MATSUGO, HUH?

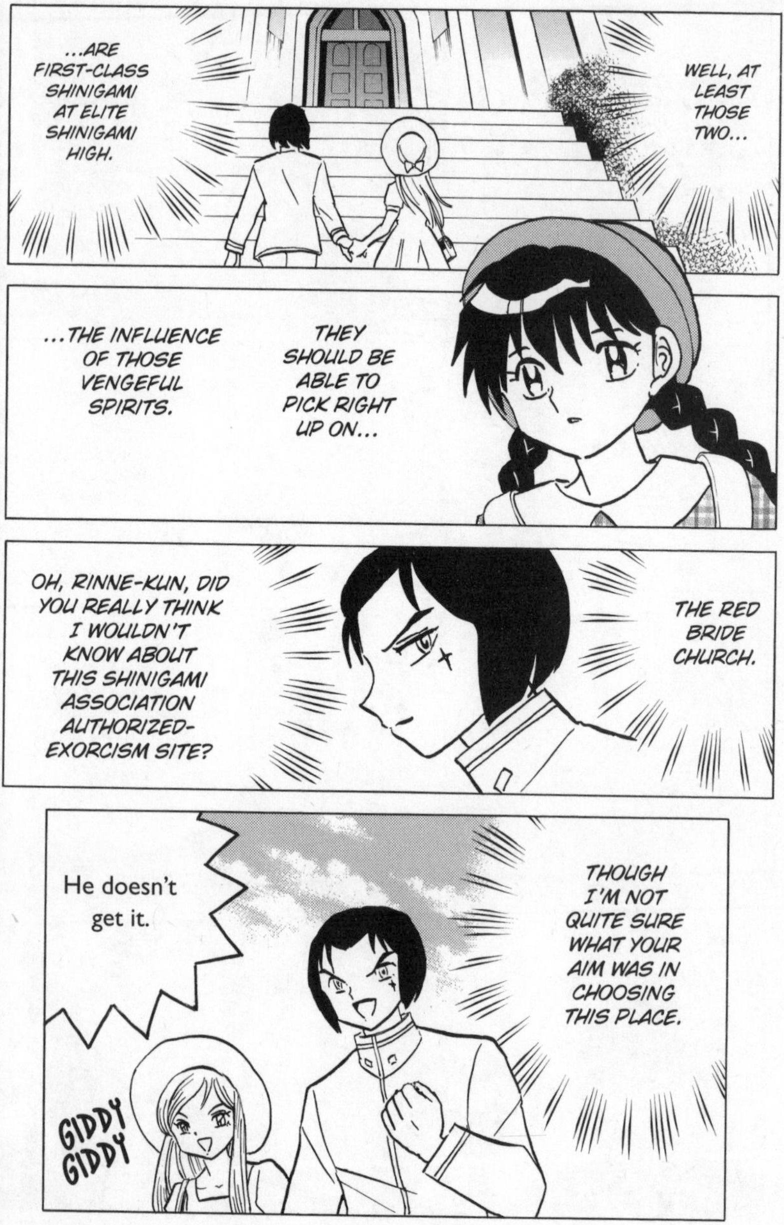
WELL, AT LEAST THOSE TWO...
...ARE FIRST-CLASS SHINIGAMI AT ELITE SHINIGAMI HIGH.
THEY SHOULD BE ABLE TO PICK RIGHT UP ON...
...THE INFLUENCE OF THOSE VENGEFUL SPIRITS.
THE RED BRIDE CHURCH.
OH, RINNE-KUN, DID YOU REALLY THINK I WOULDN'T KNOW ABOUT THIS SHINIGAMI ASSOCIATION AUTHORIZED-EXORCISM SITE?
THOUGH I'M NOT QUITE SURE WHAT YOUR AIM WAS IN CHOOSING THIS PLACE.
He doesn't get it.
GIDDY GIDDY

CHAPTER 373: RED BRIDE CHURCH

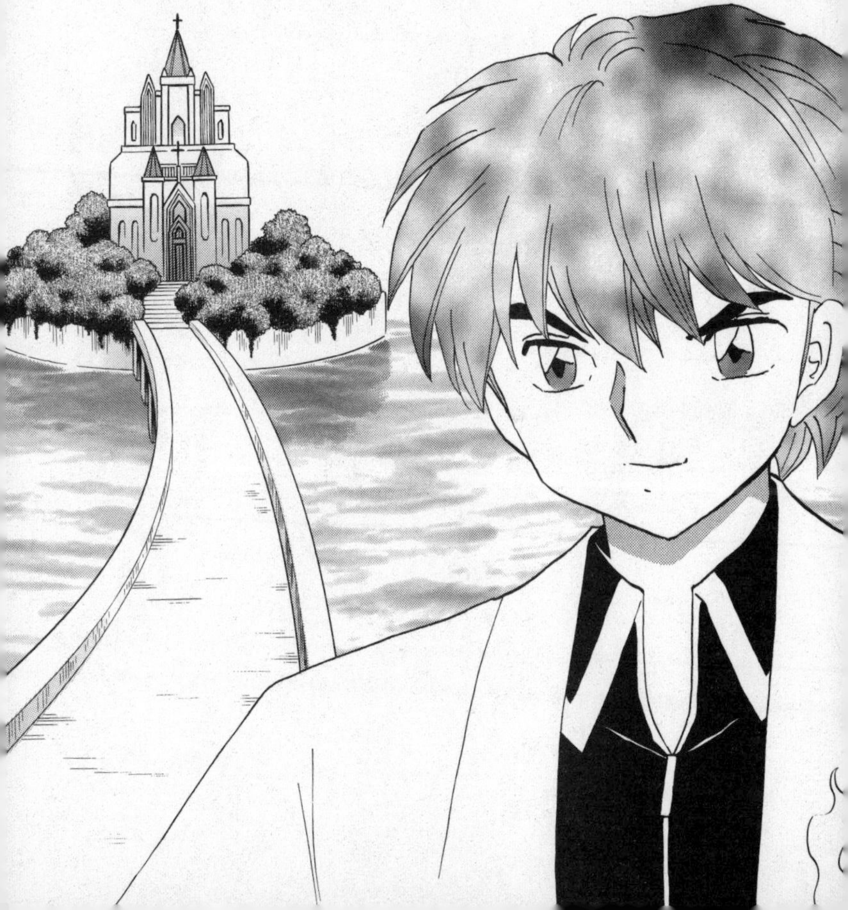

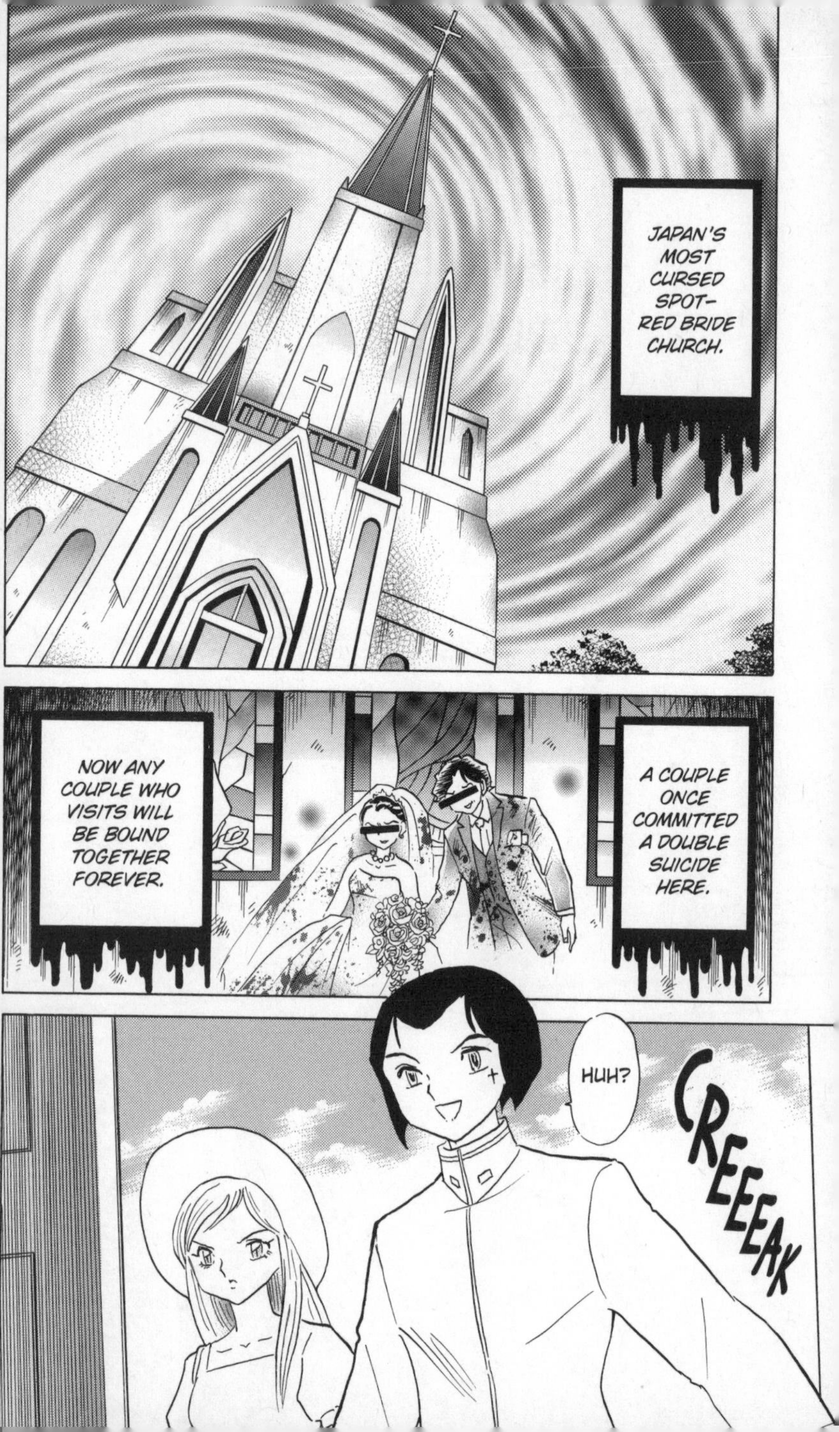
JAPAN'S MOST CURSED SPOT— RED BRIDE CHURCH.
A COUPLE ONCE COMMITTED A DOUBLE SUICIDE HERE.
NOW ANY COUPLE WHO VISITS WILL BE BOUND TOGETHER FOREVER.
CREEEAK
HUH?

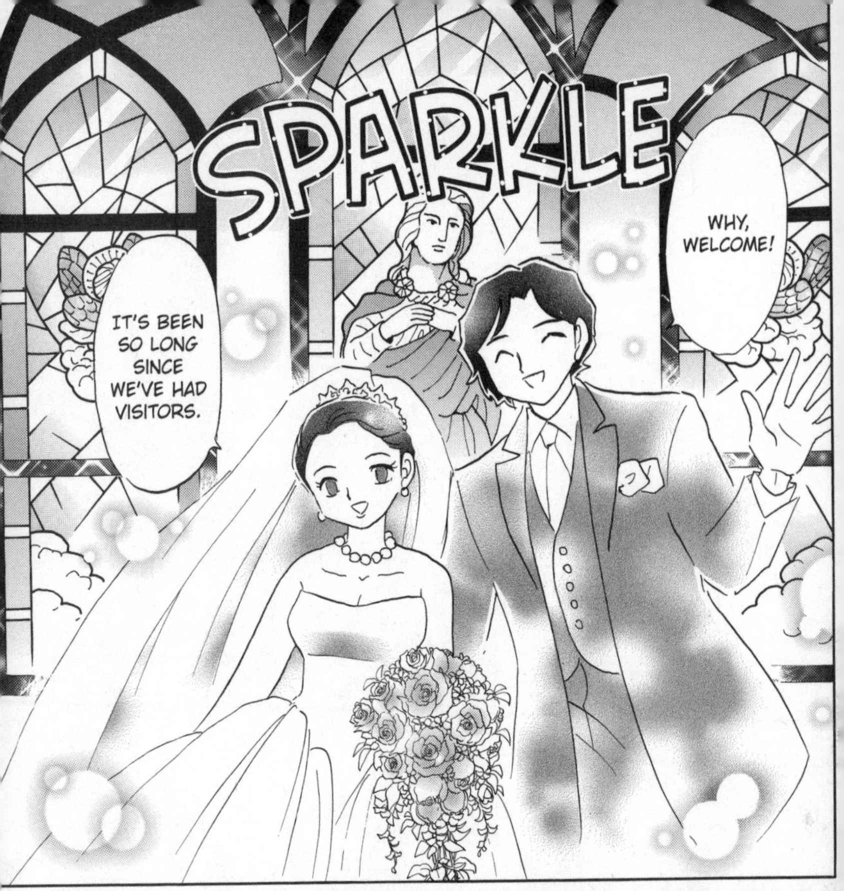
SPARKLE
WHY, WELCOME!
IT'S BEEN SO LONG SINCE WE'VE HAD VISITORS.

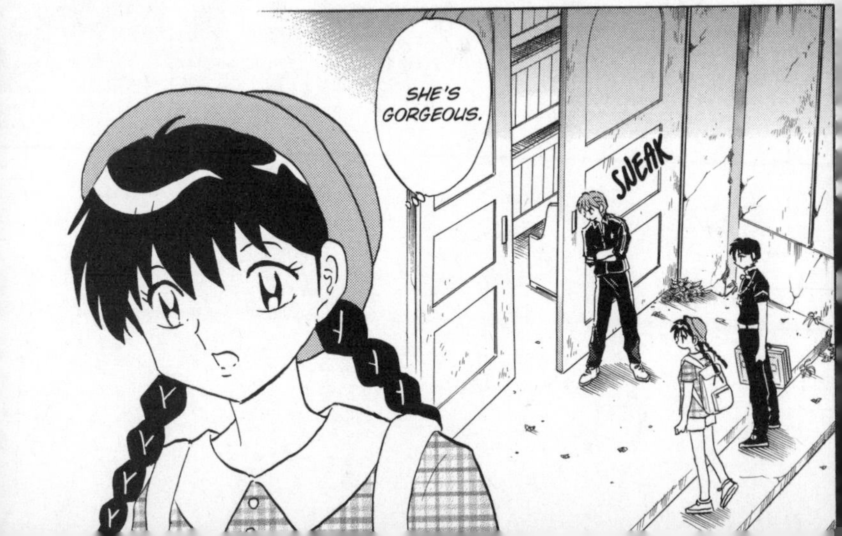
SNEAK
SHE'S GORGEOUS.

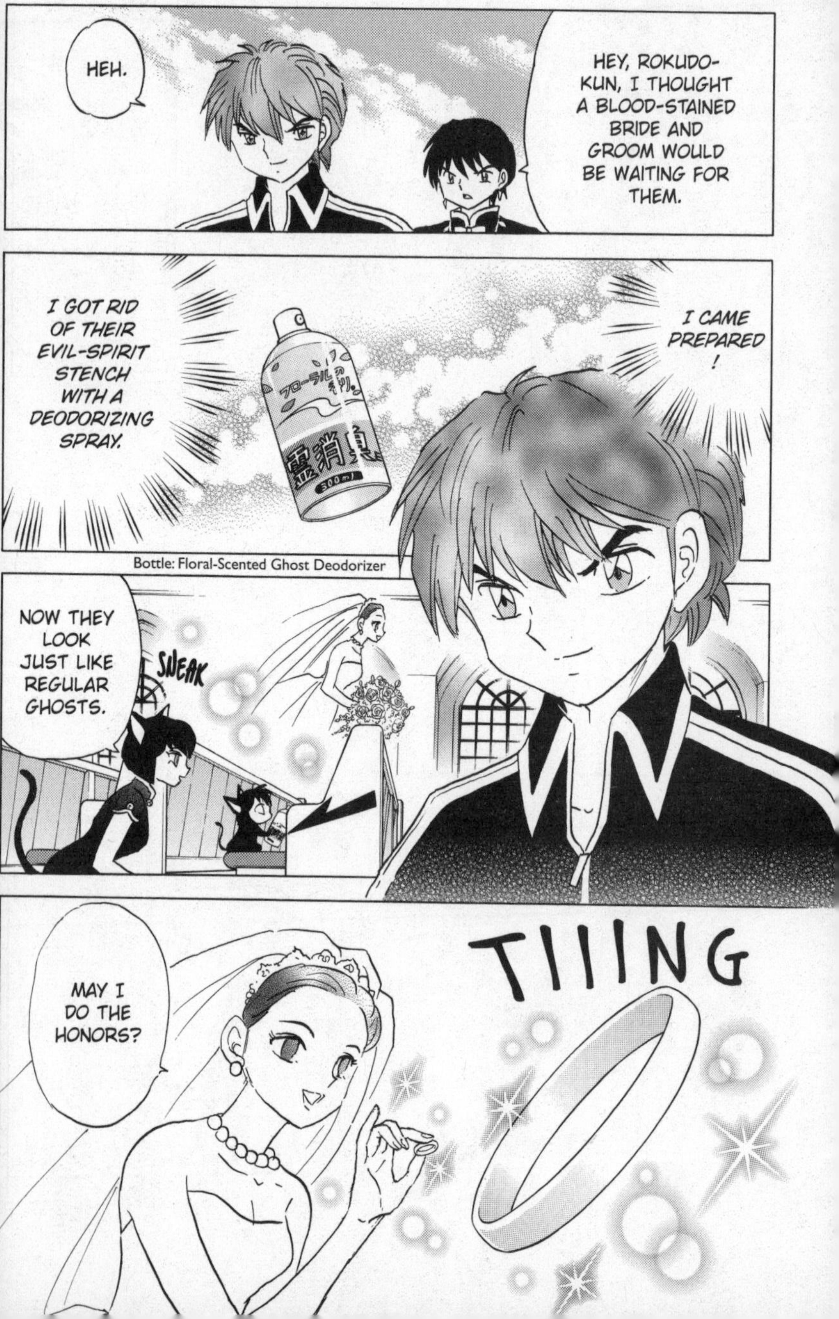
HEY, ROKUDO-KUN, I THOUGHT A BLOOD-STAINED BRIDE AND GROOM WOULD BE WAITING FOR THEM.
HEH.
I CAME PREPARED!
I GOT RID OF THEIR EVIL-SPIRIT STENCH WITH A DEODORIZING SPRAY.
NOW THEY LOOK JUST LIKE REGULAR GHOSTS.
SNEAK
TIIING
MAY I DO THE HONORS?
Bottle: Floral-Scented Ghost Deodorizer

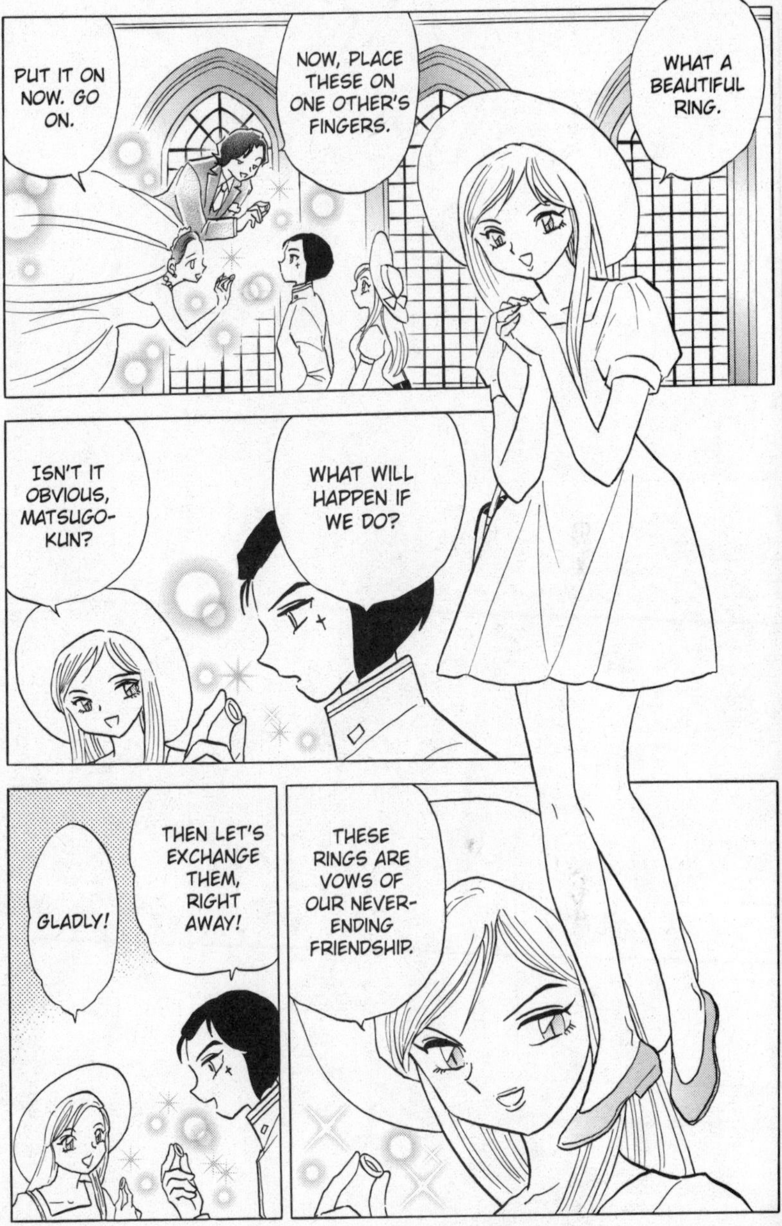
WHAT A BEAUTIFUL RING.
NOW, PLACE THESE ON ONE OTHER'S FINGERS.
PUT IT ON NOW. GO ON.
WHAT WILL HAPPEN IF WE DO?
ISN'T IT OBVIOUS, MATSUGO-KUN?
THESE RINGS ARE VOWS OF OUR NEVER-ENDING FRIENDSHIP.
THEN LET'S EXCHANGE THEM, RIGHT AWAY!
GLADLY!

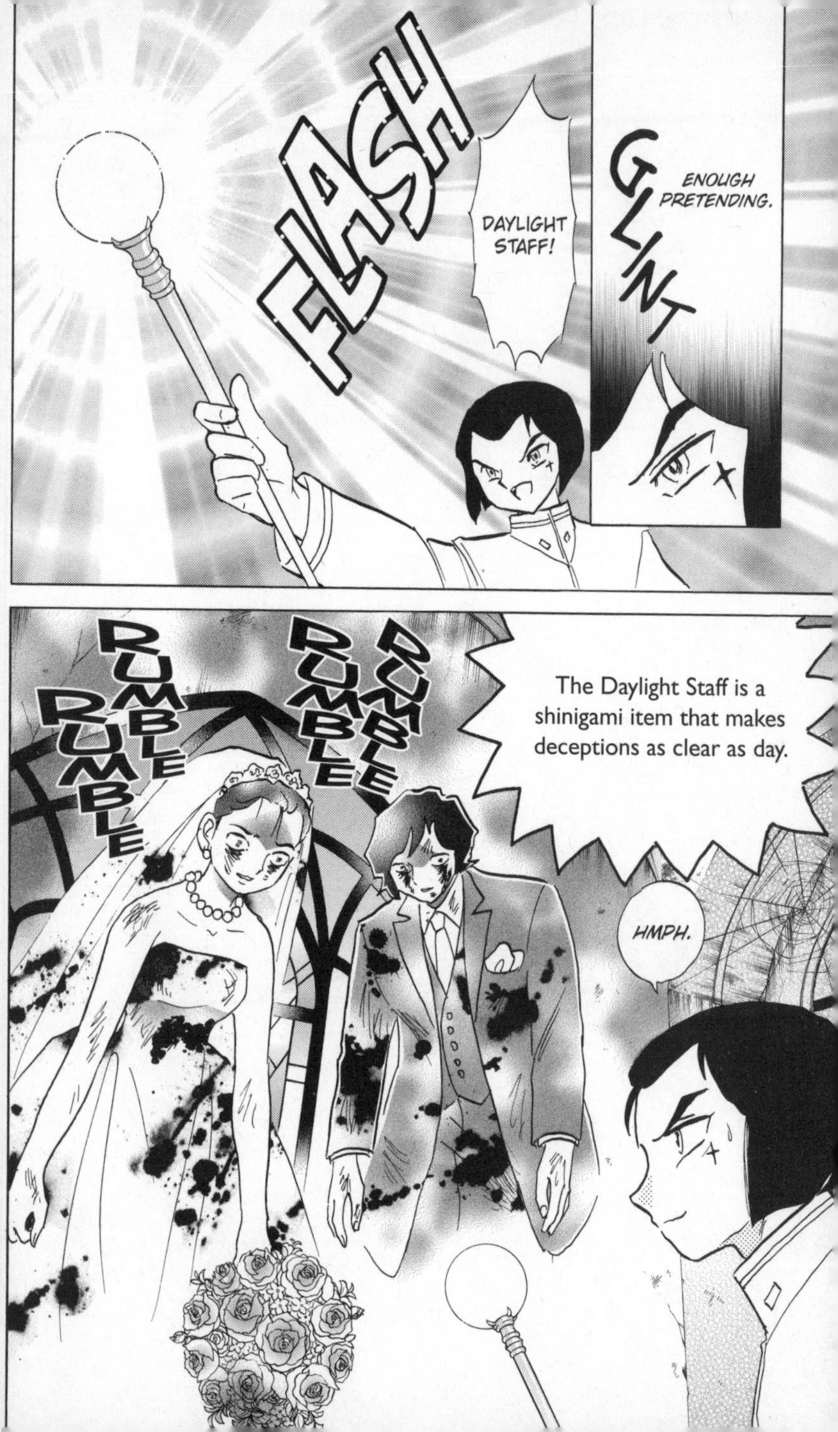

ENOUGH PRETENDING.
GLINT
DAYLIGHT STAFF!
FLASH
The Daylight Staff is a shinigami item that makes deceptions as clear as day.
HMPH.
RUMBLE RUMBLE
RUMBLE RUMBLE

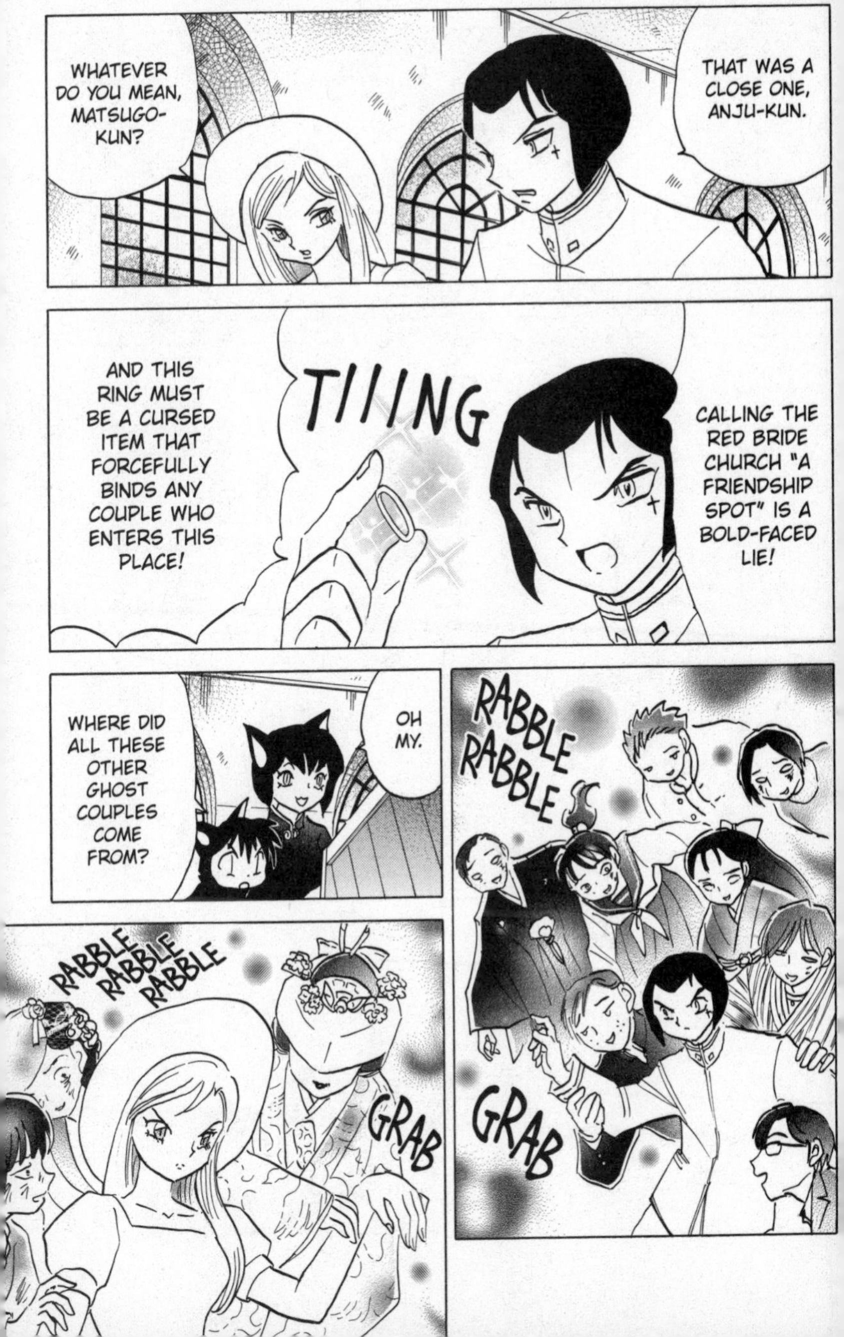
THAT WAS A CLOSE ONE, ANJU-KUN.
WHATEVER DO YOU MEAN, MATSUGO-KUN?
CALLING THE RED BRIDE CHURCH "A FRIENDSHIP SPOT" IS A BOLD-FACED LIE!
TIIING
AND THIS RING MUST BE A CURSED ITEM THAT FORCEFULLY BINDS ANY COUPLE WHO ENTERS THIS PLACE!
RABBLE RABBLE RABBLE
GRAB
OH MY.
WHERE DID ALL THESE OTHER GHOST COUPLES COME FROM?
RABBLE RABBLE RABBLE
GRAB

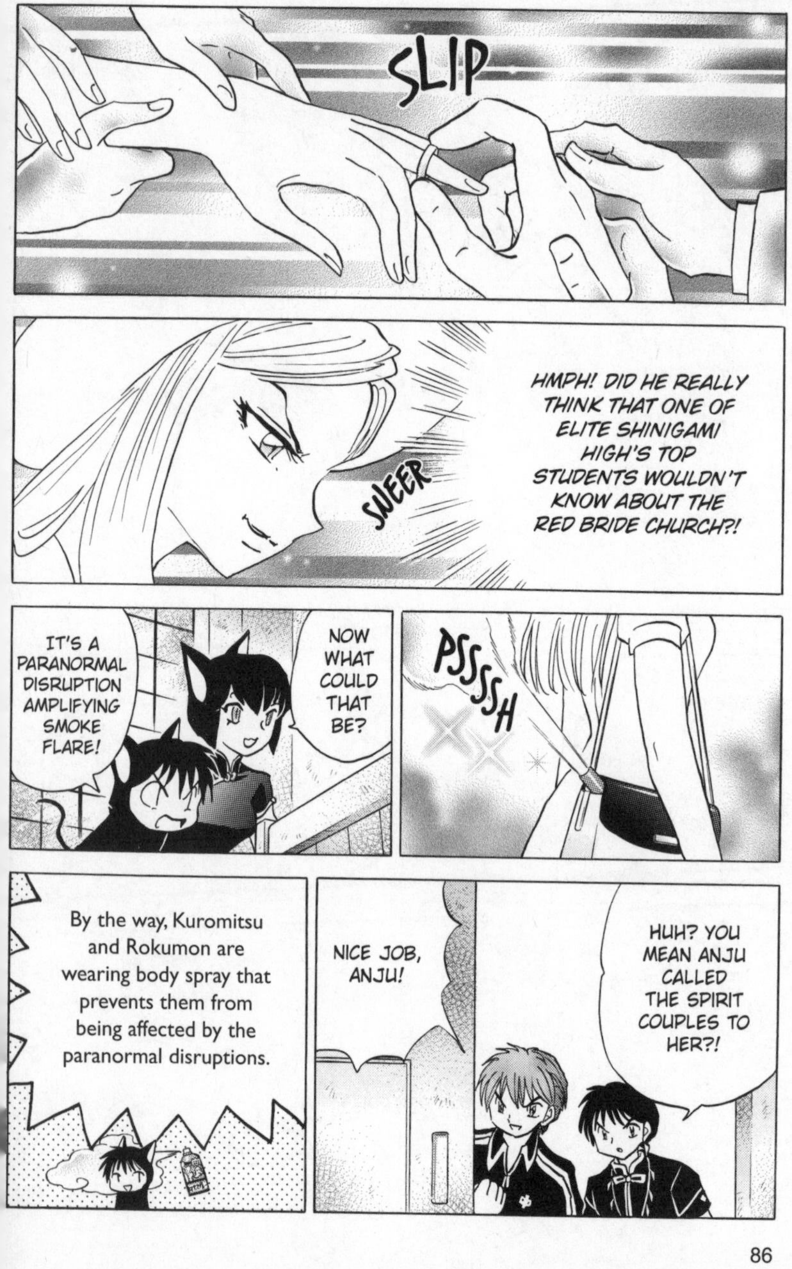
SLIP
HMPH! DID HE REALLY THINK THAT ONE OF ELITE SHINIGAMI HIGH'S TOP STUDENTS WOULDN'T KNOW ABOUT THE RED BRIDE CHURCH?!
SNEER
PSSSSH
NOW WHAT COULD THAT BE?
IT'S A PARANORMAL DISRUPTION AMPLIFYING SMOKE FLARE!
HUH? YOU MEAN ANJU CALLED THE SPIRIT COUPLES TO HER?!
NICE JOB, ANJU!
By the way, Kuromitsu and Rokumon are wearing body spray that prevents them from being affected by the paranormal disruptions.

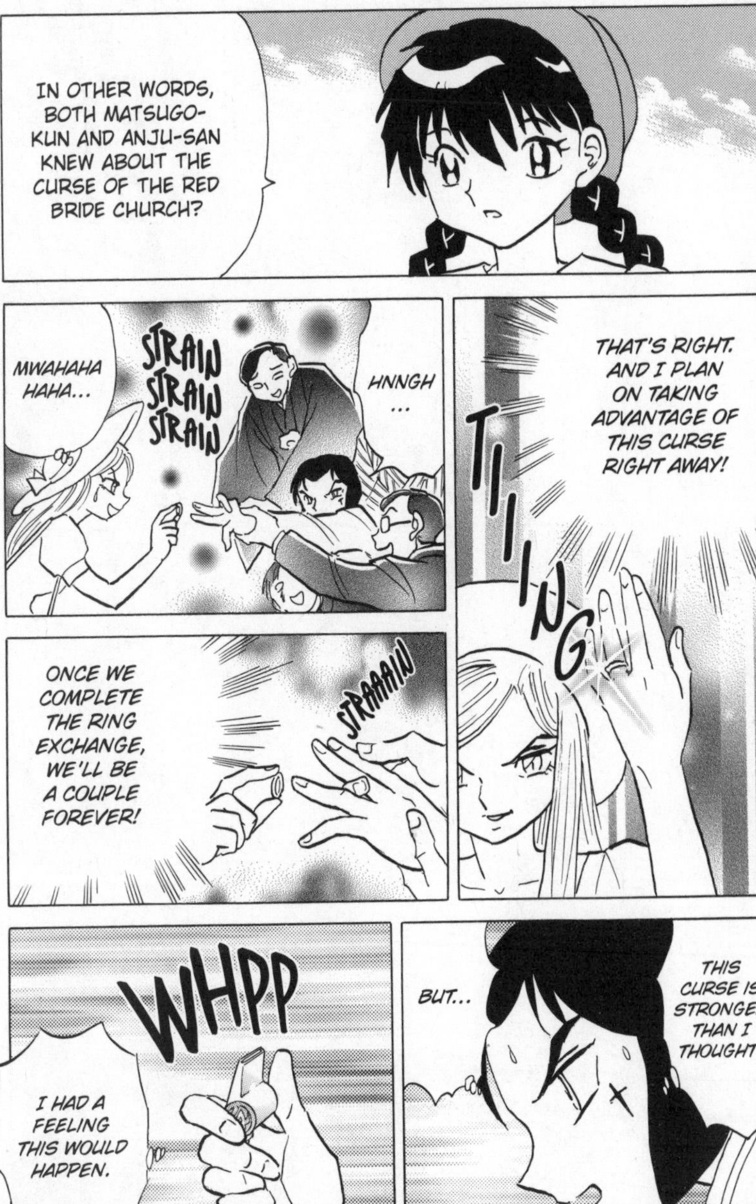
IN OTHER WORDS, BOTH MATSUGO-KUN AND ANJU-SAN KNEW ABOUT THE CURSE OF THE RED BRIDE CHURCH?
THAT'S RIGHT. AND I PLAN ON TAKING ADVANTAGE OF THIS CURSE RIGHT AWAY!
TIIING
HNNGH ...
STRAIN STRAIN STRAIN
MWAHAHA HAHA...
STRAAAIN
ONCE WE COMPLETE THE RING EXCHANGE, WE'LL BE A COUPLE FOREVER!
THIS CURSE IS STRONGER THAN I THOUGHT!
BUT...
WHPP
I HAD A FEELING THIS WOULD HAPPEN.

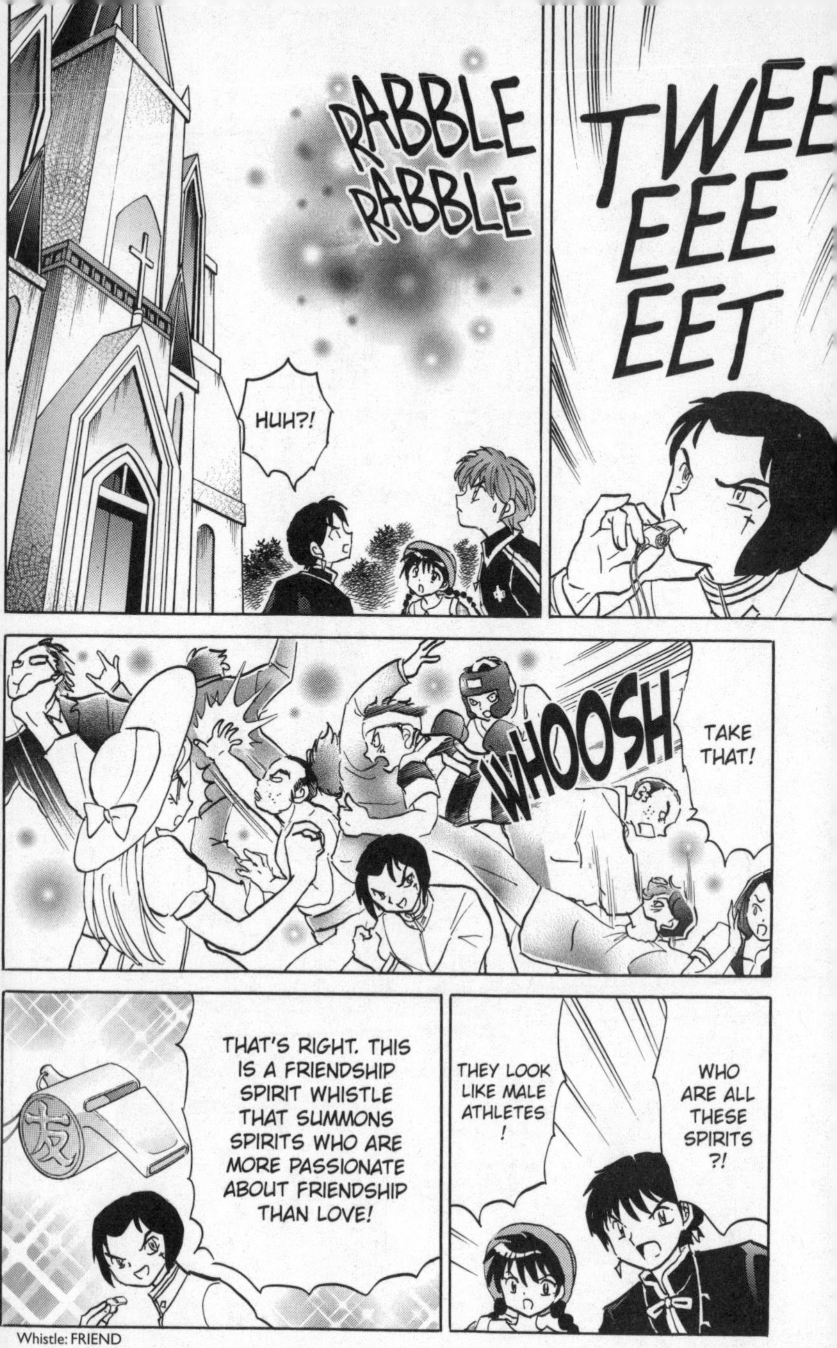
TWEEEEEEET
RABBLE RABBLE
HUH?!
TAKE THAT!
WHOOSH
WHO ARE ALL THESE SPIRITS?!
THEY LOOK LIKE MALE ATHLETES!
THAT'S RIGHT. THIS IS A FRIENDSHIP SPIRIT WHISTLE THAT SUMMONS SPIRITS WHO ARE MORE PASSIONATE ABOUT FRIENDSHIP THAN LOVE!

Whistle: FRIEND

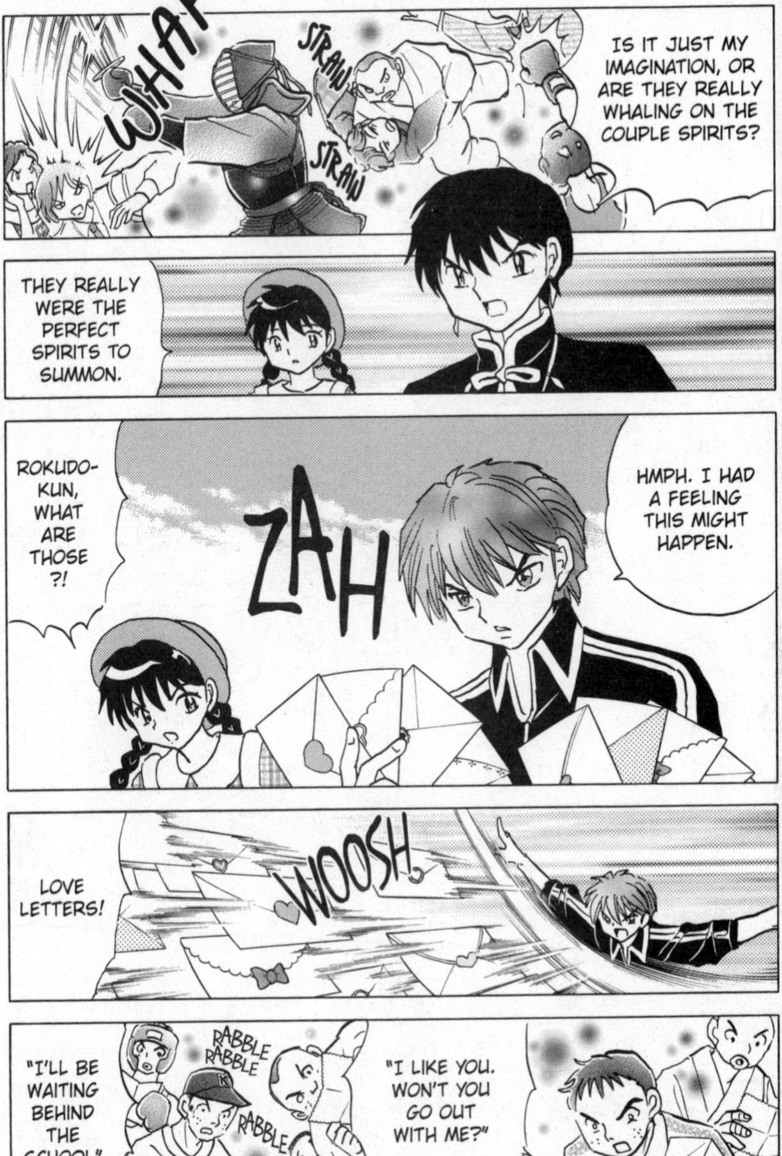

IS IT JUST MY IMAGINATION, OR ARE THEY REALLY WHALING ON THE COUPLE SPIRITS?
STRAW
STRAW
WHAP
THEY REALLY WERE THE PERFECT SPIRITS TO SUMMON.
HMPH. I HAD A FEELING THIS MIGHT HAPPEN.
ZAH
ROKUDO-KUN, WHAT ARE THOSE?!
WOOSH
LOVE LETTERS!
"I LIKE YOU. WON'T YOU GO OUT WITH ME?"
RABBLE RABBLE
RABBLE
"I'LL BE WAITING BEHIND THE SCHOOL"?

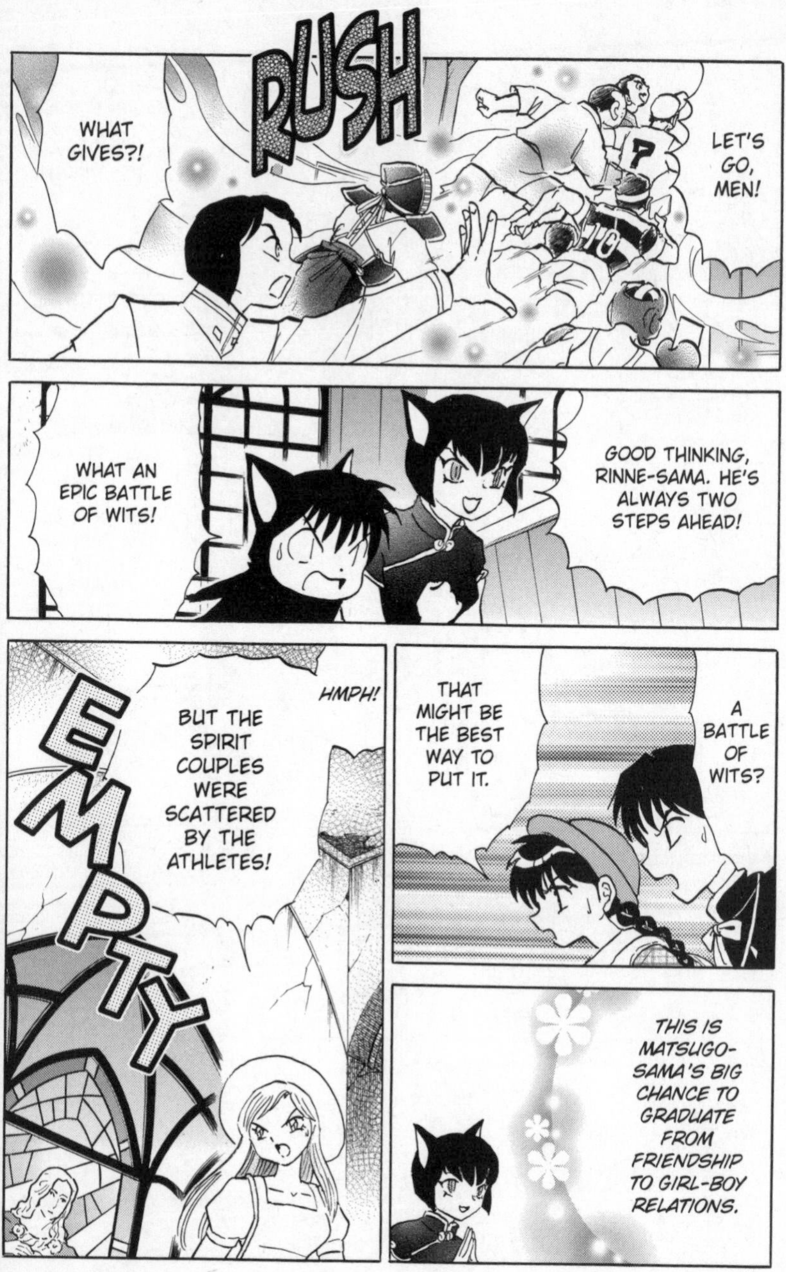
LET'S GO, MEN!
RUSH
WHAT GIVES?!
GOOD THINKING, RINNE-SAMA. HE'S ALWAYS TWO STEPS AHEAD!
WHAT AN EPIC BATTLE OF WITS!
A BATTLE OF WITS?
THAT MIGHT BE THE BEST WAY TO PUT IT.
THIS IS MATSUGO-SAMA'S BIG CHANCE TO GRADUATE FROM FRIENDSHIP TO GIRL-BOY RELATIONS.
HMPH!
BUT THE SPIRIT COUPLES WERE SCATTERED BY THE ATHLETES!
EMPTY

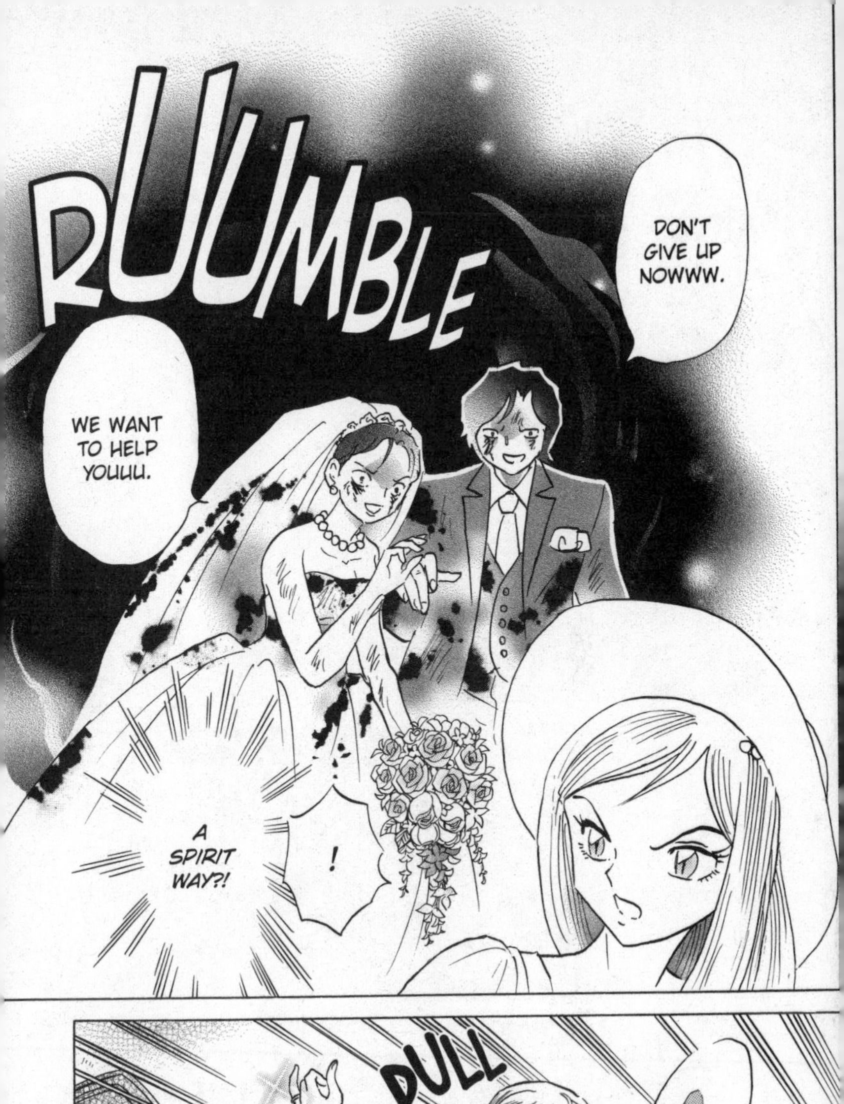
DON'T GIVE UP NOWWW.
RUUMBLE
WE WANT TO HELP YOUUU.
!
A SPIRIT WAY?!

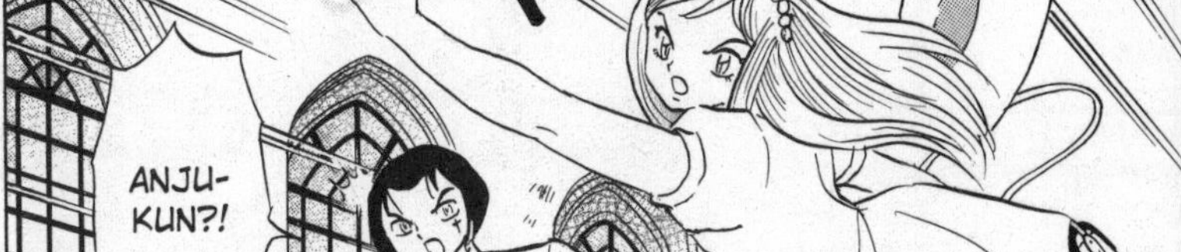
PULL
ANJU-KUN?!

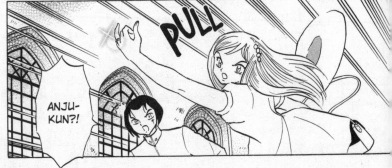

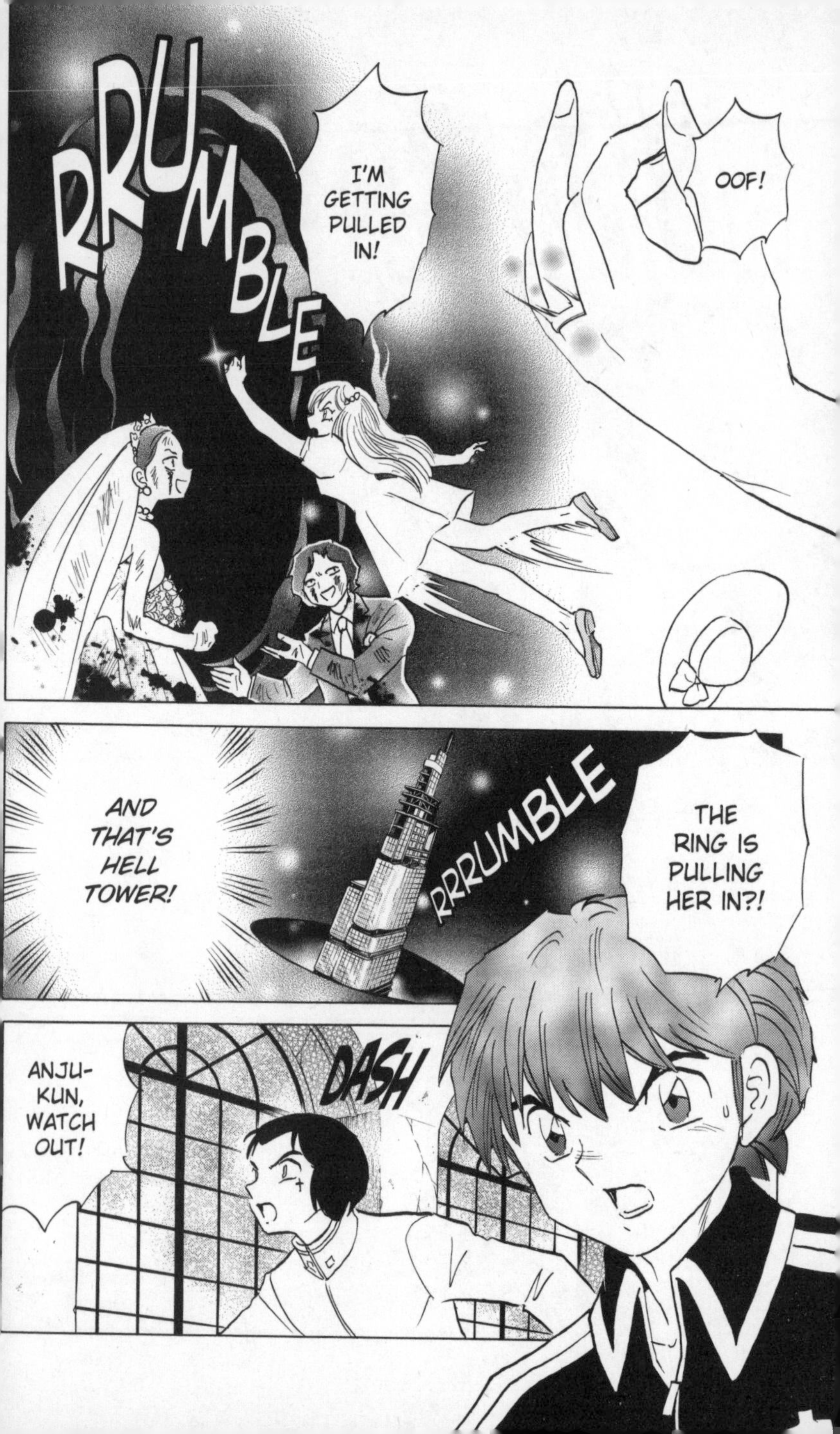
OOF!
I'M GETTING PULLED IN!
RRUMBLE
THE RING IS PULLING HER IN?!
RRRUMBLE
AND THAT'S HELL TOWER!
DASH
ANJU-KUN, WATCH OUT!

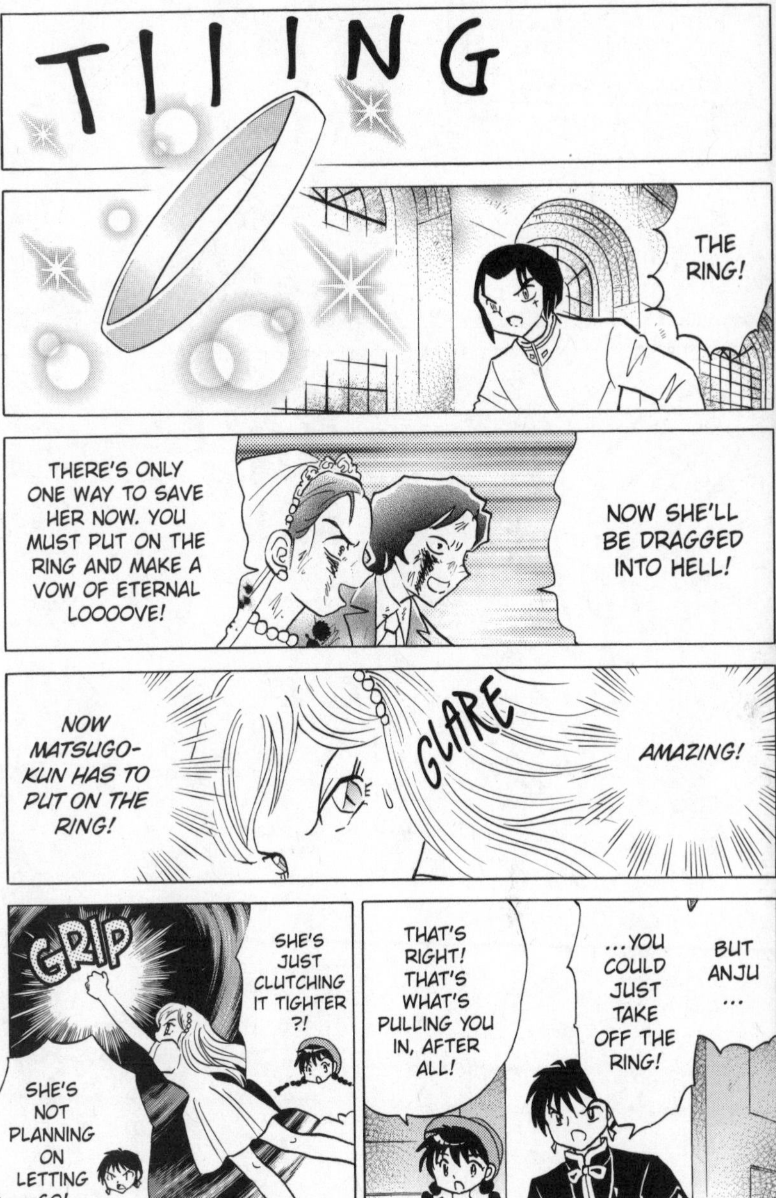
TIIING
THE RING!
NOW SHE'LL BE DRAGGED INTO HELL!
THERE'S ONLY ONE WAY TO SAVE HER NOW. YOU MUST PUT ON THE RING AND MAKE A VOW OF ETERNAL LOOOOVE!
AMAZING!
GLARE
NOW MATSUGO-KUN HAS TO PUT ON THE RING!
BUT ANJU...
...YOU COULD JUST TAKE OFF THE RING!
THAT'S RIGHT! THAT'S WHAT'S PULLING YOU IN, AFTER ALL!
SHE'S JUST CLUTCHING IT TIGHTER?!
GRIP
SHE'S NOT PLANNING ON LETTING GO!

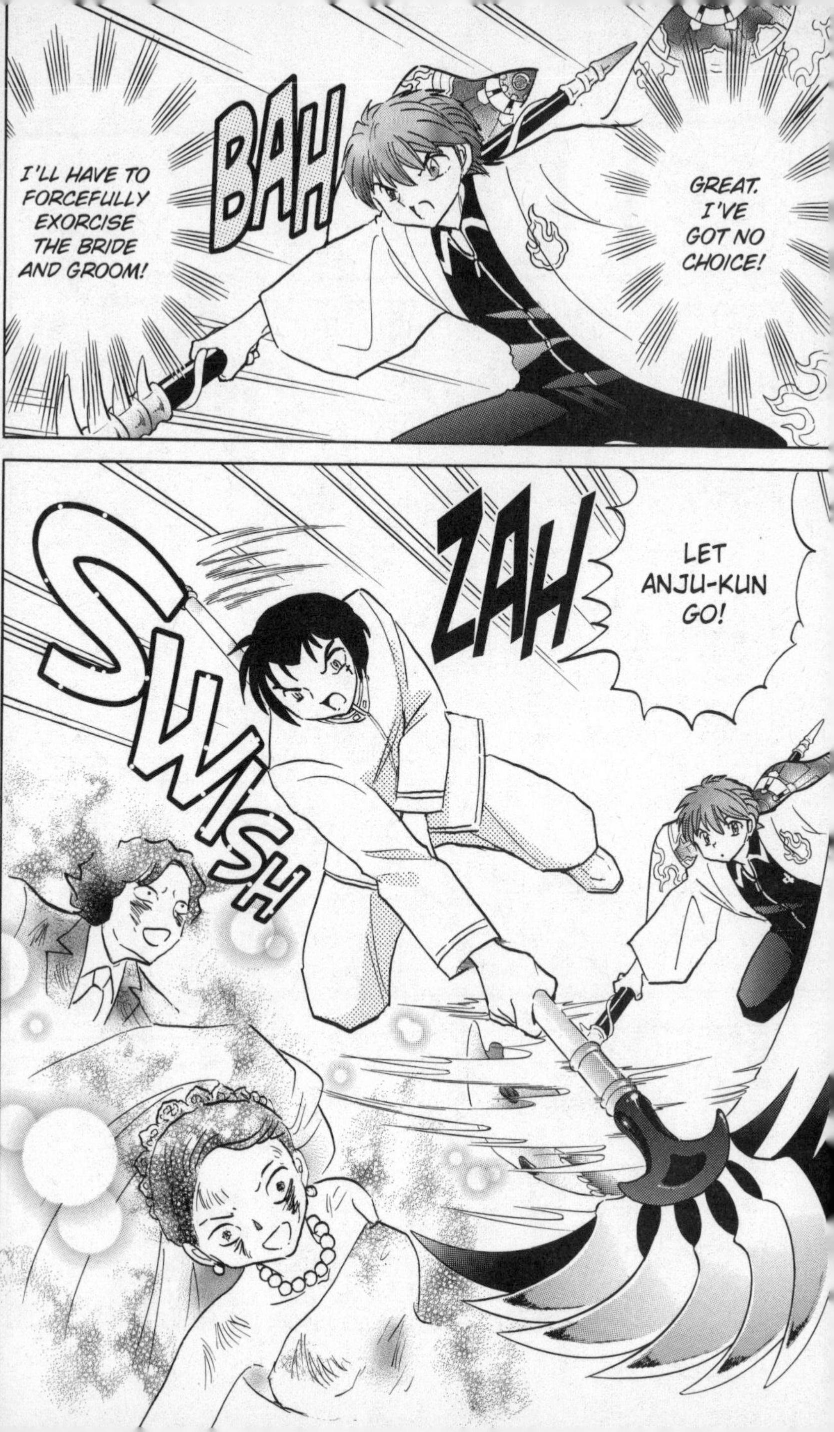
GREAT. I'VE GOT NO CHOICE!
BAH
I'LL HAVE TO FORCEFULLY EXORCISE THE BRIDE AND GROOM!
LET ANJU-KUN GO!
ZAH
SWISH

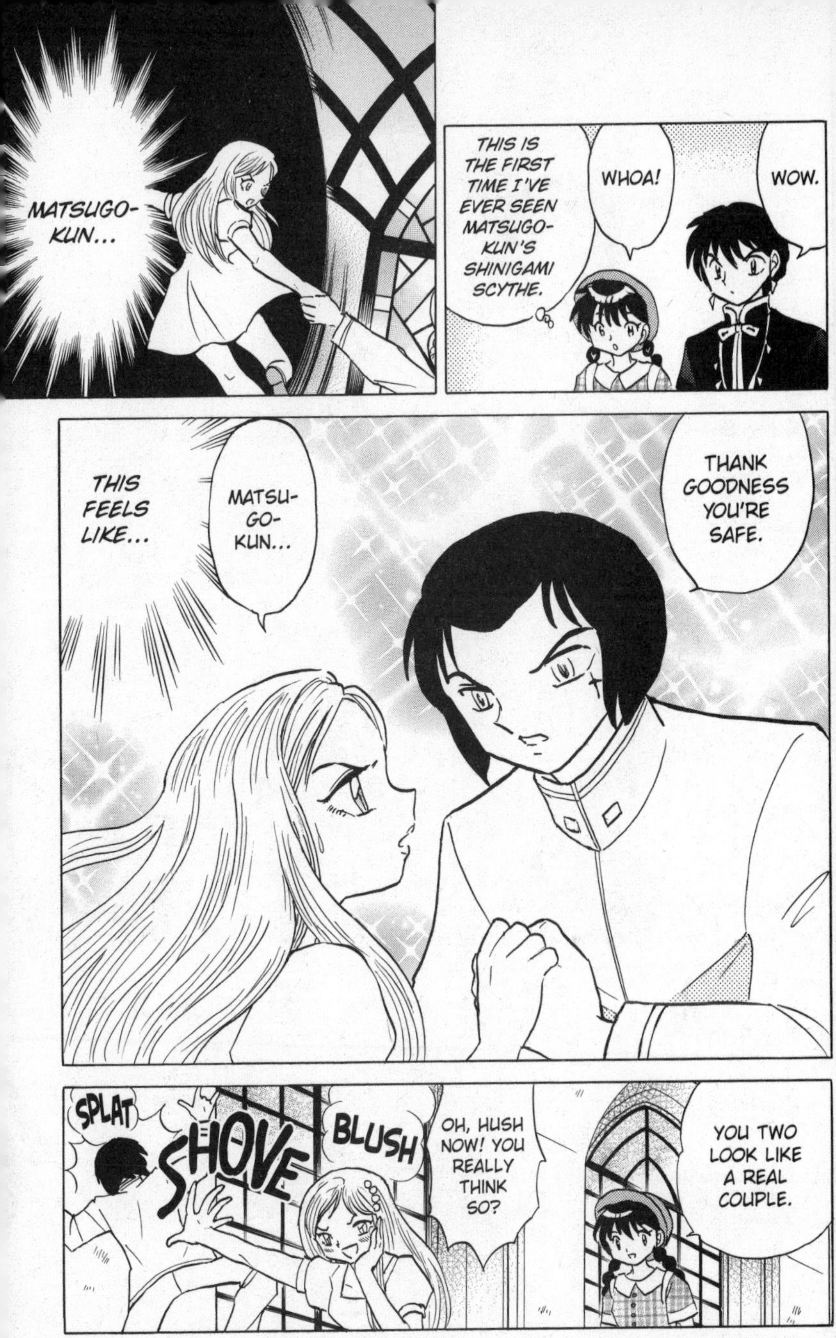
WOW.
WHOA!
THIS IS THE FIRST TIME I'VE EVER SEEN MATSUGO-KUN'S SHINIGAMI SCYTHE.
MATSUGO-KUN...
THANK GOODNESS YOU'RE SAFE.
MATSU-GO-KUN...
THIS FEELS LIKE...
YOU TWO LOOK LIKE A REAL COUPLE.
OH, HUSH NOW! YOU REALLY THINK SO?
BLUSH
SHOVE
SPLAT

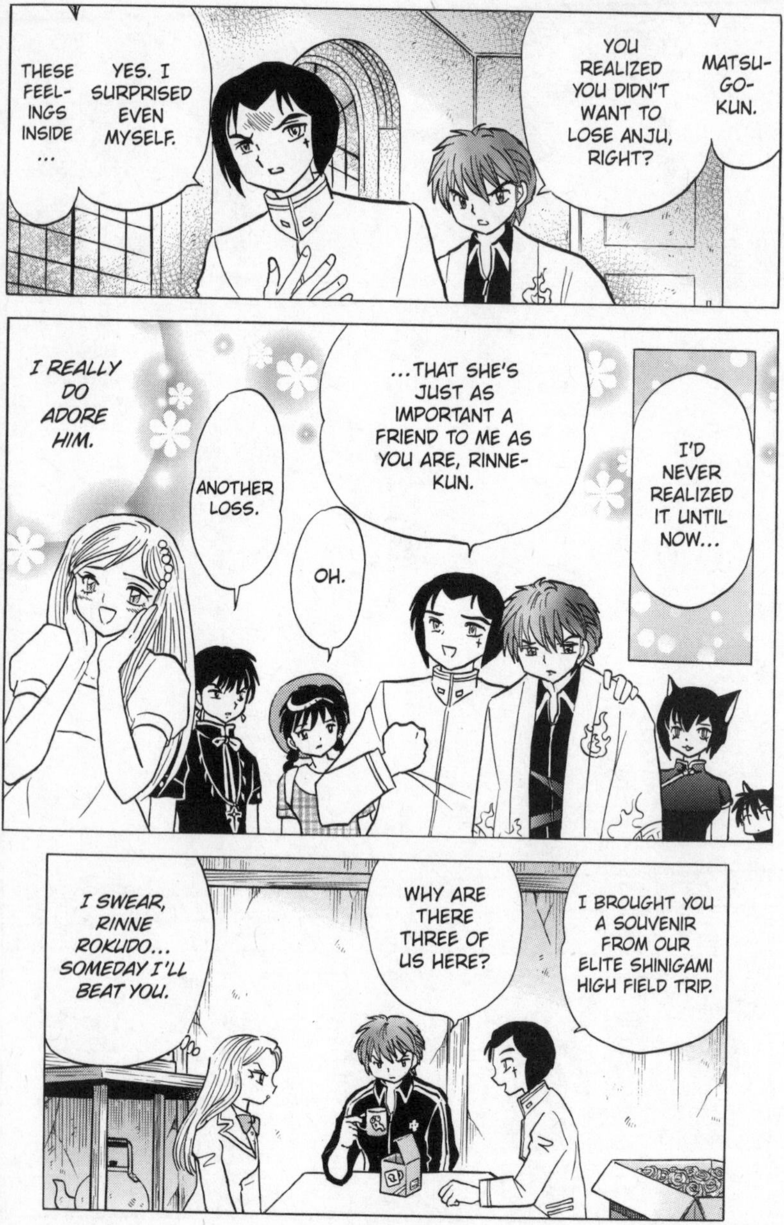
MATSU-GO-KUN.
YOU REALIZED YOU DIDN'T WANT TO LOSE ANJU, RIGHT?
YES. I SURPRISED EVEN MYSELF.
THESE FEEL-INGS INSIDE...
I'D NEVER REALIZED IT UNTIL NOW...
...THAT SHE'S JUST AS IMPORTANT A FRIEND TO ME AS YOU ARE, RINNE-KUN.
OH.
ANOTHER LOSS.
I REALLY DO ADORE HIM.
I BROUGHT YOU A SOUVENIR FROM OUR ELITE SHINIGAMI HIGH FIELD TRIP.
WHY ARE THERE THREE OF US HERE?
I SWEAR, RINNE ROKUDO... SOMEDAY I'LL BEAT YOU.

CHAPTER 374: THIS IS AN INVESTMENT!

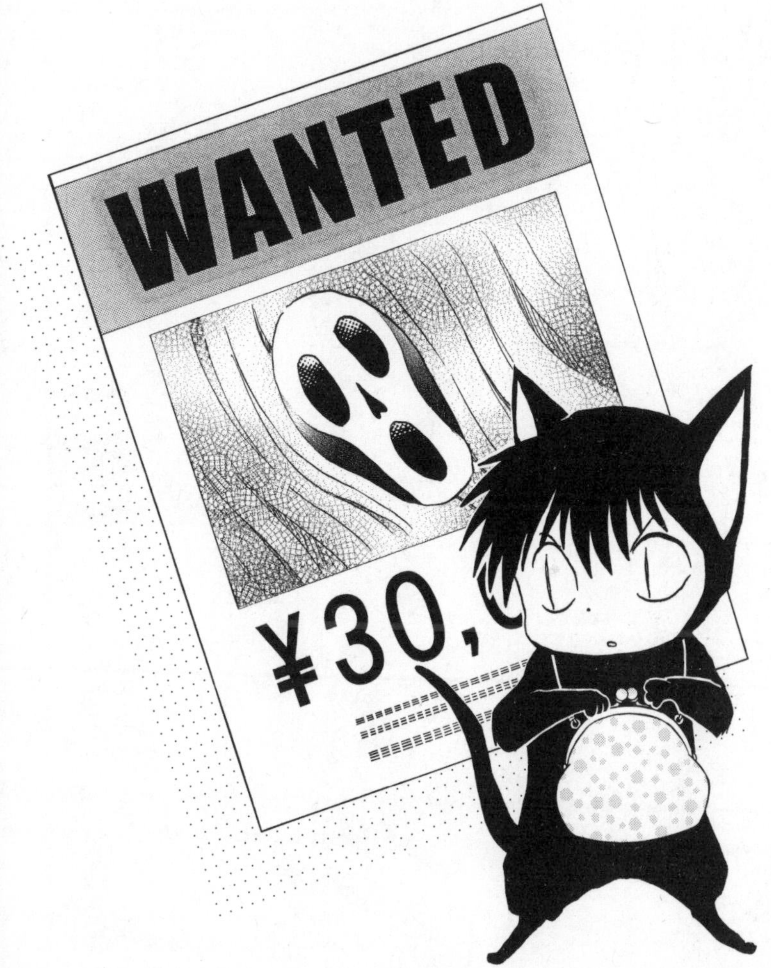
WANTED
¥30,

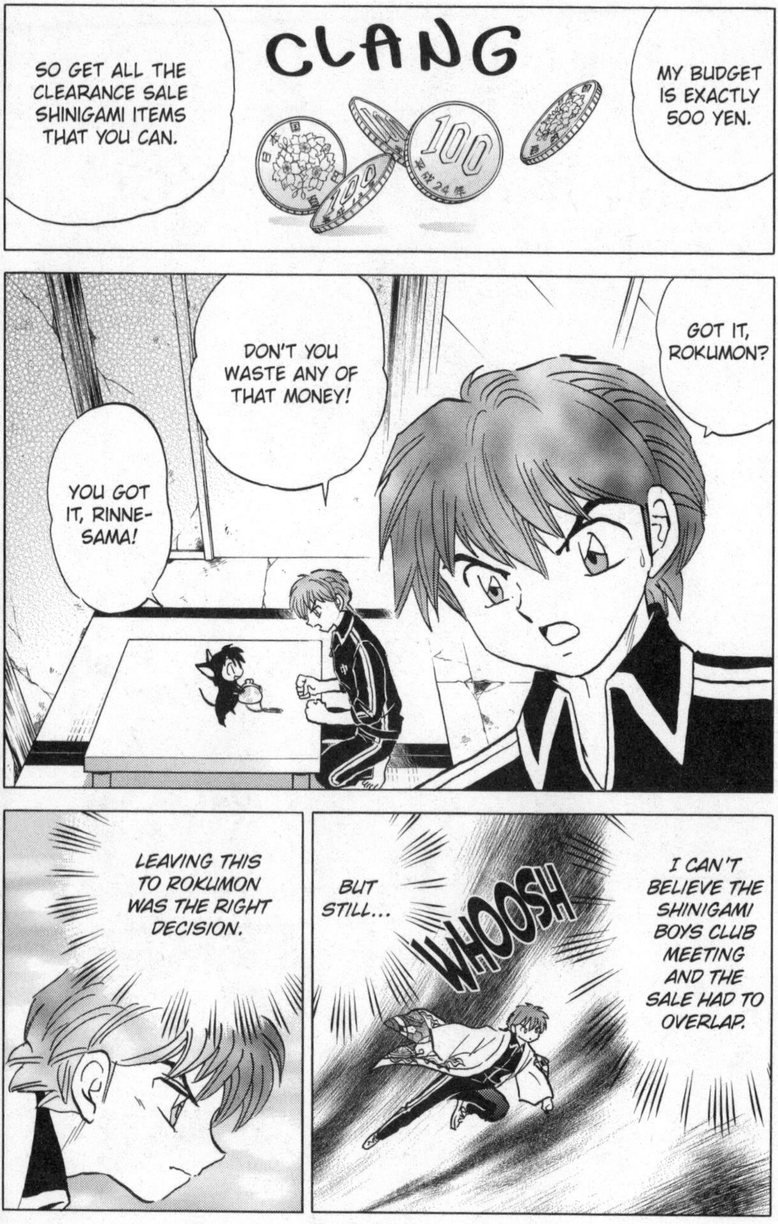
MY BUDGET IS EXACTLY 500 YEN.
CLANG
SO GET ALL THE CLEARANCE SALE SHINIGAMI ITEMS THAT YOU CAN.
GOT IT, ROKUMON?
DON'T YOU WASTE ANY OF THAT MONEY!
YOU GOT IT, RINNE-SAMA!
I CAN'T BELIEVE THE SHINIGAMI BOYS CLUB MEETING AND THE SALE HAD TO OVERLAP.
WHOOSH
BUT STILL...
LEAVING THIS TO ROKUMON WAS THE RIGHT DECISION.

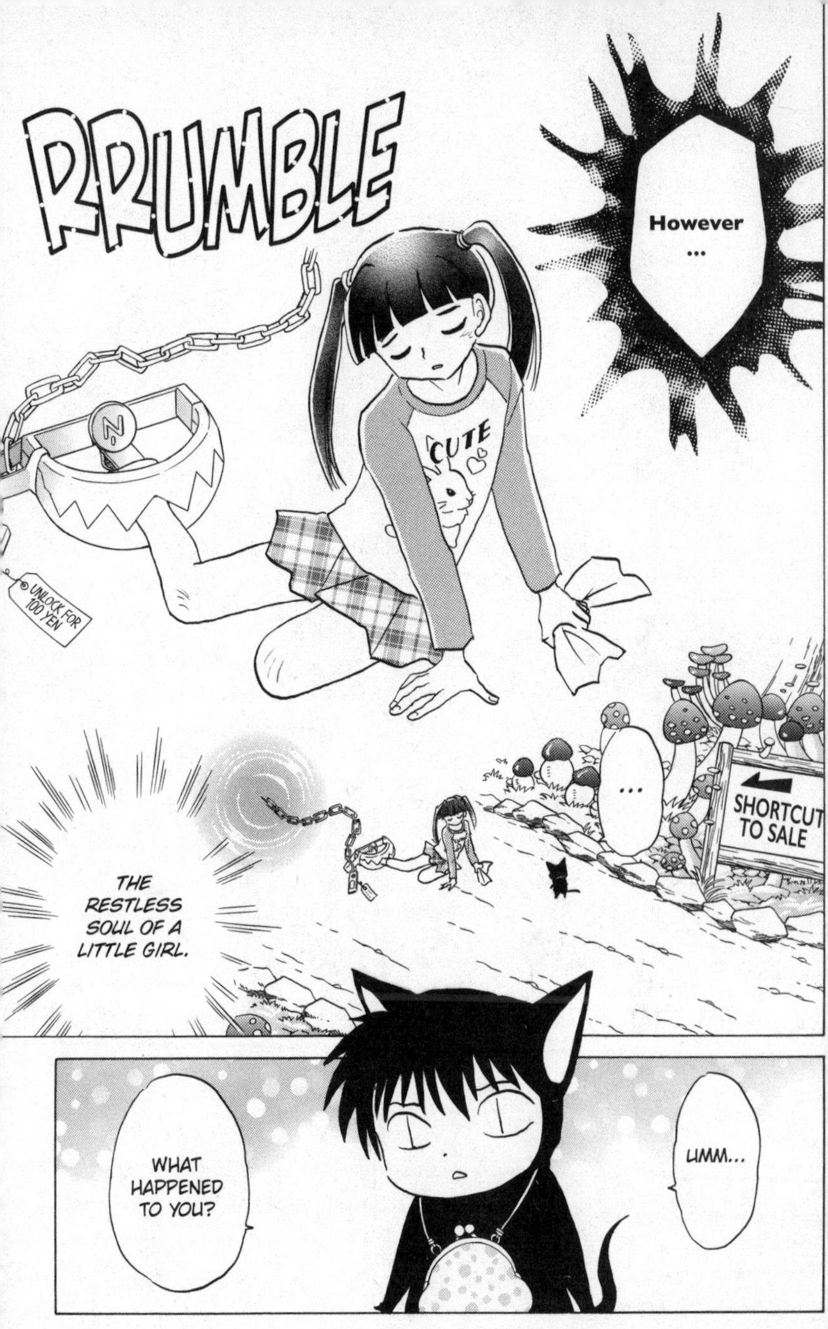
However
...
RRUMBLE
UNLOCK FOR 100 YEN
SHORTCUT TO SALE
...
THE RESTLESS SOUL OF A LITTLE GIRL.
UMM...
WHAT HAPPENED TO YOU?

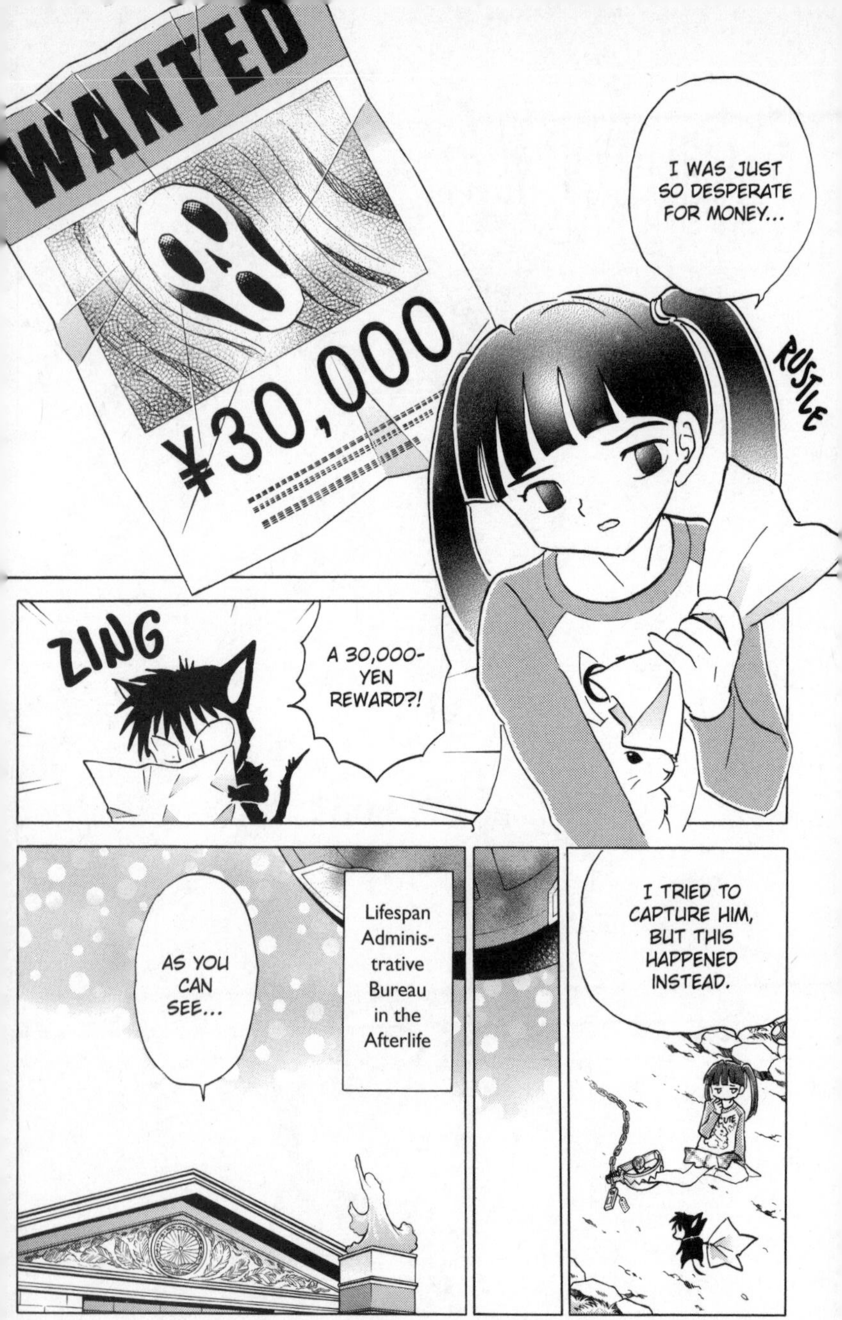
I WAS JUST SO DESPERATE FOR MONEY...
RUSTLE
WANTED
¥30,000
ZING
A 30,000-YEN REWARD?!
I TRIED TO CAPTURE HIM, BUT THIS HAPPENED INSTEAD.
Lifespan Administrative Bureau in the Afterlife
AS YOU CAN SEE...

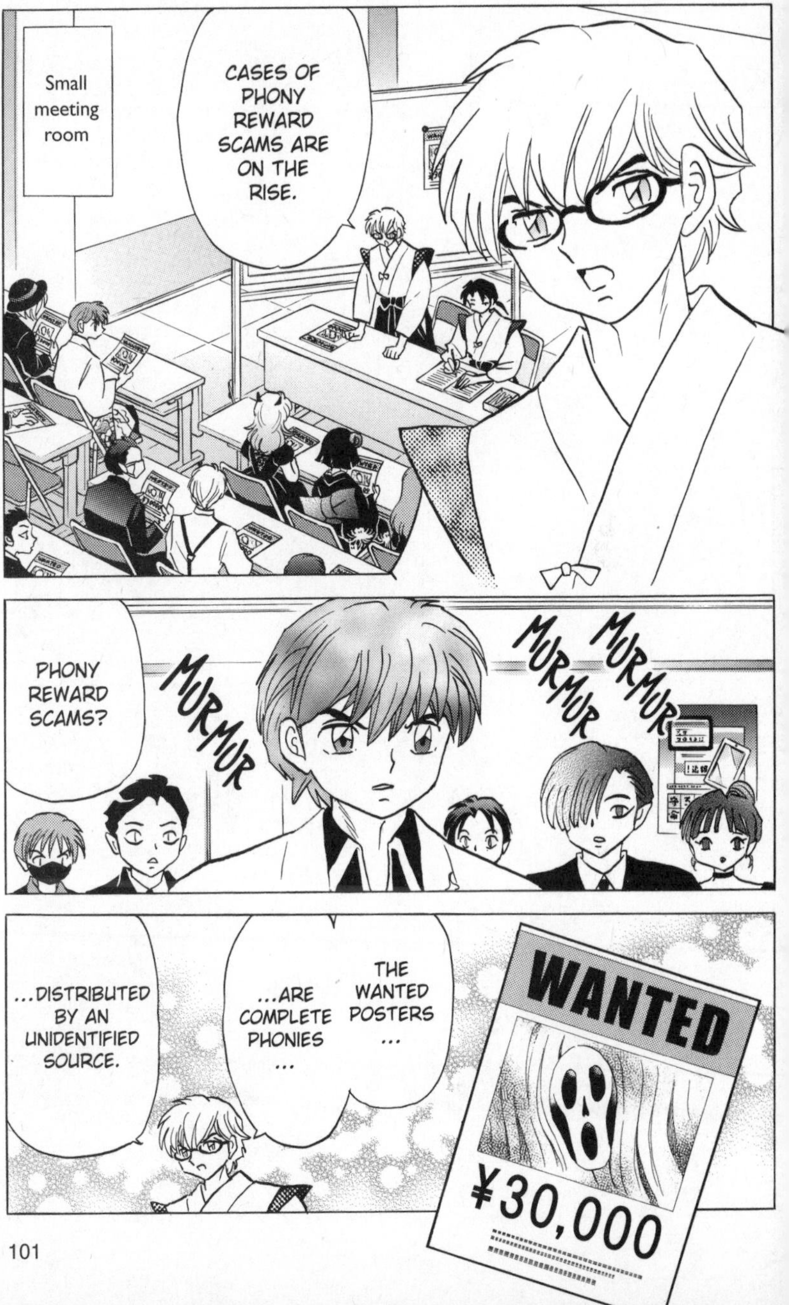
CASES OF PHONY REWARD SCAMS ARE ON THE RISE.
Small meeting room
MURMUR
MURMUR
MURMUR
PHONY REWARD SCAMS?
THE WANTED POSTERS ...
...ARE COMPLETE PHONIES ...
...DISTRIBUTED BY AN UNIDENTIFIED SOURCE.
WANTED
¥30,000

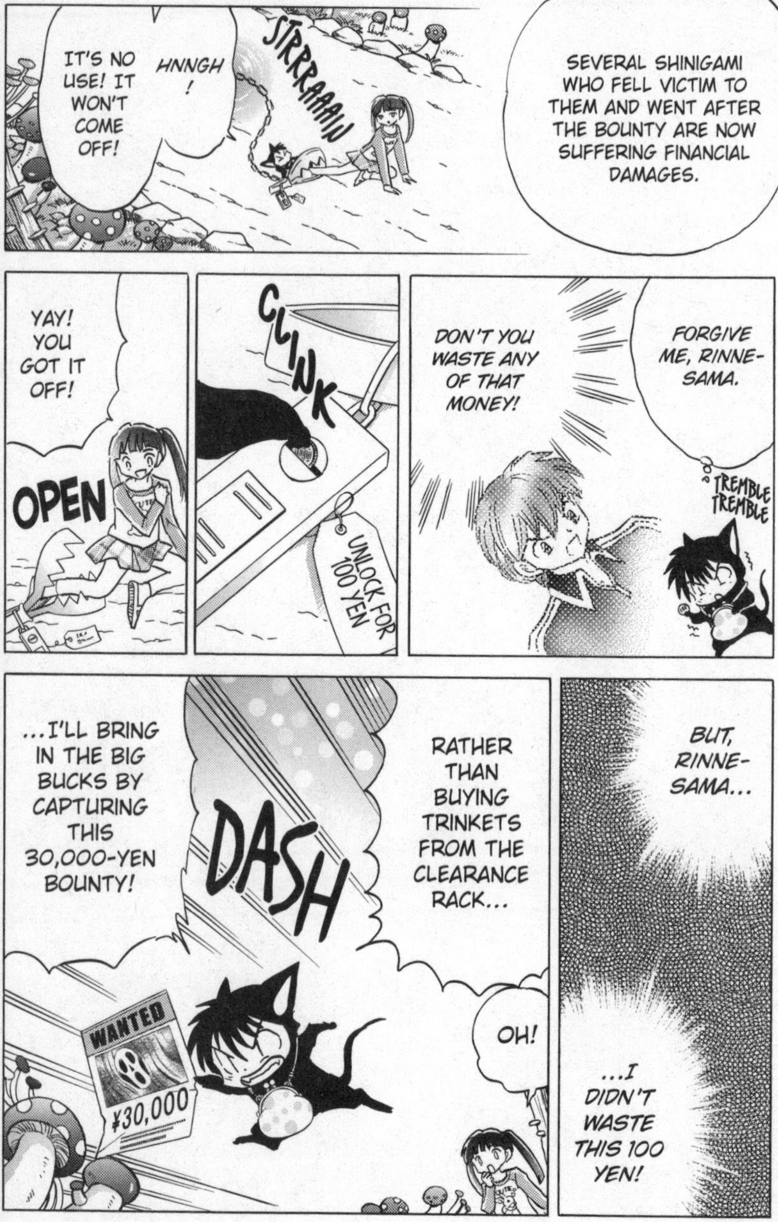
SEVERAL SHINIGAMI WHO FELL VICTIM TO THEM AND WENT AFTER THE BOUNTY ARE NOW SUFFERING FINANCIAL DAMAGES.
STRRAAAW
HNNGH!
IT'S NO USE! IT WON'T COME OFF!
FORGIVE ME, RINNE-SAMA.
TREMBLE TREMBLE
DON'T YOU WASTE ANY OF THAT MONEY!
CLINK
UNLOCK FOR 100 YEN
YAY! YOU GOT IT OFF!
OPEN
BUT, RINNE-SAMA...
...I DIDN'T WASTE THIS 100 YEN!
RATHER THAN BUYING TRINKETS FROM THE CLEARANCE RACK...
...I'LL BRING IN THE BIG BUCKS BY CAPTURING THIS 30,000-YEN BOUNTY!
DASH
OH!
WANTED
¥30,000

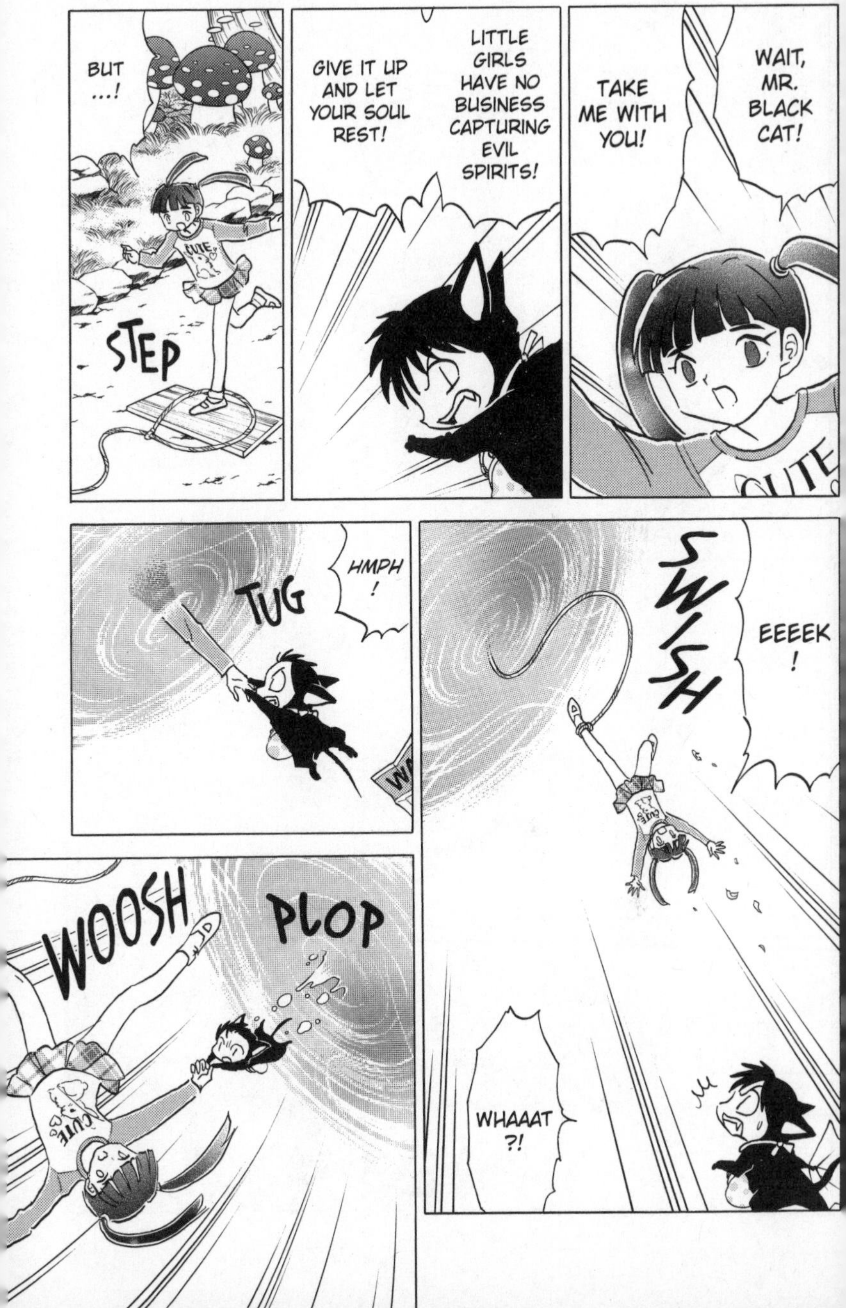
WAIT, MR. BLACK CAT!
TAKE ME WITH YOU!
LITTLE GIRLS HAVE NO BUSINESS CAPTURING EVIL SPIRITS!
GIVE IT UP AND LET YOUR SOUL REST!
BUT ...!
STEP
HMPH!
TUG
SWISH
EEEEK!
WHAAAT?!
PLOP
WOOSH

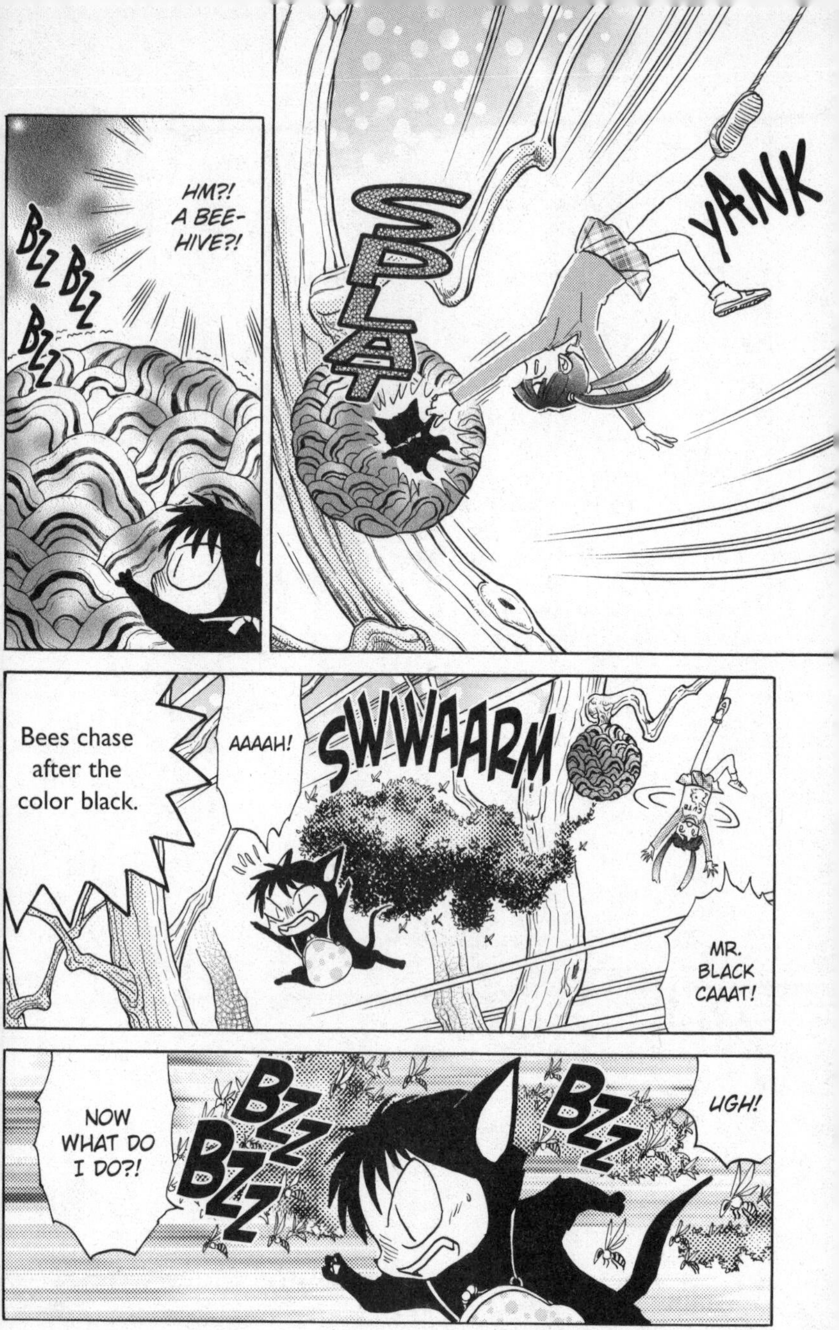
YANK
SPLAT
HM?! A BEE-HIVE?!
BZZ BZZ BZZ
MR. BLACK CAAAT!
SWWAARM
AAAAH!
Bees chase after the color black.
UGH!
BZZ
BZZ BZZ
NOW WHAT DO I DO?!

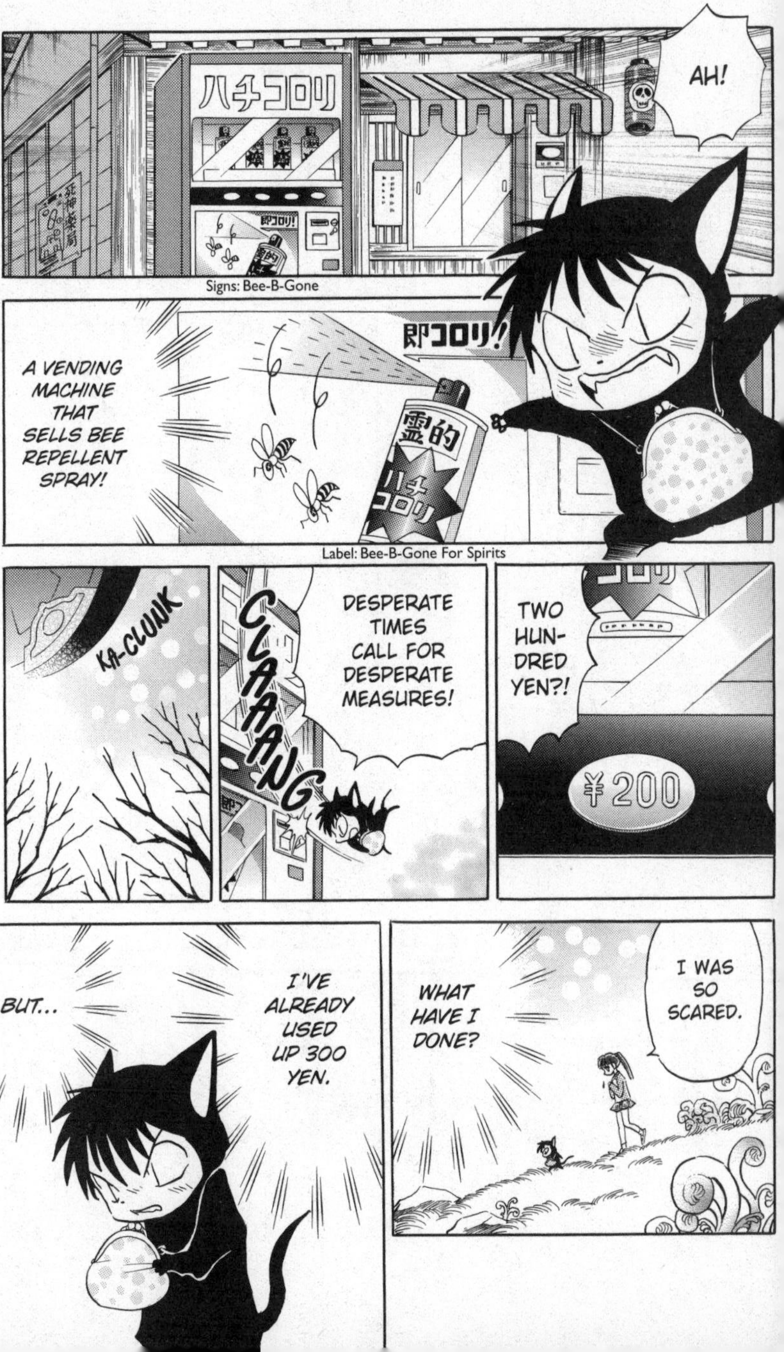
AH!
ハチコロリ
即コロリ!
A VENDING MACHINE THAT SELLS BEE REPELLENT SPRAY!
即コロリ!
霊的 ハチコロリ
TWO HUN-DRED YEN?!
¥200
DESPERATE TIMES CALL FOR DESPERATE MEASURES!
CLAAANG
KA-CLUNK
I WAS SO SCARED.
WHAT HAVE I DONE?
I'VE ALREADY USED UP 300 YEN.
BUT...

Signs: Bee-B-Gone

Label: Bee-B-Gone For Spirits

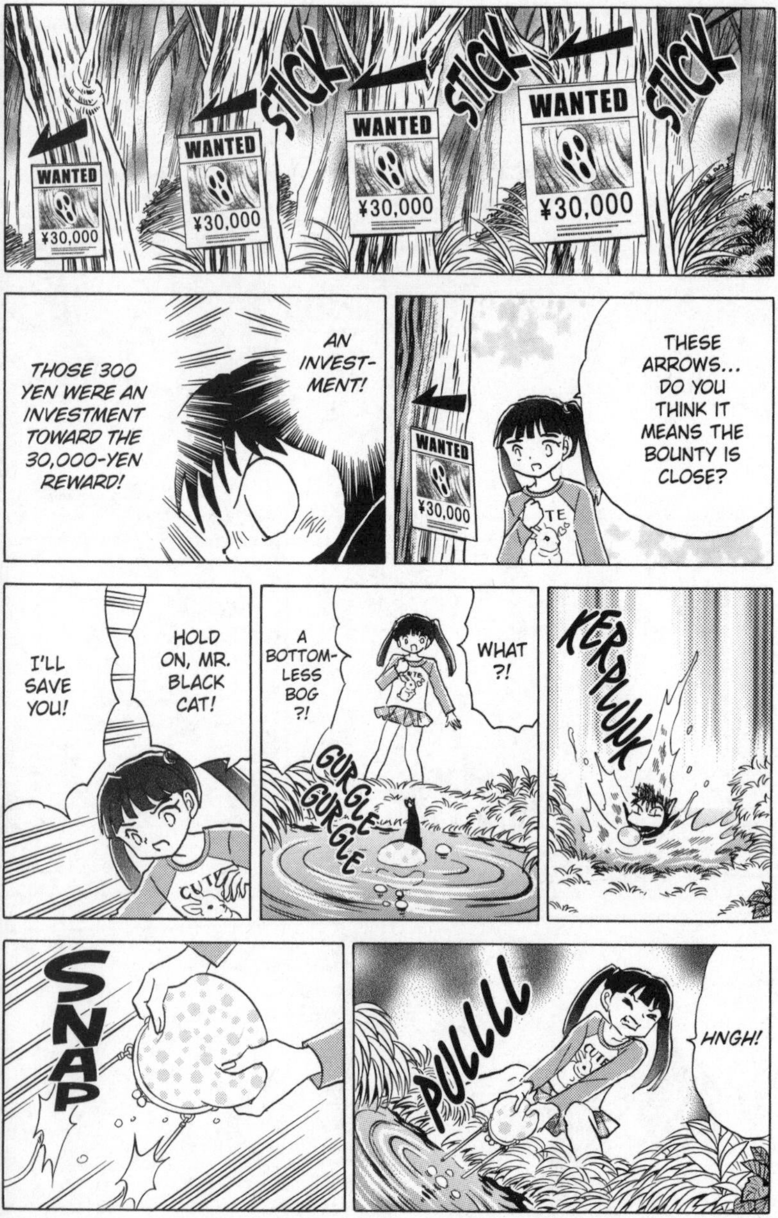
STICK
WANTED
¥30,000
STICK
WANTED
¥30,000
STICK
WANTED
¥30,000
WANTED
¥30,000
THESE ARROWS... DO YOU THINK IT MEANS THE BOUNTY IS CLOSE?
WANTED
¥30,000
AN INVESTMENT!
THOSE 300 YEN WERE AN INVESTMENT TOWARD THE 30,000-YEN REWARD!
KERPLUNK
WHAT?!
A BOTTOMLESS BOG?!
GURGLE GURGLE
HOLD ON, MR. BLACK CAT!
I'LL SAVE YOU!
HNGH!
PULLLL
SNAP

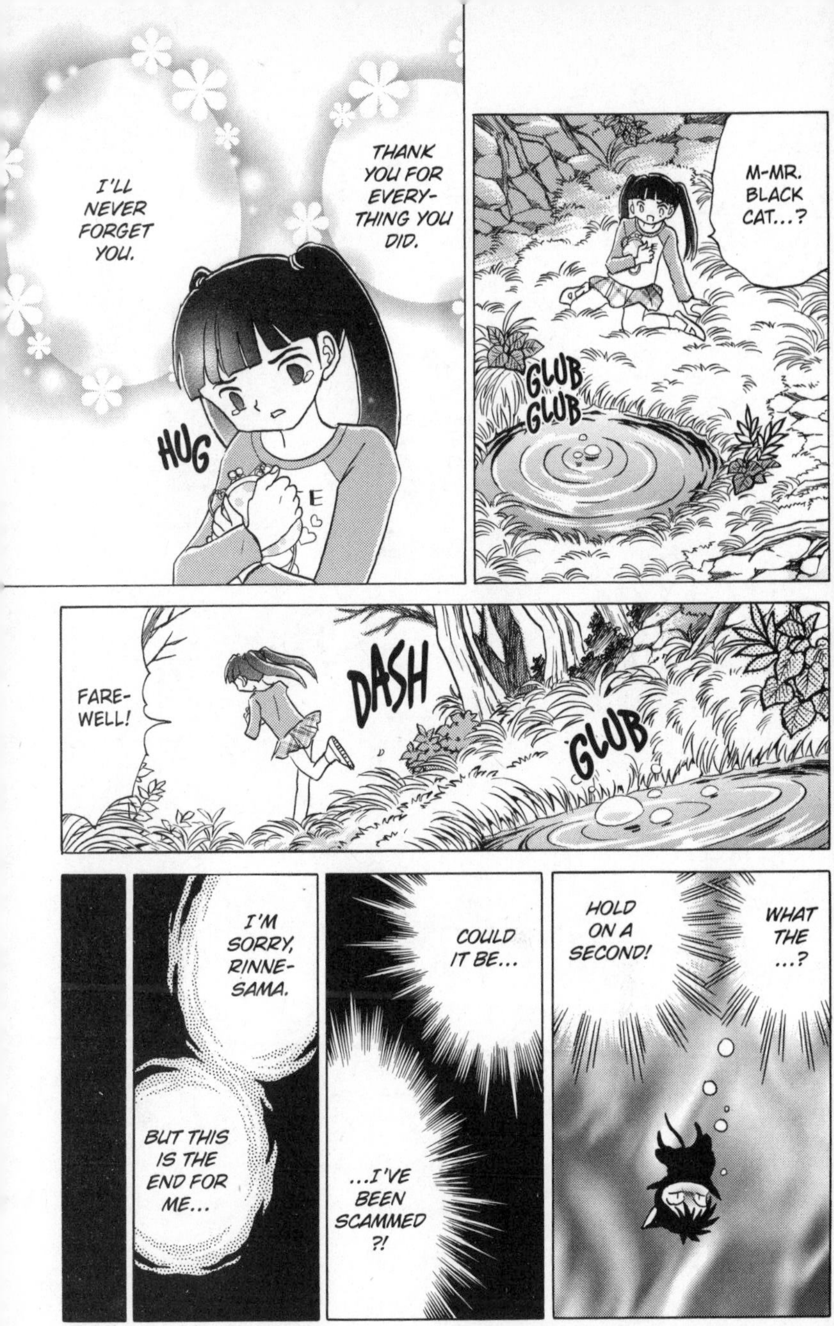
M-MR. BLACK CAT...?
GLUB GLUB
THANK YOU FOR EVERYTHING YOU DID.
I'LL NEVER FORGET YOU.
HUG
GLUB
DASH
FAREWELL!
WHAT THE ...?
HOLD ON A SECOND!
COULD IT BE...
...I'VE BEEN SCAMMED?!
I'M SORRY, RINNE-SAMA.
BUT THIS IS THE END FOR ME...

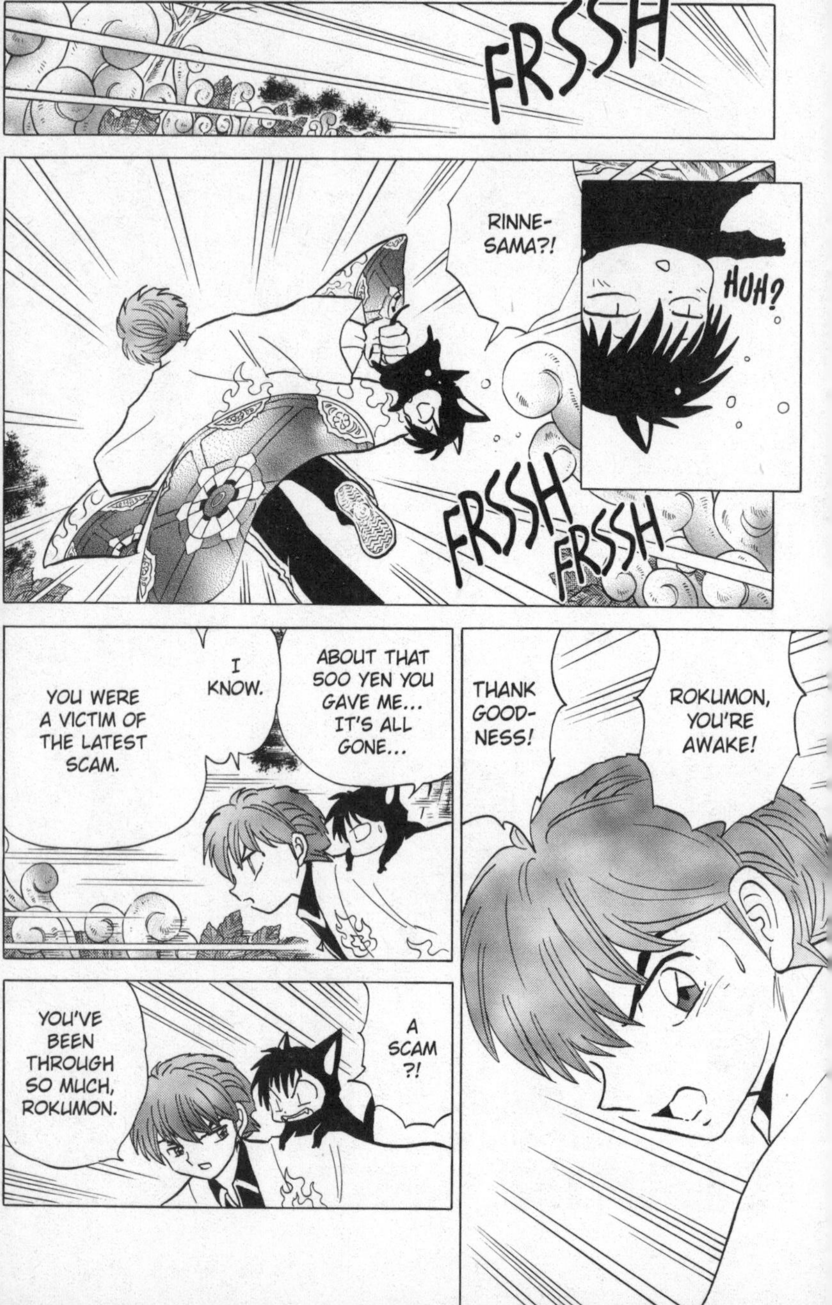
FRSSH
HUH?
RINNE-SAMA?!
FRSSH
FRSSH
ROKUMON, YOU'RE AWAKE!
THANK GOODNESS!
ABOUT THAT 500 YEN YOU GAVE ME... IT'S ALL GONE...
I KNOW.
YOU WERE A VICTIM OF THE LATEST SCAM.
A SCAM?!
YOU'VE BEEN THROUGH SO MUCH, ROKUMON.

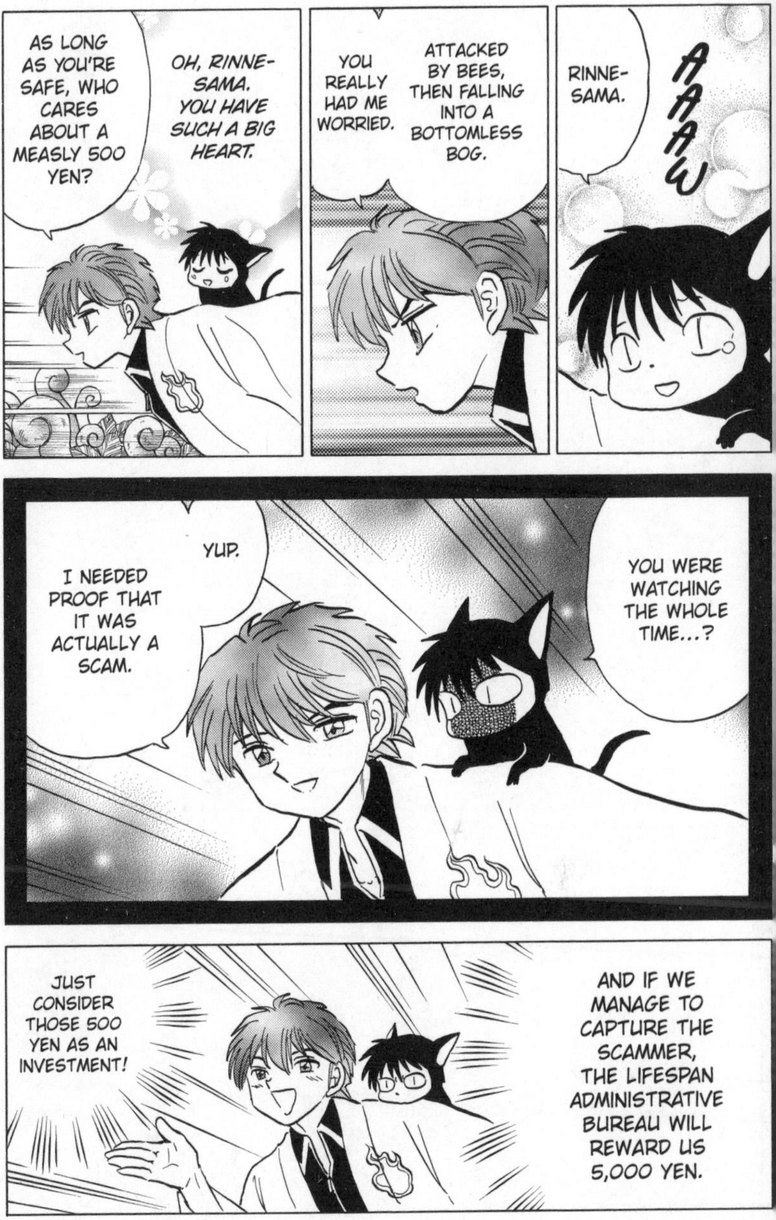
RINNE-SAMA.
AAAAW
ATTACKED BY BEES, THEN FALLING INTO A BOTTOMLESS BOG.
YOU REALLY HAD ME WORRIED.
AS LONG AS YOU'RE SAFE, WHO CARES ABOUT A MEASLY 500 YEN?
OH, RINNE-SAMA. YOU HAVE SUCH A BIG HEART.
YOU WERE WATCHING THE WHOLE TIME...?
YUP.
I NEEDED PROOF THAT IT WAS ACTUALLY A SCAM.
AND IF WE MANAGE TO CAPTURE THE SCAMMER, THE LIFESPAN ADMINISTRATIVE BUREAU WILL REWARD US 5,000 YEN.
JUST CONSIDER THOSE 500 YEN AS AN INVESTMENT!

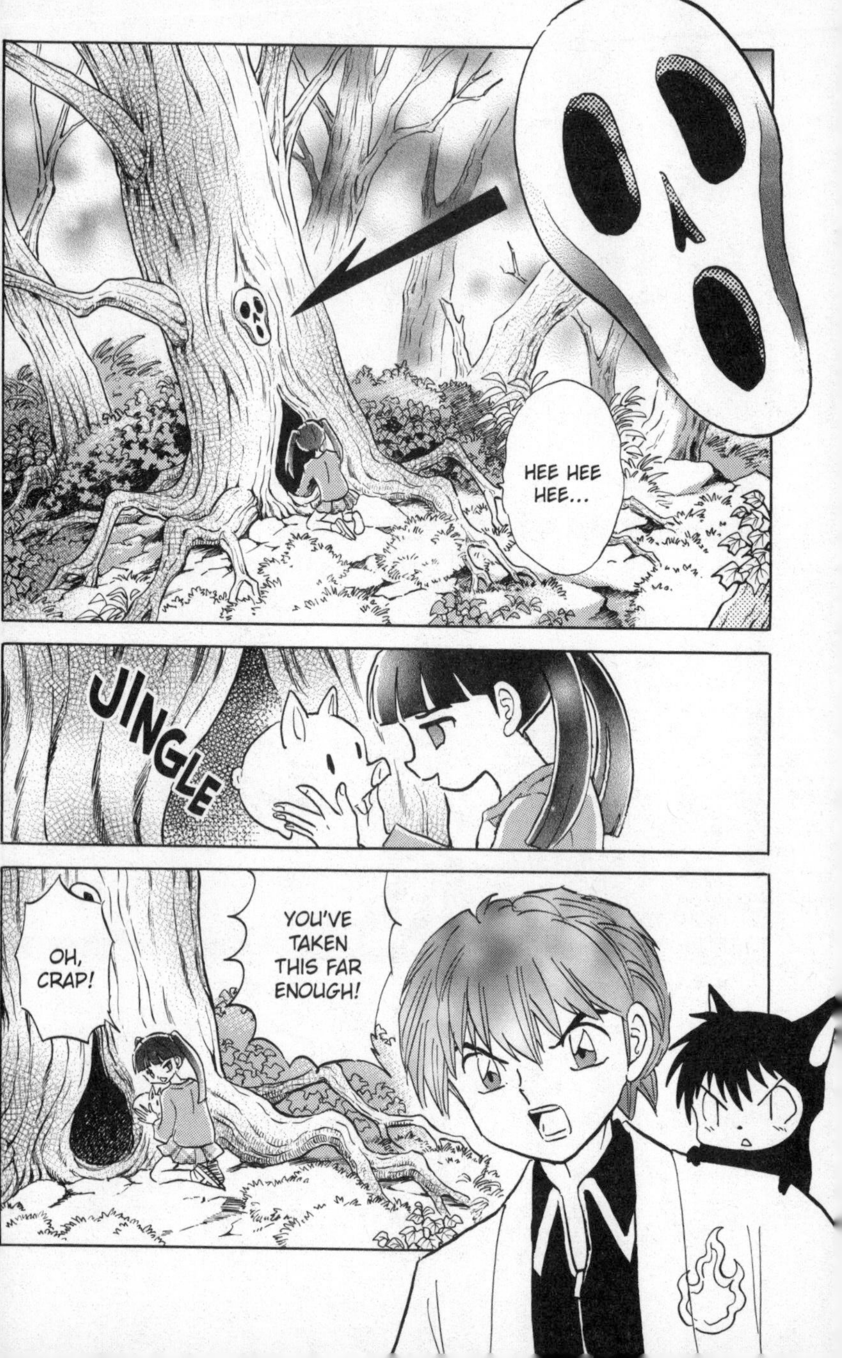
HEE HEE HEE...
JINGLE
YOU'VE TAKEN THIS FAR ENOUGH!
OH, CRAP!

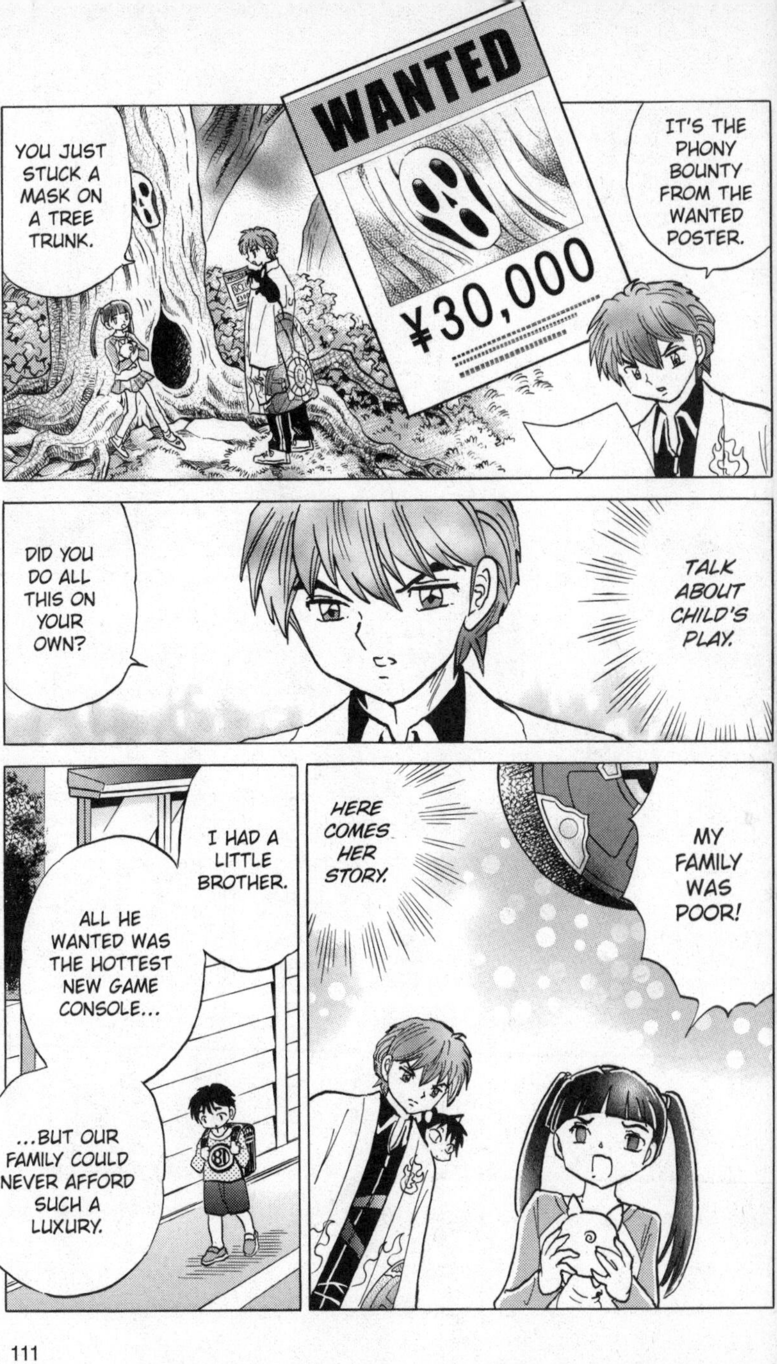
WANTED
¥30,000
IT'S THE PHONY BOUNTY FROM THE WANTED POSTER.
YOU JUST STUCK A MASK ON A TREE TRUNK.
TALK ABOUT CHILD'S PLAY.
DID YOU DO ALL THIS ON YOUR OWN?
MY FAMILY WAS POOR!
HERE COMES HER STORY.
I HAD A LITTLE BROTHER.
ALL HE WANTED WAS THE HOTTEST NEW GAME CONSOLE...
...BUT OUR FAMILY COULD NEVER AFFORD SUCH A LUXURY.

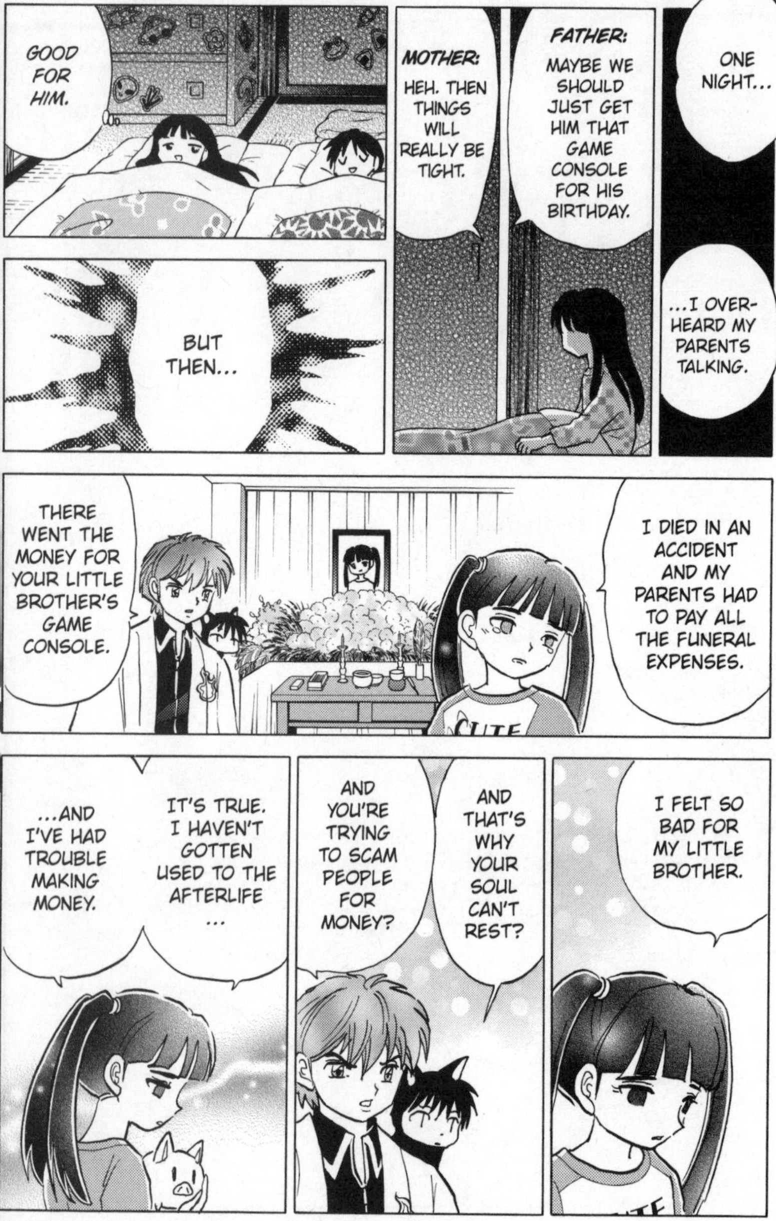
ONE NIGHT...
...I OVERHEARD MY PARENTS TALKING.
FATHER: MAYBE WE SHOULD JUST GET HIM THAT GAME CONSOLE FOR HIS BIRTHDAY.
MOTHER: HEH. THEN THINGS WILL REALLY BE TIGHT.
GOOD FOR HIM.
BUT THEN...
I DIED IN AN ACCIDENT AND MY PARENTS HAD TO PAY ALL THE FUNERAL EXPENSES.
THERE WENT THE MONEY FOR YOUR LITTLE BROTHER'S GAME CONSOLE.
I FELT SO BAD FOR MY LITTLE BROTHER.
AND THAT'S WHY YOUR SOUL CAN'T REST?
AND YOU'RE TRYING TO SCAM PEOPLE FOR MONEY?
IT'S TRUE. I HAVEN'T GOTTEN USED TO THE AFTERLIFE ...
...AND I'VE HAD TROUBLE MAKING MONEY.

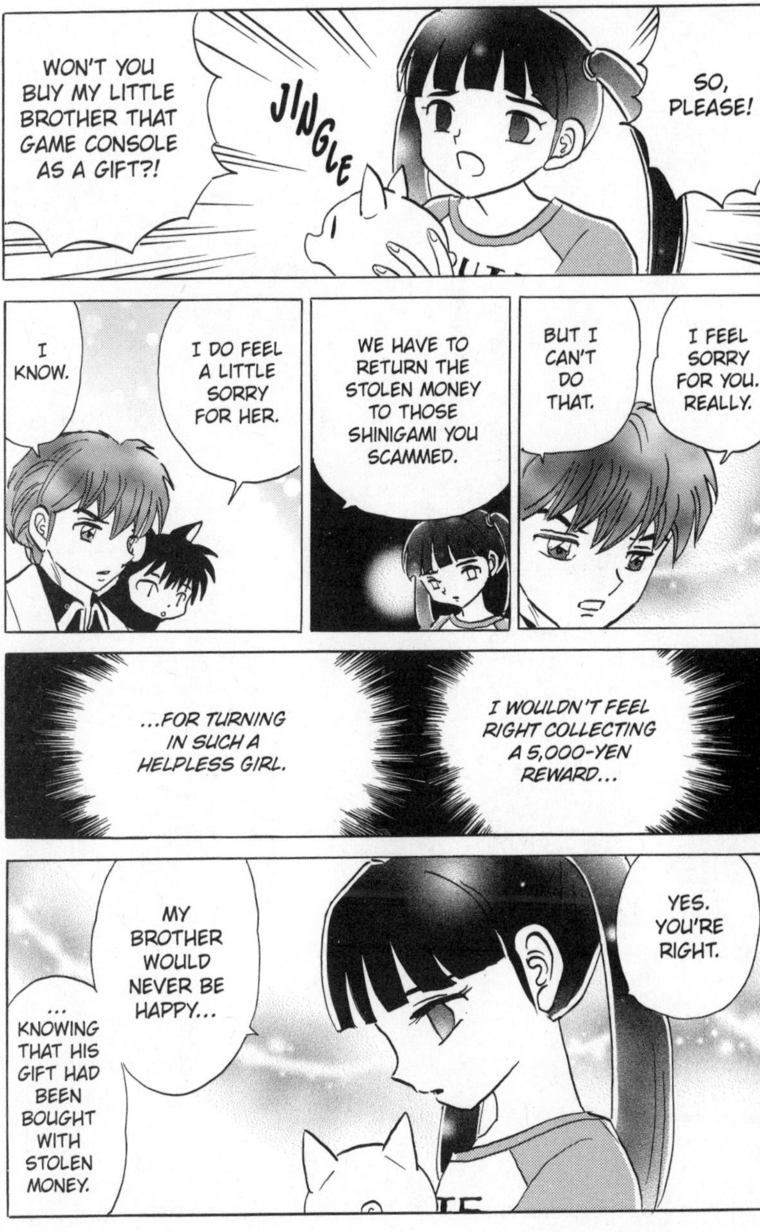
SO, PLEASE!
JINGLE
WON'T YOU BUY MY LITTLE BROTHER THAT GAME CONSOLE AS A GIFT?!
I FEEL SORRY FOR YOU. REALLY.
BUT I CAN'T DO THAT.
WE HAVE TO RETURN THE STOLEN MONEY TO THOSE SHINIGAMI YOU SCAMMED.
I DO FEEL A LITTLE SORRY FOR HER.
I KNOW.
I WOULDN'T FEEL RIGHT COLLECTING A 5,000-YEN REWARD...
...FOR TURNING IN SUCH A HELPLESS GIRL.
YES. YOU'RE RIGHT.
MY BROTHER WOULD NEVER BE HAPPY...
...KNOWING THAT HIS GIFT HAD BEEN BOUGHT WITH STOLEN MONEY.

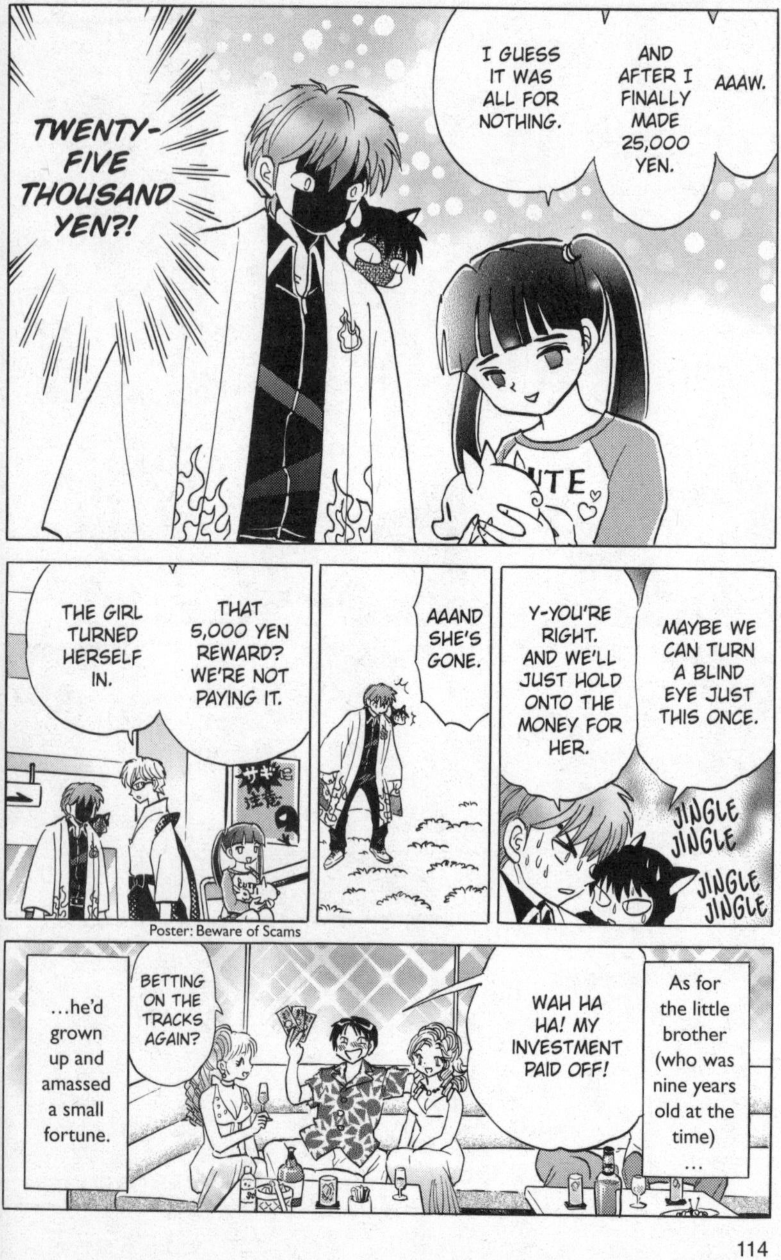
AAAW.
AND AFTER I FINALLY MADE 25,000 YEN.
I GUESS IT WAS ALL FOR NOTHING.
TWENTY-FIVE THOUSAND YEN?!
MAYBE WE CAN TURN A BLIND EYE JUST THIS ONCE.
Y-YOU'RE RIGHT. AND WE'LL JUST HOLD ONTO THE MONEY FOR HER.
JINGLE JINGLE
JINGLE JINGLE
AAAND SHE'S GONE.
THAT 5,000 YEN REWARD? WE'RE NOT PAYING IT.
THE GIRL TURNED HERSELF IN.
Poster: Beware of Scams
As for the little brother (who was nine years old at the time)...
WAH HA HA! MY INVESTMENT PAID OFF!
BETTING ON THE TRACKS AGAIN?
...he'd grown up and amassed a small fortune.

CHAPTER 375: THE PHOENIX SCYTHE

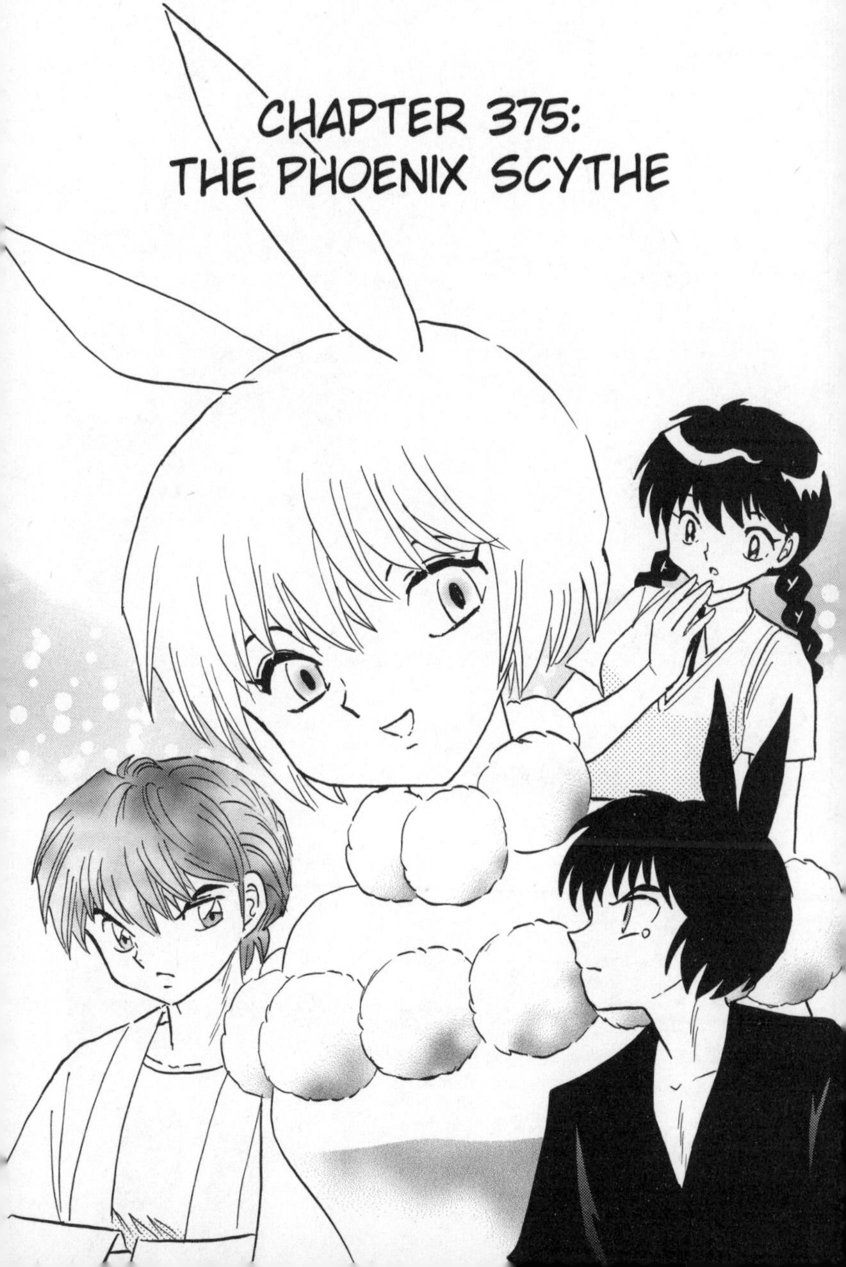

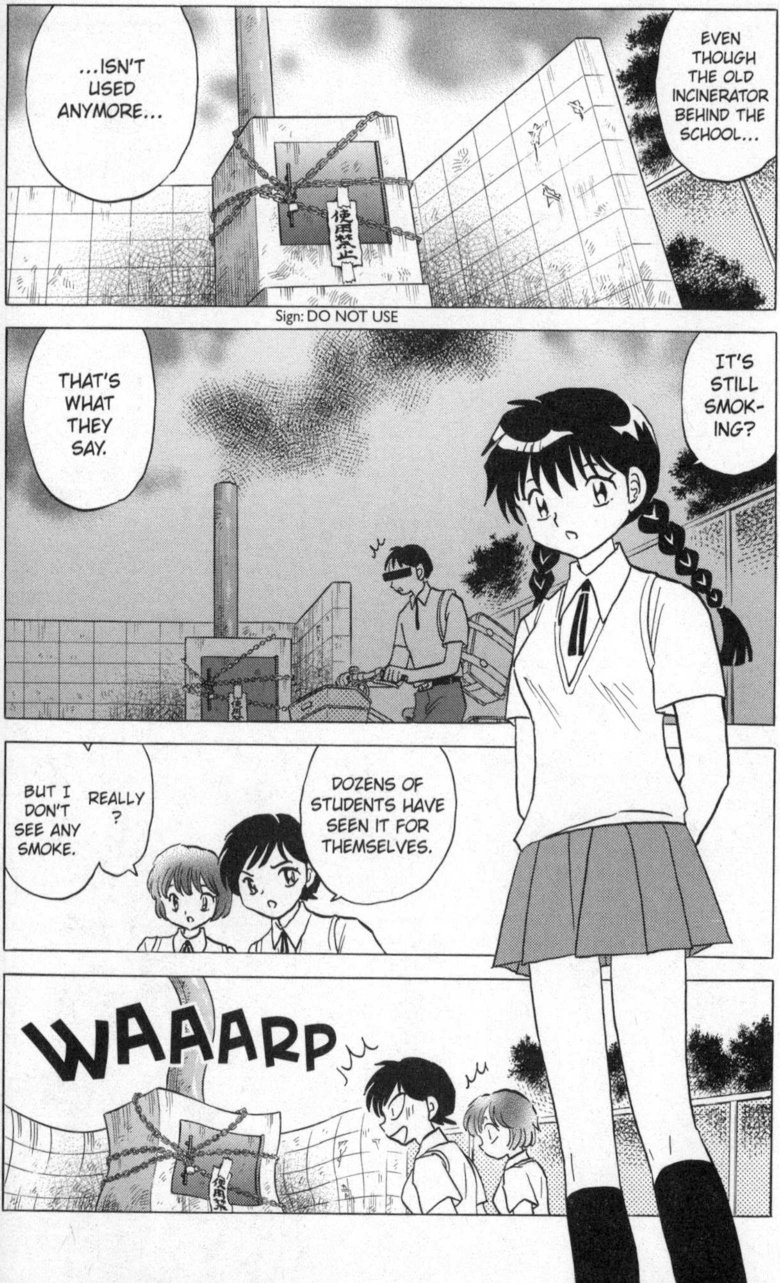
EVEN THOUGH THE OLD INCINERATOR BEHIND THE SCHOOL...
...ISN'T USED ANYMORE...
使用禁止
IT'S STILL SMOK-ING?
THAT'S WHAT THEY SAY.
DOZENS OF STUDENTS HAVE SEEN IT FOR THEMSELVES.
REALLY?
BUT I DON'T SEE ANY SMOKE.
WAAARP
Sign: DO NOT USE

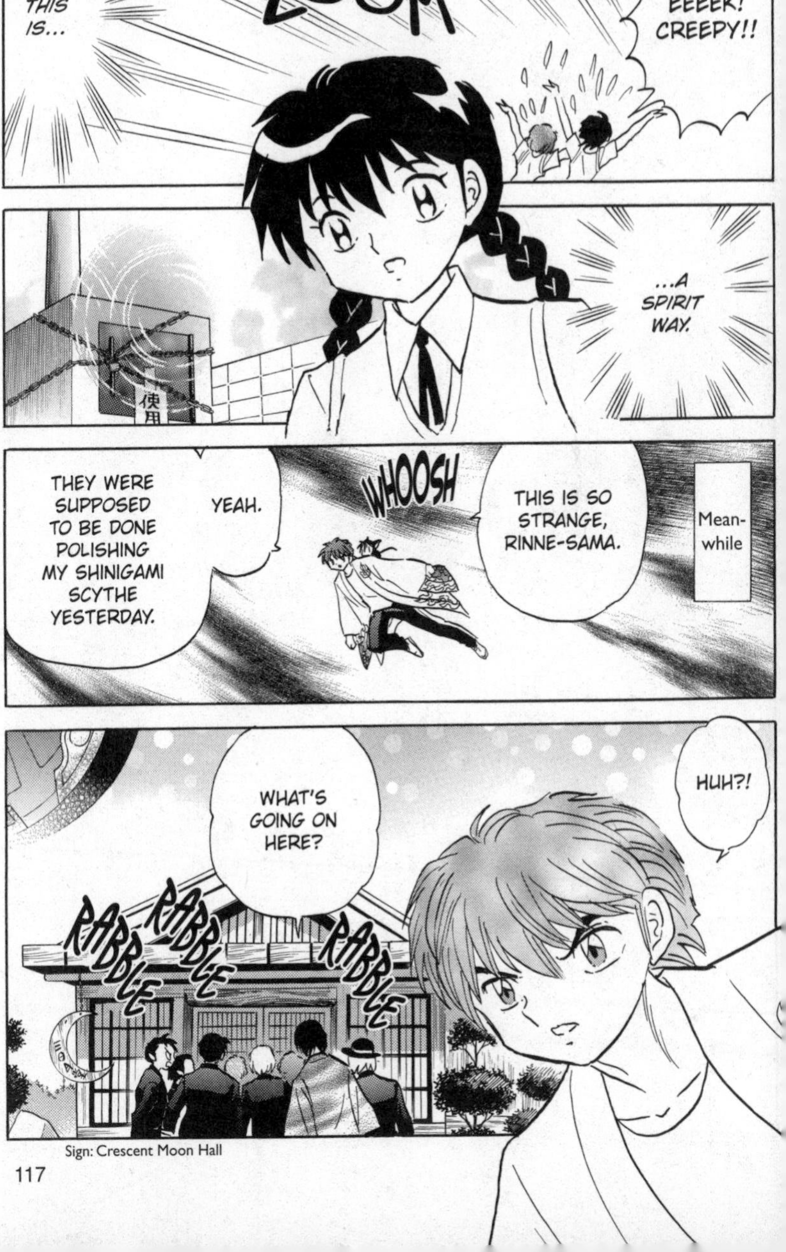
EEEEK! CREEPY!!
ZOOM
THIS IS...
...A SPIRIT WAY.
Meanwhile
THIS IS SO STRANGE, RINNE-SAMA.
WHOOSH
YEAH.
THEY WERE SUPPOSED TO BE DONE POLISHING MY SHINIGAMI SCYTHE YESTERDAY.
HUH?!
WHAT'S GOING ON HERE?
RABBLE
RABBLE
RABBLE
Sign: Crescent Moon Hall

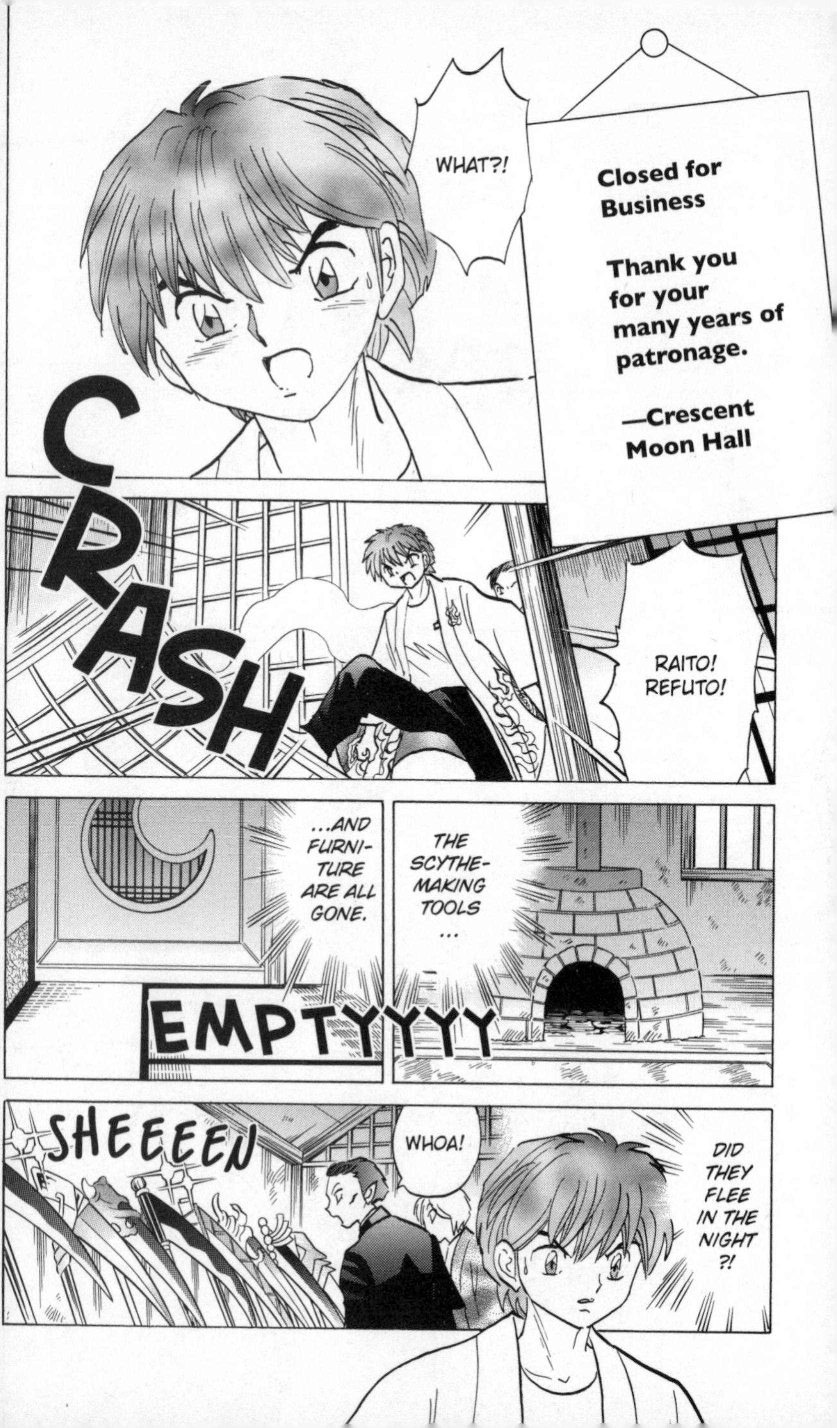
Closed for Business

Thank you for your many years of patronage.

—Crescent Moon Hall
WHAT?!
RAITO! REFUTO!
CRASH
THE SCYTHE-MAKING TOOLS...
...AND FURNITURE ARE ALL GONE.
EMPTYYYY
DID THEY FLEE IN THE NIGHT?!
WHOA!
SHEEEEN

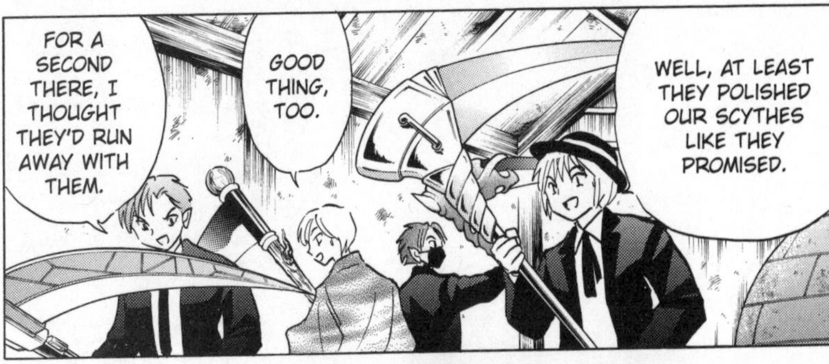
WELL, AT LEAST THEY POLISHED OUR SCYTHES LIKE THEY PROMISED.
GOOD THING, TOO.
FOR A SECOND THERE, I THOUGHT THEY'D RUN AWAY WITH THEM.

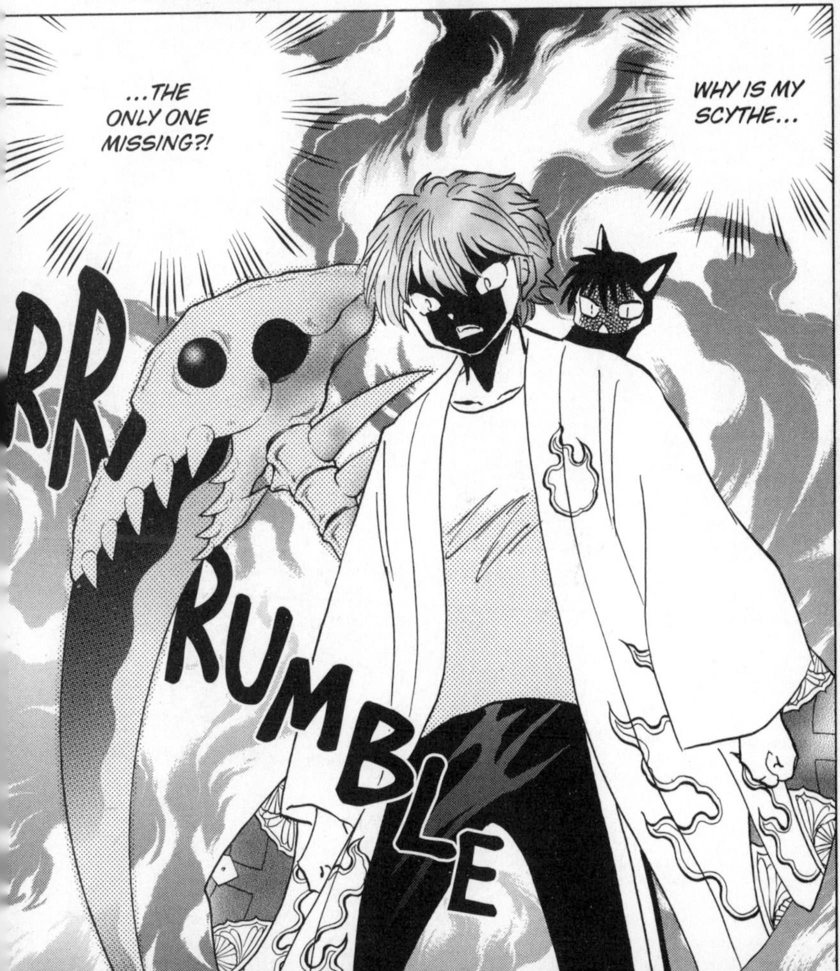
WHY IS MY SCYTHE...
...THE ONLY ONE MISSING?!
RR
RUMBLE

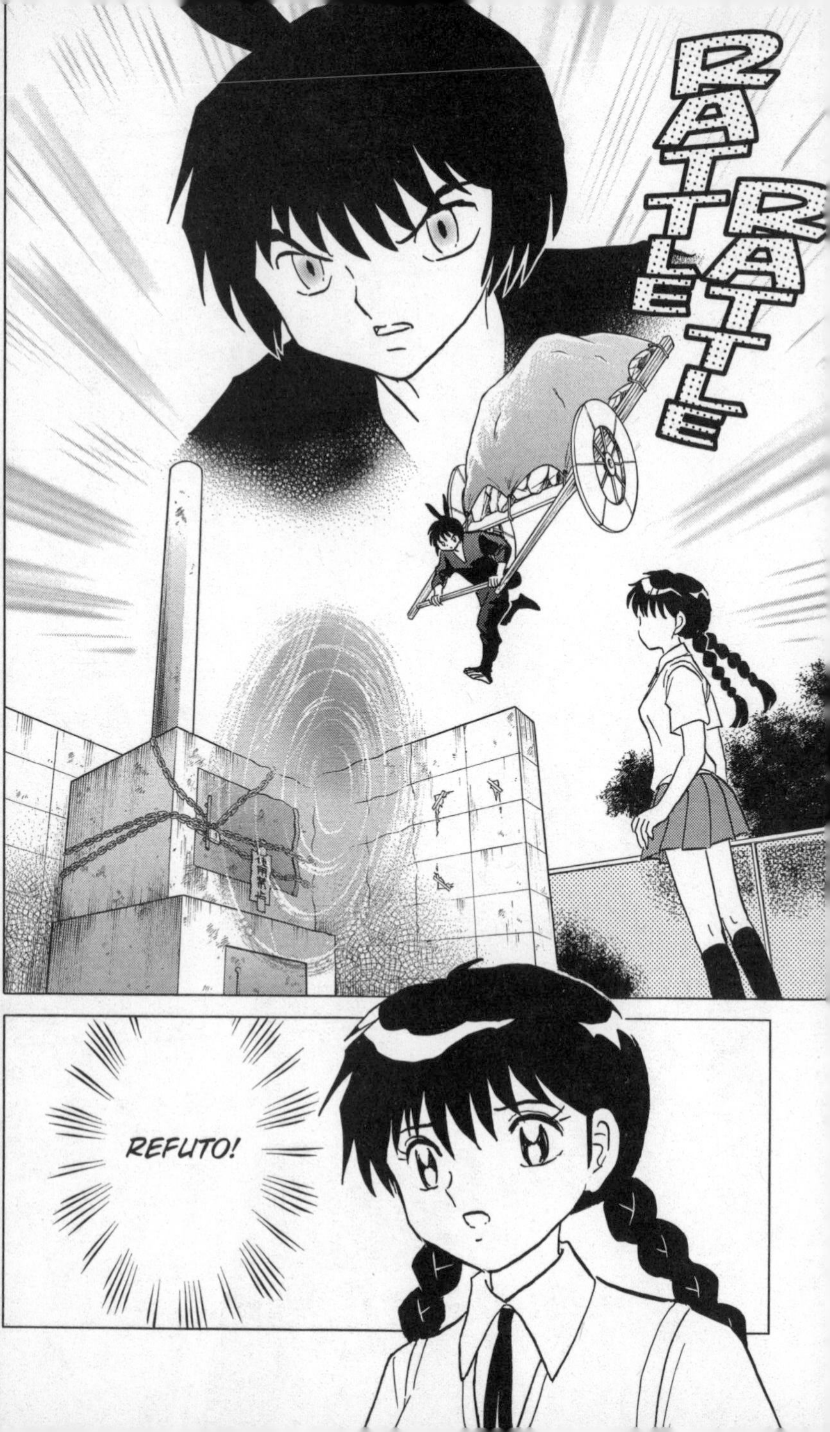
RATTLE
RATTLE
REFUTO!

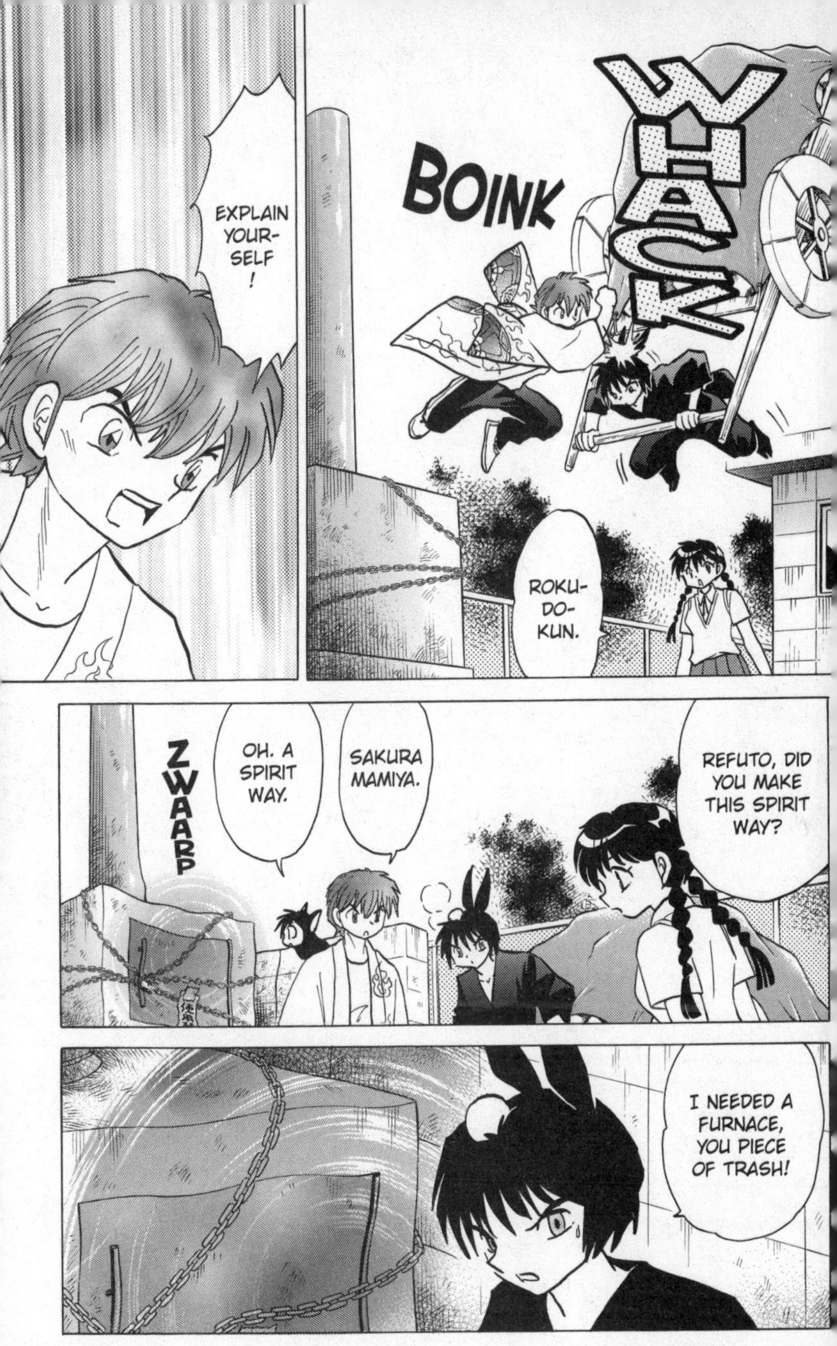
WHACK
BOINK
ROKU-DO-KUN.
EXPLAIN YOUR-SELF!
REFUTO, DID YOU MAKE THIS SPIRIT WAY?
SAKURA MAMIYA.
OH. A SPIRIT WAY.
ZWAARP
I NEEDED A FURNACE, YOU PIECE OF TRASH!

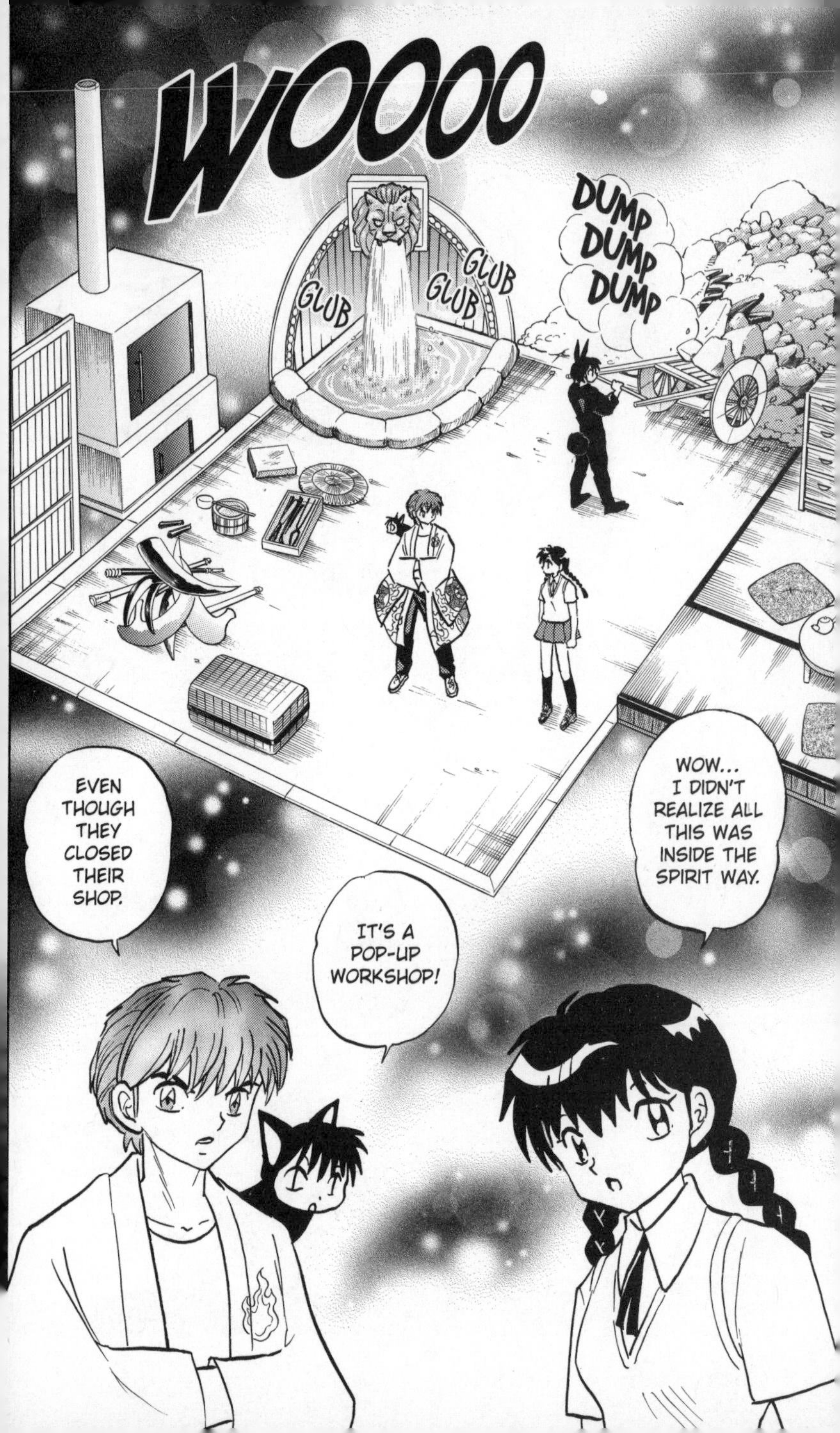
WOOOO
DUMP DUMP DUMP
GLUB GLUB GLUB
WOW... I DIDN'T REALIZE ALL THIS WAS INSIDE THE SPIRIT WAY.
IT'S A POP-UP WORKSHOP!
EVEN THOUGH THEY CLOSED THEIR SHOP.

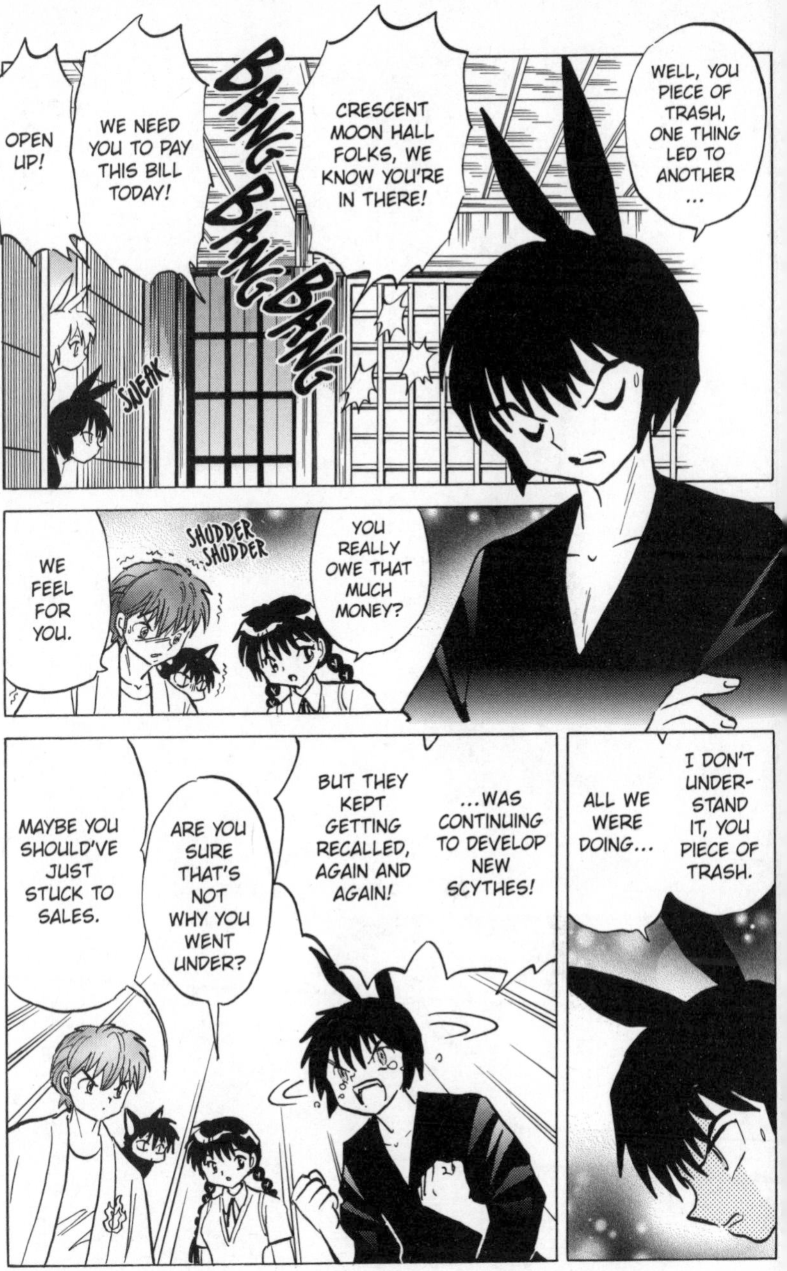
WELL, YOU PIECE OF TRASH, ONE THING LED TO ANOTHER ...
CRESCENT MOON HALL FOLKS, WE KNOW YOU'RE IN THERE!
BANG BANG BANG BANG
WE NEED YOU TO PAY THIS BILL TODAY!
OPEN UP!
SNEAK
YOU REALLY OWE THAT MUCH MONEY?
SHUDDER SHUDDER
WE FEEL FOR YOU.
I DON'T UNDER-STAND IT, YOU PIECE OF TRASH.
ALL WE WERE DOING...
...WAS CONTINUING TO DEVELOP NEW SCYTHES!
BUT THEY KEPT GETTING RECALLED, AGAIN AND AGAIN!
ARE YOU SURE THAT'S NOT WHY YOU WENT UNDER?
MAYBE YOU SHOULD'VE JUST STUCK TO SALES.

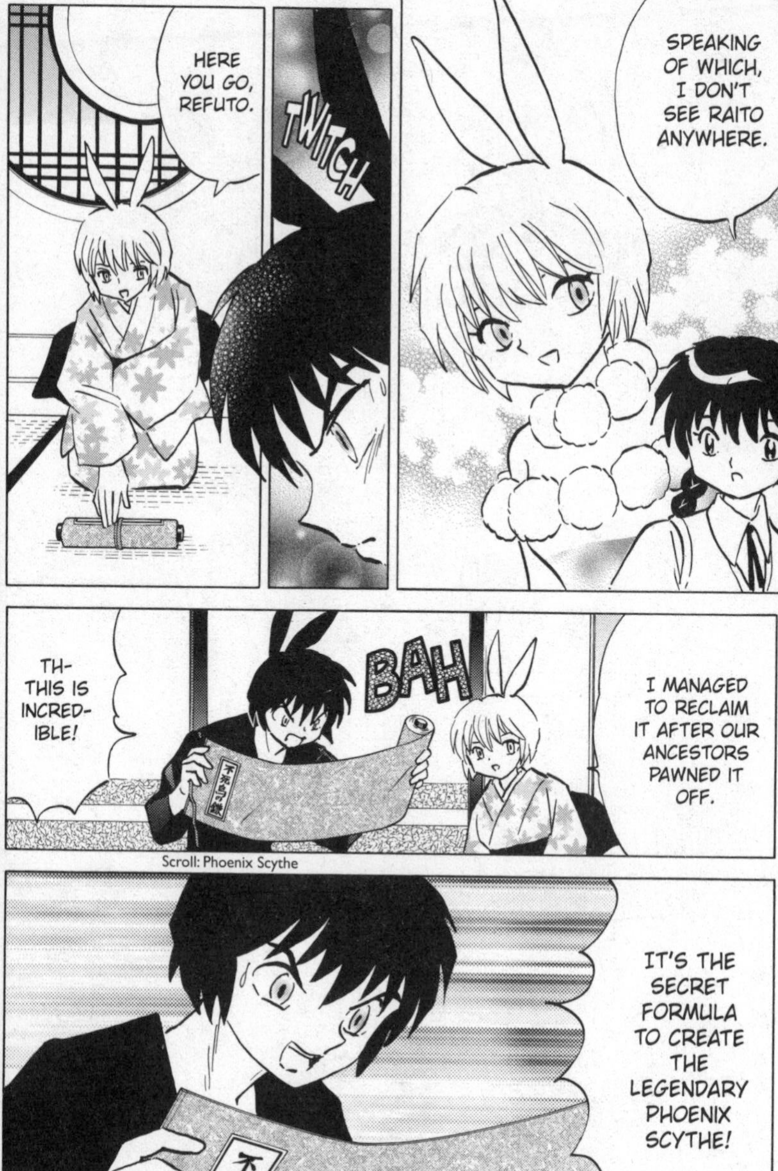
SPEAKING OF WHICH, I DON'T SEE RAITO ANYWHERE.
TWITCH
HERE YOU GO, REFUTO.
I MANAGED TO RECLAIM IT AFTER OUR ANCESTORS PAWNED IT OFF.
BAH
TH- THIS IS INCRED-IBLE!
Scroll: Phoenix Scythe
IT'S THE SECRET FORMULA TO CREATE THE LEGENDARY PHOENIX SCYTHE!

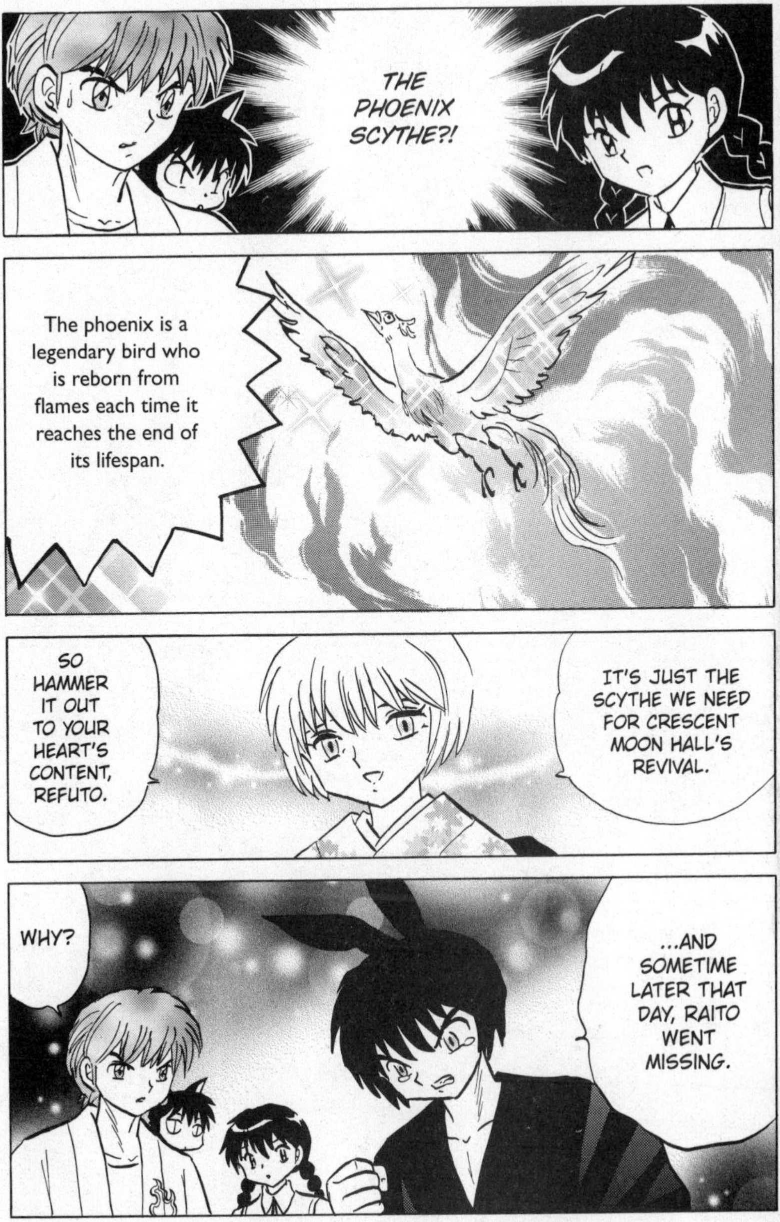
THE PHOENIX SCYTHE?!
The phoenix is a legendary bird who is reborn from flames each time it reaches the end of its lifespan.
IT'S JUST THE SCYTHE WE NEED FOR CRESCENT MOON HALL'S REVIVAL.
SO HAMMER IT OUT TO YOUR HEART'S CONTENT, REFUTO.
...AND SOMETIME LATER THAT DAY, RAITO WENT MISSING.
WHY?

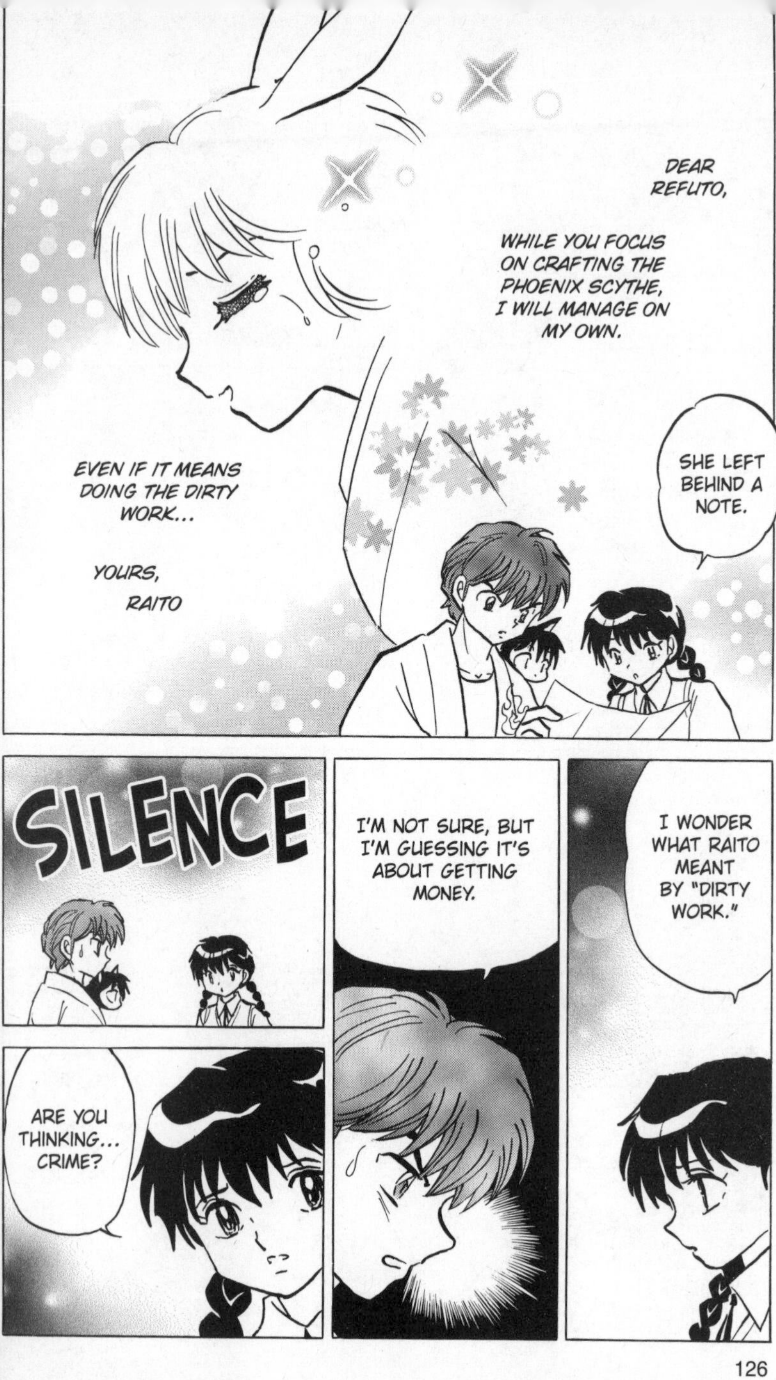
DEAR REFUTO,
WHILE YOU FOCUS ON CRAFTING THE PHOENIX SCYTHE, I WILL MANAGE ON MY OWN.
SHE LEFT BEHIND A NOTE.
EVEN IF IT MEANS DOING THE DIRTY WORK...
YOURS, RAITO
I WONDER WHAT RAITO MEANT BY "DIRTY WORK."
I'M NOT SURE, BUT I'M GUESSING IT'S ABOUT GETTING MONEY.
SILENCE
ARE YOU THINKING... CRIME?

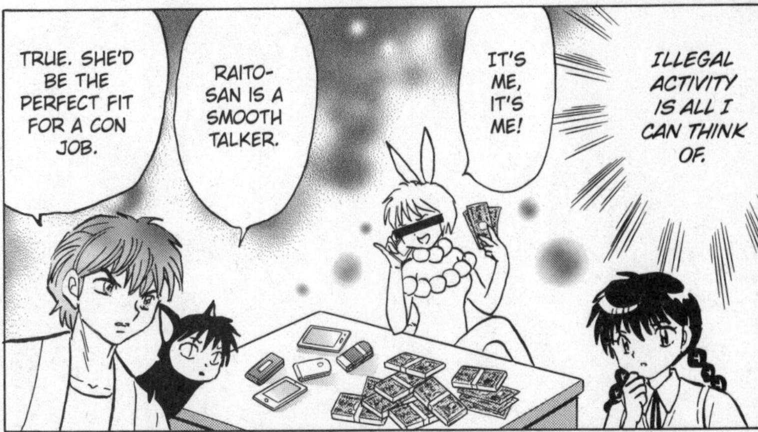
ILLEGAL ACTIVITY IS ALL I CAN THINK OF.
IT'S ME, IT'S ME!
RAITO-SAN IS A SMOOTH TALKER.
TRUE. SHE'D BE THE PERFECT FIT FOR A CON JOB.

The *ore ore* ("it's me, it's me") scam in Japan involves senior citizens being convinced their relatives need money.

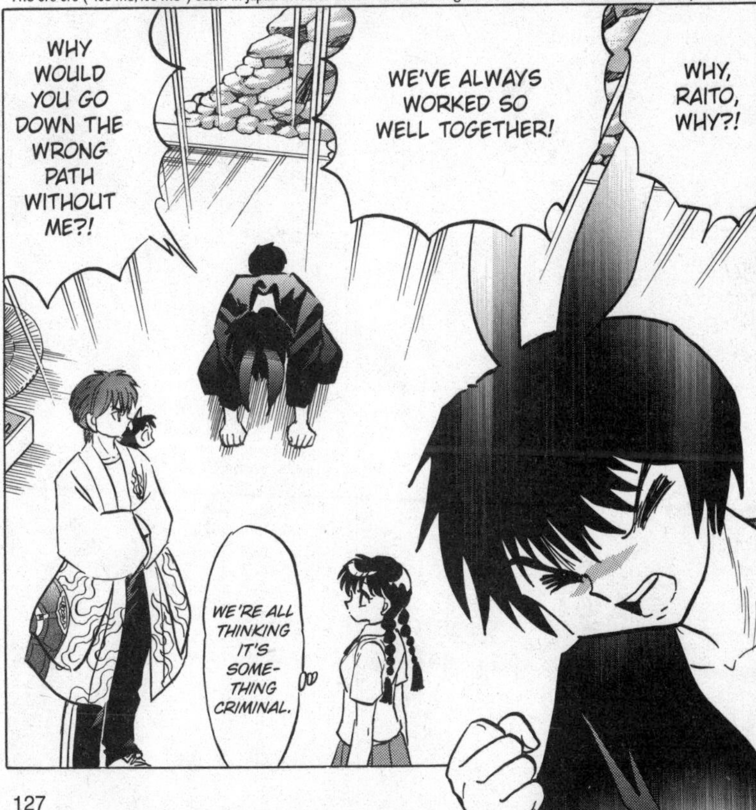
WHY, RAITO, WHY?!
WE'VE ALWAYS WORKED SO WELL TOGETHER!
WHY WOULD YOU GO DOWN THE WRONG PATH WITHOUT ME?!
WE'RE ALL THINKING IT'S SOMETHING CRIMINAL.

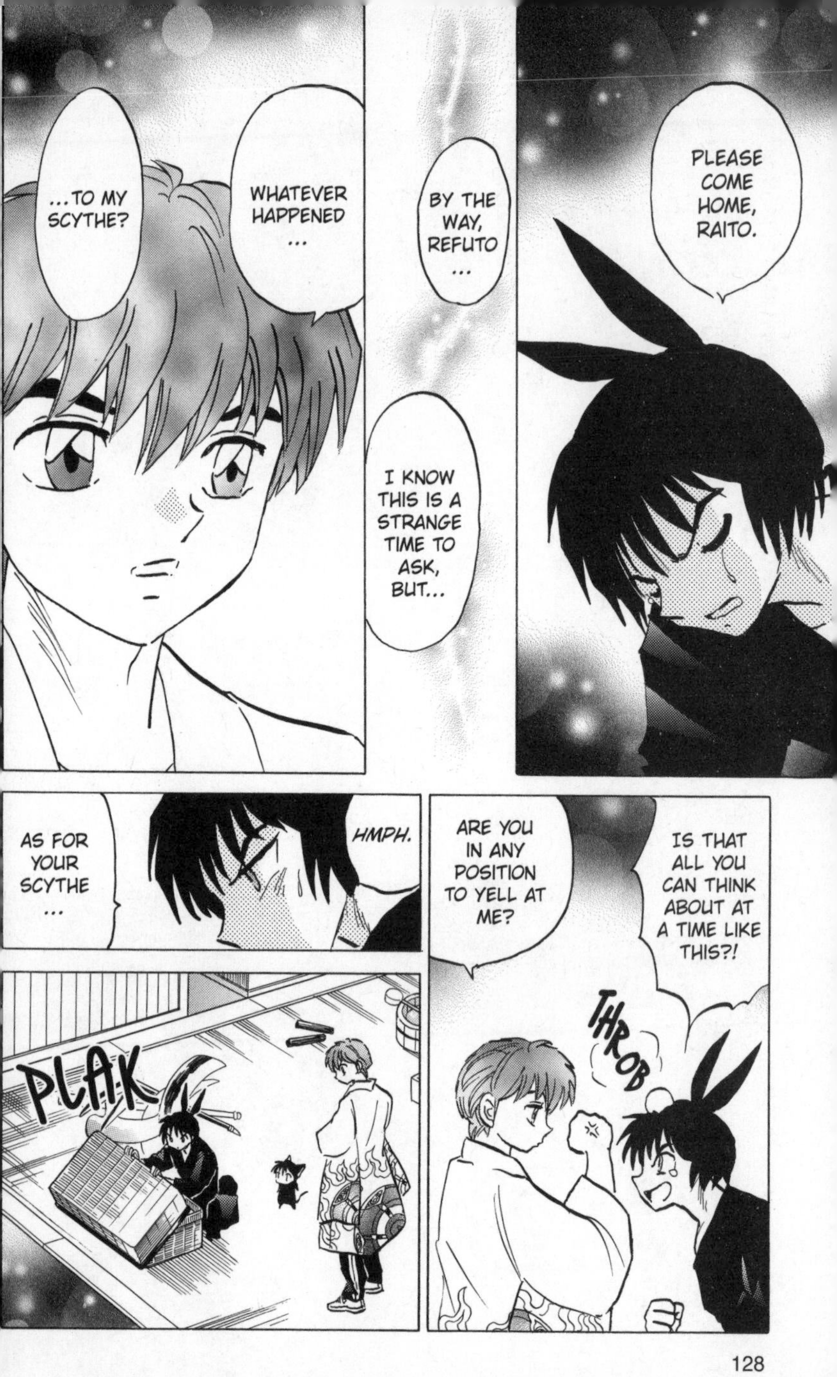
PLEASE COME HOME, RAITO.
BY THE WAY, REFUTO...
I KNOW THIS IS A STRANGE TIME TO ASK, BUT...
WHATEVER HAPPENED...
...TO MY SCYTHE?
IS THAT ALL YOU CAN THINK ABOUT AT A TIME LIKE THIS?!
THROB
ARE YOU IN ANY POSITION TO YELL AT ME?
HMPH.
AS FOR YOUR SCYTHE...
PLAK

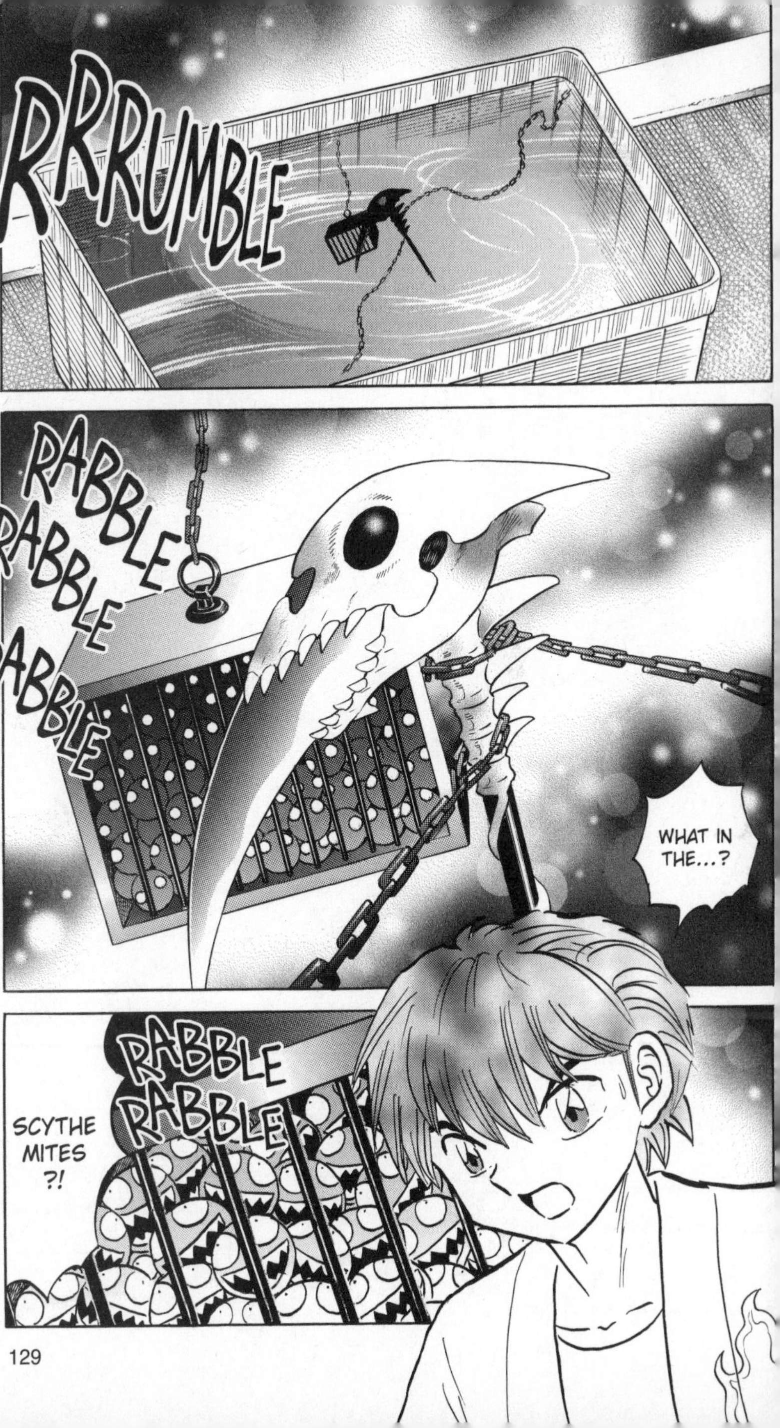
RRRUMBLE
RABBLE RABBLE RABBLE
WHAT IN THE...?
RABBLE RABBLE
SCYTHE MITES ?!

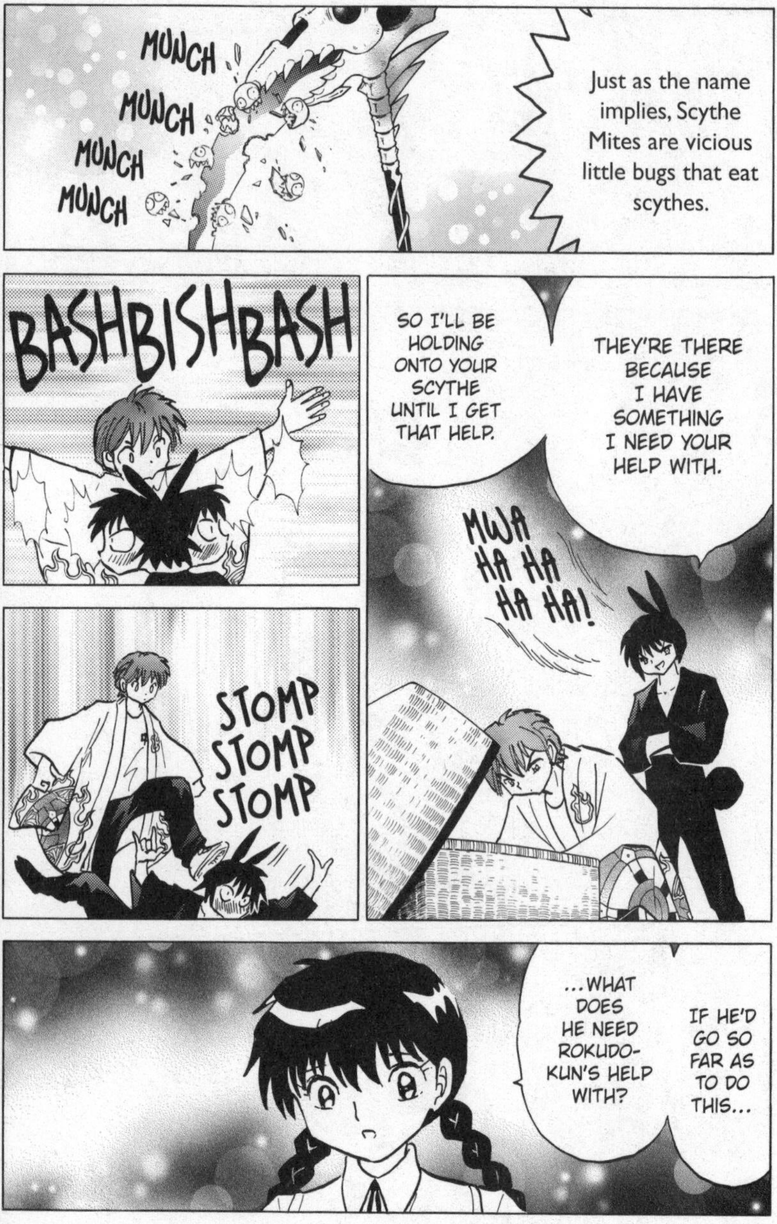
Just as the name implies, Scythe Mites are vicious little bugs that eat scythes.
MUNCH
MUNCH
MUNCH
MUNCH
THEY'RE THERE BECAUSE I HAVE SOMETHING I NEED YOUR HELP WITH.
SO I'LL BE HOLDING ONTO YOUR SCYTHE UNTIL I GET THAT HELP.
MWA HA HA HA HA!
BASHBISHBASH
STOMP STOMP STOMP
IF HE'D GO SO FAR AS TO DO THIS...
...WHAT DOES HE NEED ROKUDO-KUN'S HELP WITH?

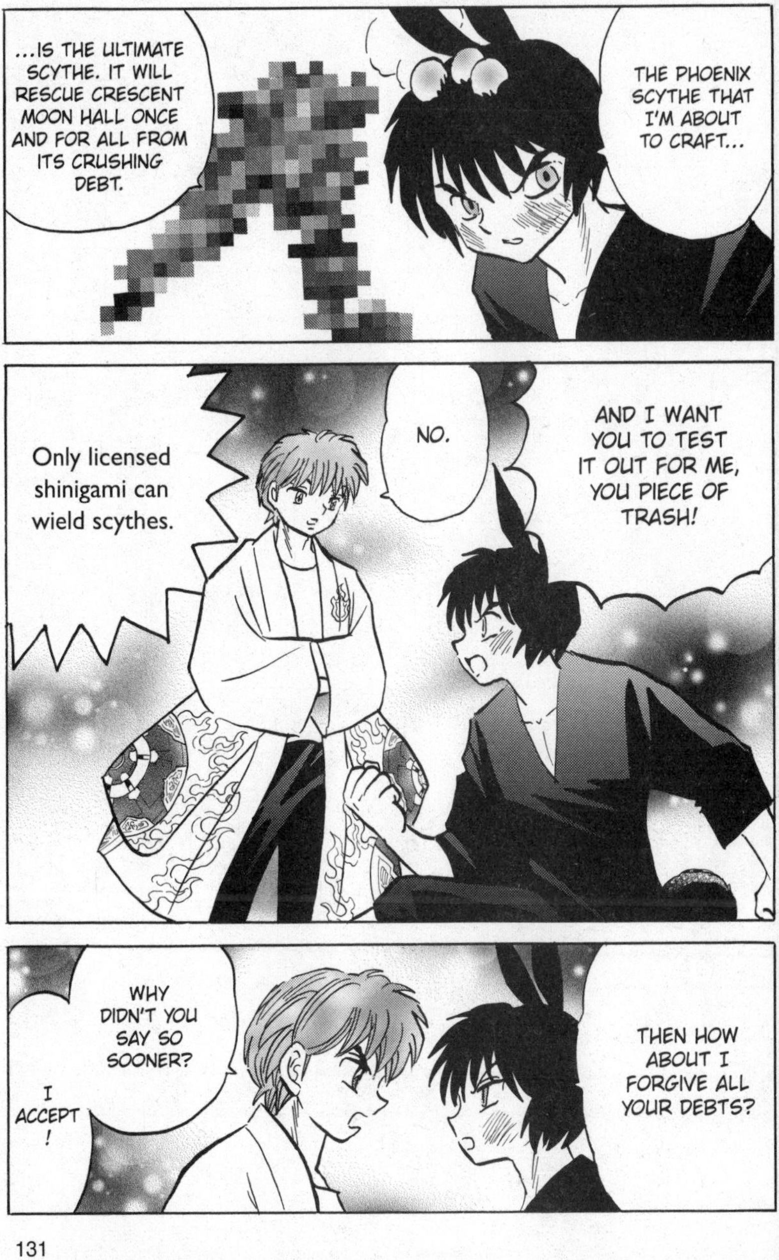
THE PHOENIX SCYTHE THAT I'M ABOUT TO CRAFT...
...IS THE ULTIMATE SCYTHE. IT WILL RESCUE CRESCENT MOON HALL ONCE AND FOR ALL FROM ITS CRUSHING DEBT.
AND I WANT YOU TO TEST IT OUT FOR ME, YOU PIECE OF TRASH!
NO.
Only licensed shinigami can wield scythes.
THEN HOW ABOUT I FORGIVE ALL YOUR DEBTS?
WHY DIDN'T YOU SAY SO SOONER?
I ACCEPT!

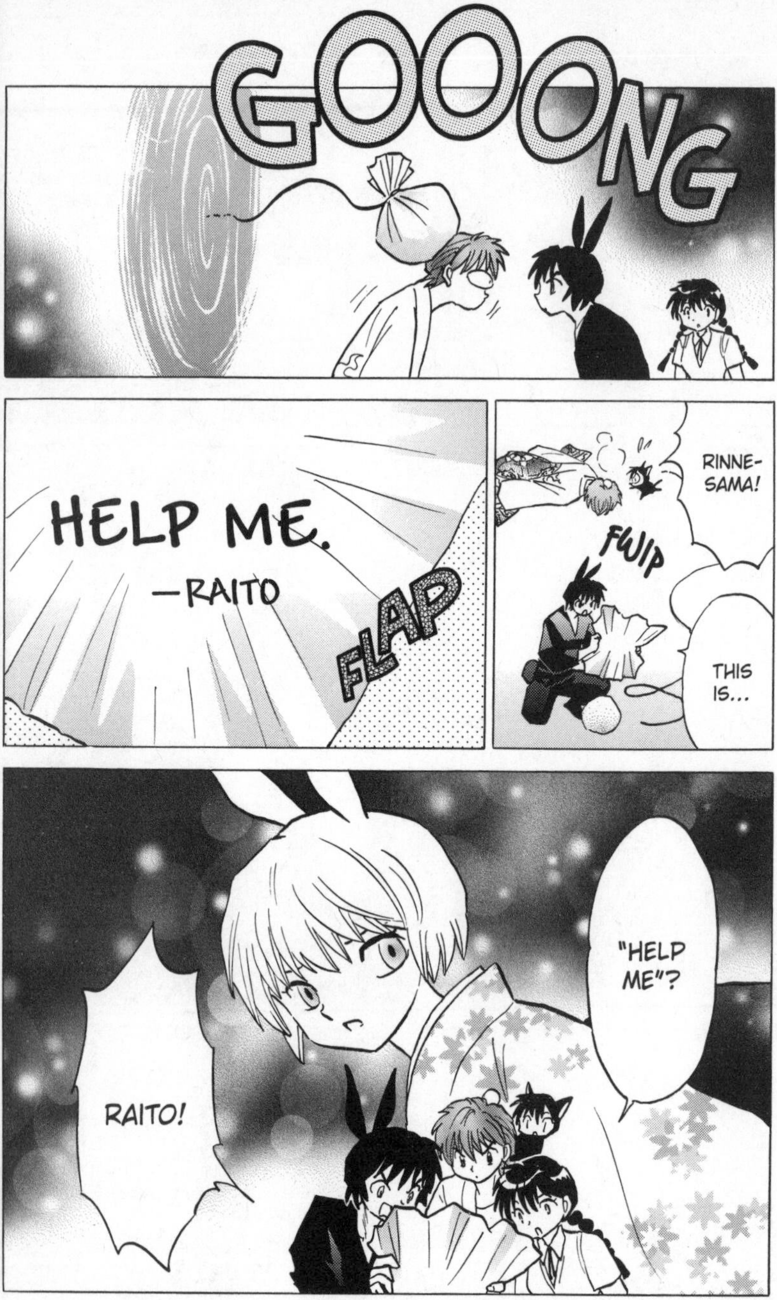
GOOONG
RINNE-SAMA!
FWIP
THIS IS...
HELP ME.
—RAITO
FLAP
"HELP ME"?
RAITO!

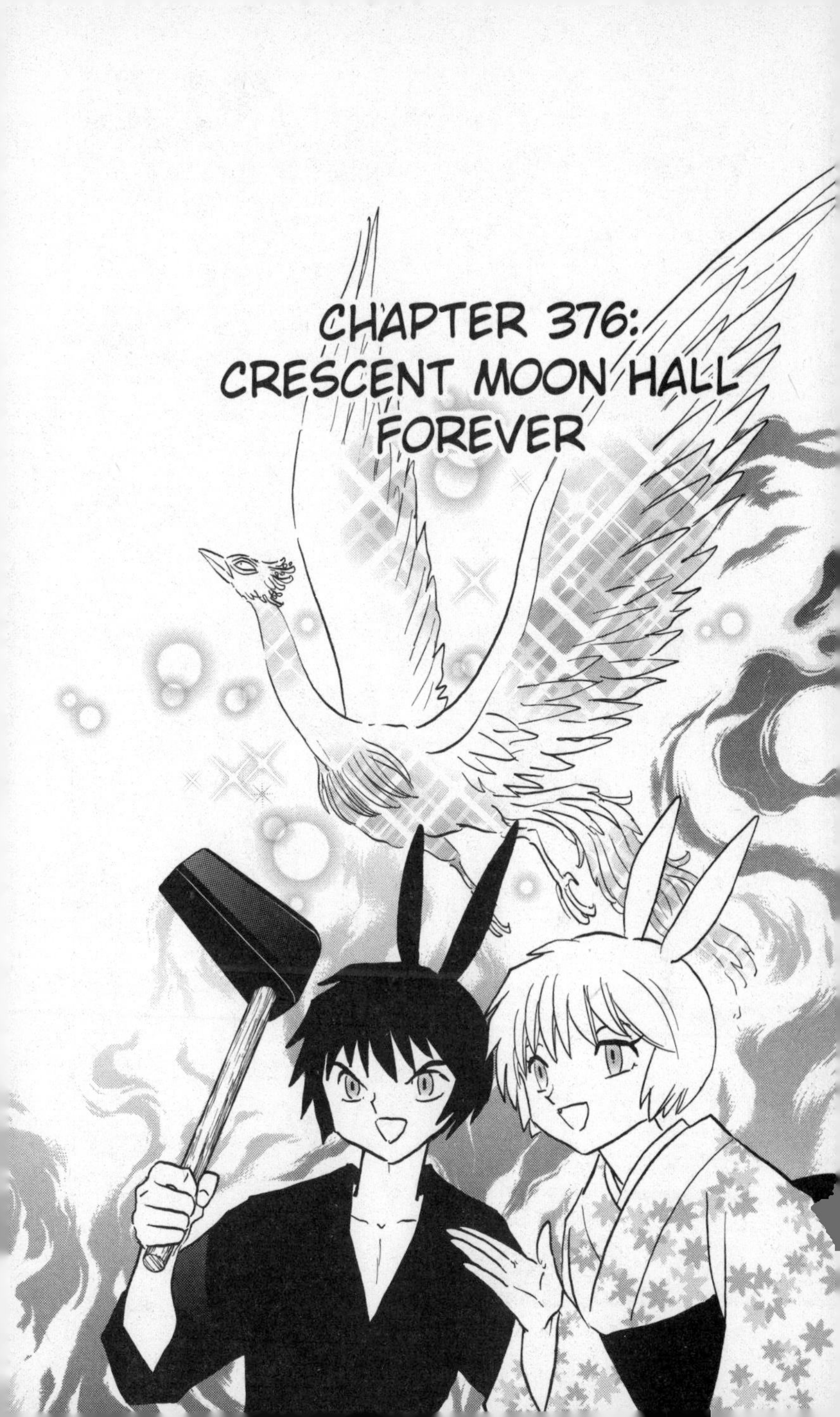
CHAPTER 376:
CRESCENT MOON HALL
FOREVER

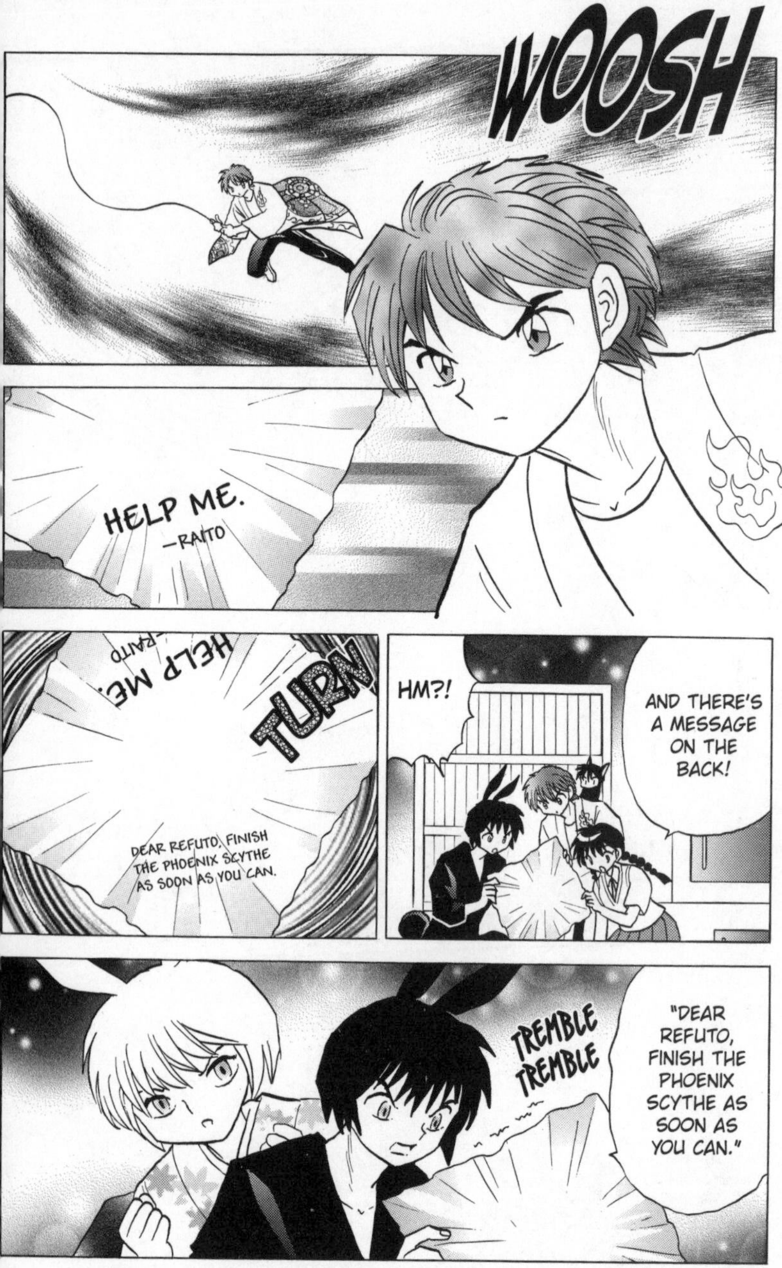
WOOSH
HELP ME.
—RAITO
AND THERE'S A MESSAGE ON THE BACK!
HM?!
HELP ME.
—RAITO
TURN
DEAR REFUTO, FINISH THE PHOENIX SCYTHE AS SOON AS YOU CAN.
"DEAR REFUTO, FINISH THE PHOENIX SCYTHE AS SOON AS YOU CAN."
TREMBLE TREMBLE

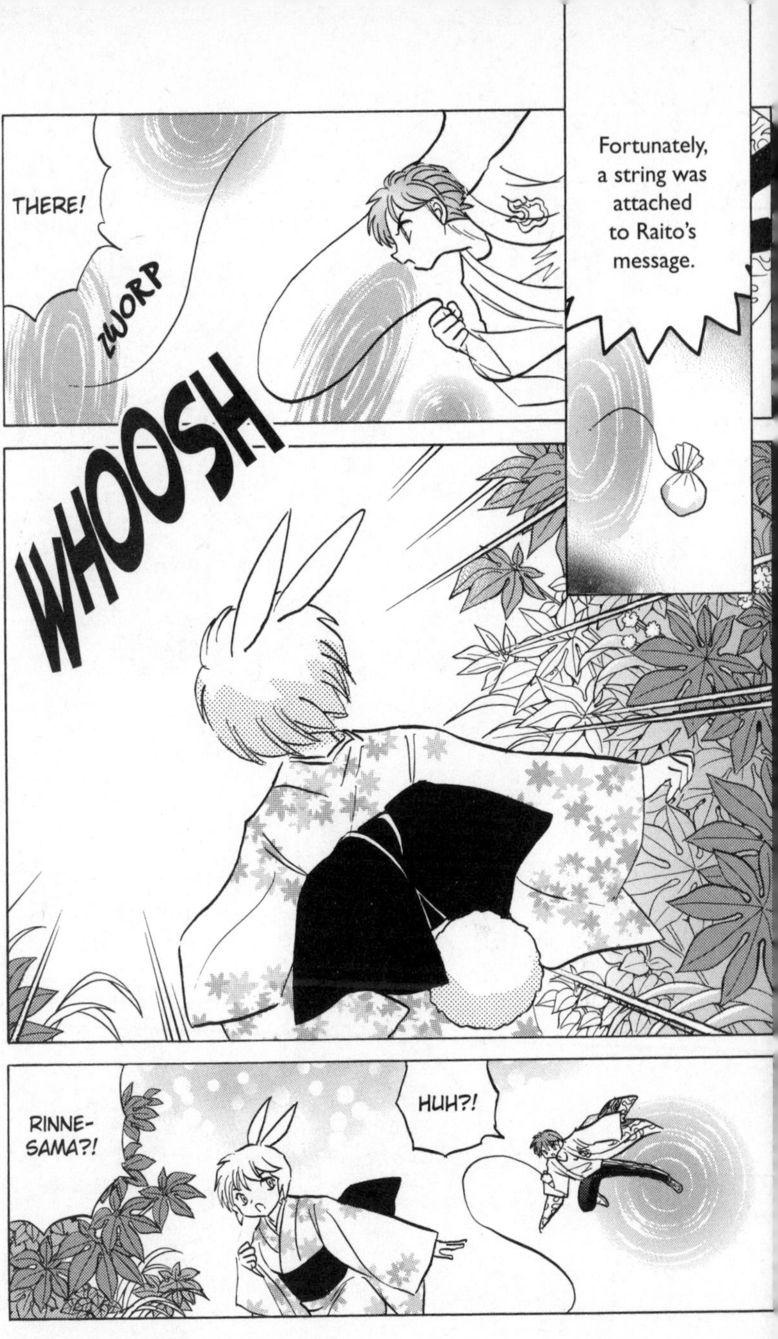
Fortunately, a string was attached to Raito's message.
THERE!
ZWORP
WHOOSH
HUH?!
RINNE-SAMA?!

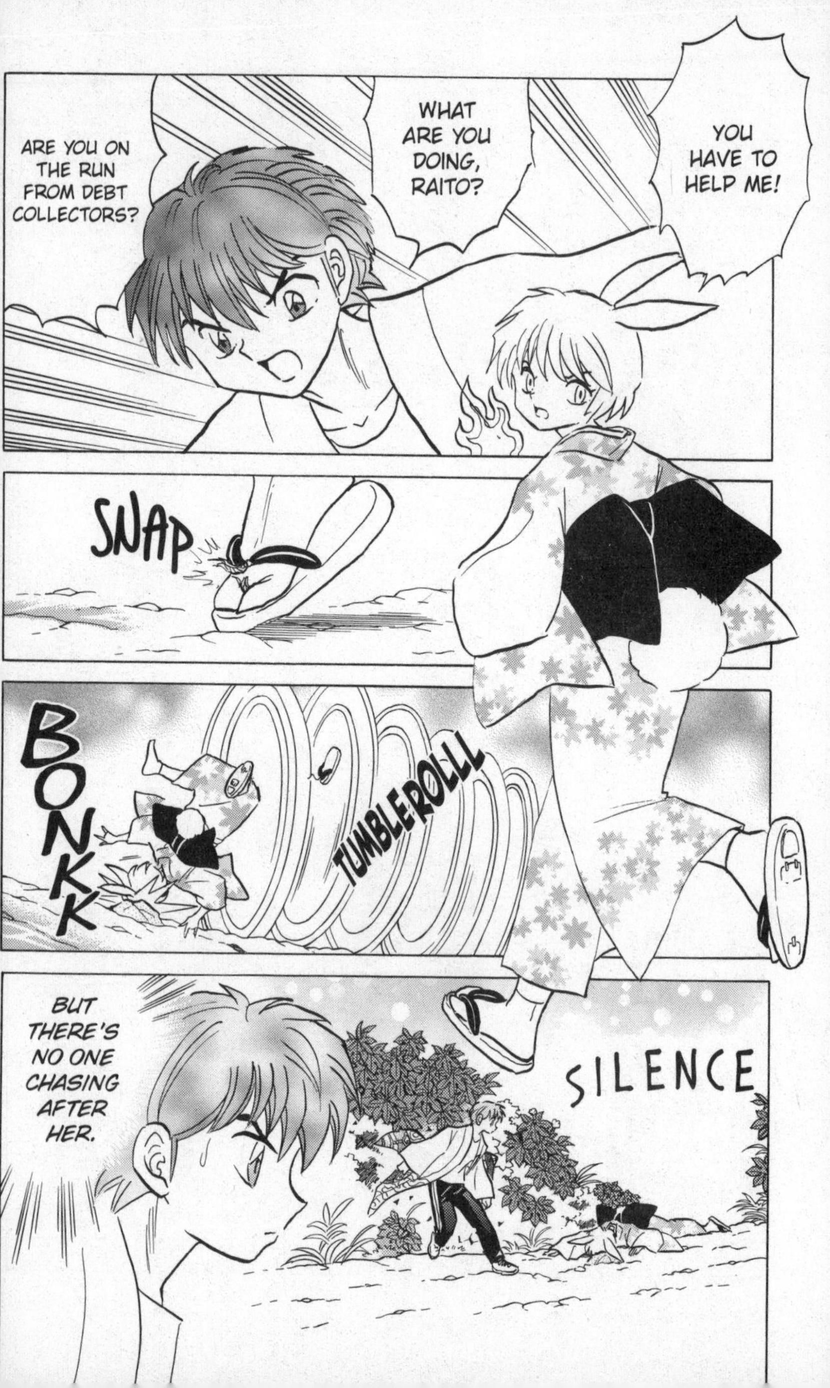
YOU HAVE TO HELP ME!
WHAT ARE YOU DOING, RAITO?
ARE YOU ON THE RUN FROM DEBT COLLECTORS?
SNAP
TUMBLEROLL
BONKK
SILENCE
BUT THERE'S NO ONE CHASING AFTER HER.

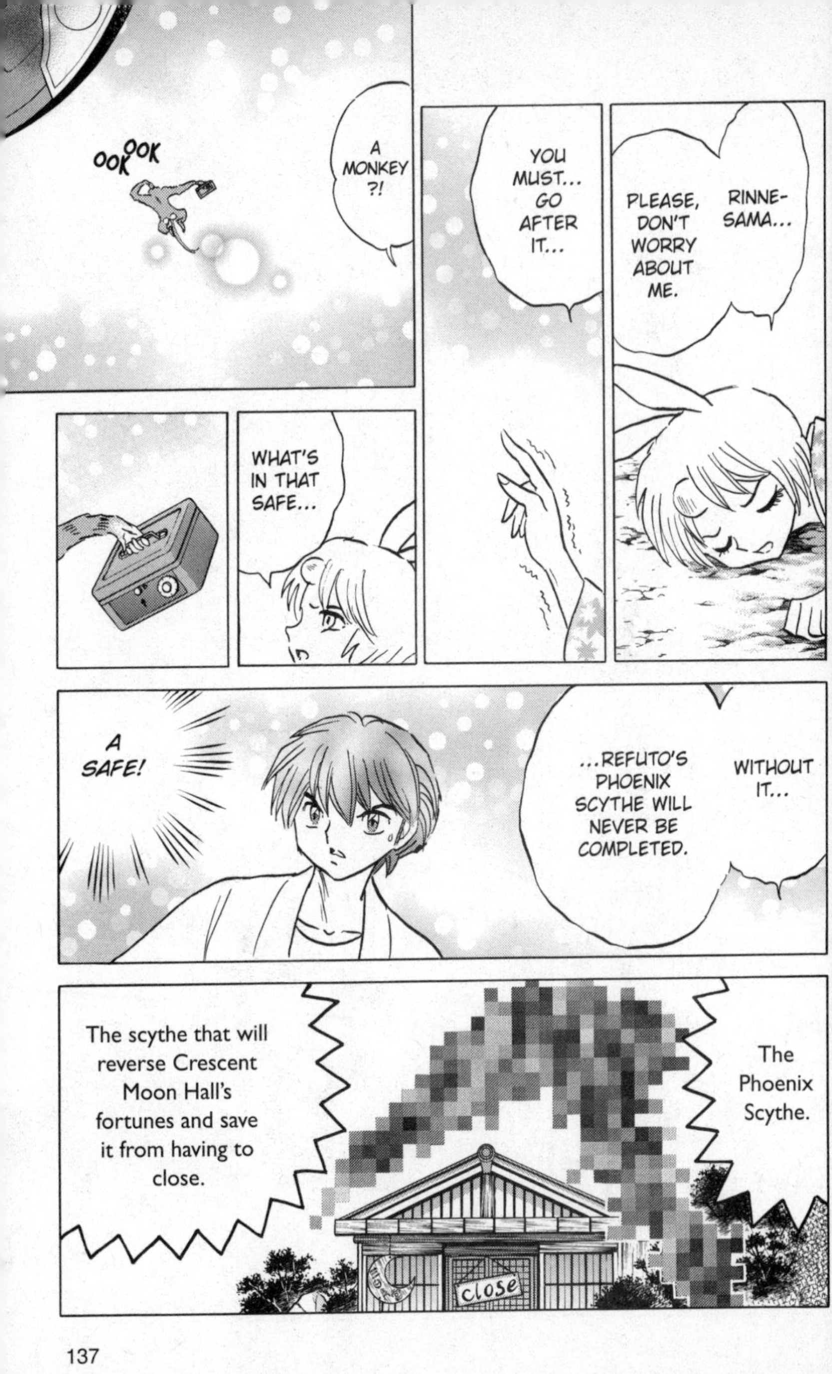
OOK OOK
A MONKEY ?!
RINNE-SAMA...
PLEASE, DON'T WORRY ABOUT ME.
YOU MUST... GO AFTER IT...
WHAT'S IN THAT SAFE...
WITHOUT IT...
...REFUTO'S PHOENIX SCYTHE WILL NEVER BE COMPLETED.
A SAFE!
The Phoenix Scythe.
The scythe that will reverse Crescent Moon Hall's fortunes and save it from having to close.
close

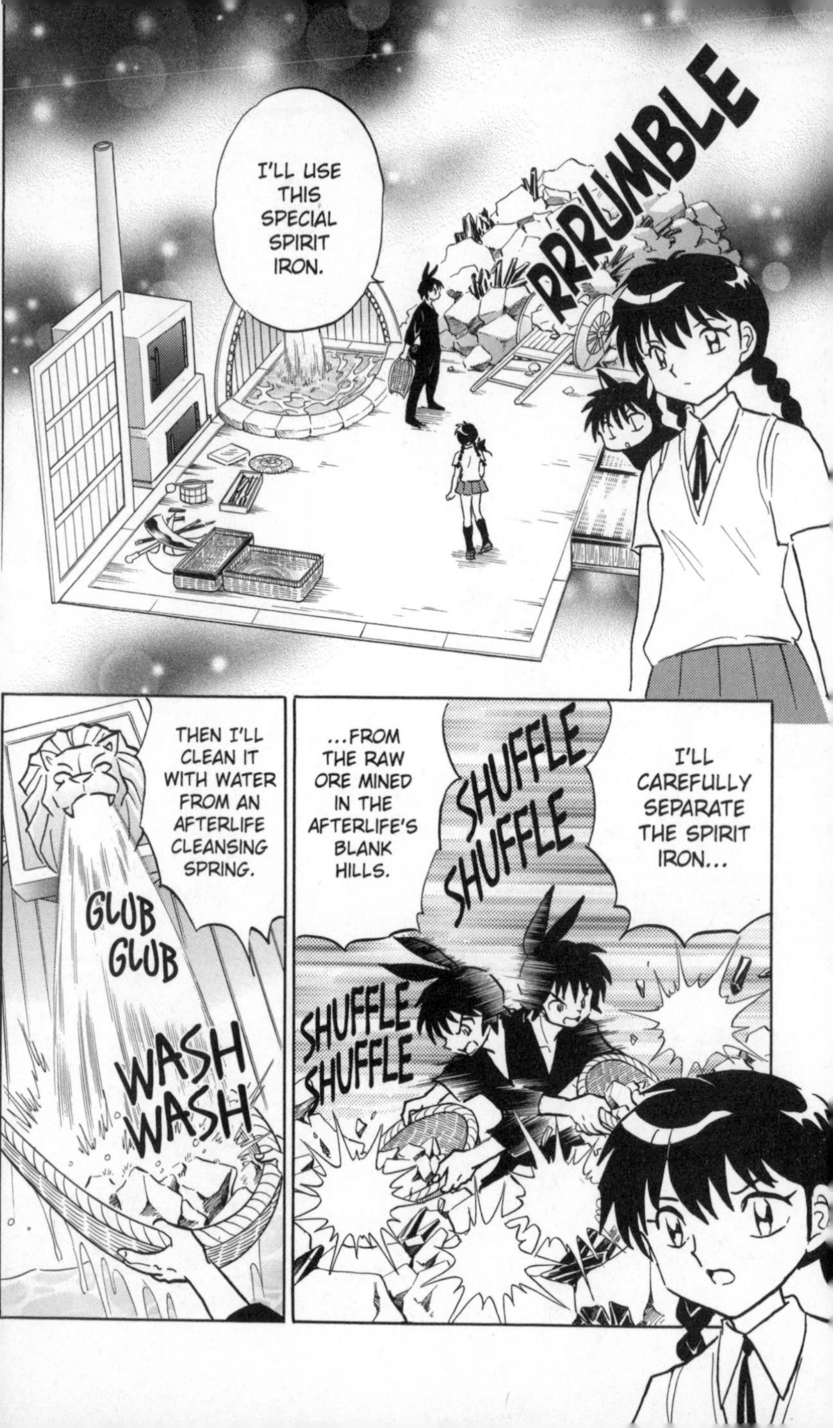
RRUMBLE
I'LL USE THIS SPECIAL SPIRIT IRON.
I'LL CAREFULLY SEPARATE THE SPIRIT IRON...
...FROM THE RAW ORE MINED IN THE AFTERLIFE'S BLANK HILLS.
SHUFFLE SHUFFLE
SHUFFLE SHUFFLE
THEN I'LL CLEAN IT WITH WATER FROM AN AFTERLIFE CLEANSING SPRING.
GLUB GLUB
WASH WASH

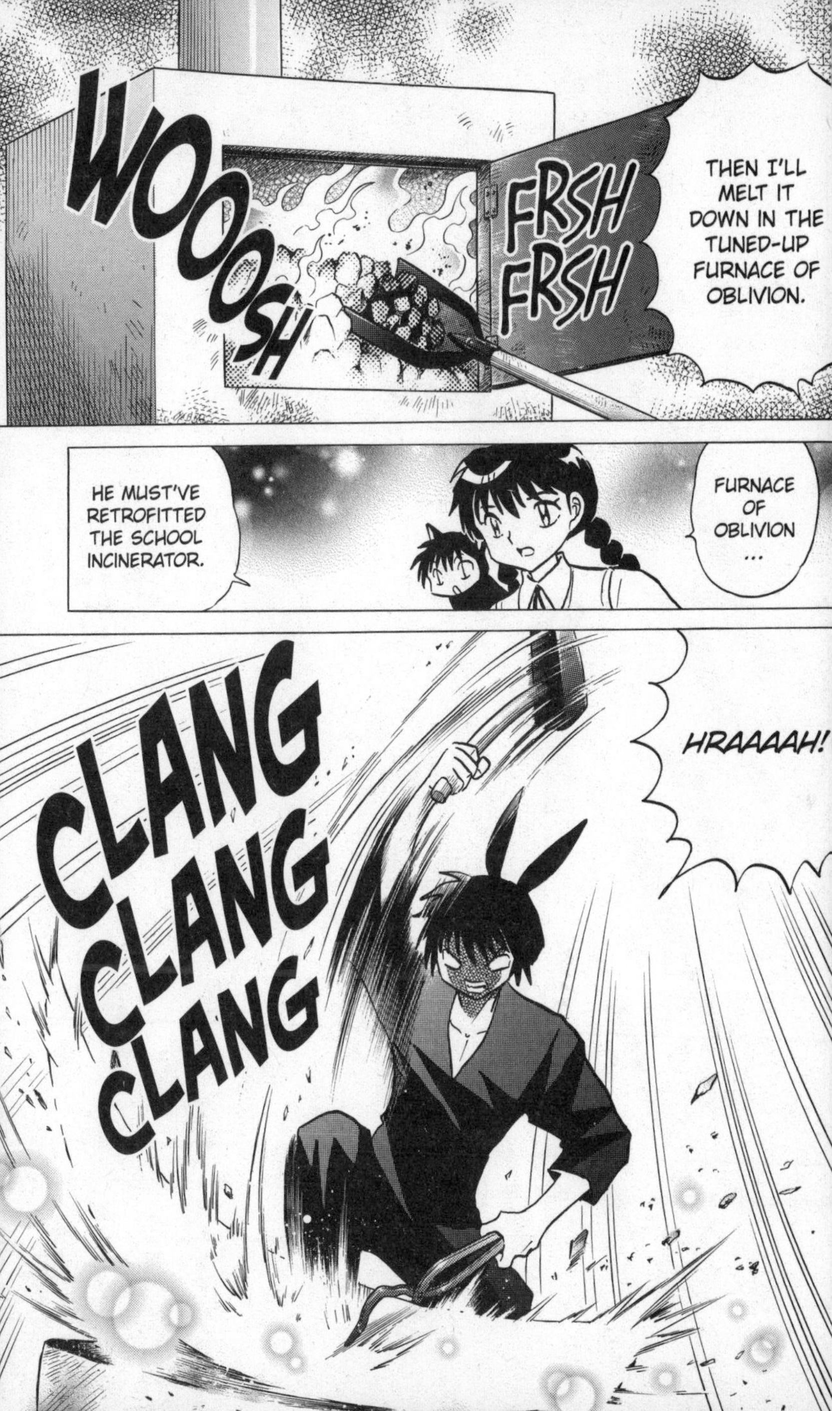
THEN I'LL MELT IT DOWN IN THE TUNED-UP FURNACE OF OBLIVION.
FRSH FRSH
WOOOSH
FURNACE OF OBLIVION ...
HE MUST'VE RETROFITTED THE SCHOOL INCINERATOR.
HRAAAAH!
CLANG CLANG CLANG

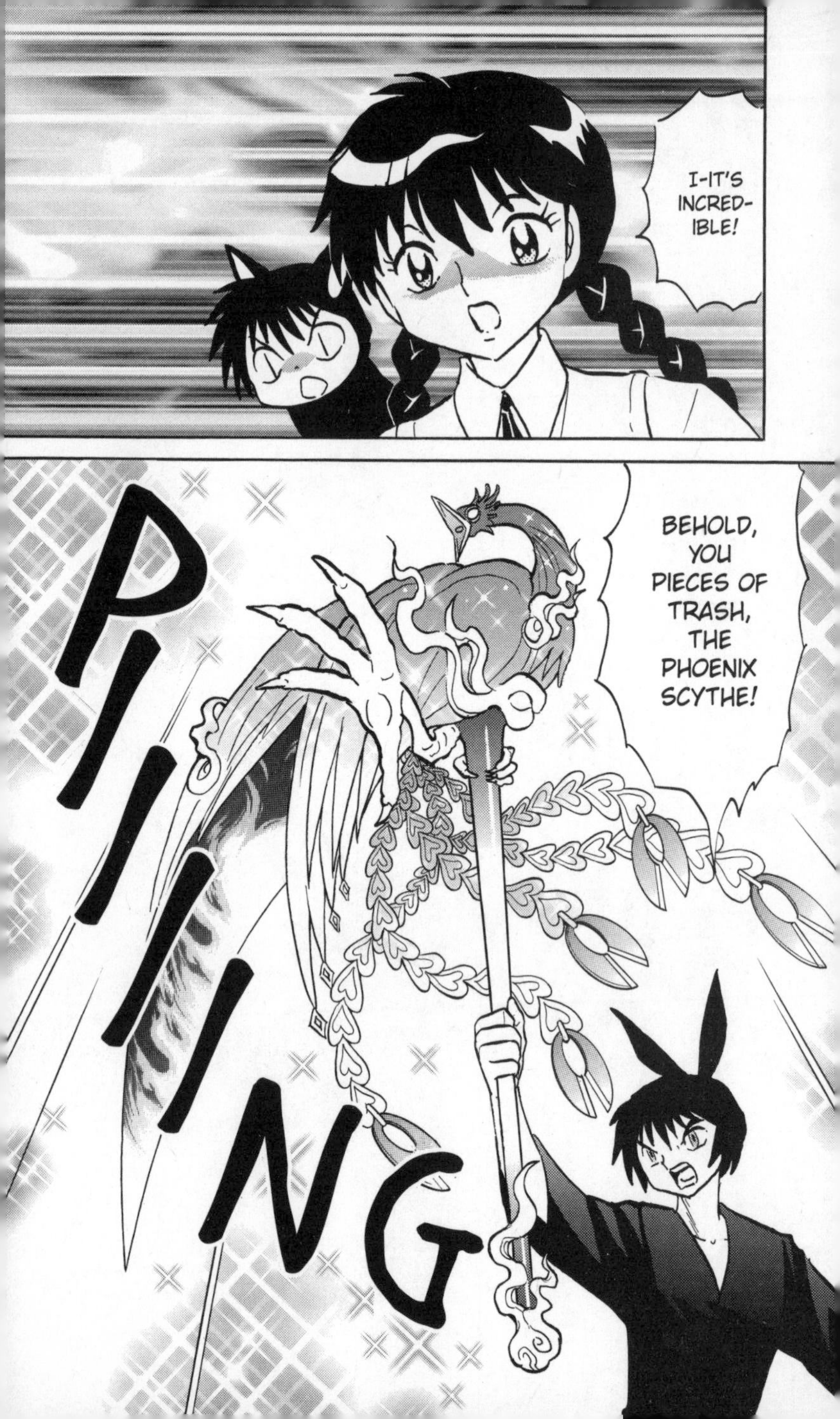
I-IT'S INCRED-IBLE!
BEHOLD, YOU PIECES OF TRASH, THE PHOENIX SCYTHE!
PIIING

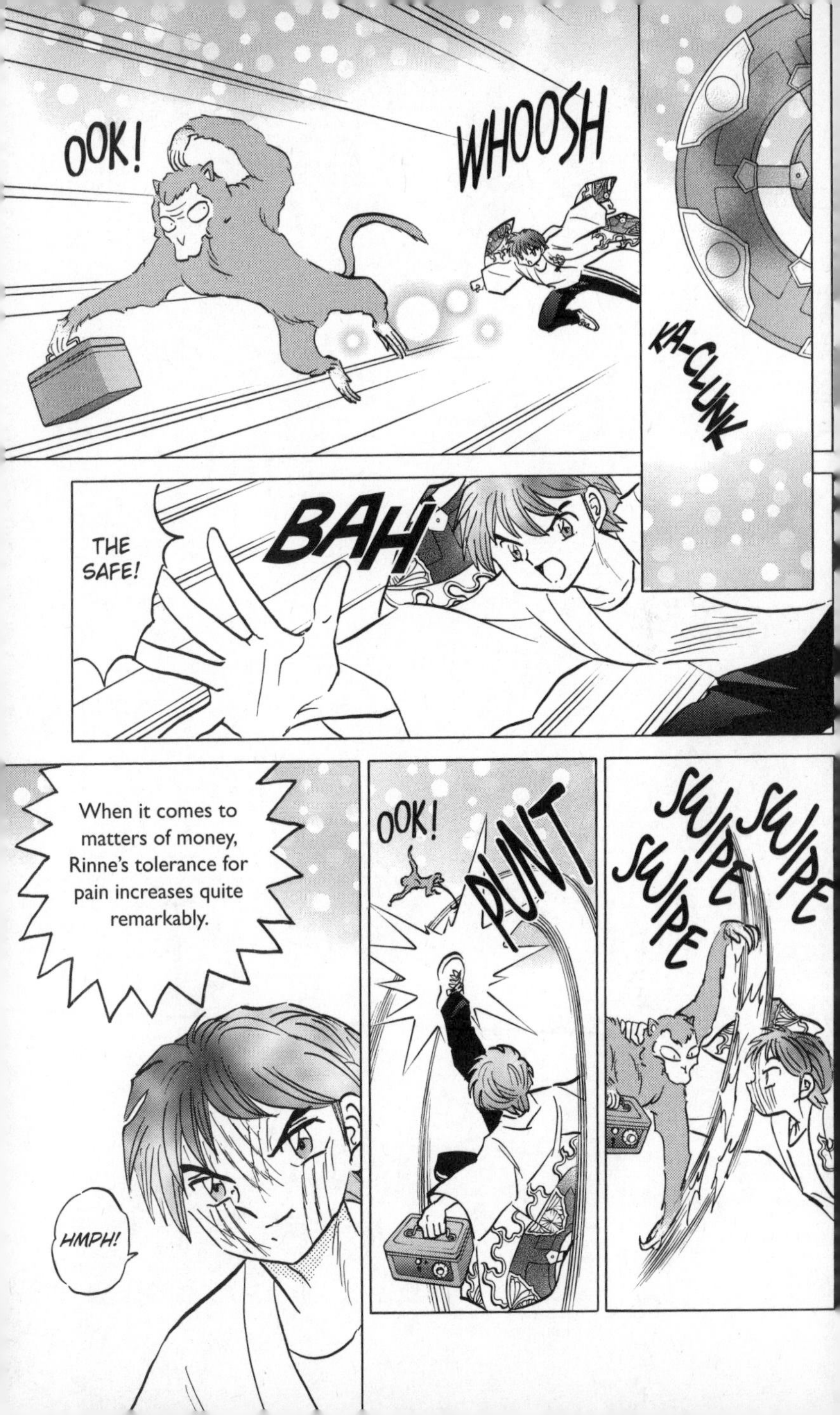
KA-CLUNK
WHOOSH
OOK!
BAH
THE SAFE!
SWIPE
SWIPE
SWIPE
PUNT
OOK!
When it comes to matters of money, Rinne's tolerance for pain increases quite remarkably.
HMPH!

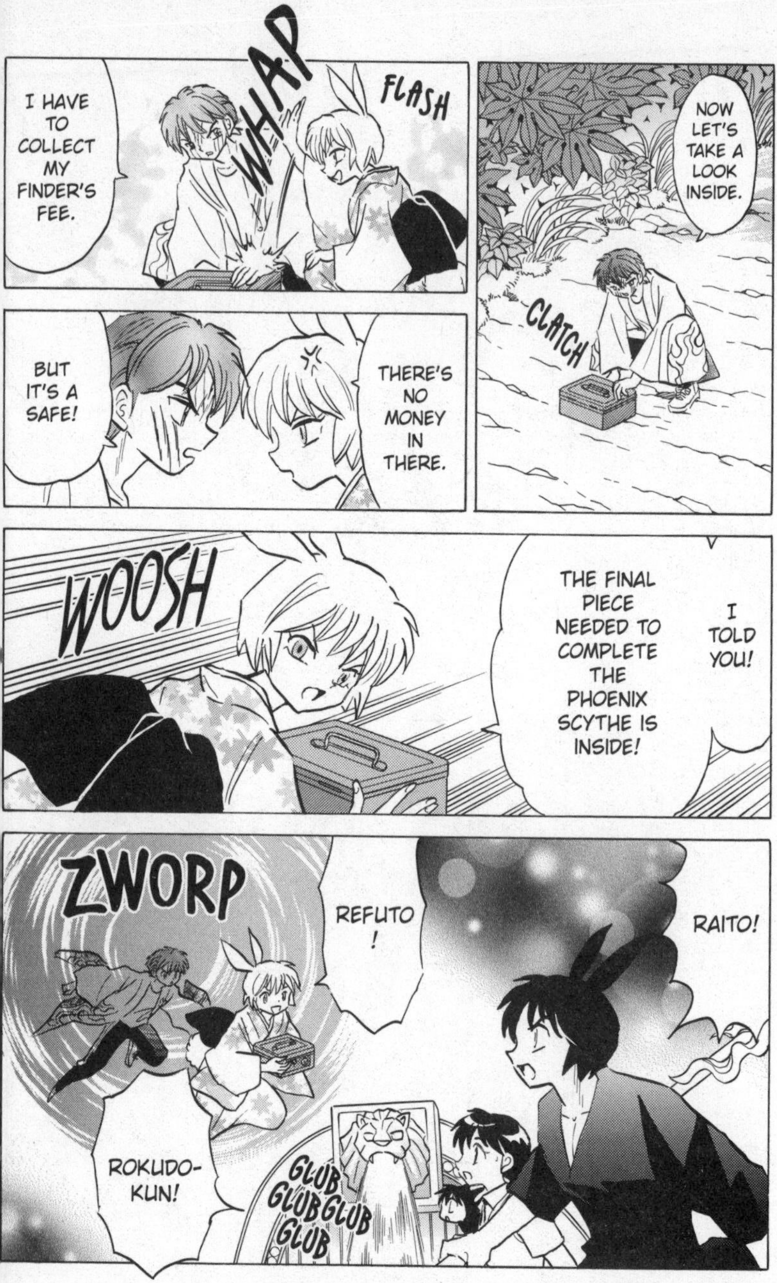
NOW LET'S TAKE A LOOK INSIDE.
CLATCH
FLASH
WHAP
I HAVE TO COLLECT MY FINDER'S FEE.
THERE'S NO MONEY IN THERE.
BUT IT'S A SAFE!
I TOLD YOU!
THE FINAL PIECE NEEDED TO COMPLETE THE PHOENIX SCYTHE IS INSIDE!
WOOSH
RAITO!
REFUTO!
ZWORP
GLUB GLUB GLUB GLUB
ROKUDO-KUN!

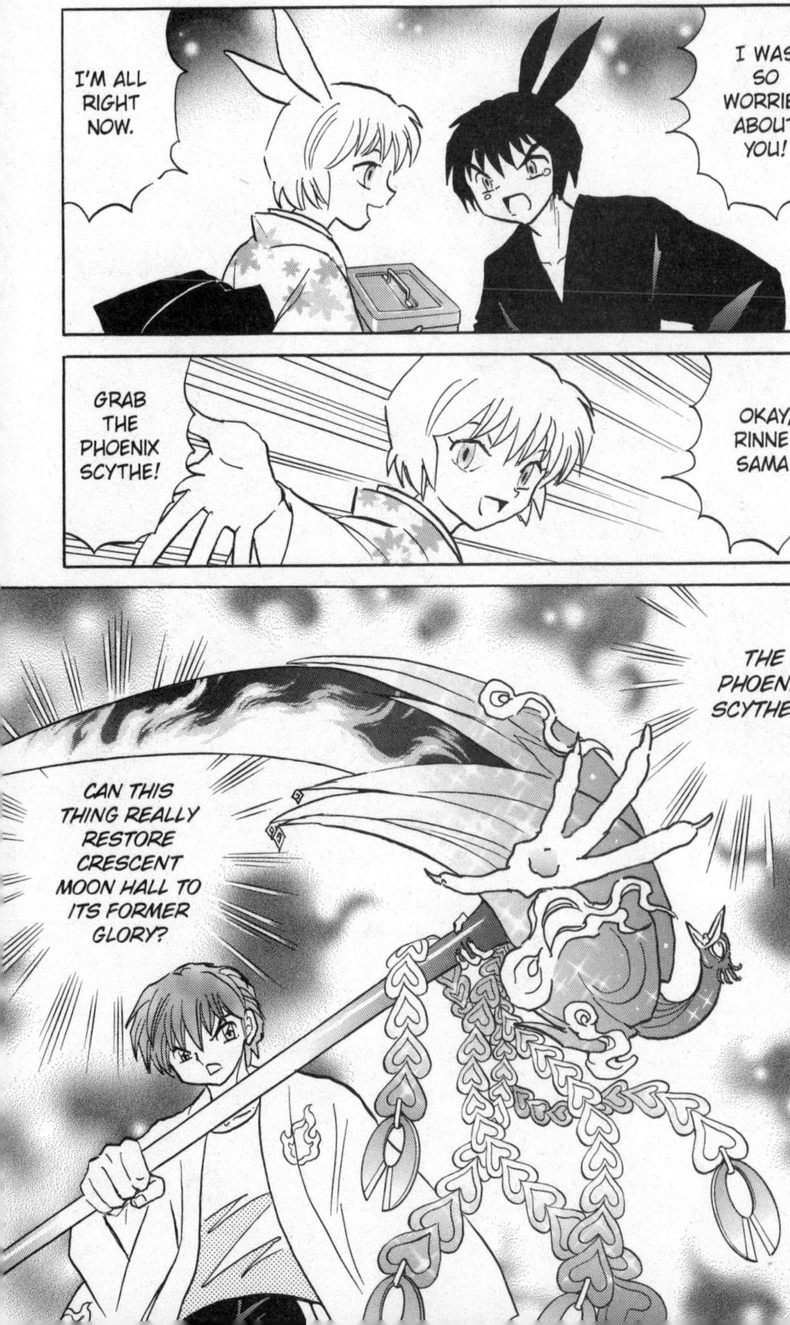
I WAS SO WORRIED ABOUT YOU!
I'M ALL RIGHT NOW.
GRAB THE PHOENIX SCYTHE!
OKAY, RINNE-SAMA!
THE PHOENIX SCYTHE...
CAN THIS THING REALLY RESTORE CRESCENT MOON HALL TO ITS FORMER GLORY?

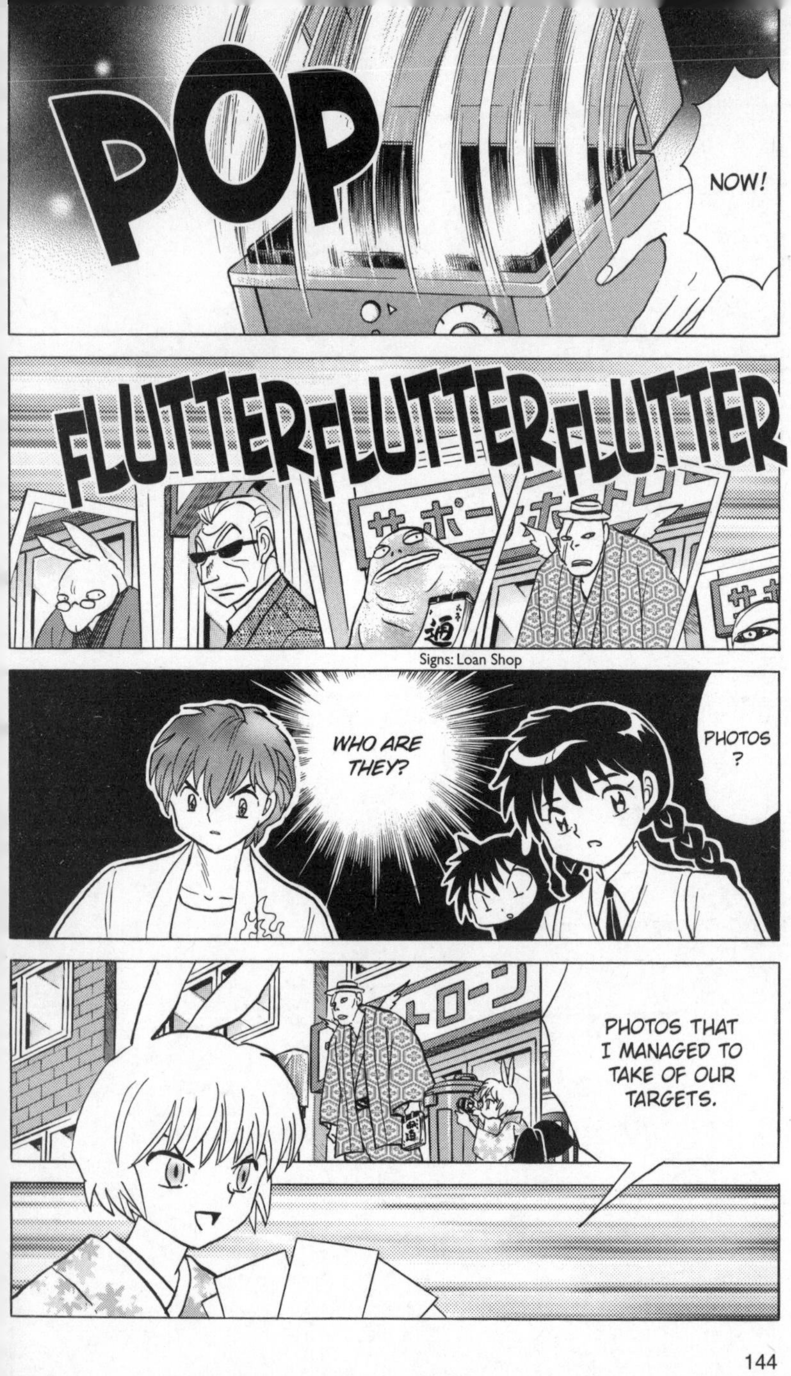
NOW!
POP
FLUTTER FLUTTER FLUTTER
Signs: Loan Shop
PHOTOS ?
WHO ARE THEY?
PHOTOS THAT I MANAGED TO TAKE OF OUR TARGETS.

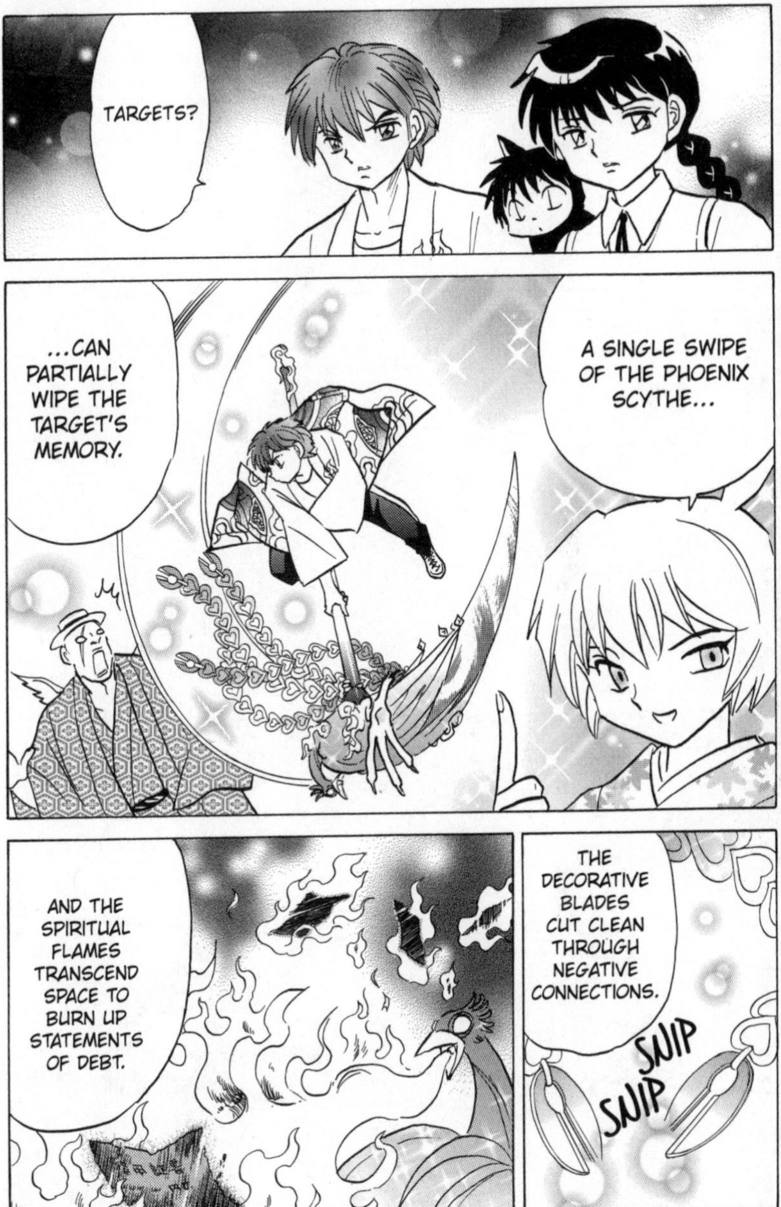
TARGETS?
A SINGLE SWIPE OF THE PHOENIX SCYTHE...
...CAN PARTIALLY WIPE THE TARGET'S MEMORY.
THE DECORATIVE BLADES CUT CLEAN THROUGH NEGATIVE CONNECTIONS.
SNIP
SNIP
AND THE SPIRITUAL FLAMES TRANSCEND SPACE TO BURN UP STATEMENTS OF DEBT.

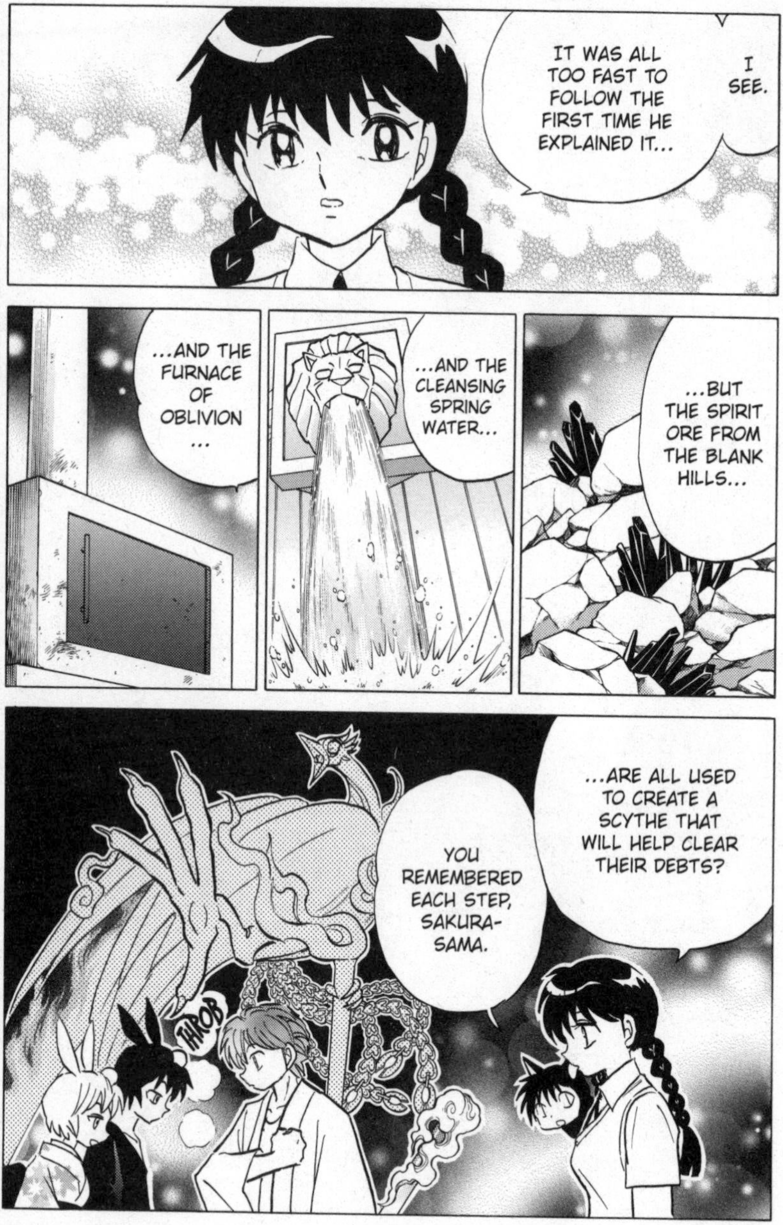
I SEE.
IT WAS ALL TOO FAST TO FOLLOW THE FIRST TIME HE EXPLAINED IT...
...BUT THE SPIRIT ORE FROM THE BLANK HILLS...
...AND THE CLEANSING SPRING WATER...
...AND THE FURNACE OF OBLIVION ...
...ARE ALL USED TO CREATE A SCYTHE THAT WILL HELP CLEAR THEIR DEBTS?
YOU REMEMBERED EACH STEP, SAKURA-SAMA.
THROB

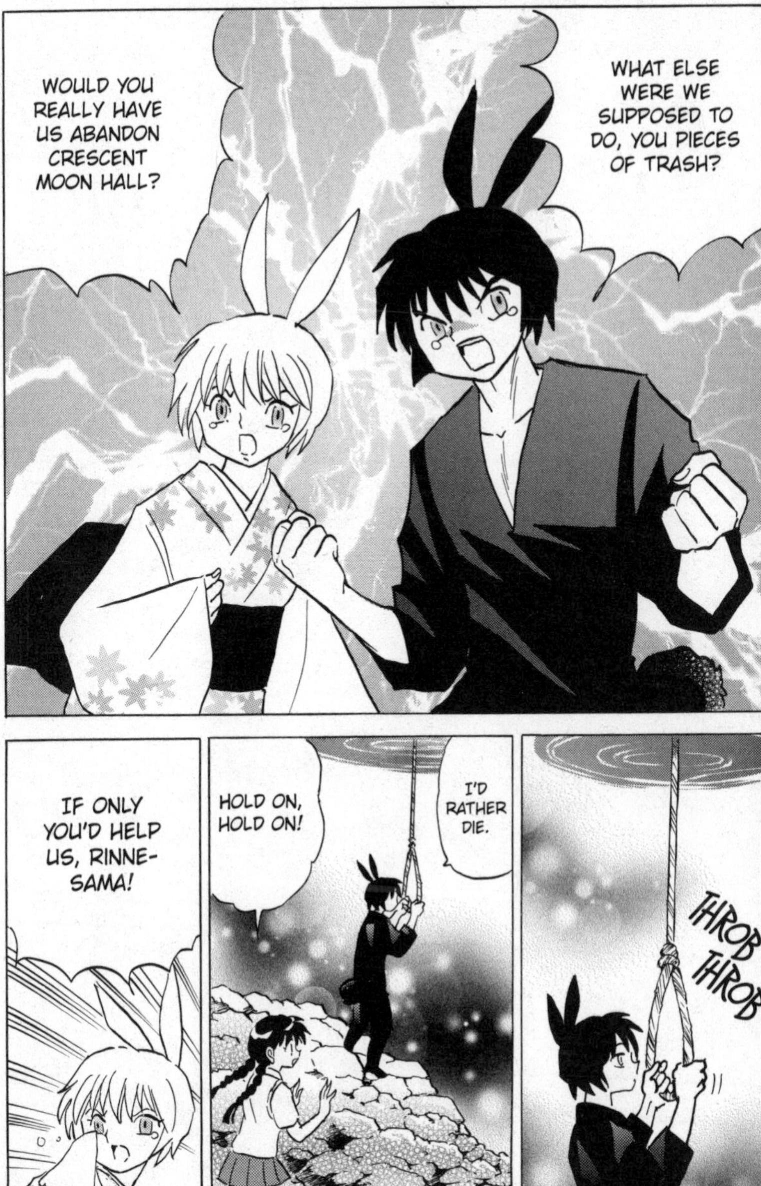
WHAT ELSE WERE WE SUPPOSED TO DO, YOU PIECES OF TRASH?
WOULD YOU REALLY HAVE US ABANDON CRESCENT MOON HALL?
THROB THROB
I'D RATHER DIE.
HOLD ON, HOLD ON!
IF ONLY YOU'D HELP US, RINNE-SAMA!

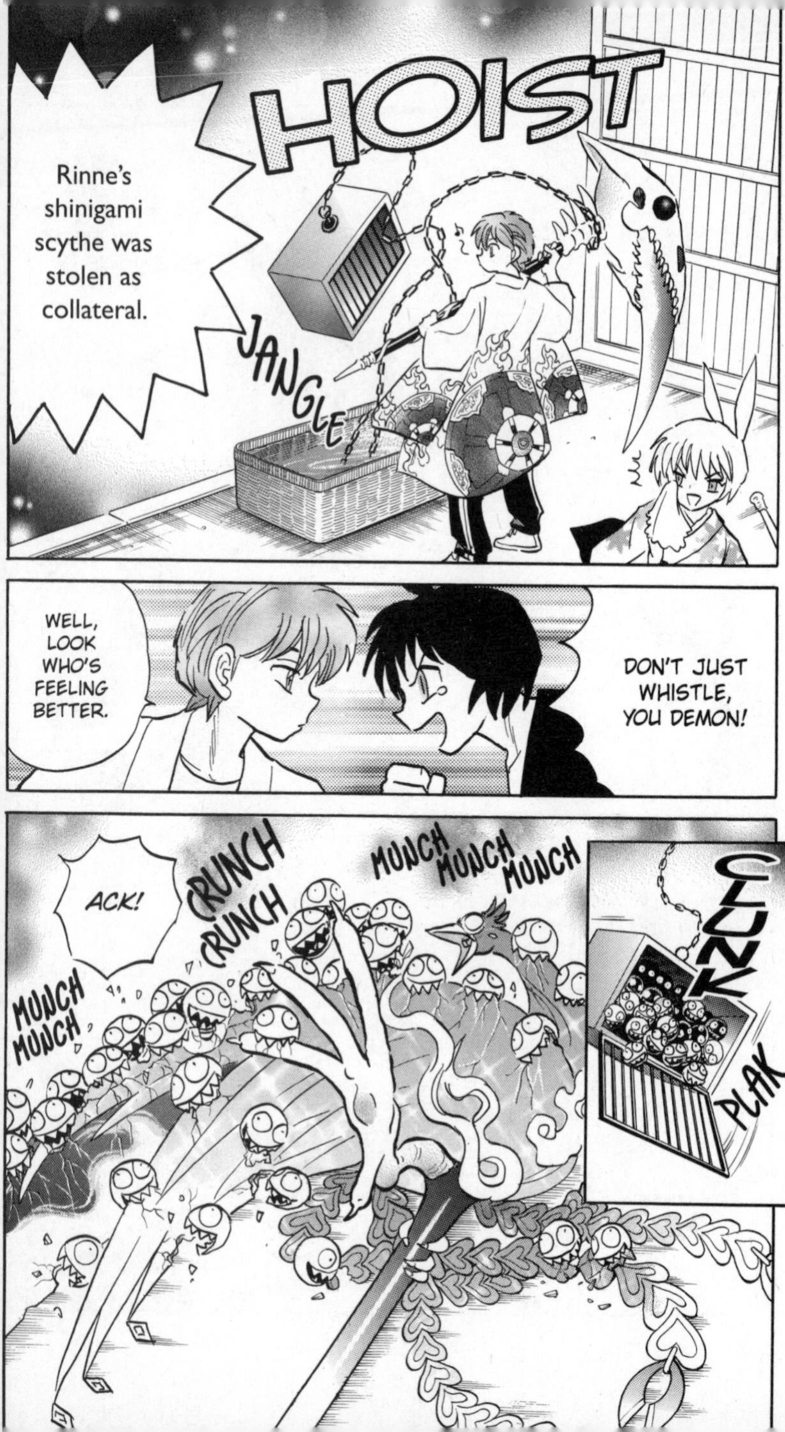
HOIST
Rinne's shinigami scythe was stolen as collateral.
JANGLE
DON'T JUST WHISTLE, YOU DEMON!
WELL, LOOK WHO'S FEELING BETTER.
CLUNK
PLAK
MUNCH MUNCH MUNCH
CRUNCH CRUNCH
ACK!
MUNCH MUNCH

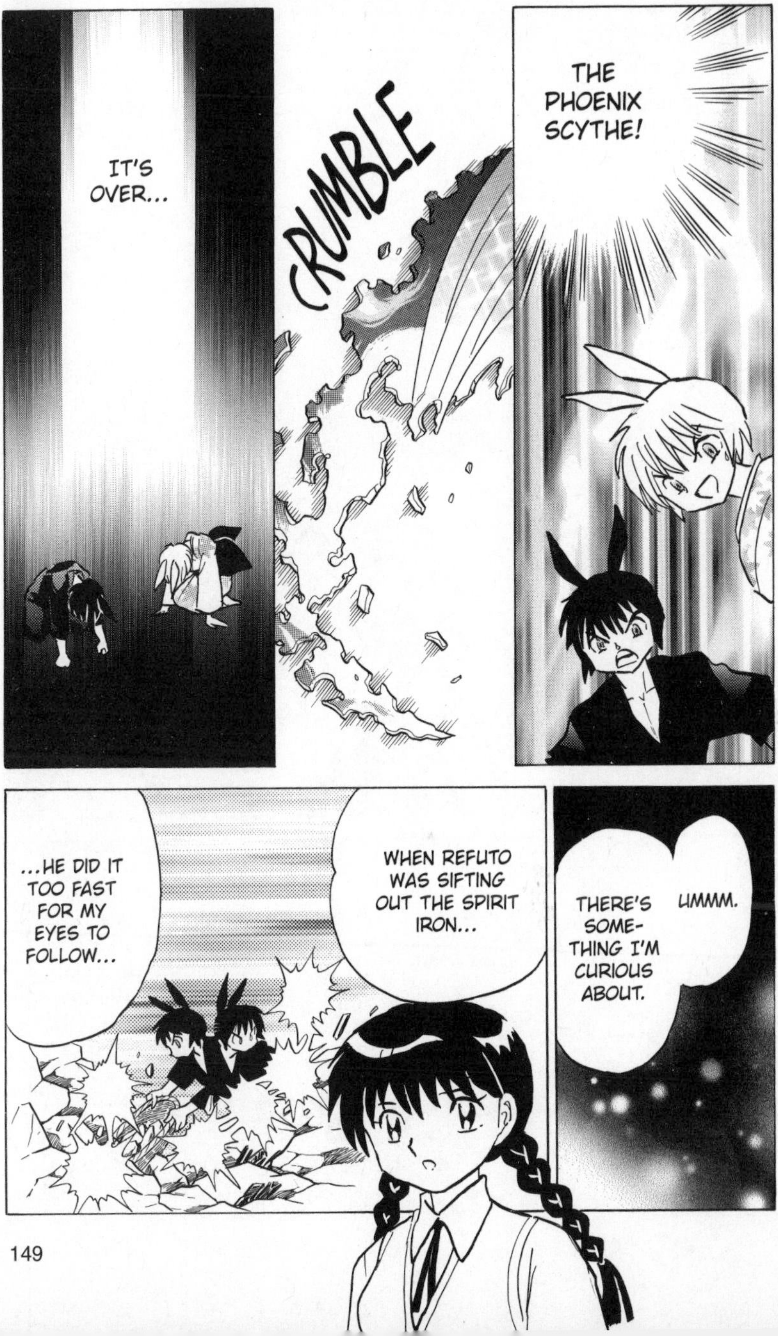
THE PHOENIX SCYTHE!
CRUMBLE
IT'S OVER...
UMMM.
THERE'S SOME-THING I'M CURIOUS ABOUT.
WHEN REFUTO WAS SIFTING OUT THE SPIRIT IRON...
...HE DID IT TOO FAST FOR MY EYES TO FOLLOW...

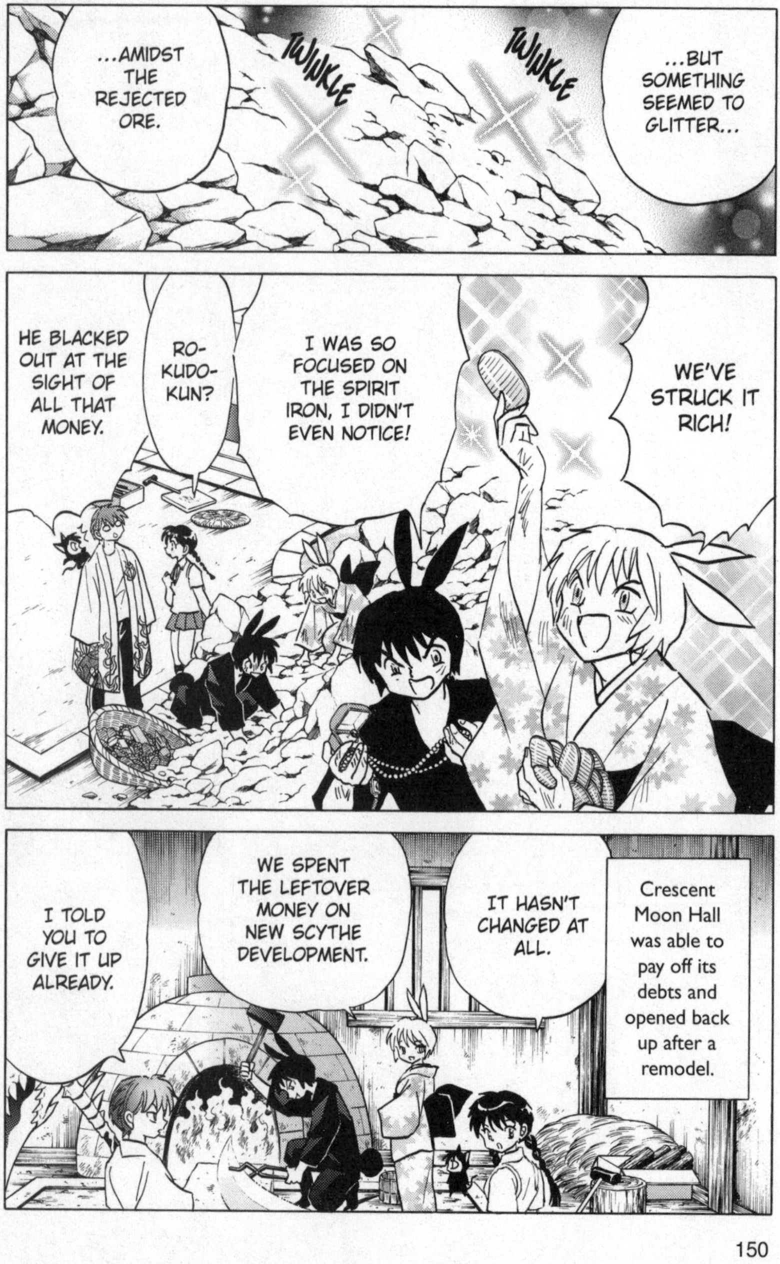
...BUT SOMETHING SEEMED TO GLITTER...
TWINKLE
TWINKLE
...AMIDST THE REJECTED ORE.
WE'VE STRUCK IT RICH!
I WAS SO FOCUSED ON THE SPIRIT IRON, I DIDN'T EVEN NOTICE!
RO-KUDO-KUN?
HE BLACKED OUT AT THE SIGHT OF ALL THAT MONEY.
Crescent Moon Hall was able to pay off its debts and opened back up after a remodel.
IT HASN'T CHANGED AT ALL.
WE SPENT THE LEFTOVER MONEY ON NEW SCYTHE DEVELOPMENT.
I TOLD YOU TO GIVE IT UP ALREADY.

CHAPTER 377: SOMETHING FELL IN THE POOL

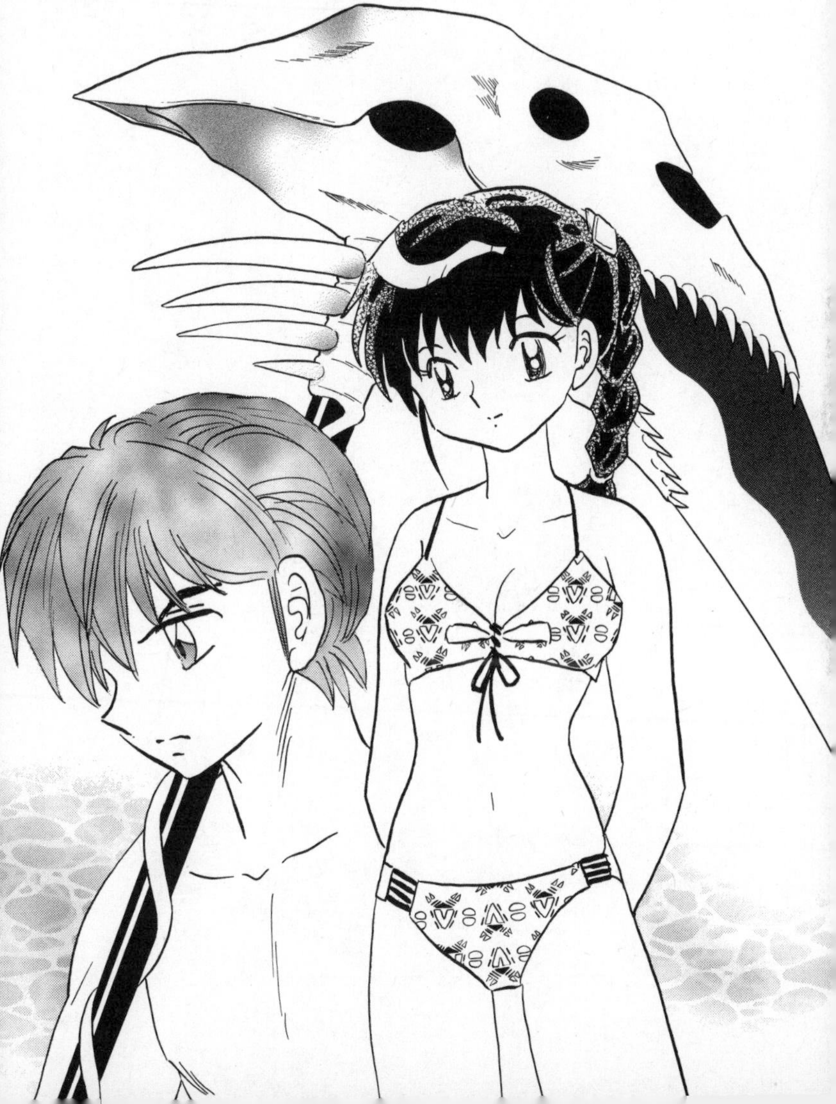

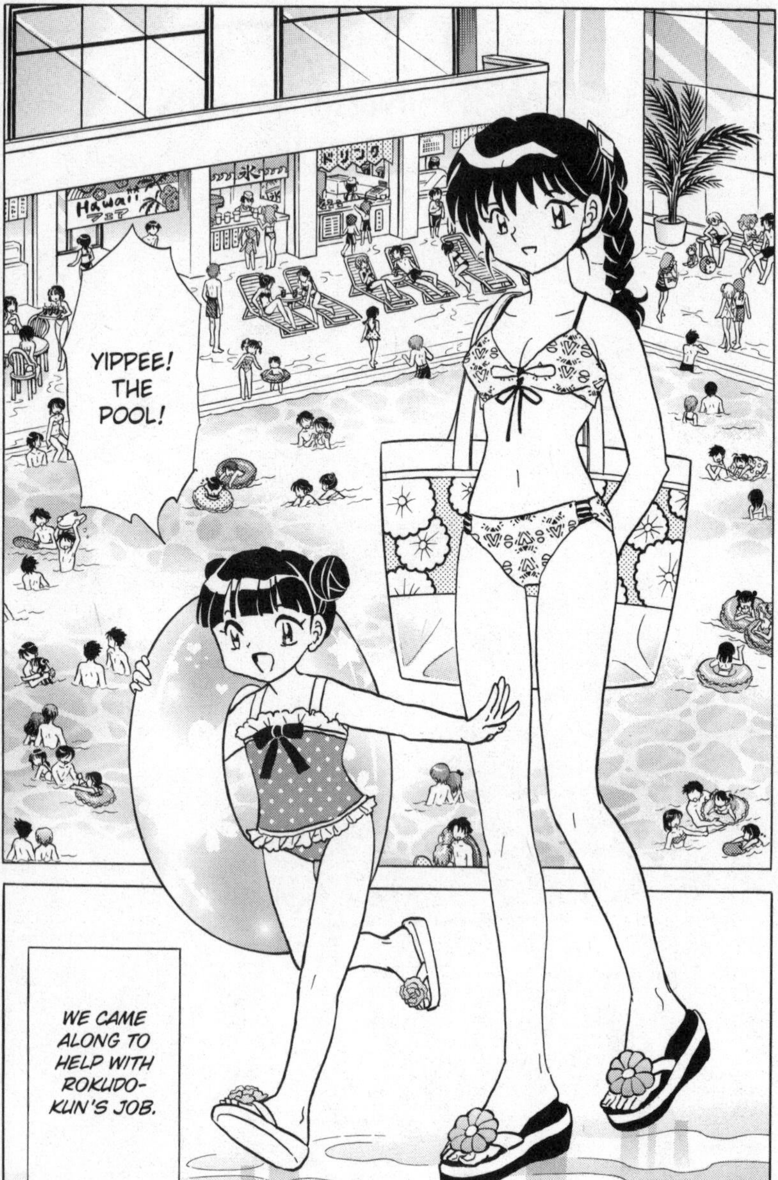
YIPPEE! THE POOL!
WE CAME ALONG TO HELP WITH ROKUDO-KUN'S JOB.

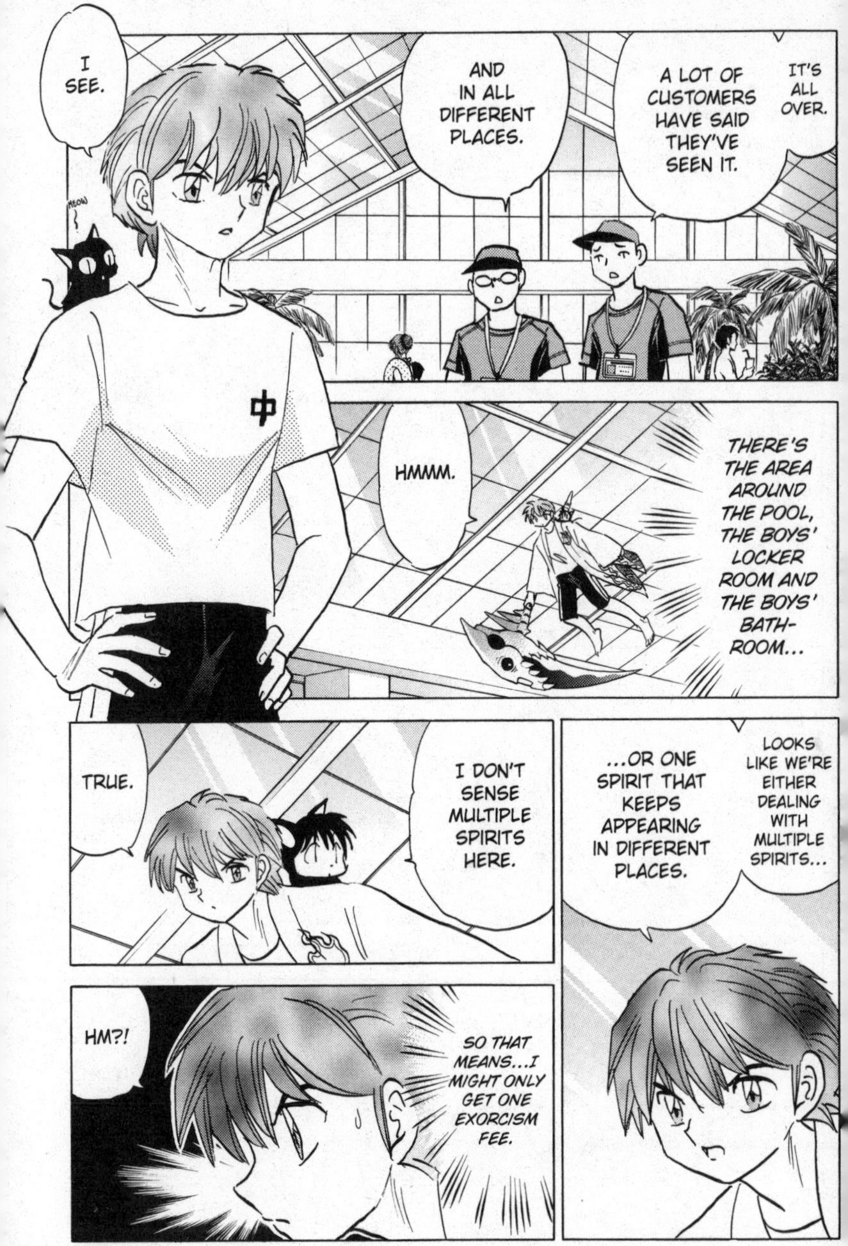
IT'S ALL OVER.
A LOT OF CUSTOMERS HAVE SAID THEY'VE SEEN IT.
AND IN ALL DIFFERENT PLACES.
THERE'S THE AREA AROUND THE POOL, THE BOYS' LOCKER ROOM AND THE BOYS' BATH-ROOM...
HMMM.
I SEE.
MEOW
LOOKS LIKE WE'RE EITHER DEALING WITH MULTIPLE SPIRITS...
...OR ONE SPIRIT THAT KEEPS APPEARING IN DIFFERENT PLACES.
I DON'T SENSE MULTIPLE SPIRITS HERE.
TRUE.
SO THAT MEANS...I MIGHT ONLY GET ONE EXORCISM FEE.
HM?!

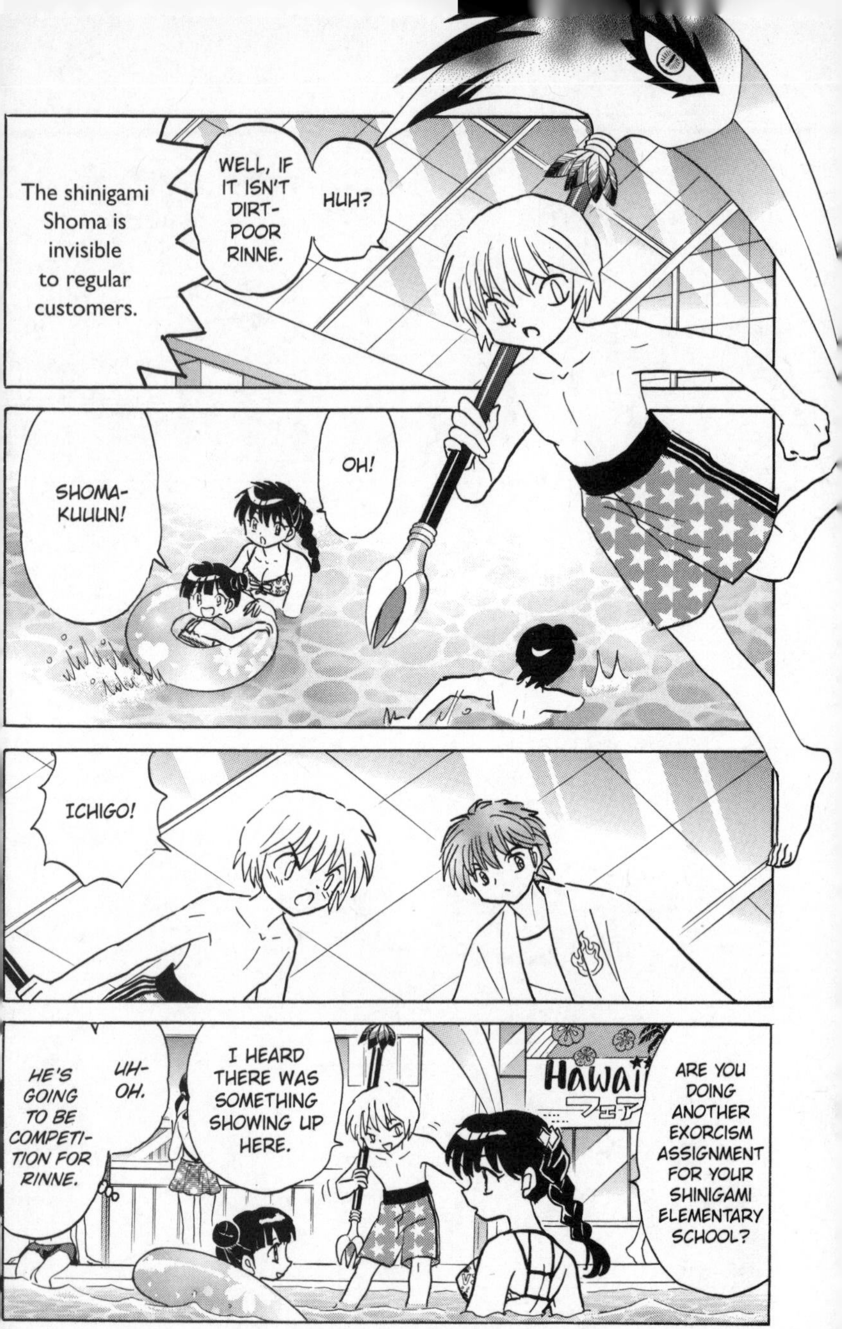
HUH?
WELL, IF IT ISN'T DIRT-POOR RINNE.
The shinigami Shoma is invisible to regular customers.
OH!
SHOMA-KUUUN!
ICHIGO!
ARE YOU DOING ANOTHER EXORCISM ASSIGNMENT FOR YOUR SHINIGAMI ELEMENTARY SCHOOL?
Hawai
フェア
I HEARD THERE WAS SOMETHING SHOWING UP HERE.
UH-OH.
HE'S GOING TO BE COMPETITION FOR RINNE.

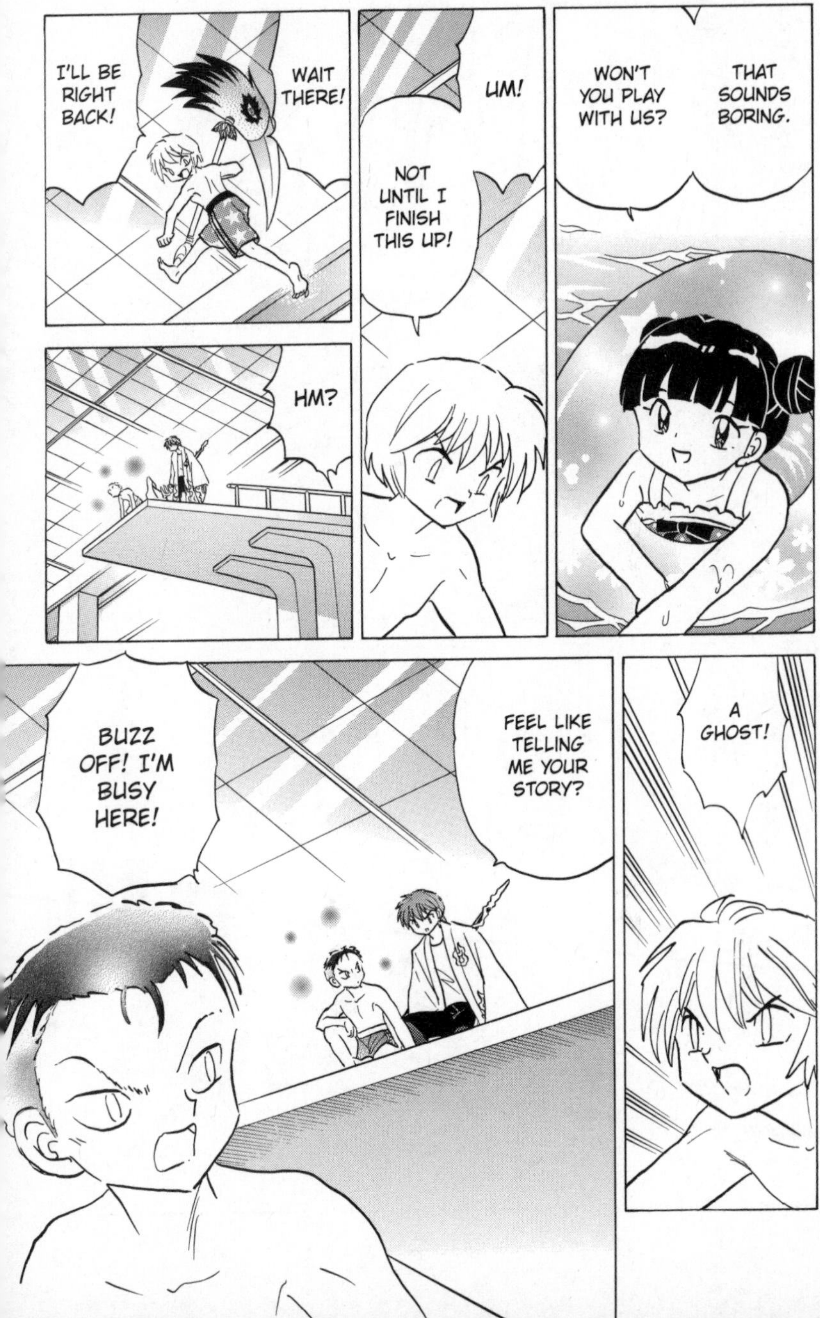
THAT SOUNDS BORING.
WON'T YOU PLAY WITH US?
UM!
NOT UNTIL I FINISH THIS UP!
WAIT THERE!
I'LL BE RIGHT BACK!
HM?
A GHOST!
FEEL LIKE TELLING ME YOUR STORY?
BUZZ OFF! I'M BUSY HERE!

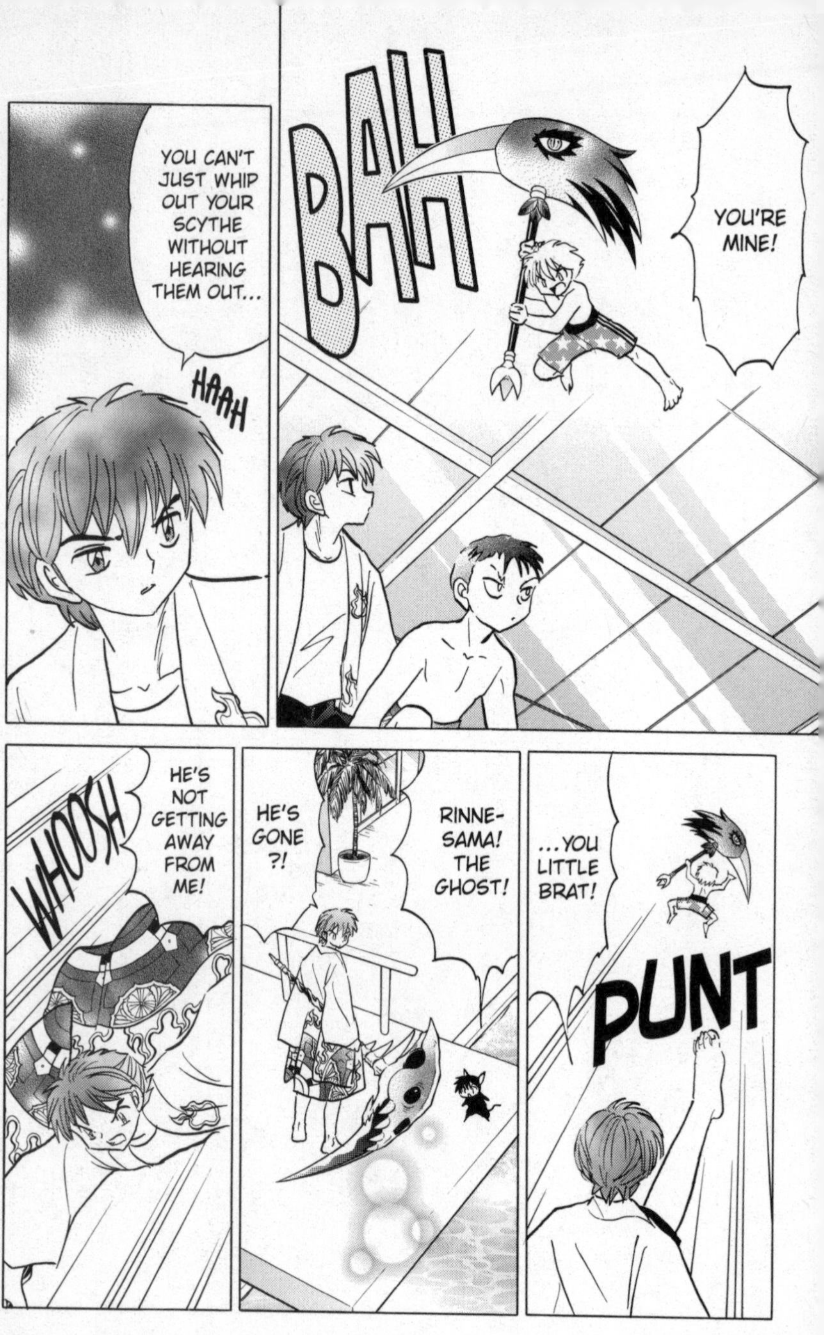
YOU'RE MINE!
BAH
YOU CAN'T JUST WHIP OUT YOUR SCYTHE WITHOUT HEARING THEM OUT...
HAAH
...YOU LITTLE BRAT!
PUNT
RINNE-SAMA! THE GHOST!
HE'S GONE?!
HE'S NOT GETTING AWAY FROM ME!
WHOOSH

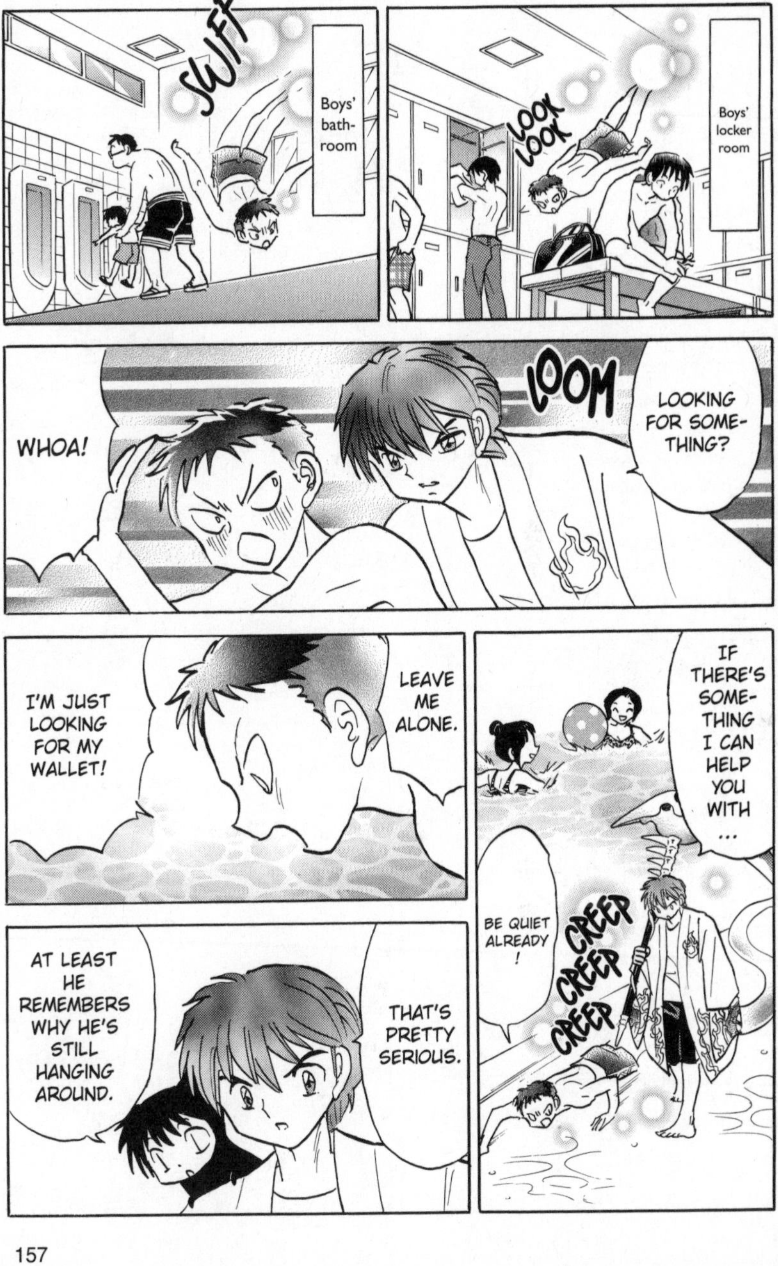
Boys' locker room
LOOK LOOK
Boys' bathroom
SWFF
LOOM
LOOKING FOR SOMETHING?
WHOA!
IF THERE'S SOMETHING I CAN HELP YOU WITH...
BE QUIET ALREADY!
CREEP CREEP CREEP
LEAVE ME ALONE.
I'M JUST LOOKING FOR MY WALLET!
THAT'S PRETTY SERIOUS.
AT LEAST HE REMEMBERS WHY HE'S STILL HANGING AROUND.

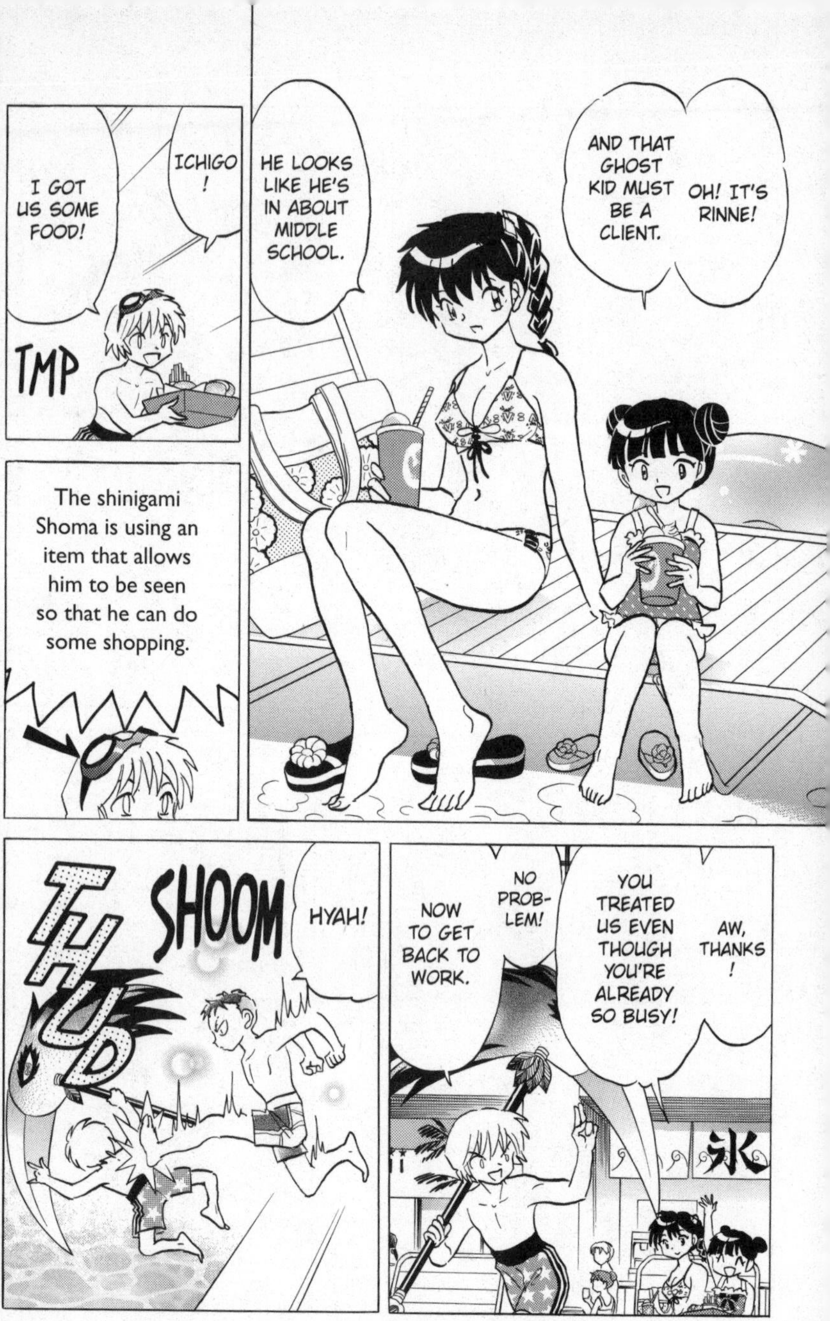
OH! IT'S RINNE!
AND THAT GHOST KID MUST BE A CLIENT.
HE LOOKS LIKE HE'S IN ABOUT MIDDLE SCHOOL.
ICHIGO!
I GOT US SOME FOOD!
TMP
The shinigami Shoma is using an item that allows him to be seen so that he can do some shopping.
AW, THANKS!
YOU TREATED US EVEN THOUGH YOU'RE ALREADY SO BUSY!
NO PROB-LEM!
NOW TO GET BACK TO WORK.
氷
HYAH!
SHOOM
THUD

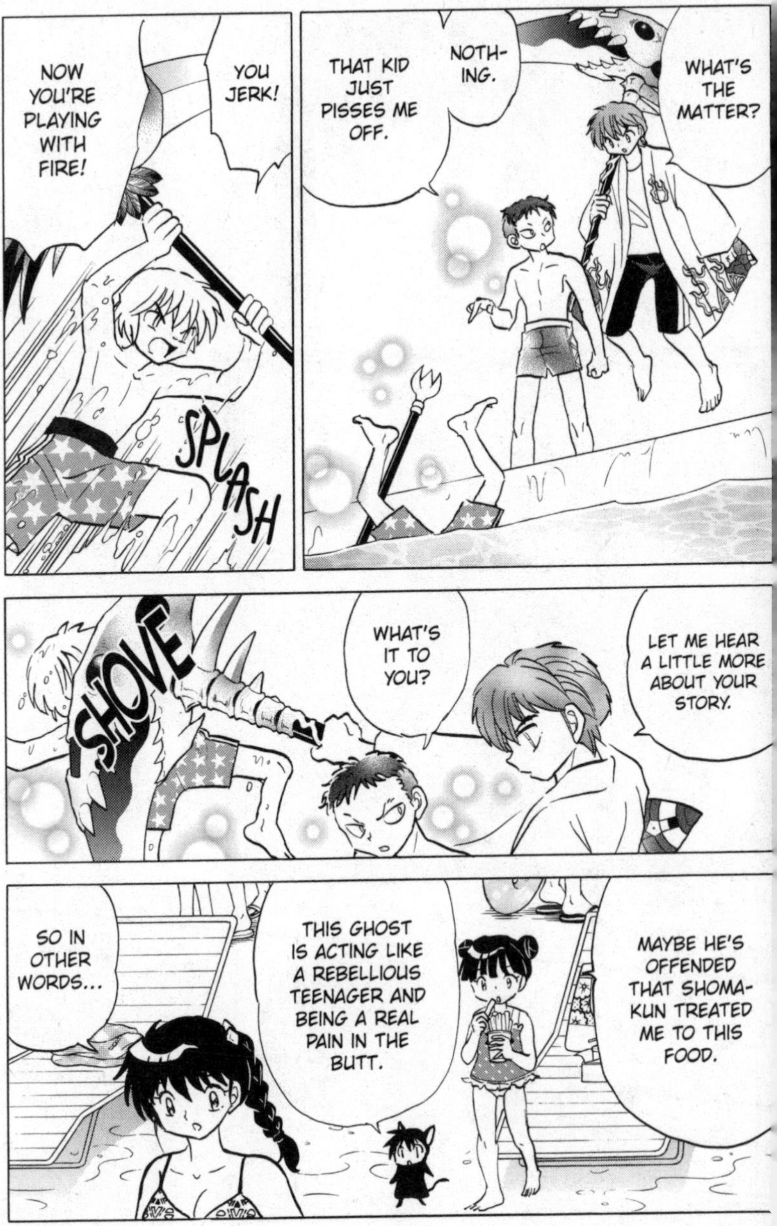
WHAT'S THE MATTER?
NOTH-ING.
THAT KID JUST PISSES ME OFF.
YOU JERK!
NOW YOU'RE PLAYING WITH FIRE!
SPLASH
LET ME HEAR A LITTLE MORE ABOUT YOUR STORY.
WHAT'S IT TO YOU?
SHOVE
MAYBE HE'S OFFENDED THAT SHOMA-KUN TREATED ME TO THIS FOOD.
THIS GHOST IS ACTING LIKE A REBELLIOUS TEENAGER AND BEING A REAL PAIN IN THE BUTT.
SO IN OTHER WORDS...

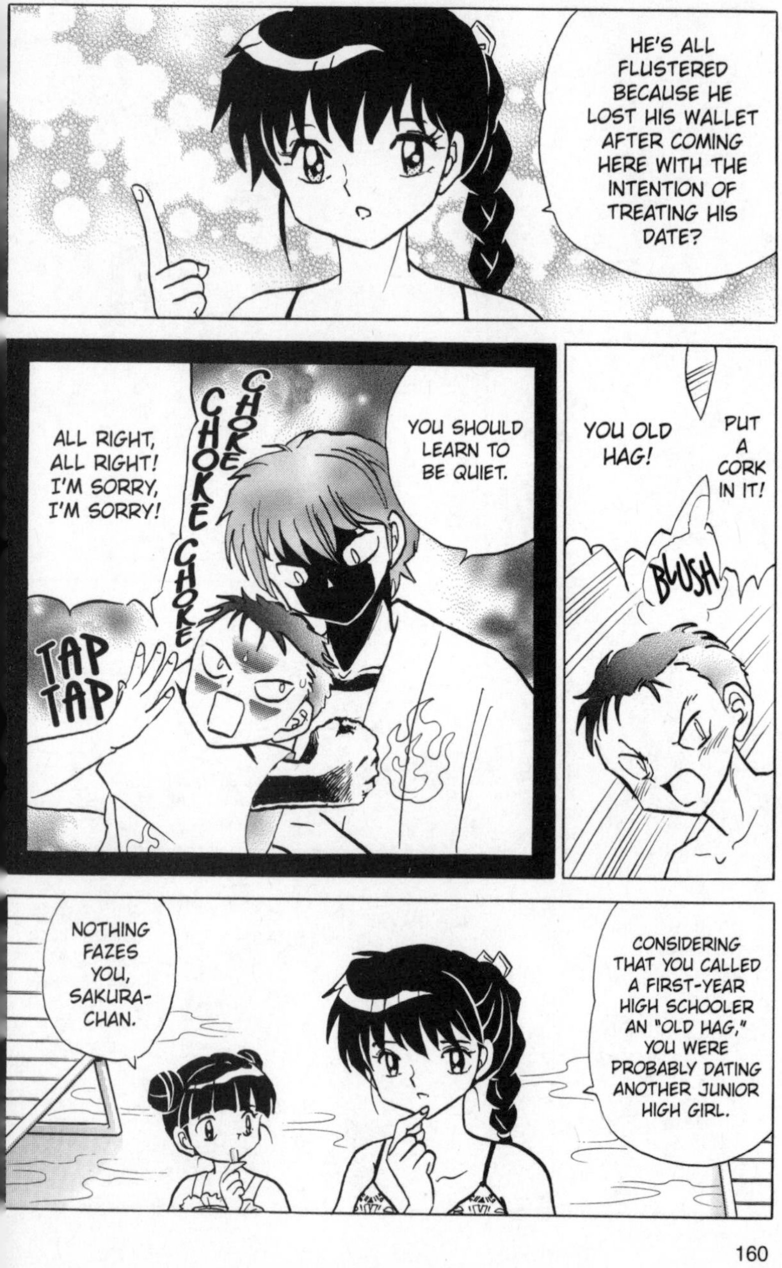
HE'S ALL FLUSTERED BECAUSE HE LOST HIS WALLET AFTER COMING HERE WITH THE INTENTION OF TREATING HIS DATE?
PUT A CORK IN IT!
YOU OLD HAG!
BLUSH
YOU SHOULD LEARN TO BE QUIET.
CHOKE CHOKE
CHOKE CHOKE
ALL RIGHT, ALL RIGHT! I'M SORRY, I'M SORRY!
TAP TAP
CONSIDERING THAT YOU CALLED A FIRST-YEAR HIGH SCHOOLER AN "OLD HAG," YOU WERE PROBABLY DATING ANOTHER JUNIOR HIGH GIRL.
NOTHING FAZES YOU, SAKURA-CHAN.

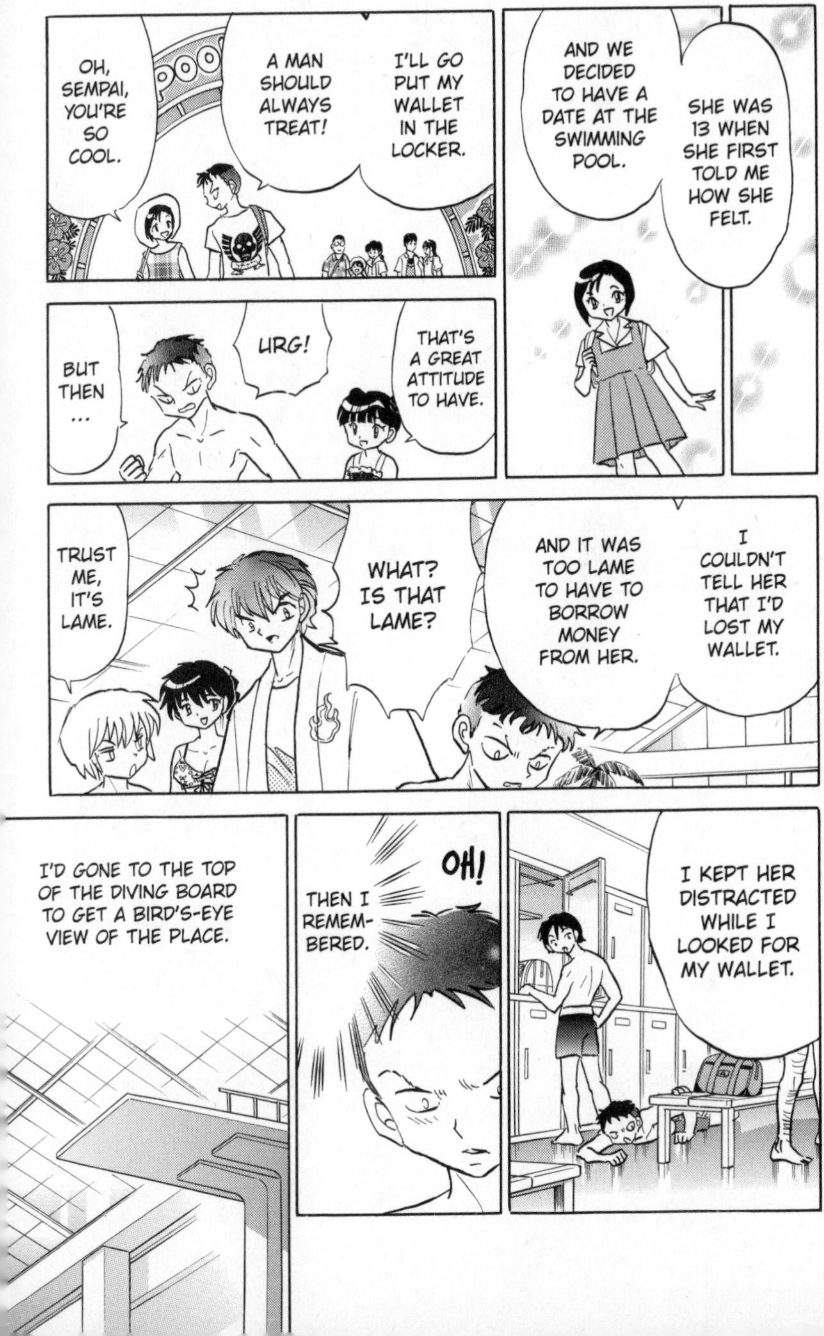

SHE WAS 13 WHEN SHE FIRST TOLD ME HOW SHE FELT.
AND WE DECIDED TO HAVE A DATE AT THE SWIMMING POOL.
I'LL GO PUT MY WALLET IN THE LOCKER.
A MAN SHOULD ALWAYS TREAT!
OH, SEMPAI, YOU'RE SO COOL.
POOL
THAT'S A GREAT ATTITUDE TO HAVE.
URG!
BUT THEN ...
I COULDN'T TELL HER THAT I'D LOST MY WALLET.
AND IT WAS TOO LAME TO HAVE TO BORROW MONEY FROM HER.
WHAT? IS THAT LAME?
TRUST ME, IT'S LAME.
I KEPT HER DISTRACTED WHILE I LOOKED FOR MY WALLET.
OH!
THEN I REMEM-BERED.
I'D GONE TO THE TOP OF THE DIVING BOARD TO GET A BIRD'S-EYE VIEW OF THE PLACE.

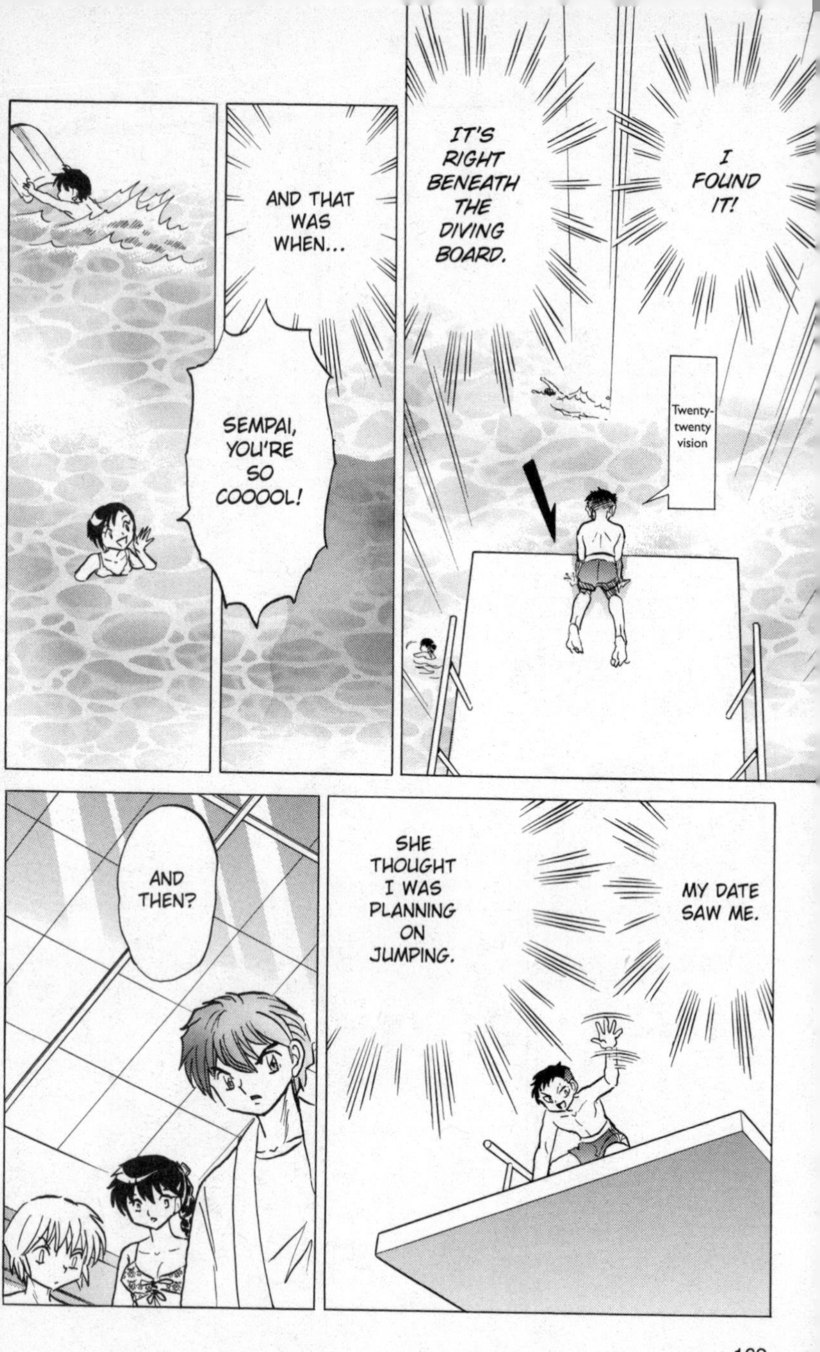
I FOUND IT!
IT'S RIGHT BENEATH THE DIVING BOARD.
Twenty-twenty vision
AND THAT WAS WHEN...
SEMPAI, YOU'RE SO COOOOL!
MY DATE SAW ME.
SHE THOUGHT I WAS PLANNING ON JUMPING.
AND THEN?

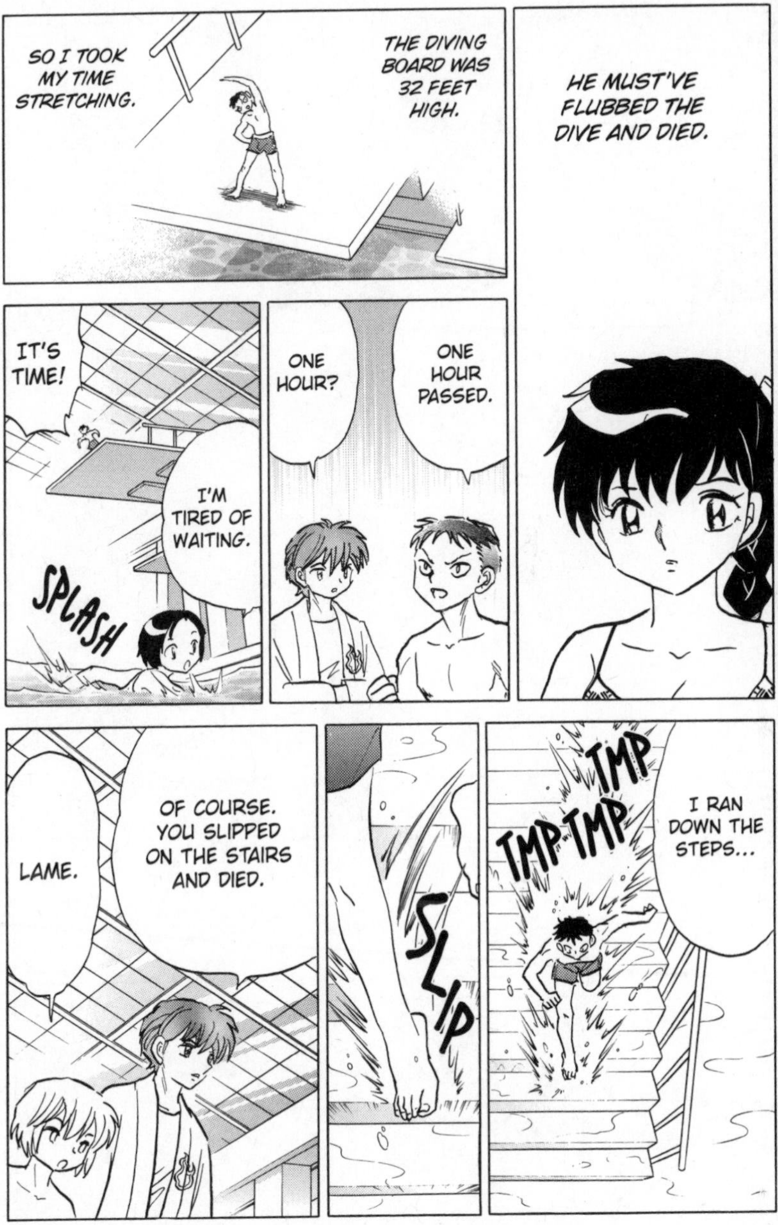
HE MUST'VE FLUBBED THE DIVE AND DIED.
THE DIVING BOARD WAS 32 FEET HIGH.
SO I TOOK MY TIME STRETCHING.
ONE HOUR PASSED.
ONE HOUR?
IT'S TIME!
I'M TIRED OF WAITING.
SPLASH
I RAN DOWN THE STEPS...
TMP TMP TMP
SLIP
OF COURSE. YOU SLIPPED ON THE STAIRS AND DIED.
LAME.

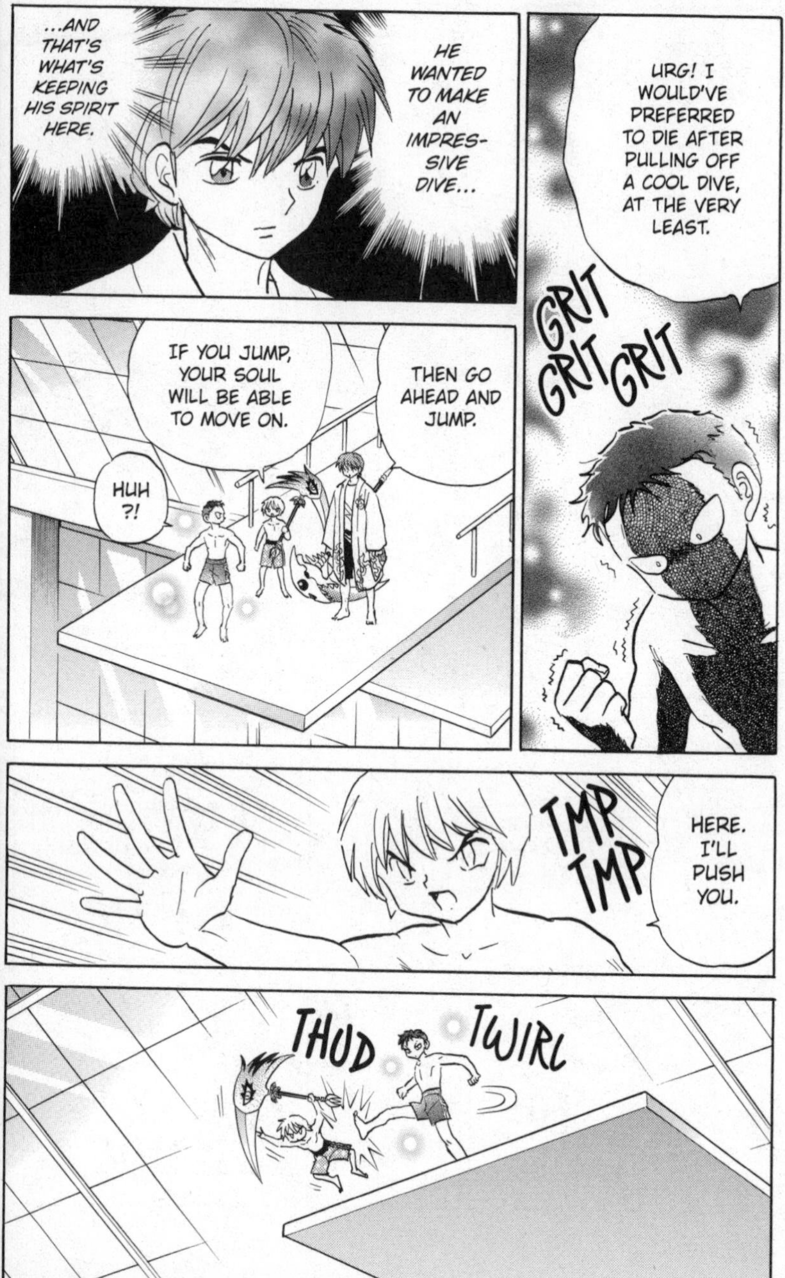
URG! I WOULD'VE PREFERRED TO DIE AFTER PULLING OFF A COOL DIVE, AT THE VERY LEAST.
GRIT GRIT GRIT
HE WANTED TO MAKE AN IMPRES-SIVE DIVE...
...AND THAT'S WHAT'S KEEPING HIS SPIRIT HERE.
THEN GO AHEAD AND JUMP.
IF YOU JUMP, YOUR SOUL WILL BE ABLE TO MOVE ON.
HUH ?!
HERE. I'LL PUSH YOU.
TMP TMP
TWIRL
THUD

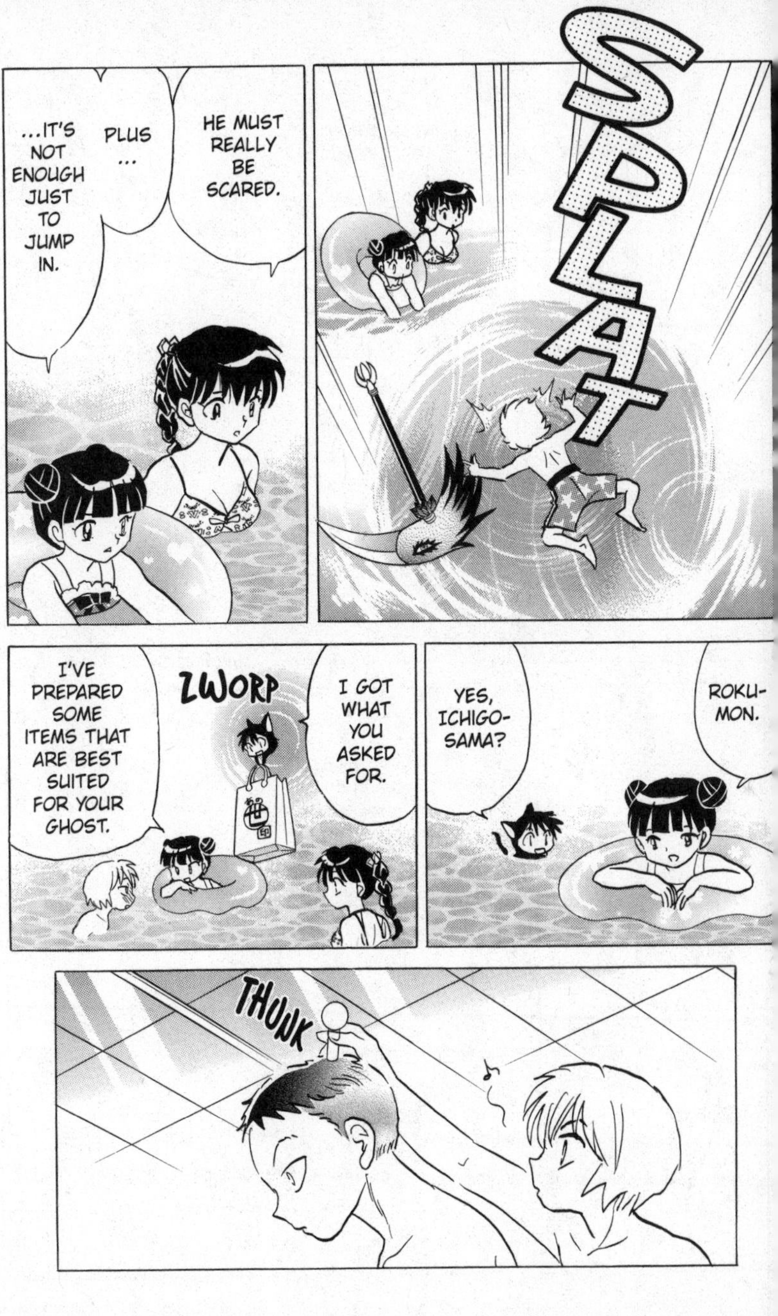
SPLAT
HE MUST REALLY BE SCARED.
PLUS ...
...IT'S NOT ENOUGH JUST TO JUMP IN.
ROKU-MON.
YES, ICHIGO-SAMA?
I GOT WHAT YOU ASKED FOR.
ZWORP
I'VE PREPARED SOME ITEMS THAT ARE BEST SUITED FOR YOUR GHOST.
THUNK

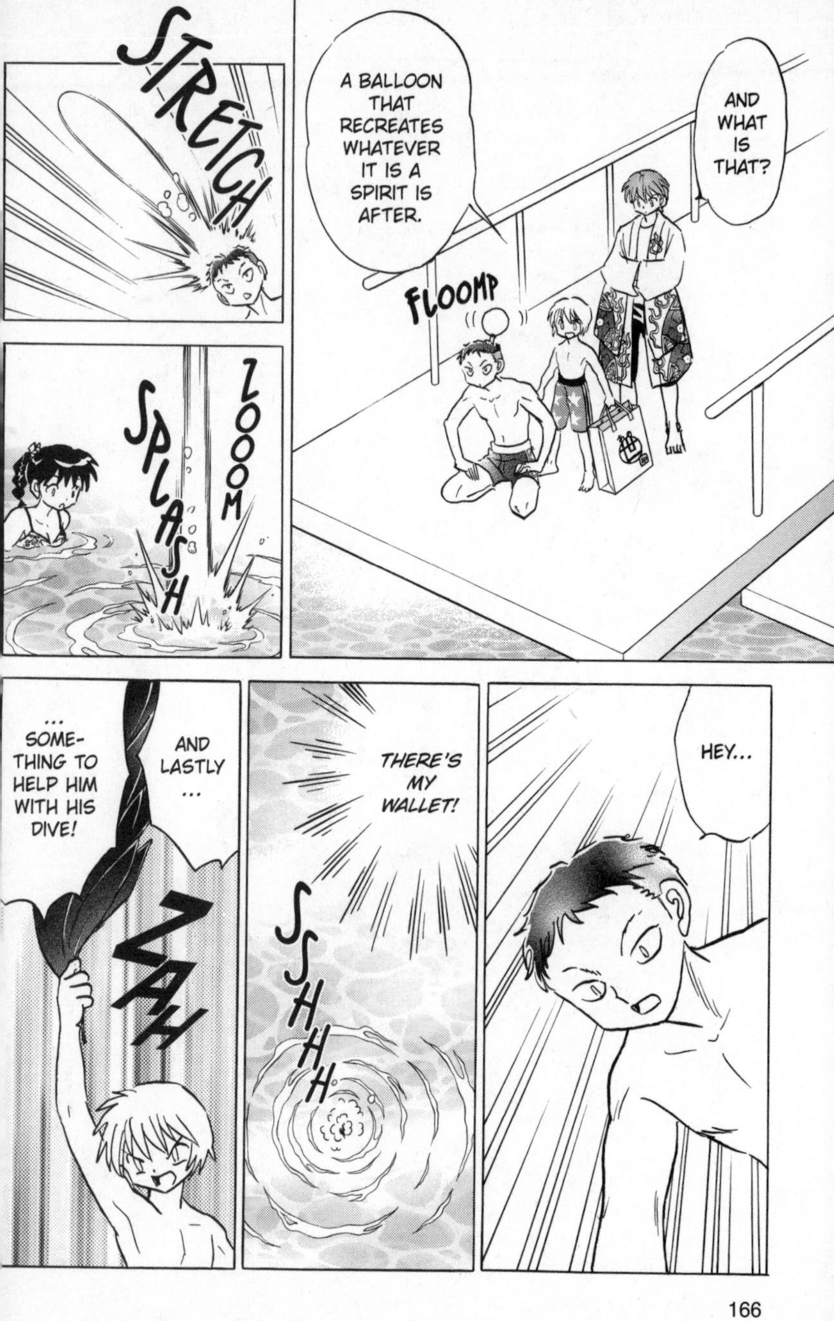
AND WHAT IS THAT?
A BALLOON THAT RECREATES WHATEVER IT IS A SPIRIT IS AFTER.
FLOOMP
STRETCH
ZOOOM
SPLASH
HEY...
THERE'S MY WALLET!
SSHHH
AND LASTLY...
...SOME-THING TO HELP HIM WITH HIS DIVE!
ZAH

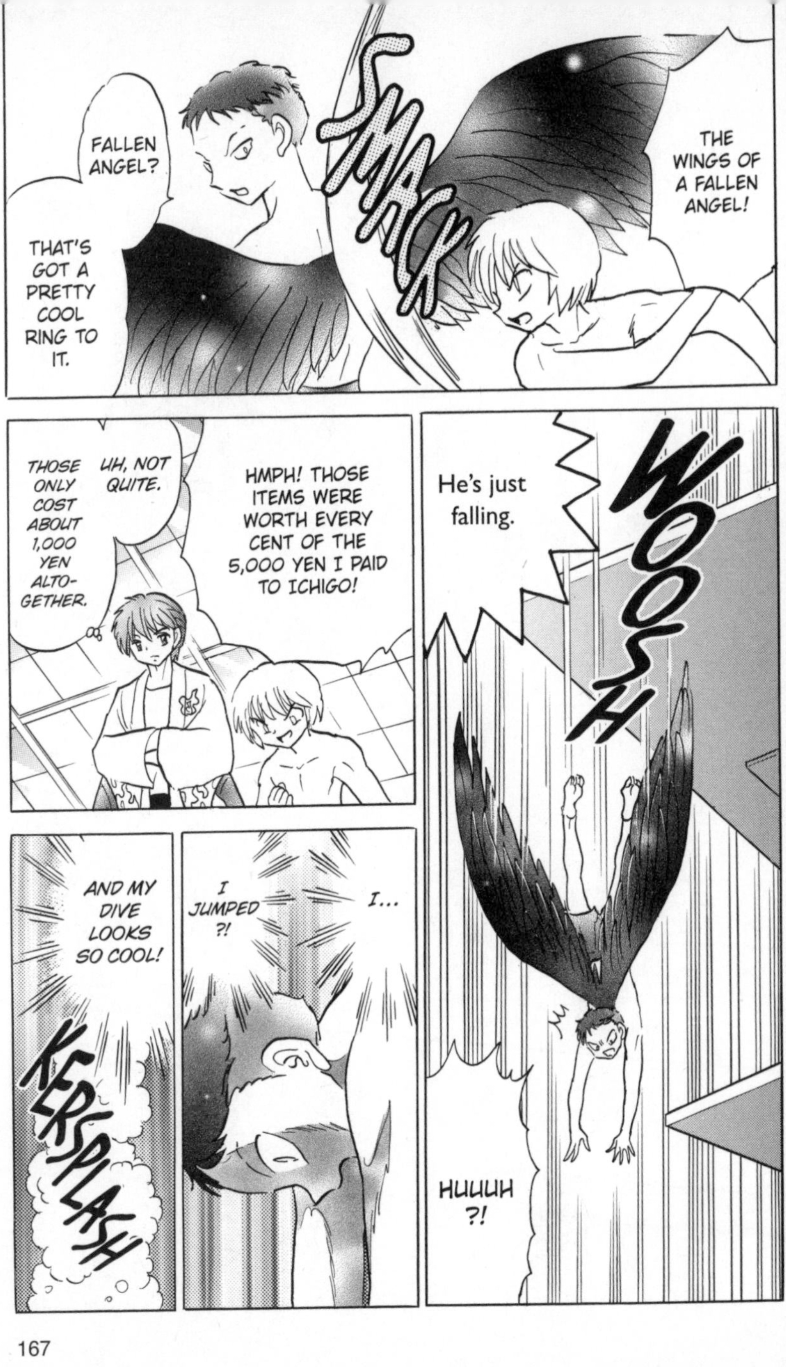
THE WINGS OF A FALLEN ANGEL!
SMACK
FALLEN ANGEL?
THAT'S GOT A PRETTY COOL RING TO IT.
He's just falling.
WOOSH
HUUUH ?!
HMPH! THOSE ITEMS WERE WORTH EVERY CENT OF THE 5,000 YEN I PAID TO ICHIGO!
UH, NOT QUITE.
THOSE ONLY COST ABOUT 1,000 YEN ALTOGETHER.
I...
I JUMPED ?!
AND MY DIVE LOOKS SO COOL!
KERSPLASH

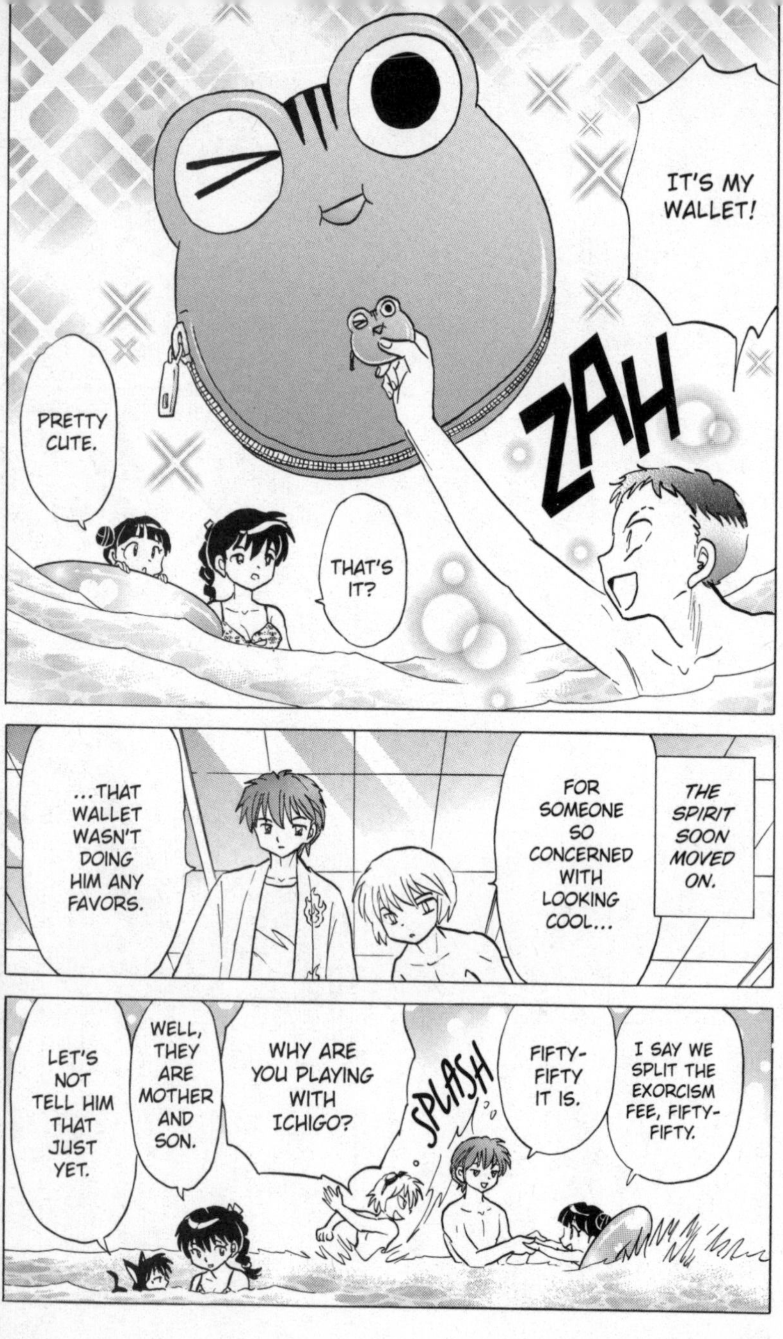
IT'S MY WALLET!
ZAH
THAT'S IT?
PRETTY CUTE.
THE SPIRIT SOON MOVED ON.
FOR SOMEONE SO CONCERNED WITH LOOKING COOL...
...THAT WALLET WASN'T DOING HIM ANY FAVORS.
I SAY WE SPLIT THE EXORCISM FEE, FIFTY-FIFTY.
FIFTY-FIFTY IT IS.
SPLASH
WHY ARE YOU PLAYING WITH ICHIGO?
WELL, THEY ARE MOTHER AND SON.
LET'S NOT TELL HIM THAT JUST YET.

CHAPTER 378:
DRESS FROM THE FUTURE

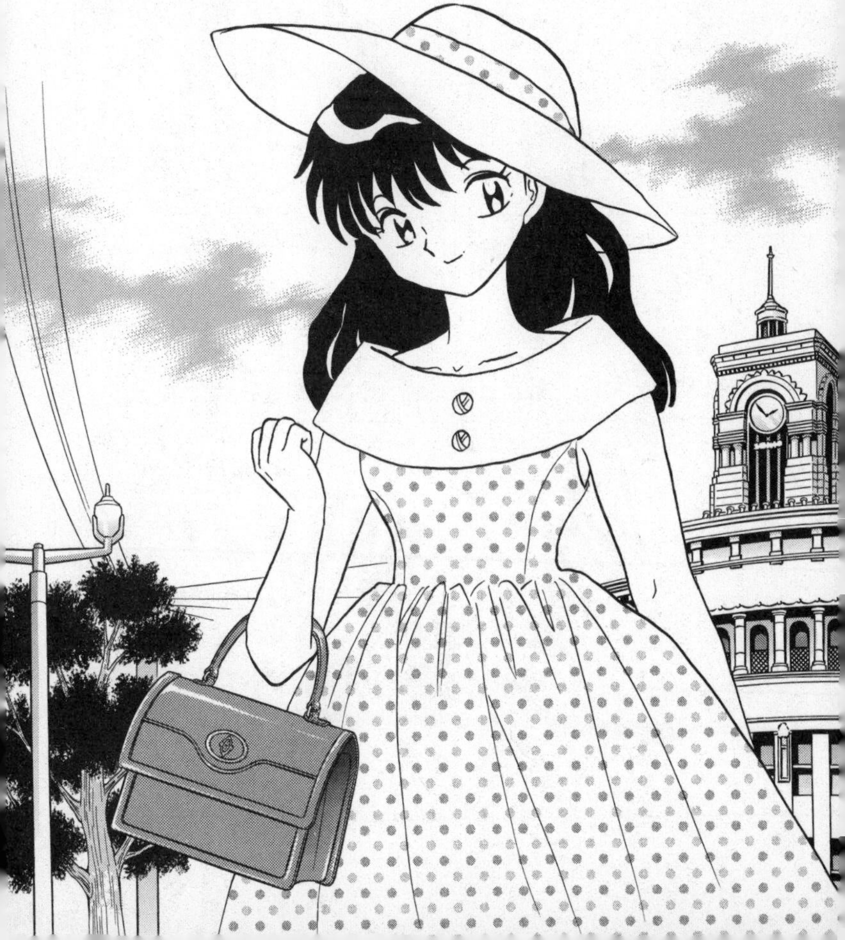

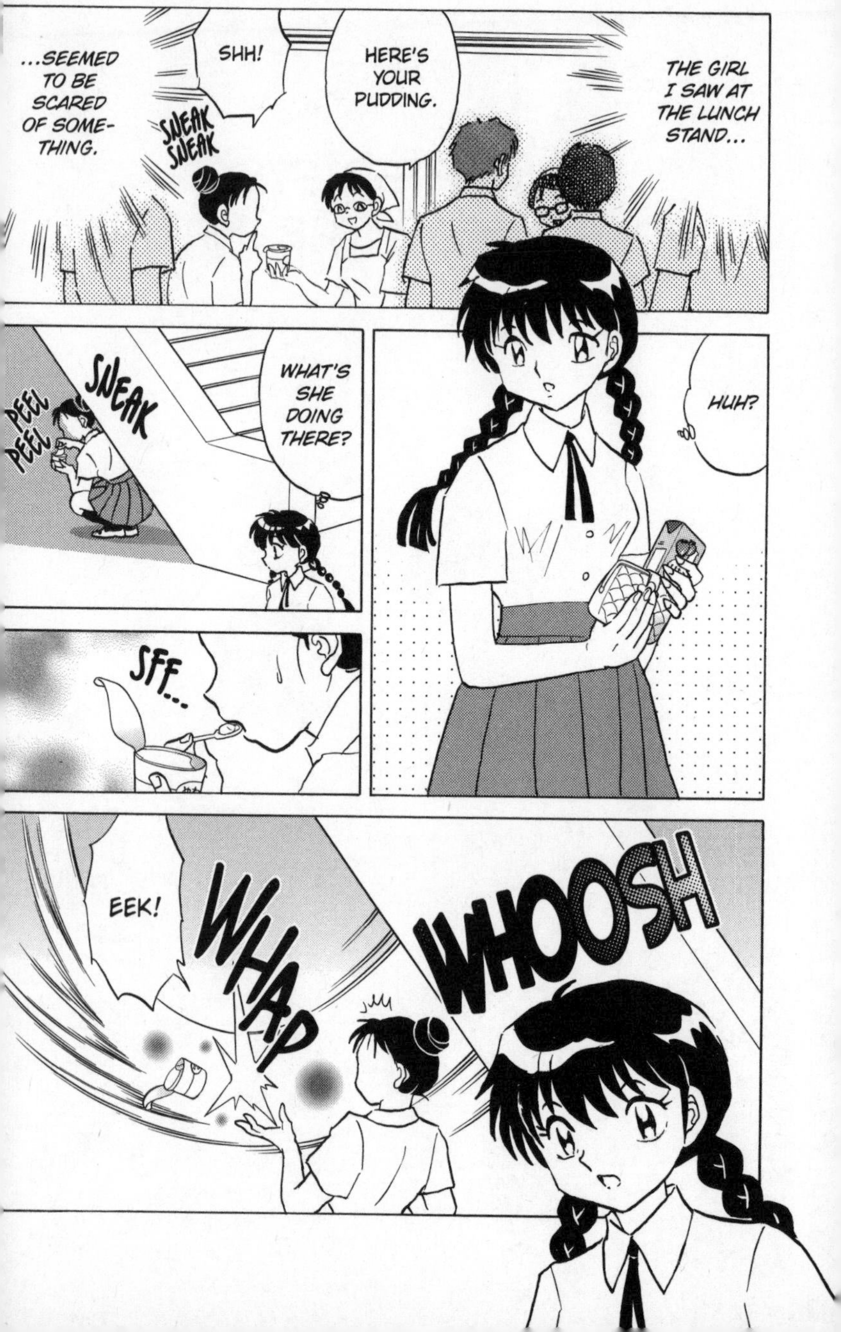
THE GIRL I SAW AT THE LUNCH STAND...
HERE'S YOUR PUDDING.
SHH!
SNEAK SNEAK
...SEEMED TO BE SCARED OF SOME-THING.
HUH?
WHAT'S SHE DOING THERE?
SNEAK
PEEL PEEL
SFF...
WHOOSH
WHAP
EEK!

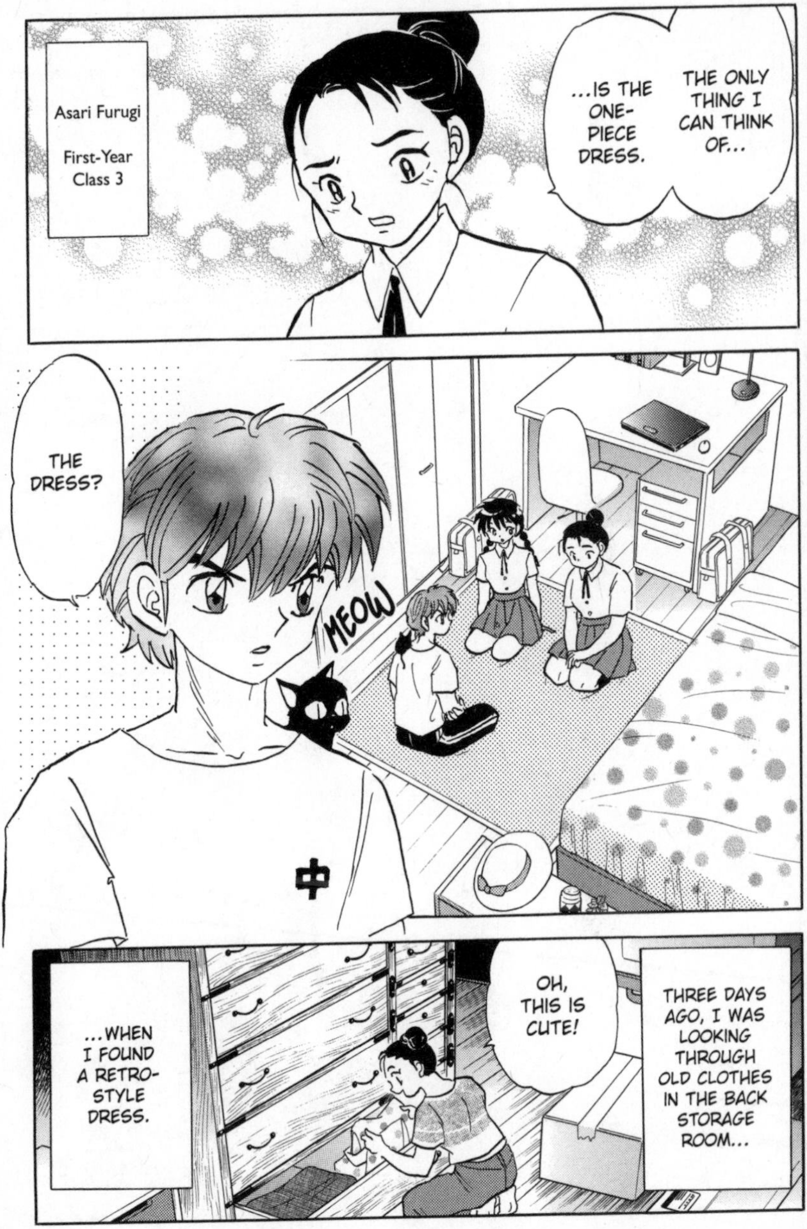
THE ONLY THING I CAN THINK OF...
...IS THE ONE-PIECE DRESS.
Asari Furugi
First-Year Class 3
THE DRESS?
MEOW
THREE DAYS AGO, I WAS LOOKING THROUGH OLD CLOTHES IN THE BACK STORAGE ROOM...
OH, THIS IS CUTE!
...WHEN I FOUND A RETRO-STYLE DRESS.

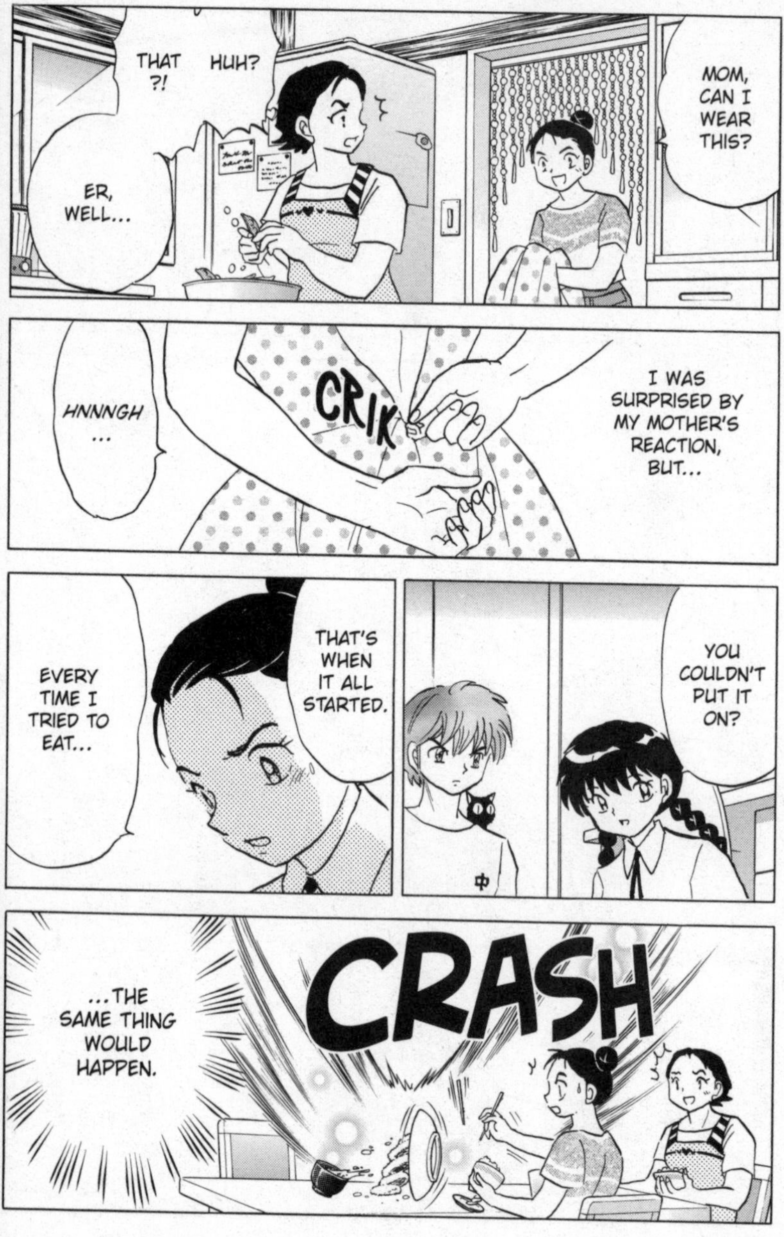
MOM, CAN I WEAR THIS?
HUH?
THAT ?!
ER, WELL...
I WAS SURPRISED BY MY MOTHER'S REACTION, BUT...
CRIK
HNNNGH ...
YOU COULDN'T PUT IT ON?
THAT'S WHEN IT ALL STARTED.
EVERY TIME I TRIED TO EAT...
CRASH
...THE SAME THING WOULD HAPPEN.

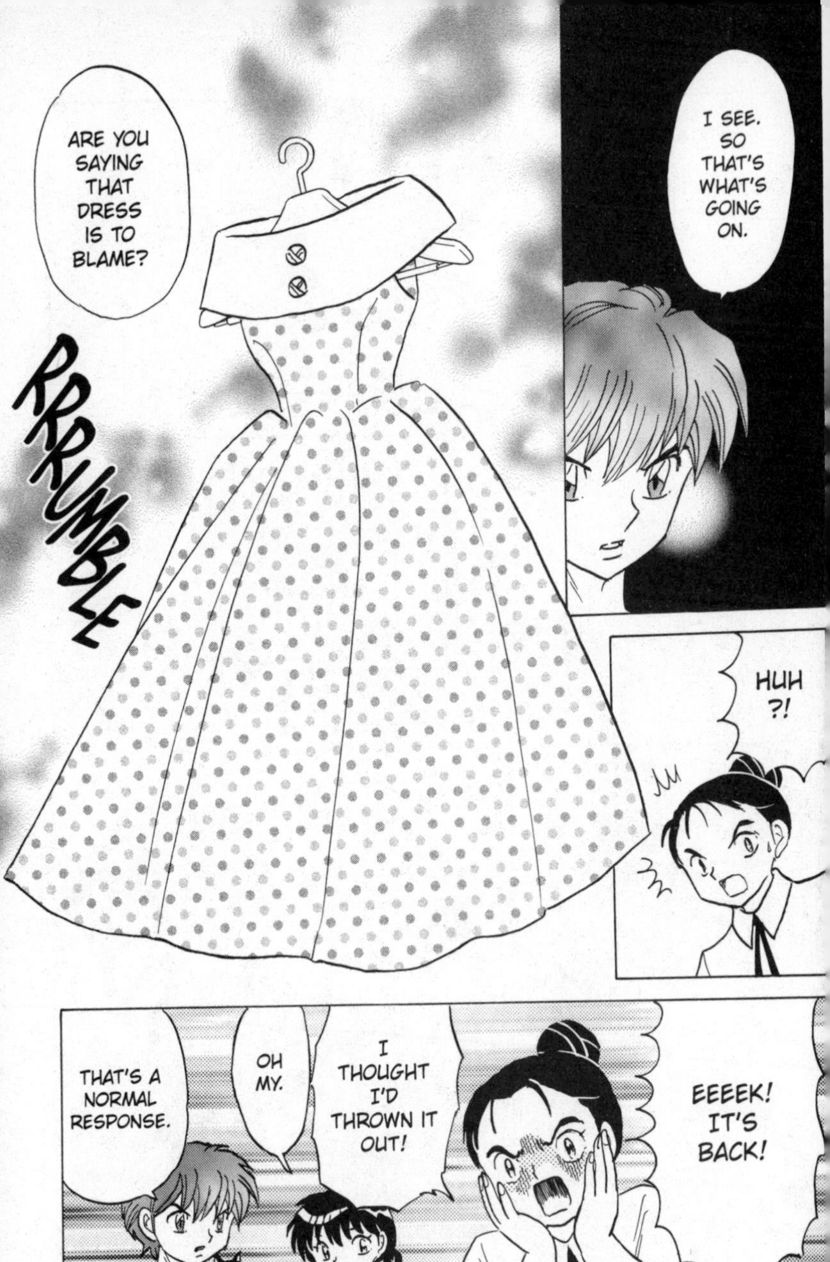
I SEE. SO THAT'S WHAT'S GOING ON.
HUH ?!
ARE YOU SAYING THAT DRESS IS TO BLAME?
RRRUMBLE
EEEEK! IT'S BACK!
I THOUGHT I'D THROWN IT OUT!
OH MY.
THAT'S A NORMAL RESPONSE.

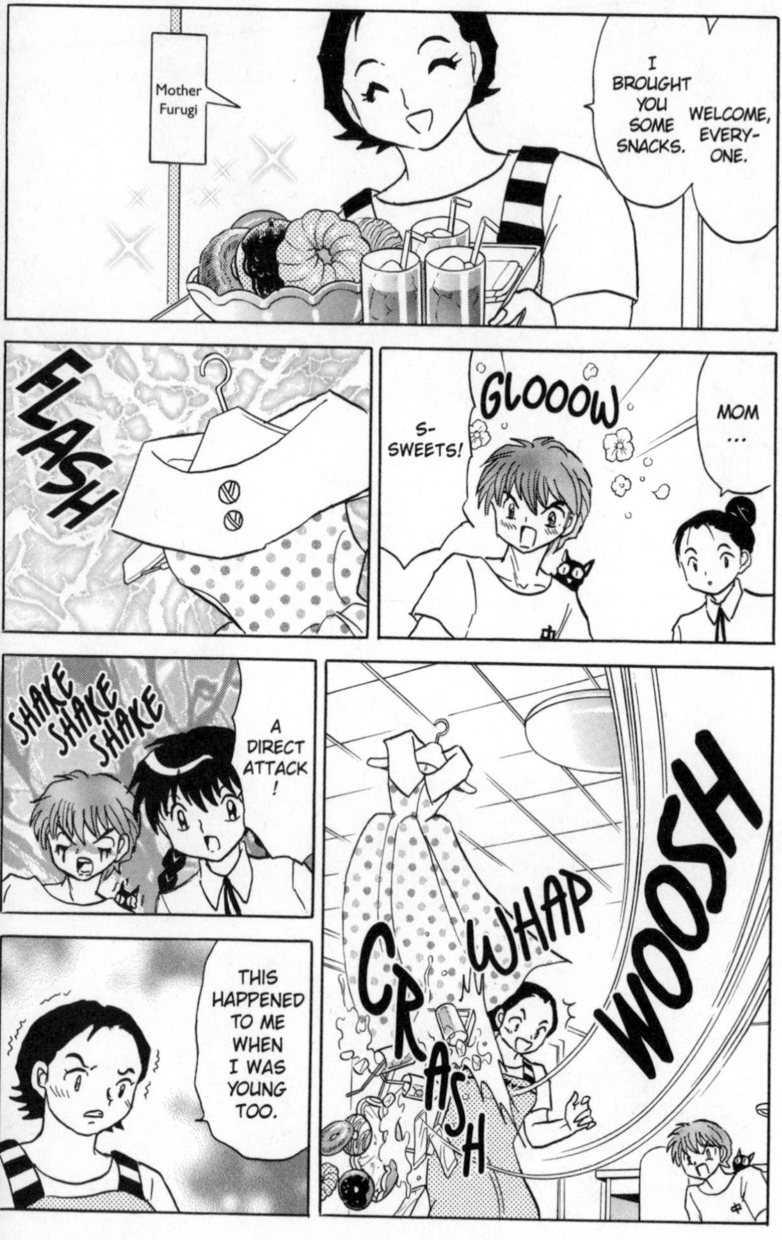
WELCOME, EVERY-ONE.
I BROUGHT YOU SOME SNACKS.
Mother Furugi
MOM ...
GLOOOW
S-SWEETS!
FLASH
WOOSH
WHAP
CRASH
A DIRECT ATTACK!
SHAKE SHAKE SHAKE
THIS HAPPENED TO ME WHEN I WAS YOUNG TOO.

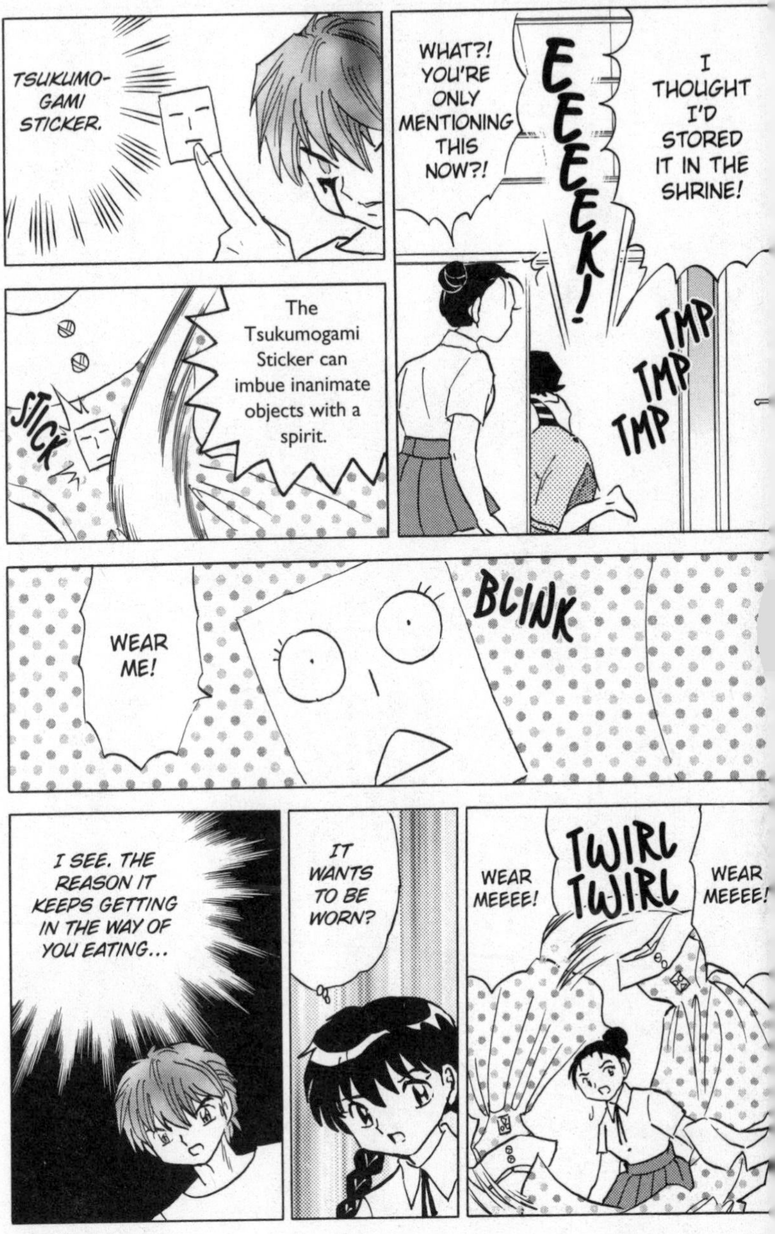
I THOUGHT I'D STORED IT IN THE SHRINE!
EEEEK!
WHAT?! YOU'RE ONLY MENTIONING THIS NOW?!
TSUKUMOGAMI STICKER.
TMP TMP TMP
The Tsukumogami Sticker can imbue inanimate objects with a spirit.
STICK
BLINK
WEAR ME!
WEAR MEEEE!
TWIRL TWIRL
WEAR MEEEE!
IT WANTS TO BE WORN?
I SEE. THE REASON IT KEEPS GETTING IN THE WAY OF YOU EATING...

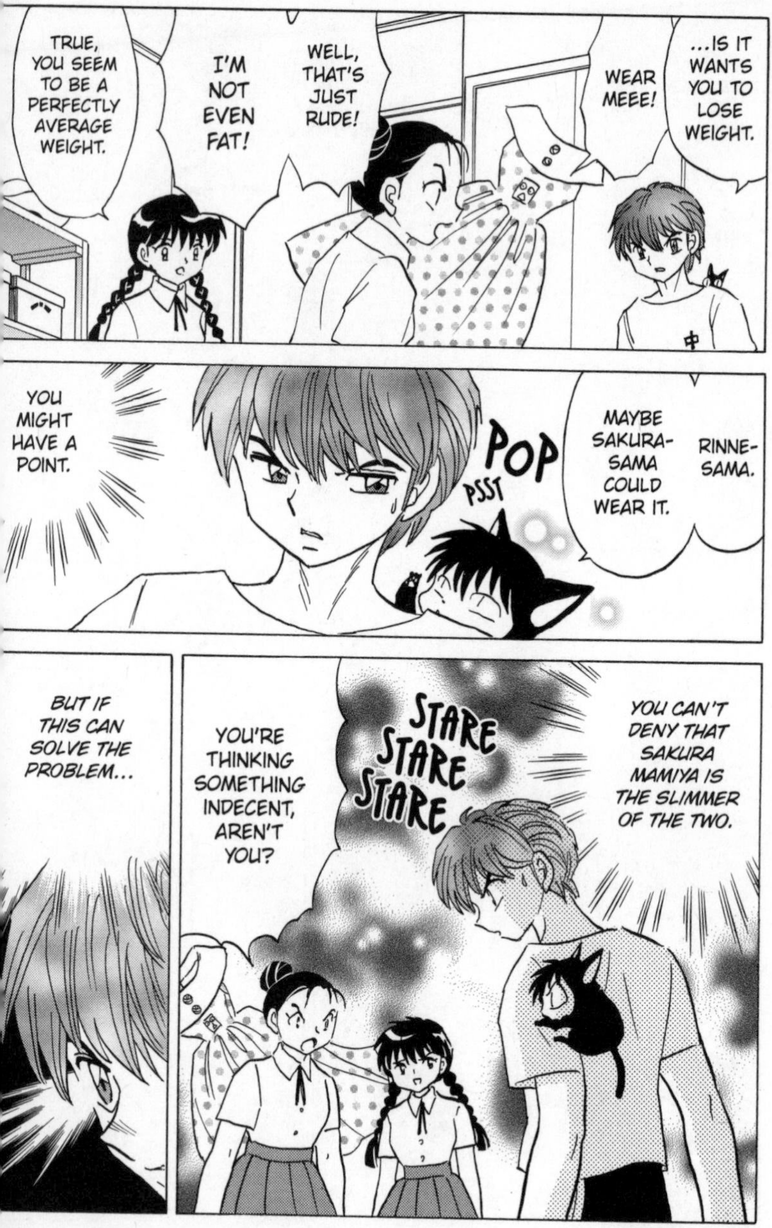
...IS IT WANTS YOU TO LOSE WEIGHT.
WEAR MEEE!
WELL, THAT'S JUST RUDE!
I'M NOT EVEN FAT!
TRUE, YOU SEEM TO BE A PERFECTLY AVERAGE WEIGHT.
RINNE-SAMA.
MAYBE SAKURA-SAMA COULD WEAR IT.
POP
PSST
YOU MIGHT HAVE A POINT.
YOU CAN'T DENY THAT SAKURA MAMIYA IS THE SLIMMER OF THE TWO.
STARE
STARE
STARE
YOU'RE THINKING SOMETHING INDECENT, AREN'T YOU?
BUT IF THIS CAN SOLVE THE PROBLEM...

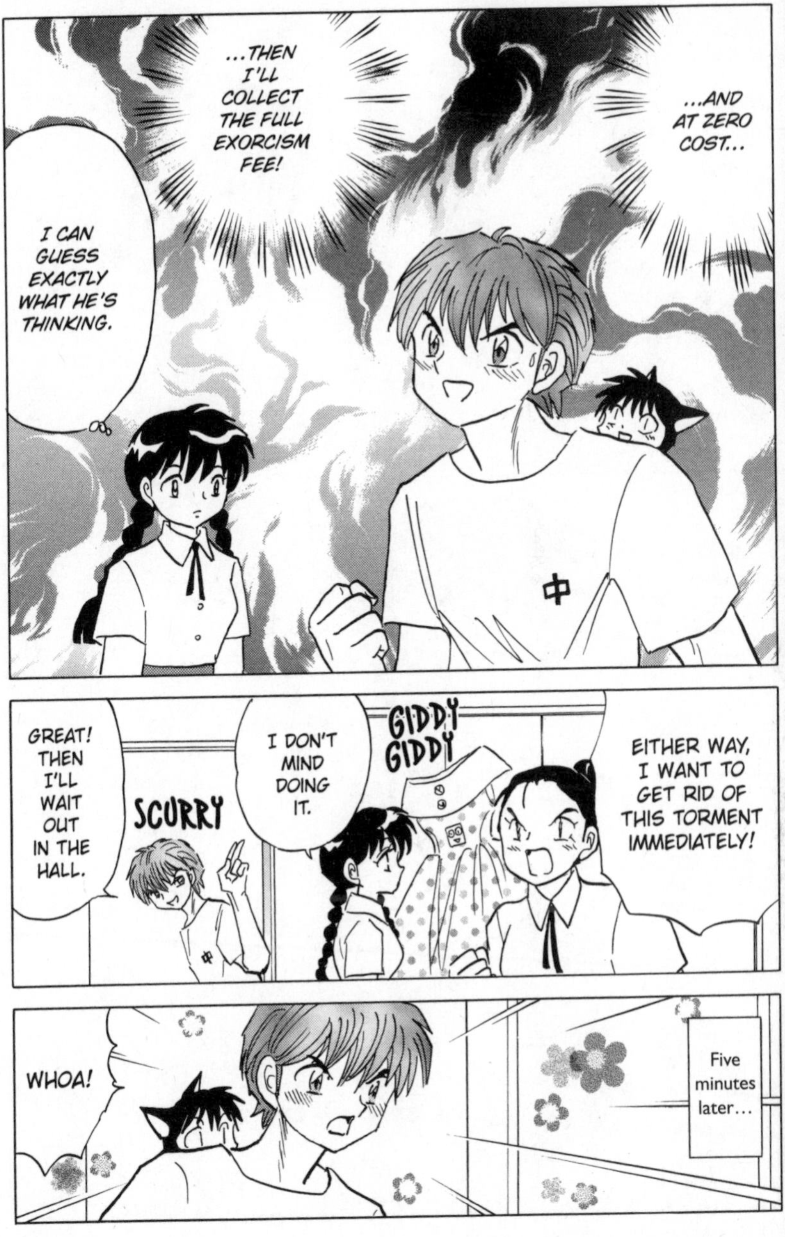
...AND AT ZERO COST...
...THEN I'LL COLLECT THE FULL EXORCISM FEE!
I CAN GUESS EXACTLY WHAT HE'S THINKING.
EITHER WAY, I WANT TO GET RID OF THIS TORMENT IMMEDIATELY!
GIDDY GIDDY
I DON'T MIND DOING IT.
SCURRY
GREAT! THEN I'LL WAIT OUT IN THE HALL.
Five minutes later...
WHOA!

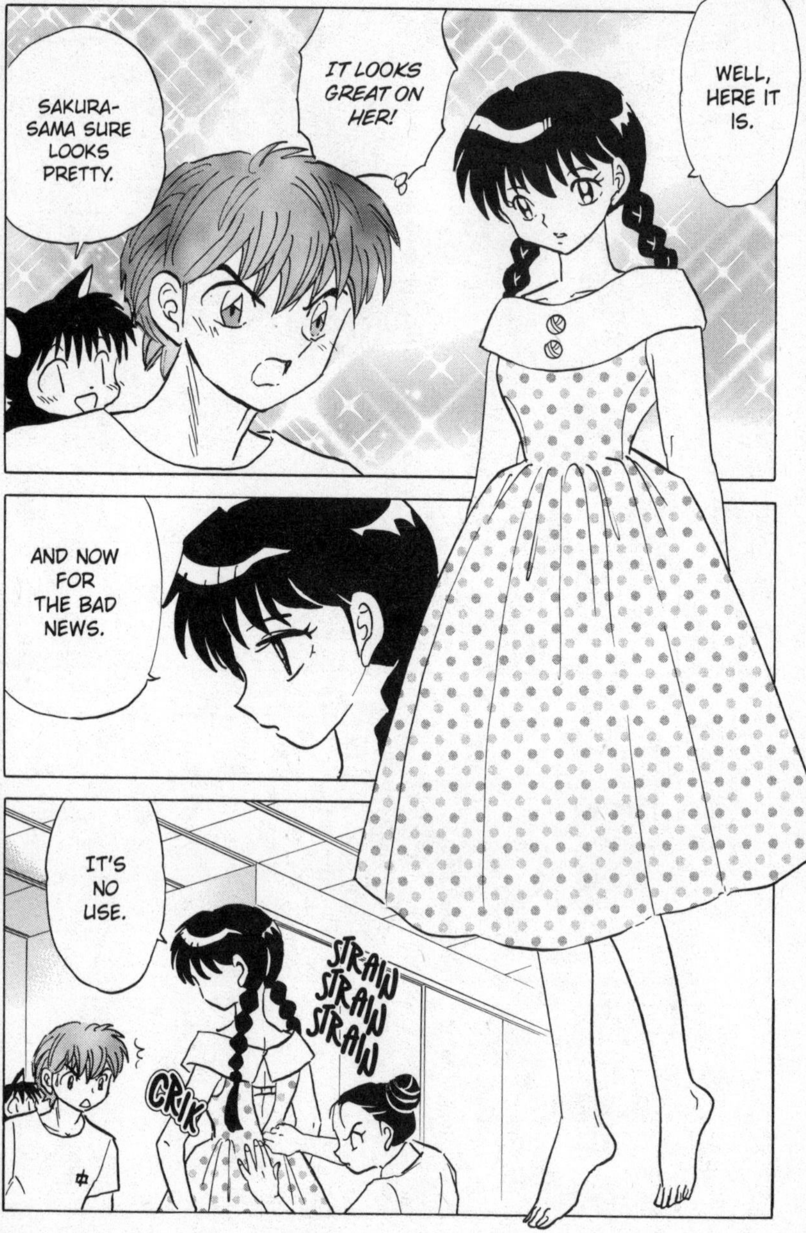
WELL, HERE IT IS.
IT LOOKS GREAT ON HER!
SAKURA-SAMA SURE LOOKS PRETTY.
AND NOW FOR THE BAD NEWS.
IT'S NO USE.
STRAW STRAW STRAW
CRIK

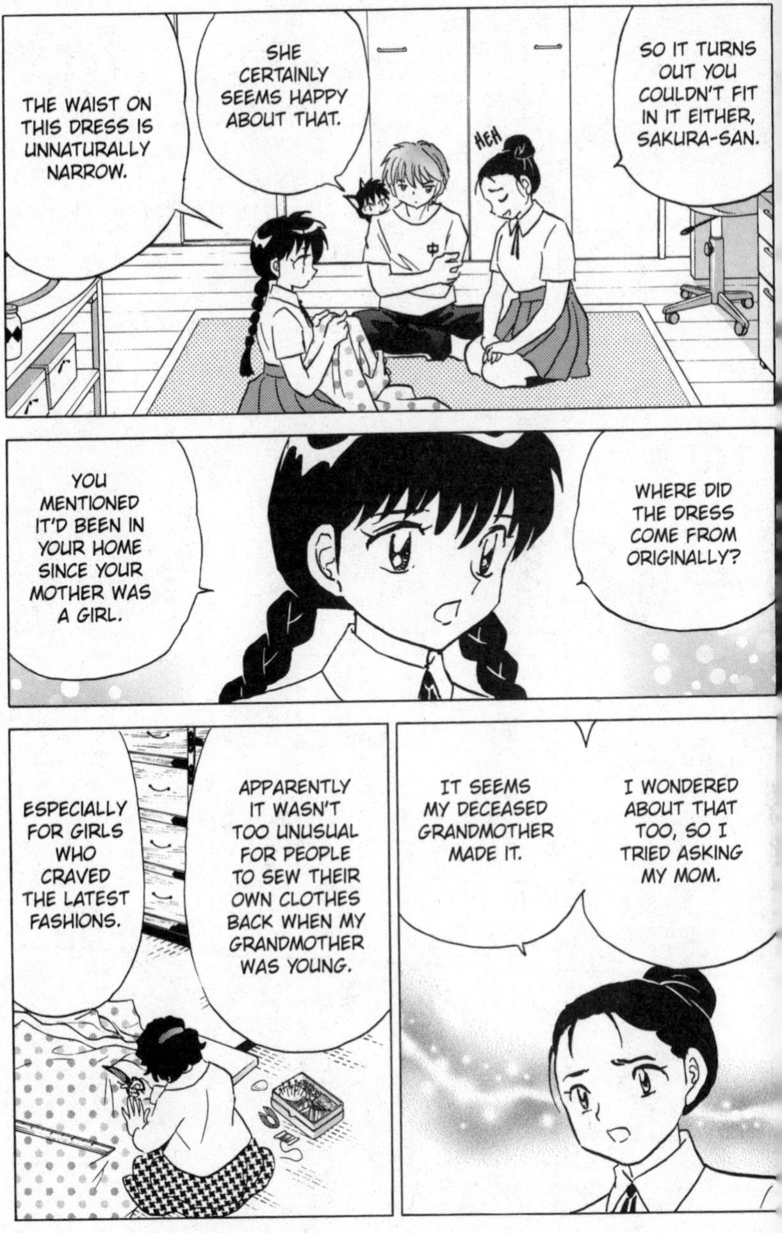
SO IT TURNS OUT YOU COULDN'T FIT IN IT EITHER, SAKURA-SAN.
HEH
SHE CERTAINLY SEEMS HAPPY ABOUT THAT.
THE WAIST ON THIS DRESS IS UNNATURALLY NARROW.
WHERE DID THE DRESS COME FROM ORIGINALLY?
YOU MENTIONED IT'D BEEN IN YOUR HOME SINCE YOUR MOTHER WAS A GIRL.
I WONDERED ABOUT THAT TOO, SO I TRIED ASKING MY MOM.
IT SEEMS MY DECEASED GRANDMOTHER MADE IT.
APPARENTLY IT WASN'T TOO UNUSUAL FOR PEOPLE TO SEW THEIR OWN CLOTHES BACK WHEN MY GRANDMOTHER WAS YOUNG.
ESPECIALLY FOR GIRLS WHO CRAVED THE LATEST FASHIONS.

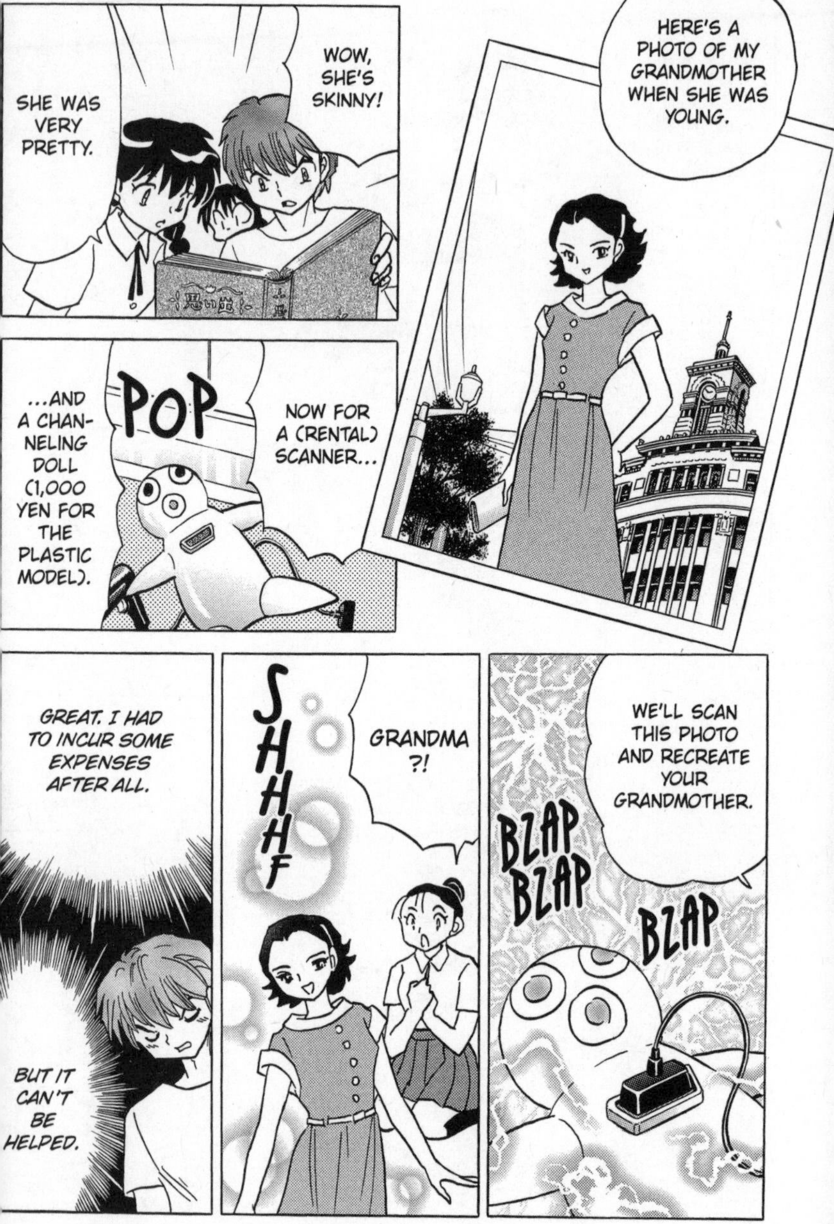
HERE'S A PHOTO OF MY GRANDMOTHER WHEN SHE WAS YOUNG.
WOW, SHE'S SKINNY!
SHE WAS VERY PRETTY.
NOW FOR A (RENTAL) SCANNER...
POP
...AND A CHANNELING DOLL (1,000 YEN FOR THE PLASTIC MODEL).
WE'LL SCAN THIS PHOTO AND RECREATE YOUR GRANDMOTHER.
BZAP BZAP
BZAP
GRANDMA?!
SHHHF
GREAT. I HAD TO INCUR SOME EXPENSES AFTER ALL.
BUT IT CAN'T BE HELPED.

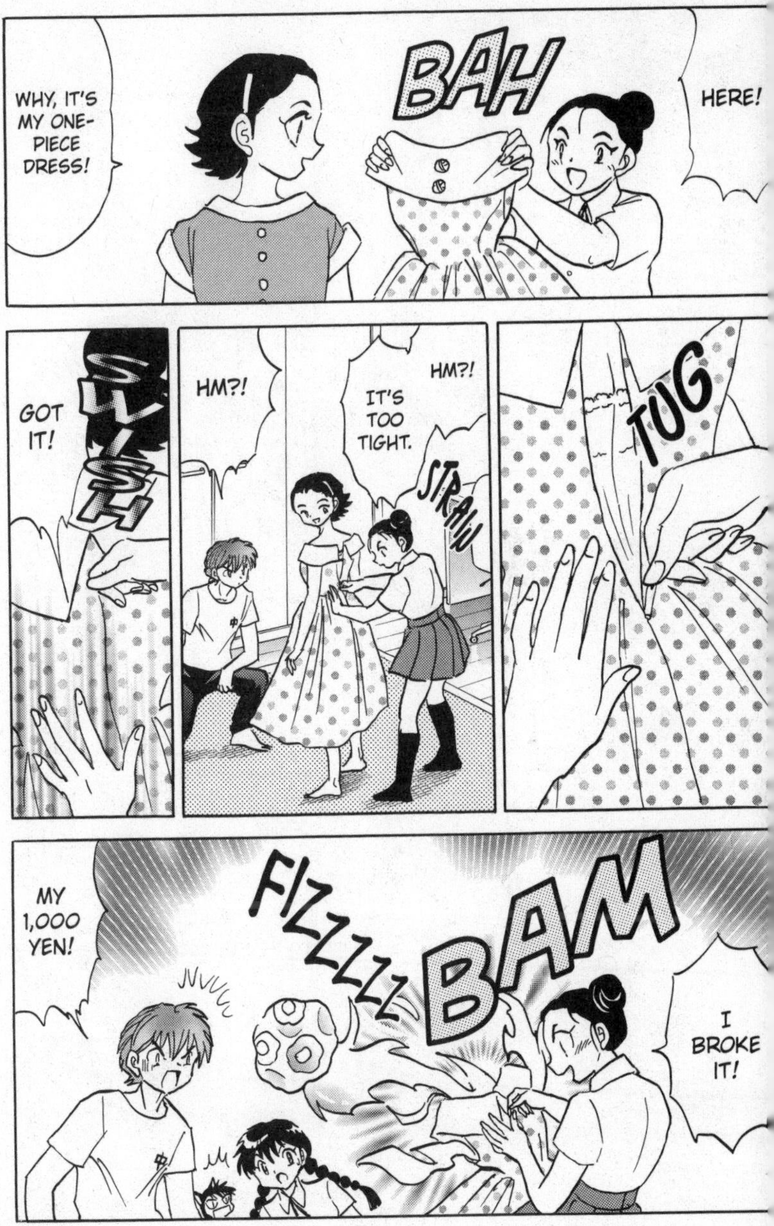
HERE!
BAH
WHY, IT'S MY ONE-PIECE DRESS!
TUG
HM?!
IT'S TOO TIGHT.
STRAIN
HM?!
SWISH
GOT IT!
I BROKE IT!
FIZZZZZZ
BAM
MY 1,000 YEN!

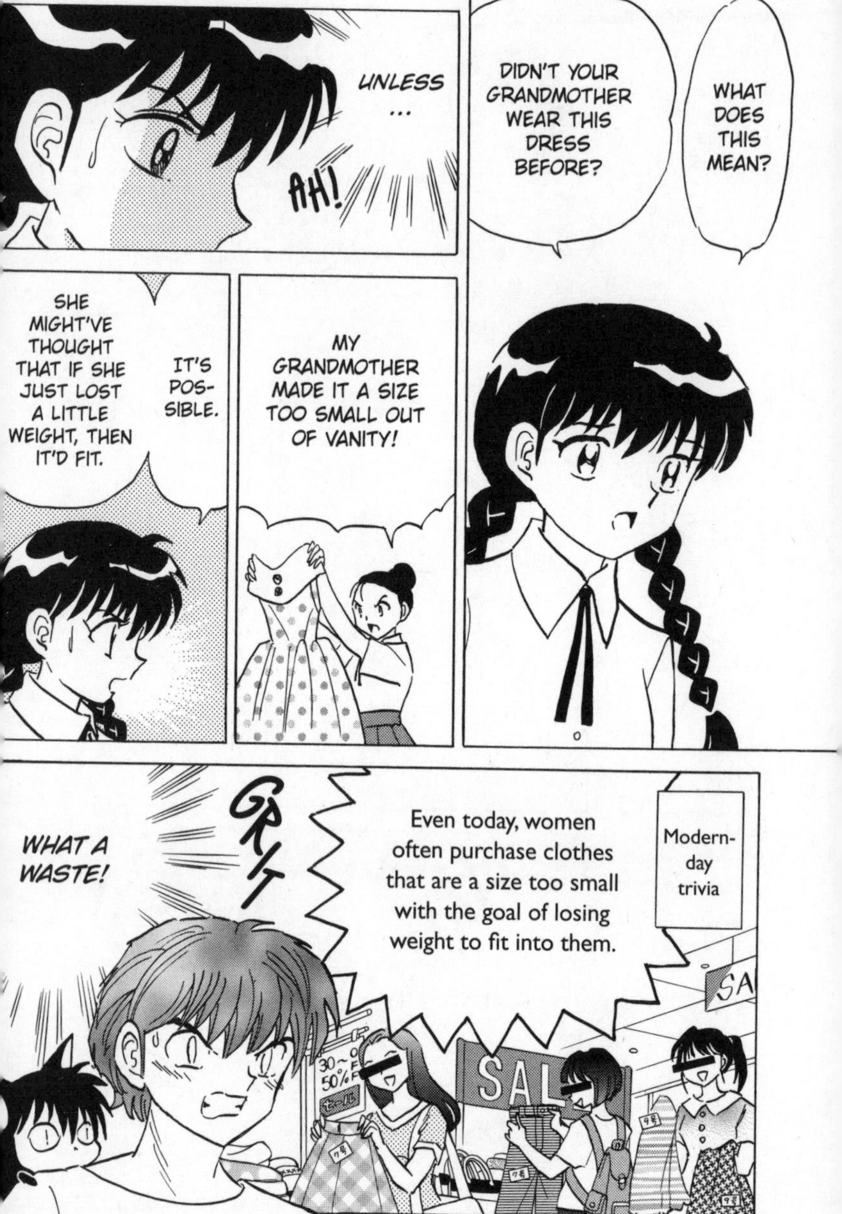
WHAT DOES THIS MEAN?
DIDN'T YOUR GRANDMOTHER WEAR THIS DRESS BEFORE?
UNLESS ...
AH!
MY GRANDMOTHER MADE IT A SIZE TOO SMALL OUT OF VANITY!
IT'S POS-SIBLE.
SHE MIGHT'VE THOUGHT THAT IF SHE JUST LOST A LITTLE WEIGHT, THEN IT'D FIT.
Modern-day trivia
Even today, women often purchase clothes that are a size too small with the goal of losing weight to fit into them.
GRIT
WHAT A WASTE!
SAL
30~ 50%

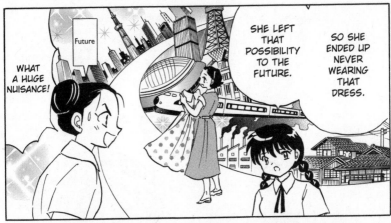

SO SHE ENDED UP NEVER WEARING THAT DRESS.
SHE LEFT THAT POSSIBILITY TO THE FUTURE.
Future
WHAT A HUGE NUISANCE!
MUTTER
SHOULD WE BURN IT?
A FORCED EXORCISM ?!
TWIRRRL
CHOKE CHOKE
OH NO! IT'S REALLY RESISTING!
PAT PAT
I BOUGHT ANOTHER ONE...
WAAARP
...OF THOSE CHAN-NELING DOLLS.
PLOP
NOW, THEN.

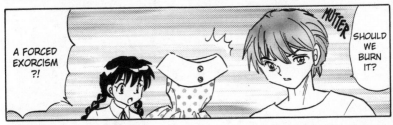

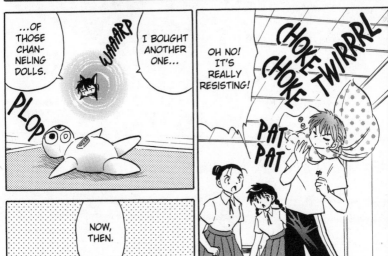

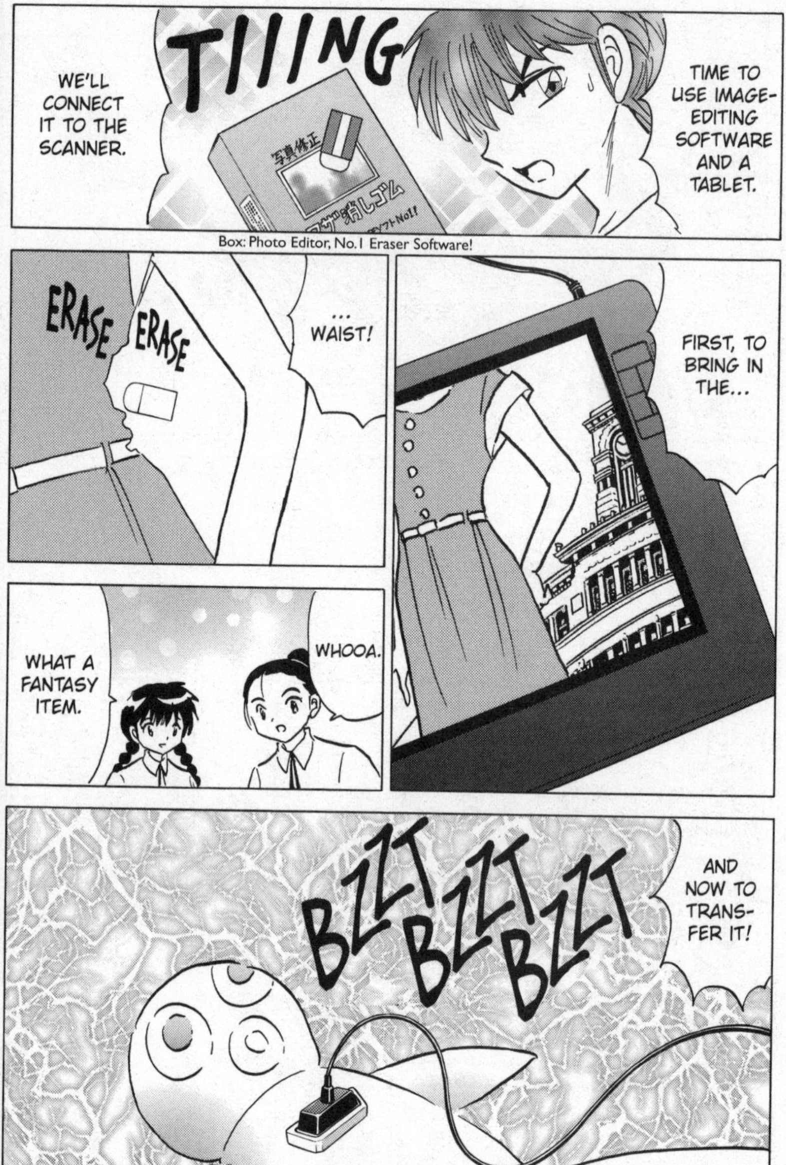
TIME TO USE IMAGE-EDITING SOFTWARE AND A TABLET.
TIIING
写真修正
WE'LL CONNECT IT TO THE SCANNER.
Box: Photo Editor, No.1 Eraser Software!
FIRST, TO BRING IN THE...
...WAIST!
ERASE
ERASE
WHOOA.
WHAT A FANTASY ITEM.
AND NOW TO TRANSFER IT!
BZZT
BZZT
BZZT

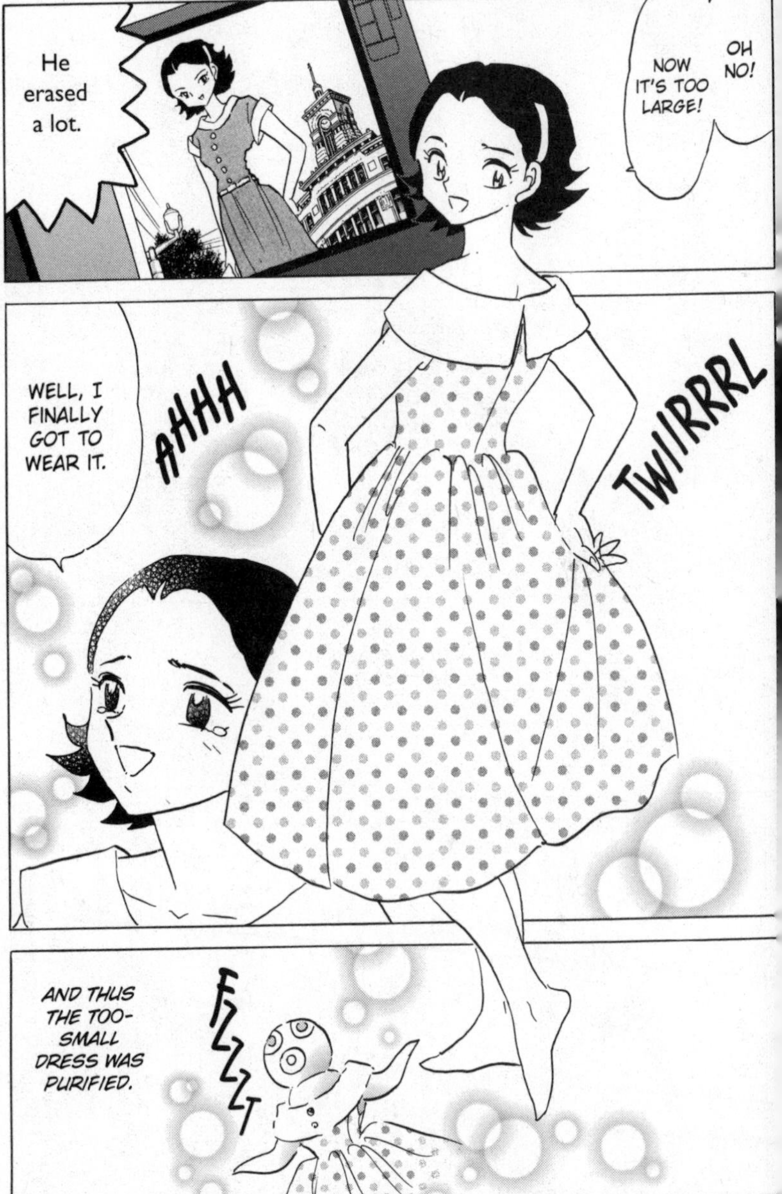
OH NO! NOW IT'S TOO LARGE!
He erased a lot.
TWIRRRL
AHHH
WELL, I FINALLY GOT TO WEAR IT.
FZZZT
AND THUS THE TOO-SMALL DRESS WAS PURIFIED.

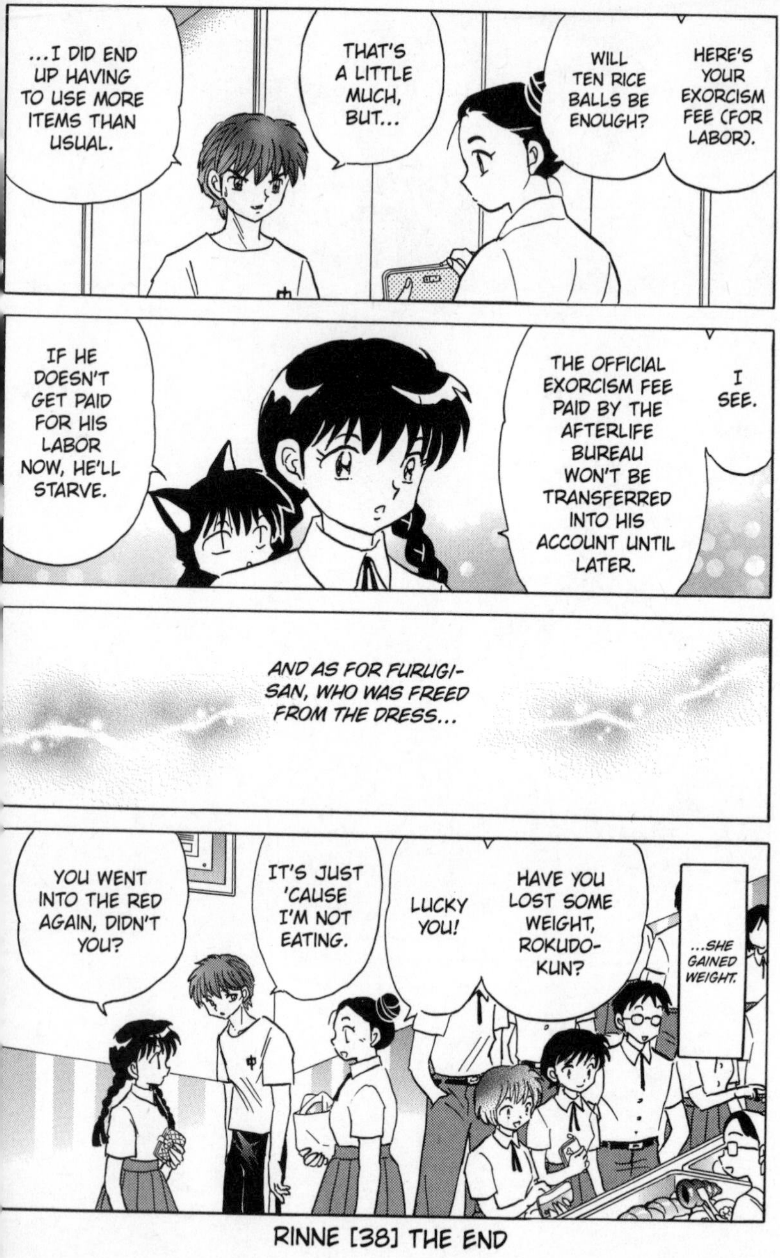
HERE'S YOUR EXORCISM FEE (FOR LABOR).
WILL TEN RICE BALLS BE ENOUGH?
THAT'S A LITTLE MUCH, BUT...
...I DID END UP HAVING TO USE MORE ITEMS THAN USUAL.
I SEE.
THE OFFICIAL EXORCISM FEE PAID BY THE AFTERLIFE BUREAU WON'T BE TRANSFERRED INTO HIS ACCOUNT UNTIL LATER.
IF HE DOESN'T GET PAID FOR HIS LABOR NOW, HE'LL STARVE.
AND AS FOR FURUGI-SAN, WHO WAS FREED FROM THE DRESS...
...SHE GAINED WEIGHT.
HAVE YOU LOST SOME WEIGHT, ROKUDO-KUN?
LUCKY YOU!
IT'S JUST 'CAUSE I'M NOT EATING.
YOU WENT INTO THE RED AGAIN, DIDN'T YOU?

RINNE [38] THE END

Rumiko Takahashi

The spotlight on Rumiko Takahashi's career began in 1978 when she won an honorable mention in Shogakukan's prestigious New Comic Artist Contest for *Those Selfish Aliens*. Later that same year, her boy-meets-alien comedy series, *Urusei Yatsura*, was serialized in *Weekly Shonen Sunday*. This phenomenally successful manga series was adapted into anime format and spawned a TV series and half a dozen theatrical-release movies, all incredibly popular in their own right. Takahashi followed up the success of her debut series with one blockbuster hit after another—*Maison Ikkoku* ran from 1980 to 1987, *Ranma ½* from 1987 to 1996, and *Inuyasha* from 1996 to 2008. Other notable works include *Mermaid Saga*, *Rumic Theater*, and *One-Pound Gospel*.

Takahashi was inducted into the Will Eisner Comic Awards Hall of Fame in 2018. She won the prestigious Shogakukan Manga Award twice in her career, once for *Urusei Yatsura* in 1981 and the second time for *Inuyasha* in 2002. A majority of the Takahashi canon has been adapted into other media such as anime, live-action TV series, and film. Takahashi's manga, as well as the other formats her work has been adapted into, have continued to delight generations of fans around the world. Distinguished by her wonderfully endearing characters, Takahashi's work adeptly incorporates a wide variety of elements such as comedy, romance, fantasy, and martial arts. While her series are difficult to pin down into one simple genre, the signature style she has created has come to be known as the "Rumic World." Rumiko Takahashi is an artist who truly represents the very best from the world of manga.

RIN-NE
VOLUME 38
Shonen Sunday Edition

STORY AND ART BY
RUMIKO TAKAHASHI

KYOKAI NO RINNE Vol. 38
by Rumiko TAKAHASHI
© 2009 Rumiko TAKAHASHI
All rights reserved.
Original Japanese edition published by SHOGAKUKAN.
English translation rights in the United States of America,
Canada, the United Kingdom, Ireland, Australia and New
Zealand arranged with SHOGAKUKAN.

Translation/Christine Dashiell
Touch-up Art & Lettering/Evan Waldinger
Design/Yukiko Whitley
Editor/Megan Bates

Printed in the U.S.A.

Published by VIZ Media, LLC
P.O. Box 77010
San Francisco, CA 94107

10 9 8 7 6 5 4 3 2 1
First printing, March 2021

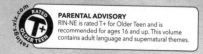

viz.com

shonensunday.com

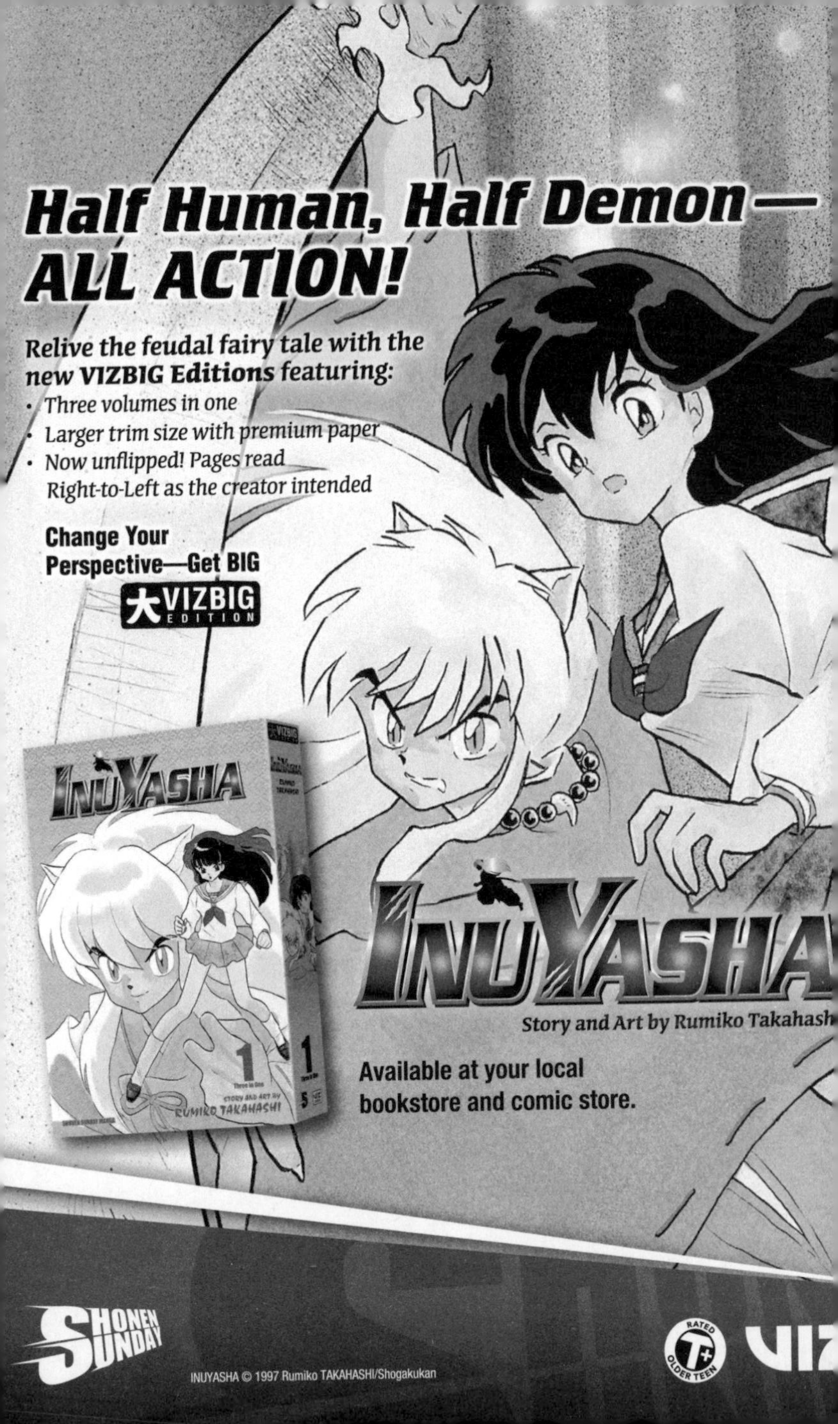
Half Human, Half Demon—
ALL ACTION!
Relive the feudal fairy tale with the new VIZBIG Editions featuring:
• Three volumes in one
• Larger trim size with premium paper
• Now unflipped! Pages read Right-to-Left as the creator intended
Change Your Perspective—Get BIG
大 VIZBIG EDITION
INUYASHA
Story and Art by Rumiko Takahash
Available at your local bookstore and comic store.
SHONEN SUNDAY
RATED T+ OLDER TEEN
VIZ
INUYASHA © 1997 Rumiko TAKAHASHI/Shogakukan

Kidnapped by the Demon King and imprisoned in his castle, Princess Syalis is...bored.

SLEEPY PRINCESS IN THE DEMON CASTLE

Story & Art by

KAGIJI KUMANOMATA

SLEEPY PRINCESS IN THE DEMON CASTLE
1
Story & Art by KAGIJI KUMANOMATA

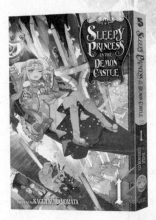

Captured princess Syalis decides to while away her hours in the Demon Castle by sleeping, but getting a good night's rest turns out to be a lot of work! She begins by fashioning a DIY pillow out of the fur of her Teddy Demon guards and an "air mattress" from the magical Shield of the Wind. Things go from bad to worse—for her captors—when some of Princess Syalis's schemes end in her untimely—if temporary—demise and she chooses the Forbidden Grimoire for her bedtime reading...

RATED T TEEN

Hey! You're Reading in the Wrong Direction!

This is the end of this graphic novel!

To properly enjoy this VIZ graphic novel, please turn it around and begin reading from right to left. Unlike English, Japanese is read right to left, so Japanese comics are read in reverse order from the way English comics are typically read.

1
2
3
4
1
2
5
6
7
8
3
4
9
5

Follow the action this way

This book has been printed in the original Japanese format in order to preserve the orientation of the original artwork. Have fun with it!

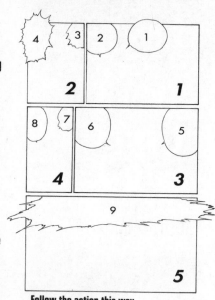